George Sandie

Horeb and Jerusalem

George Sandie

Horeb and Jerusalem

ISBN/EAN: 9783743348073

Manufactured in Europe, USA, Canada, Australia, Japa

Cover: Foto ©ninafisch / pixelio.de

Manufactured and distributed by brebook publishing software (www.brebook.com)

George Sandie

Horeb and Jerusalem

HOREB AND JERUSALEM

BY THE

REV. GEORGE SANDIE.

EDINBURGH:
EDMONSTON AND DOUGLAS.
1864.

CONTENTS.

PREFACE, ... xi

INTRODUCTORY.

Tour resolved on—Advantage anticipated—The relation of the Sacred Geography to the Sacred History—Allusions in our Lord's teaching to the Scenes and Customs of the East—Eastern Travel deepens the impression of His humanity—Pleasing reminiscences, ... 1

CHAPTER I.

ANCIENT EGYPT.

Alexandria—The landing—Night scene—Historic interest of the City—Start for Cairo—Cairo illuminated—Obelisk at Heliopolis—Trip to the Pyramids—The design of their Builders—Why so massive?—Pass on to Memphis—Tombs of the Bull Apis—Memphis, the Capital in the time of the Exodus—Its ancient grandeur—Moses in the presence of Pharaoh—The demand and the scornful reply—The Plagues—Debased character of Egyptian Idolatry, ... 11

CHAPTER II.

GOSHEN AND THE EVENTS OF THE EXODUS.

Causes of the Bondage in Egypt—The Invasion of the Hyksos—Expelled before the time of the Patriarchs—Language of

Joseph to his Brethren—Pharaoh's alarm—Goshen did not adjoin the Capital—A district in the north-east of Egypt—Route of the Israelites from Goshen by Succoth and Etham—Recent Controversies on the Pentateuch—The Numbers of the Exodus The spoil and the time when the Israelites gathered it—The moral lesson involved—The Passover—Observed in the encampment at Rameses—Number of victims required—What is meant by "a Household" in the Pentateuch sense?—What is meant by "the Congregation?"—Bearing of the answers on the number of Lambs for the Passover The eventful night—Pharaoh's despair and entreaty—The march to the Red Sea—Not a hurried flight, nor accomplished in three days The Israelites marched leisurely, and halted at Succoth and Etham—Probably three weeks before crossing—The infatuated Pursuit, . . 30

CHAPTER III.

PASSAGE OF THE RED SEA.

Our arrangements for the Journey—Arrival at Suez—The Dragoman—Baomi—Our Arab escort A tale of "Robbery and Murder"—Our suspicions—The locality around Suez—Jebel Attakah—Where did the Israelites cross?—Dr. Robinson's Theory examined and objected to They crossed close to the ridge of Jebel Attakah—Reasons for the choice of this locality—The grand issues of the event on Egypt—Israel and the World, ... 69

CHAPTER IV.

ISRAEL IN THE WILDERNESS.

Night-scene at Suez—Start on our Journey—Mount the Camels Halt at Ayoun Mousa—Beautiful sunset—Second day: The bright Mirage—The Arabs in their Desert—The Sacred Ridge of Jebel el Tih—Wady Sudr and Wady Aithi identified with the Etham and Shur of Scripture—Desolation and silence of the Scene—Third day: Pass Marah—Where is Elim?—The

Palm-trees and Wells of Gurundel—Wady Useit—Fourth day: Grandeur of Wady Tayibeh—Rocks of various colours—"The encampment by the Red Sea" (Numb. xxiii. 10)—The Manna up to this stage not vouchsafed—How then were the People supported ?—How were their Cattle supported for the forty years of the Wanderings ?—Dr. Colenso's mistakes—The Past and Present state of the Desert contrasted—Many Ceremonial Sacrifices in abeyance during the Desert sojourn—Summary of the Argument on points of recent dispute, 100

CHAPTER V.

THE ROUTE OF THE ISRAELITES TO SINAI.

From Wady Tayibeh to Wady Murkah—Mountain Scenery—Pass of the Sword's Point—Survey of the desolation of Wady Shellal—Mines of Meghara—Inscriptions on Rocks of Mokatebb—Heat overpowering—Mahmoud's anxiety about reaching our Tents—Hasten the Camels!—Selemma's Song and Merriment—Wady Feiran—"The Paradise of the Beduin"—Two Questions considered : (I.) Who wrote the Mysterious Inscriptions ? the Israelites ? Early Pilgrims ? or the Ancient Inhabitants of the Desert ?—Conclusion—(II.) Is Serbal, Sinai ?—Lepsius' Argument examined—Features of Mountain and Valley—The Traditional Argument—Convent of Justinian—Proof that the Israelites did not pass through Wady Feiran in their Route to Sinai—Their Journeyings in the Wilderness of Sin—The Stations, Dophkah, Alush, and Rephidim, identified with existing Names—The Battle at Rephidim—The Lesson to the World, ... 133

CHAPTER VI.

HOREB AND SINAI—THE ARGUMENT FROM TRADITION.

Wady Feiran to Sinai—Our First View of Horeb—The Convent—Ascend the mountain with a guide—Its Features—Value of the

Traditional Argument examined—The earliest Christian Tradition pointed to this Mountain—Proofs of the Existence of the Tradition in the Jewish Era—The Encampment of the Israelites at Sinai—Their Wanderings in its Vicinity for Thirty-eight Years—Subsequent Conflicts with the Desert Tribe—Saul's Raid—His Army swept the Sinai District—David's Pursuit of the Amalekites (1 Sam. xxx.)—Celebrates the Event in the 68th Psalm—Its reference to Mount Sinai—The Jews afterwards possess the whole Country—Solomon's Fleet at Eziongeber—Elijah's Visit to Horeb—Visit of St. Paul—The early Christian Hermits—Reverence of the Arabs for the locality at this day—Conclusion, . . 163

CHAPTER VII.

HOREB AND SINAI—THE PROCLAMATION OF THE LAW.

Theories of Drs. Robinson and Wilson—The whole locality accords with the Scripture narrative, if both summits of the mountain be included—The Plain of Rahah—The summit where Moses communed with Jehovah—Elevated and Distant from the Plain—The Law proclaimed from a lower and nearer summit—The first Warning given to the people after Jehovah descended—Important Distinction between the events of Mount Horeb and those of Mount Sinai, ... 192

CHAPTER VIII.

WILDERNESS OF THE WANDERINGS.

Route to Kadesh-Barnea—Hazeroth—Return to the Wilderness—The Moral of the Sojourn in the Wilderness—Our Return to Cairo—Surabit el Khadem—Dine with the Sheikh—Dinner-talk—Ignorance of the Arabs—No Effort made to instruct them—Reach Ayoun Mousa, Suez—The Lie confessed—Our disappointed Dragoman, . . . 225

CONTENTS.   ix

CHAPTER IX.

ALEXANDRIA TO JERUSALEM.

Land at Jaffa—Start for Jerusalem, and lose our way—Arrive next Morning—Good-Friday—Walk round by St. Stephen's Gate—The Wailing-place—Church of Holy Sepulchre—Visit the Mosque of Omar—The Temple Ruins—The Golden Gateway, ... 239

CHAPTER X.

HILLS OF THE CITY.

Dr. Robinson's Topography refused—Reasons—Two Valleys in the City still visible—A third Valley crossed the present area of the Haram—Proofs, and Importance of this Fact, . . 251

CHAPTER XI.

ZION.

Zion was a separate District of the City—David's Siege—It was the District EAST of the Central Valley—The Existence of a transverse Valley proved from Josephus, the Scripture, and the Book of Maccabees—The Sepulchres of the Kings in that Valley, ... 268

CHAPTER XII.

THE TEMPLE—THE CASTLE OF ANTONIA.

Josephus describes the Size of the Temple—His Statements confirmed by existing Remains—Proofs that there was a Valley on the North of its Area—Testimony of Scripture and the Maccabees—The filling up of the Valley by the Maccabees and Pompey—The Castle of Antonia—It did not adjoin the Temple, but was connected by Colonnades—Siege of Titus—The Temple Ruins complete the filling up of the transverse Valley, . . 286

CHAPTER XIII.

THE HOLY SEPULCHRE—TRADITIONAL ARGUMENT.

Is the Discovery desirable?—Mr. Fergusson's Theory—Architectural Proof that the "Dome of the Rock" is the original Church of Constantine—Testimony of the Early Pilgrims to this Site—The present Church the result of a Transference, . 322

CHAPTER XIV.

THE HOLY SEPULCHRE—SCRIPTURE ARGUMENT.

Constantine had sure means of discovering the Spot—Evidence from Old Testament—Evidence from the New—Scenes and Groups of the Crucifixion, . 363

CHAPTER XV.

CLOSING SCENES OF THE GOSPEL NARRATIVE.

Upper Room—The Kedron—Gethsemane—The High Priest's House—Pilate's House—Calvary—The Sepulchre—The Resurrection, ... 394

PREFACE.

It is well known that some of the localities in the East, of deepest interest to the reader of Scripture, are involved in uncertainty and dispute. Great names can be quoted in support of various opinions regarding them, and not a few have resigned themselves to the conclusion that, at this distance of time, they are beyond the possibility of satisfactory identification. It is admitted at any rate, on all sides, that the most important section of Scripture Topography is open for further inquiry and settlement, and I hope, therefore, to be the more readily excused in presenting some aspects of the subject that have appeared to me worthy of attention, and that may contribute, in some degree, to a clearer elucidation of the sacred narrative.

The localities here discussed refer to the scenes of the Exodus and the Redemption.

In the first section of the book, I have attempted to trace the route of the Israelites from Goshen to Sinai, and to examine some of those questions which have had so prominent a place in recent controversies on the Pentateuch.

In discussing the Topography of Jerusalem, I have laid great stress on the remarkable theory of Mr. Fergusson, in reference to the building generally known as the "Mosque of Omar." I have directed attention to the valley that—as I believe—anciently separated this portion of the present area from that occupied by the Temple, and exhibited the bearing of this topographical feature on the Jerusalem of Scripture and of Josephus. It essentially concerns, also, the settlement of the Holy Places—Calvary and the Sepulchre.

While receiving friendly help from various quarters, I have to acknowledge my special obligations to my friend Mr. A. B. MacGrigor, in the preparation of this volume. He was the first to direct my attention to Mr. Fergusson's theory, on my starting for the East, and when, on return, I set myself more earnestly to the study of the topography of Jerusalem, I had free access to his library, and his acquaintance with the subjects here discussed enabled him to render me valuable assistance.

I have also gratefully to acknowledge the kind service of my friend Mr. W. Simpson, widely known by his admirable sketches from "The Seat of War in the East," whose pencil has produced the three pictorial illustrations that adorn this work. Whatever may be thought of the theory they are intended to illustrate, there can, I think, be but one opinion as to the high artistic merit of the illustrations themselves.

To verify the localities of Scripture, and develop their bearing on the events associated with them, is to supply additional proof of the historical accuracy of the narrative, and is therefore of special importance in these days when that accuracy has been so strongly impugned.

Such has been my aim in the present volume, and I have endeavoured to state the arguments for the various opinions adduced, as simply and clearly as I could, leaving them to abide, as best they can, the test of criticism and future explorations. If I have thrown any light on incidents and allusions in the Sacred Volume, and helped the reader to peruse, with a more vivid conception, some of the most impressive portions of Bible history, my object will have been amply attained.

GOUROCK, *December* 1863.

LIST OF ILLUSTRATIONS.

THE CRUCIFIXION,	*Frontispiece*
PENINSULA OF SINAI—MAP,	PAGE 36
HOREB AND SINAI,	169
JERUSALEM—TOPOGRAPHY OF DR. ROBINSON,	252
JERUSALEM—TOPOGRAPHY OF JOSEPHUS,	256
JERUSALEM—TOPOGRAPHY OF SCRIPTURE,	257
JERUSALEM IN THE TIME OF THE KINGS,	279
JERUSALEM IN THE TIME OF CHRIST,	308
JERUSALEM OF THE EARLY PILGRIMS,	339

HOREB AND JERUSALEM.

INTRODUCTORY.

THE Tour in the East, which has given rise to the following chapters, was suggested in a conversation with two friends, during the spring of 1860. Having arranged to take a trip somewhere together, our first thoughts were of the Continent; but on some of the routes being named, they were set aside, as it appeared that one or other of the parties had already, in great measure, gone over the ground.

"Come," said one; "let us make *the Grand Tour* at once; let us go to the Holy Land!" The idea thus suddenly thrown out was seized on with a kind of wonder and joy. It had, no doubt, hovered before the mind at different times, yet rather as a happy dream, which one fondly wishes may some day be realized, than as a serious purpose, to be arranged for in plans of the future. And indeed, at this mention of it, there was considerable misgiving as to the possibility of carrying it out. But it was dwelt upon, it was looked at in various lights, sundry questions of its detail were started and examined, and the conclusion augured well for its accomplishment.

Subsequent reflection and consultation decided us, and we arranged to start together in the spring of 1861.

Meanwhile, in the summer, the news arrived of the massacre of Christians in the Lebanon, and the excited state of the whole of Syria. Such intelligence looked ominous enough, and at first it seemed not unlikely that the journey must be delayed. Fortunately, as our time drew near, better accounts of the state of the country were received, and we resolved to adhere to our plan. For it was a journey to Sinai, to Jerusalem, Bethlehem, Nazareth, the Sea of Galilee, and, once seriously thought of, was not to be lightly abandoned.

We anticipated much instruction, as well as gratification, from the journey. We felt that it could hardly fail to aid us in the work of the ministry.[1] We should see for ourselves the localities of the East, its manners and customs; and the direct knowledge of these must ever be of high value in the exposition of Scripture. For it can be said of the Bible, far more than of any other ancient record, that the narrative is not only consistent with, but is illustrated and enforced by, the aspect and manners of the country. "The Land" agrees well with "the Book;" the "Sacred Geography" imparts greater meaning and force to the "Sacred History." It has been well said, that the Bible itself is the best handbook of Palestine. And indeed we felt, as many have done before us, that its pages, when read there, would often derive from the locality an explanation and a commentary, shedding light upon incidents but feebly apprehended in the distance. The scene, as it lies before the

---

[1] My companions were the Rev. George M'Korkindale of Gourock, and the Rev. James M'Gregor of Monimail.

eye, would often suggest little circumstances, which fill up the graphic outline of the picture, and add to it colour and life. Admirably the theatre fits into the events described, frequently enabling us better to understand their unexpected issues.

Thus, it looks strange, at first sight, that the tribe of Judah should have maintained its independence, long after the other tribes were prostrate and in exile. But we see a reason for it when we tread that stern mountainous country where "the thousands of Judah" had their dwelling. We realize the force of the striking image of the prophecy: "Judah is a lion's whelp: he stooped down, he crouched as a lion, and as an old lion; who shall rouse him up?" Or again, it appears singular that David, with four hundred followers, should have been able to defy the power and elude the pursuit of Saul. But when we get a glimpse of the haunts of the outlaw, of the wild ravines and rugged fastnesses of the southern region, where the wild Arabs of the district defy the power of the Sultan to this day, we see how well this might be. It is thus that in innumerable instances, as has been often shown, the geography of Palestine explains the sacred narrative, and develops in fuller proportion the graphic sketches of its events. It will not be found otherwise, I trust, with the special localities to be discussed in this book. The great motive for presenting the following views respecting them, has been the hope that they may help the illustration of Scripture incidents, especially those relating to "the giving of the law," and the last scenes of "the Passion."

This harmony between the geography and the history of the Bible, which comes into clearer view the more it is investigated, is surely one of the strongest proofs that that history is true. For the geographical features of a country will not bend to the imagination of the historian. They stand there, stubborn tests to the truth of any narrative relating to them; all the more so, if it be full of circumstantial and testing incident, as the Bible history is to a greater extent than any that can be named.

Moreover, from the number and character of its local allusions, we may draw this other inference, that the narrative has been written about the time when the events occurred—that the history is contemporaneous. From the very nature of the case, the style of a contemporaneous chronicle is different from that of a history written, say two hundred years after the events. The chronicler of the time dwells on the incidents, but not on the features of the locality. He names these, of course, or at least alludes to them, but does not describe them at length, for the obvious reason that they are well known. But afterwards, information on this point becomes necessary; maps of the country are presented, the scenery is described, allusions to it are explained, and we have at last discussions on the relation of the geography to the history. In a word, a later history requires to be explanatory and descriptive, to meet the inevitable ignorance of the time. On the other hand, the contemporaneous record is occupied with incident alone, and such is the grand characteristic of the Bible narrative. The attention of the reader is fixed on its stirring events. It gives the name of the district where they occurred; but further knowledge of it is to be gleaned from some circumstances of the event itself, or the feelings and conduct of the actors, as we image the drought and privation of the desert from the cry of the Israelites for water and bread. It is for others of a later age to describe these details of locality (as does Josephus); but this record is speaking to readers of the time, to whom they are necessarily known; and its tone indeed, in this respect, is like that of a friend telling of some important incidents in a place so familiar to us, that it is enough if he merely mention its name. In consequence, when the localities of the East are visited, and the memory retains a firm hold of them, the reader of Scripture enjoys its narrative all the more for the absence of local description. At the name of Bethany, Olivet, the Sea of Galilee, the scene rises before the mind with a vividness which description would only weaken. Strongly marked throughout with these characteristics of a contemporary record, the Bible has from this circumstance "a witness in itself" "that its record is true." We are made to feel that the writer "speaks what he knows," and often indeed "testifies what he has seen."

If we speak more especially of the New Testament, it is well known how much deeper an insight we gain into the spirit and force of our Lord's teaching, from a knowledge of the localities and customs of the country. In that land it is strongly felt not only how beautiful are his parables, but also how natural and how impressive. He finds illustrations for his great thoughts in the scenery and movements of the world around him. In the view of these even now we seem to get nearer the speaker; to understand better the turn of the thought, and to enter more fully into the mood of mind with which it was uttered. For He, who bade others "consider the lilies of the field," had his own mind often swayed by the varied aspects of nature. He was wont, we know, to retire to her solitudes, finding in their deep calm a "rest" and refreshment for his spirit; and he could be cheered by the smile of flowers, as he was wounded by the faces of scornful men. It is the scene around him at the well of Samaria, where he sat wearied, that has indisposed him to partake of the good cheer which the disciples have brought, a reluctance which so amazes them. But in their absence he has been discoursing to the stranger at the well of high spiritual themes, and the influence of the surrounding landscape is perceptible in the feelings to which he gives expression. There, where he sits, stretches before him that magnificent fertile plain which no traveller in Palestine can ever forget. The view of it, acting on the ruling passion of his spirit —the accomplishment of his Father's will—has summoned up emotions in which earthly food is disregarded. The grandeur of that harvest-field into which he has now entered, the fewness of the labourers, the joy of co-operation, and the jubilee of the great in-gathering, are thoughts that fill his mind; and to the entreaty, "Master, eat," he can only reply, "I have meat to eat which ye know not of. My meat is to do the will of my Father." "Behold the fields white unto the harvest."

A simple sentence, carelessly read at other times, comes home with striking effect on the traveller in Palestine. It suggests the reflection, how fitted such teaching was to arouse attention, and to enchain it. "A certain man went down to Jericho, and fell among thieves." The traveller thinks of this once and again, as he takes the journey now. The negotiations made for his safety; the sight of the escort of the robber tribe on the slope of Bethany; the gloomy defiles and rugged ravines on either side of the solitary road; the appearance now and again of an Arab bandit on an eminence with his musket,—all this surrounds the simple statement with impressive significance, and we cannot but feel that a story opening in this wise must have riveted at once the attention of the hearers, and tended to make more memorable the moral that followed at the close.

And as the scenes of nature enter largely into our Lord's teaching, so do the manners and customs of the time. It is indeed full of such, and the fact reveals the depth of his human sympathy. The whole spirit of that teaching lies along the movements of the daily life of men, its joys and sorrows, its cares and occupations. It appears throughout that "He is not ashamed to call them brethren." And as his voice reaches us now, it is not "a voice crying from the wilderness" of the past, but strangely brings up with it, as no other does, the living work-day world of that ancient time. Reading his parables and the recorded incidents of his life, we are brought face to face, as it were, with its events, and its characters live and move vividly before us. How far is it from being a scene of mist and shadows! The fowls are in the air, and the lilies are blooming in the field; the shepherd is leading forth his sheep, and the sower is going forth to sow; the fisherman is on the lake, and the robber, too, lurks in the ravine; here it is the festivity of a marriage, again it is the company of mourners weeping at a burial. In the midst of the scene moves "the form of the Son of man," "going about doing good,"—in deepest sympathy with all its variety of joy and sorrow, its life and death—taking upon him human infirmities, and "healing all manner of sickness and disease among the people."

One of the most precious results of Eastern travel is to deepen this impression of our Lord's true humanity. Some, it seems, are disappointed with the scenes of the East; they are more prosaic and tame than they expected. But "what went they out for to see?" As suredly we need not travel there to be more deeply impressed with the *divinity* of our Saviour. Overhead and around us are as bright evidences of this great truth as elsewhere. Here, as there, "the heavens declare his glory, the firmament showeth his handywork." All trace of the miraculous is gone from the East, the lepers are by the wayside unhealed, the dead slumber in their graves, and, to the eye of sense, the land is as others, only strangely ruined and desolate. But yet it is the land

"Over whose acres walked those blessed feet
That eighteen hundred years ago were nailed,
For our advantage, to the bitter cross."

Yes! here are the very scenes, in their unchanged outlines, on which *He* looked—the villages and towns of his infancy and youth—sacred spots, where he toiled and preached, suffered and died. If the power of association can work anywhere, it should be here; and the journey surely cannot be undertaken, without the traveller feeling more impressively than ever the true humanity of our Lord, and how closely he allied himself in brotherhood to our race. Could this be indeed felt as it ought to be, there were surely ample recompense for all the toil.

There is one locality which, if it could be discovered.

would greatly tend to deepen this sacred impression, I mean the *site of the Holy Sepulchre*. Fictitious as the present site may have been proved to be, the very idea of a locality in Jerusalem, specially associated with such an event, induces the visitor to enter the present church under strange and solemn emotion. And the involuntary wish will spring to the lip, " Would that I were certain of this being the very spot!" I am aware, indeed, that some write, and many think otherwise. It is well on many accounts, they argue, that the real spot should remain unknown; yet they are very thankful that the Mount of Olives is unquestioned; that the lake of Galilee, Bethlehem, Nazareth, and Jerusalem are localities well ascertained. But these have all their claim to our regard, simply because of their associations with Him. Why, then, should it not be welcome to us, if, on real and solid grounds, we should be able to identify the actual " rock of the sepulchre," where cluster the deepest, tenderest associations of all?

Of the tomb of Moses it is indeed said, that " the Lord buried him, and no man knoweth of his sepulchre until this day." How different with the sepulchre of Christ! The Romans, the Pharisees, the people of the Jews knew it well. And such knowledge was even absolutely necessary at the time to the proof of Christianity. What is virtually implied in the argument of Peter on the day of Pentecost to the listening thousands, but an appeal to them to visit for themselves the tomb where he was buried? They will find it empty, for the tenant has risen, whereas he affirms, " The sepulchre of David remains with us unto this day." It is not easy to understand how the knowledge of such a locality, formerly so important, should be held in little estimation now; at all events, if any proof can be adduced fixing its true position, it should surely be hailed with satisfaction, not superciliously undervalued, by every intelligent Christian.

I venture to believe that this locality *has* been preserved in a most remarkable way, and if, as Professor Stanley remarks, " there is much in the ruins and desolation of Jerusalem that seems to say, He is not here, he has risen as he said," I believe that there may yet be heard the *remainder of the utterance* from " the Dome of the Rock," " Come, see the place where the Lord lay."

I have stated that we took this journey in expectation of much enjoyment and instruction, and I can speak for my companions, as well as for myself, in affirming that we were not disappointed. We have brought home pleasant memories, and profitable lessons. It is delightful to recall the vanished scenes; to wander anew through the great and terrible wilderness, and bow the soul before the majesty of Mount Sinai; to go to Bethlehem, Nazareth, and the shore of the Sea of Galilee; above all, " to sit down on Olivet, over against the city," with Kedron and Gethsemane at our feet. The Holy Land, with all its stirring memories, comes back to the soul idealized, wearing on it, as no other land can wear,

" The consecration, and the poets' dream,
The light that never was on sea or shore."

Incidents of discomfort or annoyance fade from the view, and that scene of Eastern travel lies " in the pale moonlight of memory,"

" A thing of beauty, and a joy for ever."

CHAPTER I.

ANCIENT EGYPT.

We left Scotland for the East in the middle of February 1861. Our route was *via* Marseilles to Alexandria. On the rapid steam-voyage up the Mediterranean, we caught a glimpse of Caprera, the island-home of Garibaldi. Stopping for a few hours at Malta, we paid a hurried visit to St. Paul's Bay, and on the morning of Saturday the 24th February we sighted the shores of Egypt. There, in the hazy horizon, stretched its monotonous line of coast, and on the low eminence were numerous windmills, telling still of "corn in Egypt."

The special pilot was now at the wheel, guiding the vessel in the intricate navigation; and we gazed with interest at the old lighthouse, insignificant in itself, but marking the site of the far-famed Pharos of Alexandria, one of the seven wonders of the world.

On our coming to anchor in port, crowds of boats pushed off to the ship, and, while her papers were being examined, lay at a little distance, and we looked with curiosity at the grotesque devices painted on their sterns, and the wild gesticulations of their Arab-looking crews.

It being announced that "all was right," they pulled in swiftly to the ship's side, and, clambering over the bulwarks, were amongst us, seizing our luggage. Woe, then, to the inexperienced voyager whose packages lay dispersed! These are clutched by the boatmen, each eager to fill his own boat, and the proprietor has to run hither and thither, shouting and distracted. The "practised traveller" is seen, on the other hand, with all collected before him, standing a grim sentinel over his property, and sternly silent to the most impassioned appeals. After considerable difficulty, our "traps" were collected, and, on landing, we passed from the vociferations of the boatmen to the wrangling and gibberish of the donkey-boys. Donkeys swarmed on the landing-place; the drivers pushed them into our service, with broken English and vehement gesture. Somehow the animals have all got the oddest English names! You are entreated to avail yourself of the services of "Uncle Sam." "Him not good," cries another. "Steam-Boat good, you try." "I say, Sir, here! Billy Button! very good donkey, him run like railway," so shouts a third. We preferred to walk to our hotel, and see the town leisurely. In the narrow and confused streets, at the first look of the houses, of the camels slowly passing with their burdens, the turban, the fez, and general dress of the people, the hubbub and crowd of the market-place—we felt that we were now fairly in the East. We passed on to a fine open street, and reached our destined hotel, near it, in a spacious square.

As the evening fell, the moon rose in splendour, giving a deeper interest to the eastern scene. We were surprised to see, at the same time, numbers of the people going about with lanterns. This we afterwards found to be the custom at Cairo also, and it was rigorously enforced during our stay at Jerusalem. There, owing to the then disturbed state of the country, groups of soldiers were wont to patrol the streets nightly, and any one without the precaution of a lantern was sure of being lodged in the guard-house. The explanation given of the custom was, that it keeps the people within doors at night, prevents mob-riots, and frees from suspicion of evil intention any who are abroad. It was not, however, so strictly attended to in Alexandria, where western ideas and habits are beginning largely to prevail. When passing home from an evening saunter, we started at the sight of a muffled figure crouching at a corner. "Some ruffian," was the first thought, "waiting for his opportunity?" He remained quiet, however, and in front of our hotel we were still leisurely enjoying the scene,— "How splendid the moonlight! how beautiful the palms! and all this is in Egypt!" etc. etc.—when there burst from this crouching figure one of the most unearthly cries that ever "made night hideous." And it had hardly ceased before there arose "another of the same," and still another and another, echoing away and away, far over the city. It turned out to be the call of the watchmen of Alexandria, who sit all night long, keeping their posts in a very literal sense, each shouting at intervals, in this inhuman manner, to announce that he, for his part, is not asleep.

The antiquities of Alexandria are not connected with the Bible incidents that will chiefly interest us. The Goshen of the Israelites was not here, nor the scenes of the Exodus. Yet I may, in passing, notice how ancient is the city, and how interesting are its memories to the student of literature, of philosophy, and of the first centuries of Christianity. Founded by Alexander the Great, it rapidly attained a grandeur beyond his fondest dream. In its harbours there now lie some of the finest steamships of Britain, and along the country are the railway and telegraph of British enterprise. In the ancient time, "the first was last, and the last was first." When Britain was an unknown island, her inhabitants painted savages, paddling their rude canoes, and not venturing out of sight of land, this city had attained to a greatness which rivalled that of imperial Rome. The magnificent Pharos threw its far-off gleam upon crowds of vessels, entering its harbour to bring or receive the richest products of the East. It became the seat, too, of a vast literature, with a library of 400,000 volumes, among which was a Greek translation of the Hebrew Bible. The Greek schools of Philosophy found a congenial asylum here, speculating and disputing with a subtlety not surpassed in any other part of the ancient world.

A colony of Jews had been planted in it at an early period, on whose ancient faith the tempting speculations of the school exerted a strong influence. These were also introduced into the Christian Church, and then was first made the attempt, often repeated since, to incorporate the dogmas of Philosophy with the pure creed of Revelation. Christianity, let us remember, has her clear field of knowledge bounded on all sides by an awful realm of mystery, and if those subtle speculations have helped to mark off the frontier between the light and the darkness, they have not been without their uses to the world.

Having "done the lions" of Alexandria—Pompey's Pillar, Cleopatra's Needle, and the Catacombs, on which I need not dwell—we started for Cairo on the Monday, at two o'clock.

One porter, who carried my baggage, insisted on keeping up with the donkeys, and ran with a heavy load under the burning sun. I was paying him at the railway station,—handsomely, as I thought, for it seemed a frightful effort under the circumstances. He was not, however, satisfied, and was pressing for more. Before I could comply, an official burst from the office, and, with a kick and a blow, made him vanish through the doorway. I felt for the poor fellow, and after securing the ticket, looked out to see what had become of him. He seemed little the worse, and grinning, as if the whole thing had been a good joke, beckoned still, in a whisper, for more "bucksheesh." The effect was that another piece of money changed hands, much to his satisfaction, without the official knowing anything further of the matter. We soon found that kicks and blows and beatings with a stick were not uncommon with the officials of the East.

It is difficult, with the strong Biblical association, to entertain the idea of a railway in this ancient land of the Pharaohs. Shut your eyes, or read your book, and you are at home; on looking out, however, all is so strange in the aspect of the fields, the mud villages, the swarthy faces, with fez and turban, the numerous boats on the Nile, that you assure yourself of being indeed in the East, the scream and puff of the engine notwithstanding. Our journey in great part was under the magnificent oriental moonlight; and on reaching Cairo about ten o'clock, we found excellent quarters in "Shepherd's Hotel."

Next morning about six, I was awakened by a salute of cannon from the citadel. It announced, as we afterwards learned, the return of the Pasha from a pilgrimage; and great, accordingly, were to be the rejoicings. No notice had been taken, it seems, of his return on a similar occasion the year before. This had somewhat chagrined him, and *now* his loyal subjects were resolved to make up for the deficiency. There were to be illuminations for three nights, and of a splendour the like of which was never before seen in Egypt. As evening fell, we sallied forth, a large party on donkeys; and certainly the hubbub of the scene will long live in our remembrance. What a spectacle was that beneath the coloured lamps! The streets were narrow, and choked with the motley crowds. We were swayed helplessly backwards and forwards in the pressure, fortunate indeed if we got along a dozen yards in half an hour. There was, in particular, the most dreadful crushing and confusion when the carriage of the Pasha or any of his nobles was passing; sometimes the wheels were in a dead lock, and the horses rearing wildly; then came the shoutings and beatings of the police and soldiery among the dense and helpless mass; so that afterwards, for a time, the indescribable wrestling and battling for very life of that night came back, and haunted the mind as the recollection of a frightful dream.

But during the day, and in ordinary circumstances, it is delightful to have a donkey ride through Cairo; to gaze at the quaint, fantastic, many-coloured scenes that everywhere meet the eye. The merry little creatures set off with you at a rattling pace, the attendant shouting behind. He insists on keeping at the canter, while entering the most crowded streets, so that you fear that somebody will surely come to grief. Yet accidents rarely happen. The donkey-boy shouts indeed as if the

Pasha himself were coming. "Ouah! Reglah! Shamallek! Yaminak! O man, to the right! O woman, to the left! he comes! he comes! the Howagee comes!" We wound our way through the wonderful bazaars to the citadel of Cairo, where we inspected the famous Mosque of Mohammed Ali, and the scene of the Mameluke tragedy. Looking westward, lo! the Pyramids! They are distant some twenty miles, and on the frontier line between the rich green plain and the brown desert. They do not much impress you at first; pictures have made you feel that you have seen them before. The associations of the Exodus were much more forcibly suggested to my mind by another incident of our sojourn here. When talking with a friend in the narrow street, there burst from a window opposite a sharp startling scream. Ere long it fell into a low sobbing wail, but now and again was heard a wild shriek. A death had occurred. In such a place one thought of the awful night when "there was a great cry in Egypt, for there was not a house where there was not one dead."

We had a pleasant trip one afternoon to Heliopolis, ascertained to be the *On* of Scripture. Here dwelt Potiphar the Priest, the father-in-law of Joseph. It was indeed the "city of the Priests,"—the sanctuary, therefore, of the science and wisdom of Egypt. One obelisk alone remains as a relic of the past, but this is the most ancient in the world. Plato wandered here long ago in search of "wisdom;" and standing at its base, gazed with "thoughtful brow" on the clear-cut hieroglyphics. It now seems as a tombstone, telling of the buried religion of that ancient land.

Shortly after our arrival in Cairo, we were joined by

some friends, who accompanied us through the Desert to Palestine. We were eight in number, and our first trip together was to the Pyramids. The ascent has been often described. It is little else than mounting a stupendous staircase, with the steps from three to four feet high on the average (the Arabs sometimes choosing the most difficult, that you may the better appreciate their assistance), and with no proper landing till you reach the top. I suppose they shout some doggrel with all travellers when pulling and pushing them up to the summit. We mounted to the following strain; and as the shouting of it kept them "in wind" for one thing, it was joined in by some of the party, although it was a compliment to themselves, and "they said it that should not say it:"—"Mulla! Walla! Mash Walla! gentlemen! very good! not afraid! of the money! all right! Bucksheesh! Mulla! Walla!" etc.; each exclamation, be it understood, signifying one step more of the arduous ascent. The Pyramids certainly disappoint in the first view; but as we linger near and think about them, our wonder and interest are strongly excited. Human hands, you cannot but reflect, have reared these marvellous structures, which, along with the hills around, have defied the ravages of time for several thousand years, and apparently will endure for several thousand more. "All things dread time; time dreads the Pyramids." They thus lead the mind far back into the human life of the past; Abraham, Joseph, and many of the Israelites have looked on them.

What was meant by the Pyramids is a question frequently discussed, and to which various answers have been returned. Had their builders any worthy idea at all ? or was it a whim of a tyrant, embodying itself in brick and mortar ? Such seems the general idea, tersely expressed in the phrase that "the Pyramids represent a despotism." It may be questioned whether this theory of their construction is the true one, or that other, which would connect them principally with astronomical observations. A pyramid is simply, it may be said, an enormous tombstone, having a central chamber for the sarcophagus with the mummy. But then why so massive, if this be all ? In the religious ideas of the Egyptians respecting death and immortality, we may, I incline to think, find the true answer to the question. In their idolatry, as in that of other nations, we come upon ideas that point back to an earlier and purer faith. When we think of the embalming of the body, the strength and enduring character of the rock-tombs where it was laid, and the religious and other emblems with which these are decorated, we are led to conclude it to have been part of their religious belief, that the body of earth was somehow to participate in the life of immortality. They did not indeed approach the profound disclosure of the Christian resurrection, by which the body is reclaimed from corruption and decay. For the Christian faith no embalmment is necessary—ashes to ashes, dust to dust; yet "God shall raise it up again." But in ancient Egypt, preparation for death was the engrossing idea ; and the utmost skill was put forth to insure, beyond secular computation, the preservation of the body itself. Especially was this the case with the king, who began to prepare a fitting tomb for himself as soon as he ascended the throne. His corpse was expensively embalmed ; a series of chambers, like those of a palace, were deeply cut into the rock, and in the inmost of them was deposited the sarcophagus with the mummy. Great care was taken to prevent the chambers from ever being entered, or even discovered. All around were painted representations of gods, and the manifold varieties of Egyptian life, to meet the eyes of the king on awakening. Thus the great underlying idea was, that the body would be resuscitated after distant ages; and the grand solicitude was to secure it a safe and enduring mausoleum in the interval of its long repose.

Such an idea may explain for us the structure of the Pyramids. It was an attempt to accomplish the object by a pile of masonry, whose gigantic dimensions should rival the strength of the rock-cut tombs, and last through the prolonged period likely to intervene before the re-awakening of the body in the central chamber. And tombs of this construction so prominent to the view, tended besides to gratify the pride of the monarch, who doubtless believed that by them his fame would be perpetuated to all time. The fond dream of the royal builder has however been falsified. His very name is in dispute. The passage to the inner chamber has been discovered. With painful effort you struggle through the narrow entrance, and, getting within, find the sarcophagus already opened, and not a shred of the mummy remaining. The dreaded dishonour has been perpetrated; and grinning Arabs shout their gutturals and dance their torch-dance beside you, in the greatest tomb of the Pharaohs.

> "Let not a monument give you or me hopes,
> For not a pinch of dust remains of Cheops."

After our exit we lingered by the Sphinx, in the short

but beautiful twilight. The full moon rose from the horizon opposite, and we watched the effect, as it brought out one by one the features of that massive, mysterious, awful face.

Our quarters for the night were in an adjacent rock-cut tomb. Fleas abounded, and the wakeful restlessness of sojourners in such circumstances was our fate. After a twentieth attempt at sleep, we welcomed the glorious dawn in the east, and, breakfast over, were soon on our way to Memphis.

We rode across the plain, eastward by the Pyramids of Sacchara. The first impression was that we were in the unchanged Libyan desert. But no; these wastes of sand cover up miles of burial-ground :

"Stop! for thy tread is on an Empire's dust."

For twenty miles, it is said, this cemetery extends. Numbers of gods and kings, of priests and people, are promiscuously sepulchred below.

Descending into some of the tombs recently excavated, we found them covered with the representations of the Egyptian life before referred to. The ancient race are delineated as fishing, ploughing, building, cooking, and engaged in the various amusements and trades of social life; and so vivid was the colouring, that it seemed as if the brush of the painter had left them but yesterday. The ornamentation was more like that of a palace than of a sepulchre; the intention being, as already remarked, that when the sleeper awakes, he should have suggested before him the scenes of his earthly existence. Anywhere the tomb of a human being is beheld with reverence, and the pilgrim in the East gazes with deep feelings on the graveyards of the poor Arabs in the desert of

Sinai, marked by a rude stone tilted on edge, no less than on those princely mausoleums of Egypt. But it was with other feelings that we descended to inspect another class of the tombs in this locality, that have been described as by far the most splendid in the world. Lowering ourselves through an entrance in the sand, we soon reached a wide and lofty tunnel cut in the rock. As we passed along, the gleam of the torchlight on either side of it, revealed large vaulted apartments. Almost every one contained a sarcophagus of black marble, of vast dimensions: eight feet deep, as many broad, and fifteen feet long; at the same time exquisitely polished, cut out of one block, and, when struck, ringing with a bell-like clearness. Each was a tomb for the Egyptian god Apis, the "ox that eateth grass." Strabo, speaking of Memphis, says: "The bull Apis is kept in an enclosure, treated as a god, permitted to go out of the enclosure when strangers are desirous of seeing him, and after showing himself a little, is taken back again;" and it would appear that the brute felt the confinement and attention of the priest to be somewhat of a "bore." After his natural decease, here was the splendid entombment.

We now passed on to Memphis, whose ancient grandeur none could have guessed from its present appearance. There remain only what seem extensive mounds of ruin, wrapped in the sands of the desert, and melting into a vast green plain, which is fertilized by the periodic inundation of the Nile. There is still, on the surface, however, a statue of Rameses, the Sesostris of the Greeks, the king of greatest fame in the history of ancient Egypt. He is said to have carried his victories far into Asia and Europe, leaving behind, in various places, the exulting inscription on the rocks, "I conquered this country by my arms." The chronicles of the greatness of this king are repeated in every form in the statues and hieroglyphics among the ruins of the distant upper capital, Thebes. One statue is there seen, sixty feet high; throughout he is represented as of great size, and other mortals are as pigmies in comparison. His prowess and triumphs are variously represented. Now he is returning from the wars with numbers of captives; again, he is driving his chariot over the prostrate bodies; again, he is standing scornfully, with his heel on their necks. They implore him, "Behold, give us breath, O king; we are fast bound beneath thy sandals." But at this lower capital there remains visible only this statue of large size, although it is probable that there are others entombed in the ruins around; and the face here, as elsewhere, is placid, pensive, with an expression of high disdain,—a look altogether befitting the traditions of the ruthless conqueror. Erect at one time, the statue is now prostrate in the mud, face downward, like the image of the captives he tramples on; and fears have been expressed, that some day it may be burned for lime, or in other ways destroyed.

As the main object of this work is the endeavour to fix, with something like accuracy, the localities of Scripture, we must linger for a little round this scene at Memphis; for here, I believe, was the capital of Pharaoh at the time of the Exodus.

There is one great mistake, as it seems to me, that has entered into the discussion relating to this locality. It has been too hastily presumed that Moses and Aaron were actually in the capital (wherever it may have been) during the awful night of the death of the first-born. Now, it is said, considering that the Israelites marched out in thirty hours after this event, and that Moses and Aaron had to travel to them, after receiving Pharaoh's permission to depart; considering, also, the necessary arrangements and trouble in the moving of so vast a multitude, we must conceive of the capital as situated within a few miles of Goshen, whence they started. The alternatives usually presented are these: if Goshen was in the north, the capital was also there (Zoan); on the other hand, if the capital was in the south (Memphis), Goshen was there likewise, and consequently in the vicinity of Cairo and Heliopolis. I hope afterwards to point out the errors of this reasoning, and to show that there are no valid reasons for making the localities thus adjoin. Meanwhile, let us look at the strong testimony which indicates Memphis as the capital of Lower Egypt.

1. The most ancient tradition points to Memphis alone. It was built by Menes, the first king. At vast expense he directed the course of the Nile eastwards, embanked it carefully, and on the ground thus reclaimed erected the city. This tradition, says Sir J. Gardner Wilkinson, is confirmed by the appearance of the bend of the river fifteen miles north from the site of the city.

2. Some of the most ancient ideas in the mythology of Greece came from the customs of Memphis. Between the town and the tombs in the Libyan hills was a lake, across which, after certain payments and ceremonies, the dead were ferried. From this custom, according to ancient historians, arose the story of Charon, his ferry-boat, and the penny in payment for carrying the ghosts across the Styx.

3. That it is the ancient capital, seems also deducible from the situation of the pyramids, and the miles of tombs, now covered by the sands of the desert in the vicinity. The monarchs of Egypt were certainly buried near their capital, and neither at Zoan nor elsewhere in Lower Egypt are there such evidences of royal sepulchres as lie around Memphis.

4. The capital of the country was much less likely to be built beside the comparatively small offshoot of the Nile which passes Zoan, than close to the full volume of waters flowing past Memphis.

5. The only reference of the Scripture narrative, that bears on the subject, points to this locality. "A west wind," it is said, "drove the locusts into the Red Sea." At Memphis, this would be the effect of such a wind, but the passage cannot be understood if the capital were farther north, as a glance at the map will show.

Many considerations, therefore, combine to support the view that Memphis was the capital at the time of the Exodus. Doubtless Zoan was a town of distinction. The Bible refers not only to "the princes of Noph," but also to "the princes of Zoan," and from it a name was given to the surrounding district. As it bordered on Goshen, the Israelites saw there the judgment inflicted on the Egyptians, of which, elsewhere, they could hear only the report. Hence it is written, "Marvellous things did he in sight of their fathers in the land of Egypt, in the field of Zoan." But this in no way militates against the belief that Memphis, the Noph of Scripture, was the metropolis.

It is difficult, when wandering over these desolate plains, to conjure up that city of splendour, where dwelt the proud monarch of Egypt. The prophet, telling his vision, exclaims, " Noph is desolate !" and so it has come to pass.

It has not, as already observed, the gorgeous wealth of ruined grandeur that is so astounding to the visitor at Thebes. The ancient materials here were probably used up in building the more modern city, which, even at the Christian era, rivalled Alexandria in size and population. The embankments of the Nile, too, have here fallen down, allowing the inundations to cover its site, and over much of it the sands of the adjacent desert have accumulated to the depth of thirty or forty feet. But though its colonnades, pillars, and halls have disappeared, or, it may be, are entombed, there yet survive memorials that indicate its ancient glory. What a city that must have been which is represented by the pyramids! If such were the tombs, what were its palaces to correspond?

Around, everything would combine to flatter the immense pride of a Pharaoh, a feature of Egyptian royalty to be always remembered, if we would appreciate the Scripture narrative. There is on this point an obvious harmony between the language of the Bible and that of the sculptured representations which bear reference to the "glory of the king." The colossal forms tell how high the imagination placed him above all other mortals; the inscriptions flatter him as a god. Corresponding with all this, are the expressions of Scripture, " I am Pharaoh ;" the oath of the Egyptians was " by the life of Pharaoh ;" and the prophet Ezekiel heaps images of splendour and strength in answer to the question, " Say unto Pharaoh, To whom art thou like in thy greatness ?"

To the Pharaoh of the Exodus, when the metropolis had reached the zenith of its glory, such a question might be emphatically put; and it was the intoxicating estimate of his own power, inherited from the traditions of centuries, that made him "lift up his heart against the Lord," and refuse to humble himself when smitten by fearful judgments.

In the streets of this splendid capital are seen the two Hebrew brothers, venerable in years, but full of energy, passing through its crowds, and bending their steps toward the palace of the king. They bear the badge of the oppressed race whose cause they have undertaken. With what peculiar emotions would Moses move among those Memphian splendours! He was the son of Pharaoh's daughter, and, if tradition is to be believed, even the throne might have been his. But he now appears in the dress of a Bedouin of the desert, not in the raiment of a royal prince; he beholds without envy this earthly greatness; "He chooses rather to suffer affliction with the people of God." This return from exile was not of his seeking. He would have preferred the stillness of the desert life, with solemn musings amid the sublime grandeurs of Sinai. When he sought his first interview with the king, our wonder is how it should have been granted. But the statement of the Jewish historian indicates that he, the messenger, was not unknown to the servants of Pharaoh. At one time he was the commander of the armies of Egypt, and achieved victories which delivered the upper provinces from an Ethiopian invasion. To this St. Stephen probably referred when he declares that he was known among them by "mighty deeds." His was a name, too, associated with fear, because of what the oracles had uttered respecting it. Such a personage would not be refused; and we may suppose that the new Pharaoh would be anxious to see one of whose achievements he could not have failed to hear.

He delivers the message: "Thus saith the Lord God of Israel, Let my people go, that they may serve me. And Pharaoh said, Who is the Lord, that I should obey his voice to let Israel go? I know not the Lord, neither will I let Israel go." The pride and scorn of the answer are what might have been expected. Well enough had it been a message from the priests of Apis, of the sacred Ibis, or other gods of the temples; but from the God of Israel!—the God of the slaves! who was he? It were vain for Moses to argue with such a potentate in mere words. The answer was to be in deeds. "God shall be known by his judgments."

First there are the signs, which the skilled magicians can at least imitate. Then come the plagues, which they have no wish or power to repeat. They pause awe-struck, and say, "It is the finger of God!" Together with the servants of Pharaoh, they prostrate themselves, and seek to alter the decision of that proud heart. In vain; and the judgments become heavier as they continue to fall. The last is preceded by a silent and palpable darkness for three days, an appalling phenomenon, especially in such a country. "They saw not one another, neither rose any from his place for three days;" each sitting helpless and passive as the statues of their temples. Then came that crushing blow, the death of the first-born; "from the first-born of Pharaoh that sitteth upon his throne, even unto the first-born of the maid-servant that is behind the mill. And there was a great cry throughout all the land of Egypt, such as there was none like it, nor shall be like it any more."

In these judgments that fell on idolatrous Egypt, we may "behold the goodness and severity of God." In all idolatries, and certainly in that of Egypt, we come upon the traces of a purer and earlier faith. But, in this instance, the truth had been darkened by the most hideous and debasing corruptions that ever provoked the patience of Heaven. It was a system of worship that had passed to the lowest stage of the inspired description, "images of four-footed beasts and creeping things." As we walk through the sacred galleries of the tombs of the Bull Apis, as we view the pits of the mummy-gods, and see on the monuments the images of hawks, dogs, monkeys, serpents, all adored and worshipped, we feel that we look on the lowest depths of ancient idolatry. And that nation who, as *a fact*, were afterwards to give to the world the purest revelation of heaven, are sunk in all this; breathing its horrible atmosphere, and becoming tainted to the core with its worst vices, as their subsequent history too plainly shows!

Blessed surely were the judgments that set them free, stern though they were. Bitter as was the earthly bondage of the chosen people, more killing by far was this enslavement of their souls. Their Exodus meant the liberation of humanity; the determination of Heaven that the soul of man should not thus perish in brutishness and darkness, but go forth to the faith and the rapture of Prophets and Psalmists, to the hopes and the holiness of the gospel of Christ.

CHAPTER II.

GOSHEN, AND THE EVENTS OF THE EXODUS.

THEIR residence and bondage in Egypt, it may be proper to remark, prepared the Israelites for the development of their future national life. They entered Goshen a family of shepherds, and went out from it a large nation. Had they remained in Palestine, it is not easy to see how they could have grown to be a nation at all. As the families increased, they would have been broken up, dispersed, and absorbed by the existing populations of the country. But in Goshen, the colony had room to expand, their occupation of shepherds keeping them quite distinct from the Egyptians. Their bitter bondage likewise powerfully tended to promote the feeling that they were a separate people; the fellowship of suffering evoked deep sympathy and mutual help, which bound them closer to each other, and raised still more firmly a barrier between them and other nations. This sense of national unity, so remarkably developed in their history, was of vast importance for the defence of the mighty interests intrusted to their keeping; and thus the means employed by the oppressor for their degradation and ruin, were overruled by Him who makes "the wrath of man to praise Him," for their ultimate good, and tended to make them, in a still higher degree, his chosen instruments for conveying spiritual blessings to the world.

It is an interesting inquiry, What caused the Egyptians to treat that people so cruelly? They not only spurned them as slaves, but dreaded them as enemies; here was the peculiarity. They doubtless possessed other slaves, captives of war; as it was a common boast on the monuments of Egypt, "no native worked hereon." But these were not ground to the dust as the descendants of Israel were. The Egyptians became jealous of their *power*, a feeling for which their numbers can hardly account, and we do not read of their having attempted a revolt. How then explain a policy so murderous, one which really aimed at the extermination of that people as a distinct race? The answer is found in the consideration of an event in the history of ancient Egypt, which, as it is supplied from an Egyptian source, strikingly confirms the historic truth of the Pentateuch.

Josephus, in his book against Apion, gives a long quotation from the writings of Manetho, a historian of Egypt, and who by his own account gathered his materials from the Sacred books. Part of it is to the effect, that in the far antiquity a foreign race came from the East and conquered Egypt, holding possession of it for 500 years. They were known as the Hyksos or Shepherd kings. After a struggle of 80 years, they were conquered by a king of Ethiopia, and driven back to their own country of Palestine and Arabia.

The students of Egyptian history have earnestly discussed the question, At what period were the intruders expelled? One theory, supported by eminent names, affirms that it was during the stay of the Israelites. It is alleged that it was owing to these Shepherd Kings being on the throne, that the family from Palestine were received with favour, and had assigned to them such a fertile district. But "a new king arose that knew not Joseph." This is held to mean that the old Egyptian dynasty was once more restored, and naturally began to oppress the pastoral colony.

It is difficult, however, to see how such a theory consists with the plain facts of the Scripture narrative. The kindness shown to Jacob and his household on their descent to Egypt, was certainly *not* owing to their "occupation," but rather in spite of it, for it is expressly stated that "every shepherd was an abomination to the Egyptians." That notwithstanding this, they were so kindly welcomed, was due solely to the high influence of Joseph with the king. Again, if the shepherd dynasty were expelled at the time supposed, how came it that the Israelites were left behind? They must have made common cause in the struggle, and would not have remained in the country to endure their certain fate of insult and oppression.

The fact is, that when we read of Egypt in the time of the Patriarchs, it is of a country of high prosperity and power, warranting the inference that even before that period the expulsion of the Hyksos had taken place, and that the dynasty of Pharaoh again bore sway. Even then had arisen the hate and prejudice against all who followed the pastoral life. Keeping this in view, many somewhat strange incidents in the narrative are clearly explained. Thus the shepherd patriarchs, Abraham, Isaac, and Jacob, seemed to have a dread of this country, and to go thither only on the pressure of famine. Joseph, their descendant, is sold there as a slave, and but for the events of an overruling Providence, would have died in the bondage of a prison. His brethren go down to Egypt, as a last resource from the terrible famine of their time. His strange language on their arrival is, on our hypothesis, clearly explained. He says, "Ye are spies," that is, "ye are emissaries of the expelled race, and are again plotting to reconquer the country." Regarding the feelings of the Egyptians, he does not eat with them, even after he makes himself known as their brother. Moreover, he skilfully manages to make the existing prejudices tell for their advantage, in securing for them a rich pastoral district, where they would be free from all annoyance. He announces plainly to Pharaoh that his brethren are shepherds, and instructs them also to place this fact in the foreground of their answer to his inquiries. "When Pharaoh shall say, What is your occupation? ye shall say, Thy servants' trade hath been about cattle from our youth even until now, both we and also our fathers; that ye may dwell in the land of Goshen: for every shepherd is an abomination unto the Egyptians" (Gen. xlvi. 33).

Above all, this event of the invasion and expulsion of the Shepherd Kings, explains the jealousy with which the growth of the Israelites in Goshen came to be regarded. "A king rose up that knew not Joseph," *i.e.*, one who did not know or care to remember the service done to his country by a relative of that shepherd colony. He only saw that "they increase and multiply exceedingly." Remembering the past, he became afraid of the consequences. He dreaded a second invasion. If the expelled Hyksos should return from the East, they would be sure to find an ally in these shepherds of Goshen. "Come now," said the alarmed Pharaoh, "let us deal wisely with them, lest they multiply, and it come to pass that when there falleth out war, they join also unto our enemies and fight against us." Hence the bitter oppression that was resolved upon, the cry of which reached to heaven, and resulted in the terrible judgments of the Exodus.

It may be well to add, that in another extract of Manetho's history quoted by Josephus, we have an account of the expulsion from Egypt of a vast multitude of leper slaves, who also went towards the East. This is thought by some to be the account of the Scripture Exodus (though Josephus himself will not have it so), told in a way such as might be expected from the boastful pride of ancient Egypt. Now, the historian asserts that the leprous race sought alliance with the Hyksos, or expelled Shepherd Kings, and actually obtained it to the consternation of the Egyptian monarch. Indeed, the whole of Manetho's story, or legend, points to a group of facts such as those of the Scripture narrative; and we can understand how the fear expressed by Pharaoh roused the whole nation, and secured the co-operation of all in the work of enslaving and exterminating the suspected race. They were made to cease from their loved pastoral life, and compelled to build the cities of Pethom and Rameses,[1]—"treasure cities,"—walled or fortified towns on the frontiers of Arabia, and erected, no doubt, with the design of preventing the dreaded invasion from the East. Thus, then, Egyptian history aids in the proof that the narrative of the Pentateuch is true, and supplies

[1] Named Raamses, in Ex. i. 11, simply from a difference in the points.

us with an event which throws light on incidents which otherwise would not have been so easily explained.

Goshen was the district assigned to the Israelites when they entered Egypt, and was occupied by them during all their sojourn. It is not uncommon, indeed, to represent them as scattered through Egypt; working at their tasks away northwards as far as Thebes. A monument, some have fancied, exists there, on which appears a representation of their bondage. On closer examination, it has been found that such is not its meaning, and certainly the Scripture narrative would warrant no such idea. For on *one* occasion only, the oppressed people are said to " be scattered abroad throughout all the land of Egypt, to gather stubble instead of straw." In Goshen was the scene of their toil throughout; their great task being to build and fortify the new frontier cities for Pharaoh. Only beneath the ruins in this district, then, or under those of the lower capital, Memphis, can the discovery of such sculptured representations be expected, if they exist at all.

And now, where was Goshen? Some contend, as does Lepsius, that this district adjoins Cairo and Heliopolis. The Israelites, it is thought, actually set out from the vicinity of the capital, Memphis. Accordingly, in pictorial representations of the scene, the Pyramids are usually seen in the background of their imposing procession,—a circumstance naturally enough investing it with additional interest. They marched, according to this theory, right eastwards by the valley Tawarik to the Red Sea; and this route, pointed out to passengers sailing down that gulf, is often pronounced " to be as like the thing as possible."

Notwithstanding such recommendations, the placing of Goshen in this locality is subject to insuperable objections.

1. It seems questionable, from the very fact that it is so near the capital, Memphis ; near also to Heliopolis (On), the town of the priests. Not to dwell on the circumstance that this district would be densely peopled, and so could not afford room for the strangers, here surely, more than anywhere else in Egypt, they would have been the victims of those prejudices, at once patriotic and religious, from which it was certainly the object of Joseph and the King to deliver them as much as possible. If throughout the land "every shepherd was an abomination to the Egyptians," how much more would this be the case in the vicinity of the capital, and under the shadow of its temples ? Could this, then, be the locality which Joseph would select for his brethren, that they might follow in peace the pastoral life of their forefathers ?

2. We are told, "when Joseph heard that his father had come to Goshen, he made ready his chariot, and went up to meet him." On this theory, the distance is but short, and no very great honour was paid after all. The Patriarch had not only passed the frontier, but entered far into the country, almost within view of the capital itself. Joseph then takes his chariot, and goes some twenty miles to welcome him ! This cannot be the meaning of the narrative, and is not in keeping with the reverent affection of such a son.

3. Still further, we cannot make out the route of the Israelites to the Red Sea, if they start from this district. There are but two stations in the way thither, viz., Succoth and Etham. The distance is eighty miles, to be overtaken in three stages, or thirty miles at a stretch !

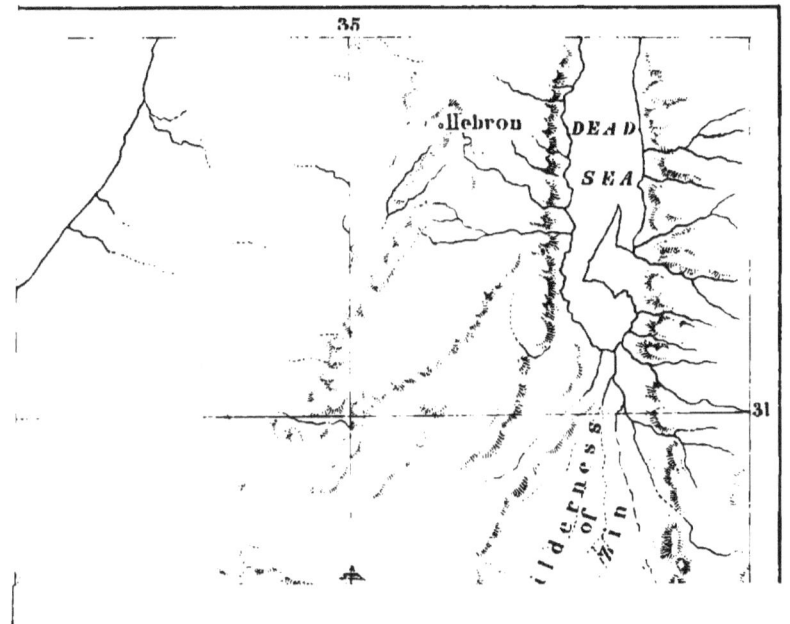

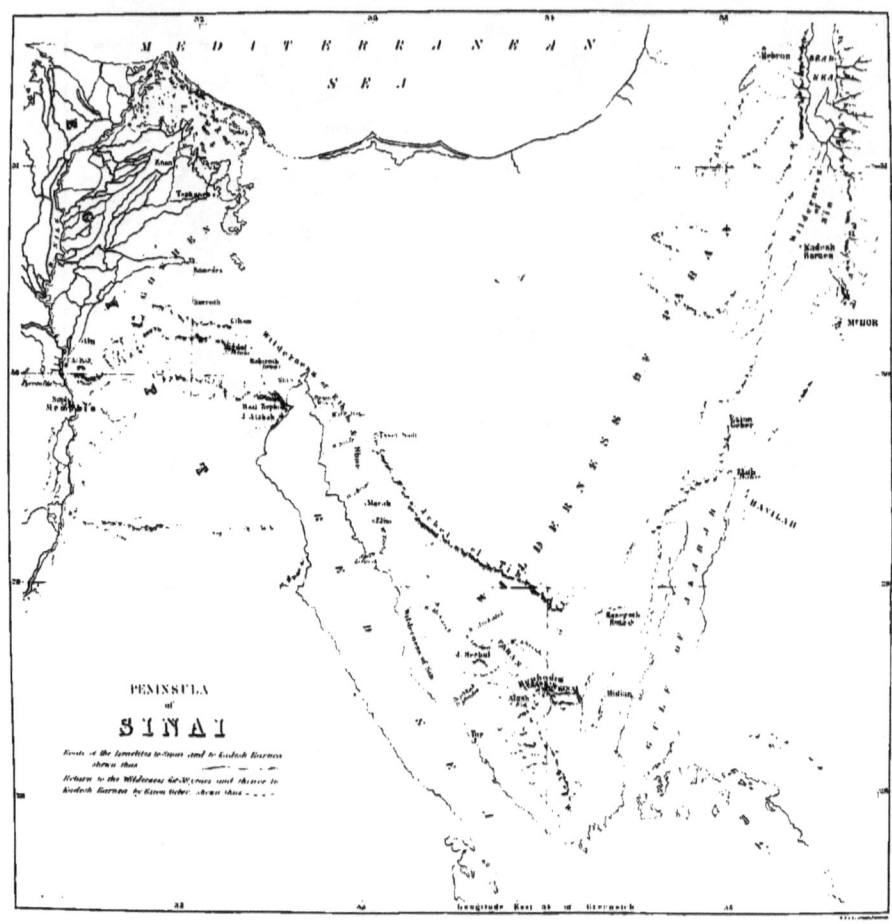

4. Again, they are commanded, when at Etham, "to turn by way of the Red Sea." The phrase has no meaning if they have gone by this route, for they are going direct to the Red Sea all the while, as a glimpse at the map will show. In such a case Pharaoh, when he decided on pursuit, would have thought of the sea as the great barrier in the direction of their march. He would have said, the sea, not the wilderness, hath shut them in.

5. Once more, the narrative shows that they reached "Etham on the edge of the wilderness," *before* coming to the Red Sea. But starting from Cairo, they *must* have come to the shores of that gulf first of all, and so the successive order of their encampments would have been reversed.

Away on the north-east of Egypt, on the way to Palestine, and adjacent to the desert of Arabia, lies a fertile province, where are still produced luxuriant supplies of such savoury herbs—garlic, leeks, onions—as the Israelites longed for in the desert. The Nile here disperses its full flood in numerous streams, which prove a source of continued fruitfulness. This is Goshen, as Robinson and others have held. It is one of the richest agricultural provinces of Egypt to this day, and the most ancient tradition clearly points to this locality. Thus the Septuagint speaks of Goshen as "the Goshen of *Arabia*," which implies its adjoining the desert. Also, the same authority names Hieropolis as the place where Joseph met his father in Goshen: and by Strabo and Ptolemy this town is placed north of the Red Sea, and in this locality. Again, the towns of Goshen, mentioned in Scripture, are Rameses and Pithon. The latter is understood to be the Patumia of Herodotus, which he expressly calls an Arabian city.

4. Again, they are commanded, when at Etham, "to turn by way of the Red Sea." The phrase has no meaning if they have gone by this route, for they are going direct to the Red Sea all the while, as a glimpse at the map will show. In such a case Pharaoh, when he decided on pursuit, would have thought of the sea as the great barrier in the direction of their march. He would have said, the sea, not the wilderness, hath shut them in.

5. Once more, the narrative shows that they reached " Etham on the edge of the wilderness," *before* coming to the Red Sea. But starting from Cairo, they *must* have come to the shores of that gulf first of all, and so the successive order of their encampments would have been reversed.

Away on the north-east of Egypt, on the way to Palestine, and adjacent to the desert of Arabia, lies a fertile province, where are still produced luxuriant supplies of such savoury herbs—garlic, leeks, onions— as the Israelites longed for in the desert. The Nile here disperses its full flood in numerous streams, which prove a source of continued fruitfulness. This is Goshen, as Robinson and others have held. It is one of the richest agricultural provinces of Egypt to this day, and the most ancient tradition clearly points to this locality. Thus the Septuagint speaks of Goshen as " the Goshen of *Arabia*," which implies its adjoining the desert. Also, the same authority names Hieropolis as the place where Joseph met his father in Goshen ; and by Strabo and Ptolemy this town is placed north of the Red Sea, and in this locality. Again, the towns of Goshen, mentioned in Scripture, are Rameses and Pithon. The latter is understood to be the Patumia of Herodotus, which he expressly calls an Arabian city.

From the East, as we have seen, the invasion was dreaded, and it was to meet this that such cities were erected,—a view of their design corroborated by the statements of Manetho, who speaks of strong fortified cities built by the Egyptians in this very direction.

Situated thus on the frontier, we can appreciate the exhibition of filial regard shown by Joseph to his aged father. The announcement that Jacob had come to Goshen, meant that he had fairly entered Egypt, and at once the son hastened from the distant capital, to greet him with impassioned reverence and affection. He " made ready his chariot, and went up to meet Israel his father, to Goshen, and presented himself unto him : and fell on his neck, and wept a good while."

And now also we can understand the route to the Red Sea. They reach Succoth ; then they come " to Etham on the edge of the wilderness." Away from the point here marked on the map, stretched the desert, downward upon the eastern shore of the Red Sea ; and named the wilderness of Etham, very likely, from a town of this name, at which the Israelites had now arrived. It is obvious, that had they gone right forwards, they would have been in the wilderness of Etham, without crossing the Red Sea at all. Such was exactly the supposition of Pharaoh. He fancies that it is the waste of the vast desert that frightens them, and detains them in the borders of his territory. " They are entangled in the land" (Egypt), and the wilderness hath shut them in." But they are told " to *turn by way* of the Red Sea," and accordingly his pursuing army finds them encamped on its shores.

Recent controversies have awakened attention to

other points in the Pentateuch than those now discussed, and require that we treat of the events as well as the scenes of the Exodus. It has been long felt that the narrative contains "some things hard to be understood." There are cases in which we are puzzled to explain how events could have happened as the writer has represented. Such difficulties, indeed, are more or less inevitable in every ancient record. Nor could it be expected that the Pentateuch would be free of them,—a narrative professedly of high antiquity,— necessarily elliptical and fragmentary, dealing with the manners and spirit of an age so foreign to our own in many respects, and belonging to a period now lying behind us several thousand years. Notwithstanding these problems, therefore, which the commentator on the Pentateuch had to encounter, its high value as a truthful history was acknowledged; held to be established on the most unassailable grounds, and to lie, indeed, at the very foundation of the whole scheme of revelation. The questions referred to were regarded as fair topics for free discussion, on which different explanations might be attempted, and the difficulties attendant on which, we might expect, would greatly give way, if not altogether disappear, before deeper investigation and more extended research.

But of late the matter has assumed a somewhat startling aspect. Bishop Colenso, carefully mustering these difficulties, has sought to fashion them into an array of formidable objections, which, as he contends, fatally vitiate the reliable character of the record in which they occur. In his hands, the Pentateuch, to whose incidents prophets and psalmists so often refer with such earnestness and rapture, and which is quoted with such unsuspecting confidence by our Lord and his apostles in the enforcement of their teaching, sinks into a legend for the leisure hour; one cleverly concocted, and graphically written, but a *legend* still. As a historical record, he affirms, the Book is altogether unworthy of credit. It is not surely to be wondered at, that the rude violence thus inflicted on many sacred associations should have been most keenly felt, and that a decision so startling and peremptory should have provoked a loud remonstrance and protest alike from the learned and unlearned of the Christian world. However, the appearance of his book has been productive of one good result. It has awakened a fresh inquiry into passages of difficulty that were formerly too lightly handled, and developed an amount of critical and historical investigation which will prove of great advantage to the cause of truth on the various points under discussion.

The Bishop busies himself too much with the opinions of commentators, who, it is generally understood, are not infallible. To dispose of an argument, or a "private interpretation," is not equivalent to disposing of the history of the Pentateuch. The meaning of the sacred writer may have been misunderstood: a more comprehensive view of his hints and statements may lead to a juster interpretation and a more satisfactory solution; and the objections may tell oftentimes only against the errors of the commentator, not the veracity of the author. The following considerations may tend to show that in many cases, when the Pentateuch is allowed to speak for itself, the objections urged against it appear plainly to be baseless and irrelevant, and may aid in removing some difficulties deeply felt by many conscientious minds, and in restoring a *truer* conception of the real character and events of the Exodus.

Let me be allowed a preliminary remark on the much agitated question of the number of the Israelites on leaving Egypt. It is alleged in the narrative, as it has come down to us, that there were 600,000 *f'ghting-men*,—implying a total population of about 2,000,000. It is long since these numbers were suspected, and a proposal has been made to correct them by cutting off a cipher, reducing the number of adults to 60,000, and the total population to about half a million. This is *not*, as some may assert, giving up the inspiration of the sacred writer. It is only implying an error of the copyist and the translator, for which the original author cannot be held in any way responsible. All admit that clauses, and even verses, have crept into the text which are not genuine, and yet the doctrine of the inspiration of the sacred writer, in the highest and most literal sense, may be firmly held. Where such blunders are made, it is to be observed, that there lie *in the record itself* the means of rectification. The narrative will be self-corrective. The present, I am inclined to believe, is a case in point, as the following fact may show. The number of all the male Levites, from a month old and upwards, is declared to be 22,000. This must be held as correct, for it is compared with the numbers of the first-born in all the tribes, which amount to 22,273. This figure, of course, cannot be altered, as it has no cipher to strike off; and besides, for the surplus (273) payment was exacted. Out of this number of all the males in the tribe of Levi, then, how many *adults* or fighting-men might there be? On the average we may say as 1 : 4, or about 5000. Let this calculation be placed alongside the number of adults in the other tribes. Judah has 74,600 ; Reuben 46,500 ; the lowest, Manasseh, had 32,200, etc. Here is obviously an immense disproportion in numbers, which it is possible did not belong to the original statement. But reduce the numbers by cutting off a cipher, as suggested, and due proportion is apparent. Levi about 5000 ; Judah 7460 ; Reuben 4650 ; Manasseh 3220. Dr. Colenso says the numbers in our common version must be those of the original writer, as they are checked and counter-checked. But the above reduction will stand the same test, as every one can find on experiment. The Exodus, then, *may* have consisted of 60,000 fighting-men ; a population like that of Liverpool, instead of that of London, to which the Bishop so earnestly persists in comparing it for the reader's appreciation of his argument.

Let us now notice the statements of the Pentateuch on the following points :—I. The gathering of the spoils. II. The children of Israel going out harnessed in battle array from Egypt. III. The keeping of the passover. IV. The march afterwards to the Red Sea. On these matters, says the Bishop, the language of the narrative is incredible and contradictory. The simple answer is, that he has misread that language.

I. As to the gathering of the spoil.

It was very great,—" they went out laden." But when was it collected ? On the day before the Exodus, is the usual reply ; one, however, which the narrative by no means sanctions. The Israelites asked for that treasure by command of Jehovah. Now, this command was first given to Moses at the "*burning bush of Horeb.*" "I will give this people favour in the sight of the Egyptians: and it shall come to pass, that, when ye go, ye shall not go empty: But (or rather *also*) every woman shall borrow of her neighbour, and of her that sojourneth in her house, jewels of silver, and jewels of gold, and raiment: and ye shall put them upon your sons, and upon your daughters; and ye shall spoil the Egyptians" (Ex. iii. 22). Moses returned with Aaron to Egypt; and we read that they "gathered all the elders of the children of Israel. And Aaron spake all the words which the Lord had spoken unto Moses, and did the signs in the sight of the people. And the people believed" (Ex. iv. 29-30). It is plain, therefore, that the people knew at the very outset that they were eventually to gather great spoil; and we must infer that they would act upon the divine command at the first opportunity. This was soon furnished in the state of mind produced by the judgments on their oppressors, which extended over a lengthened period. The monarch, indeed, hardened his heart and was unyielding to the last; but it must have been far otherwise with the terror-stricken populations. Each plague was heavier than the one before, and they became overwhelmed with bewilderment and fear. The magicians declared, even in the presence of Pharaoh, "This is the finger of God." His servants expostulated, "How long shall this man be a snare unto us? Let the men go that they may serve the Lord their God; knowest thou not yet that Egypt is destroyed?" Thus, long before the night of the Exodus, during the slow months when the judgments were falling, the Egyptians evinced a state of feeling which would make them anxious to propitiate the favour of the Israelites, and yield the gifts for which, by the command of God, they were to ask. And we may think of weeks instead of hours as the time within which the spoils were collected.

In further confirmation of this, let us notice that Moses, by divine direction, *repeats* the command on this very matter before he goes into the capital of Pharaoh to utter the last warning. They are earnestly to embrace this opportunity, for it is the last; one more judgment and they bid farewell to Egypt. It is expressly added "that the Lord gave the people favour in the sight of the Egyptians," from which we are to infer that they complied with the command at this *very time*, and that much treasure was in consequence accumulated. Looking at the events that follow, we may well believe that all this was done several weeks before the Exodus. For Moses thereafter goes in to warn Pharaoh, as stated in the 11th chapter, and delivers the minute instructions to the people about the Passover, contained in the greater part of the 12th. He tells them that this month was to be to them the beginning of months, that they are to select a lamb on the tenth day, and slay it on the fourteenth. Such language, candidly considered, allows and even requires us to believe that Moses was back among his own people at the commencement of the Passover months, two weeks at least before the Exodus.

On the whole, then, there was *not* the hurry and scramble in the collecting of the spoils on the day of the Exodus, which has been often supposed. On that day, indeed, it is highly probable that the Egyptians pressed more of their gifts on the Israelites. The first-born in their families lay dead. Their own life was in danger. What to them now were worldly possessions? They would give anything if only that dread people were fairly out of their country, for the Egyptians said, "We be all dead men." We need not wonder, then, that in these circumstances it should be recorded for the *second* time that "the Lord gave the people favour in the sight of the Egyptians" (Ex. xii. 35).

II. Such a view of the case disposes of another objection that has been urged. The Israelites are described as going out "harnessed" from Egypt. It seems impossible to avoid taking the word here in its usual sense, meaning "armed" or "in battle array." Such is its established rendering, and any other suggested for the passage before us only increases the difficulties in our apprehending the real sense of the writer. He would have us clearly to understand that the Israelites went out furnished with weapons of war.

Bishop Colenso asks, how were these obtained? The idea of their "turning out at a moment's notice," as he expresses it, so equipped and ready for battle, is in the highest degree extravagant, and not to be received. But why this idea at all?

If we are to suppose such an extension of time for collecting the spoils of Egypt, as has been indicated, then the fair inference is, that the Israelites had gathered the kind required for purposes of war long before their departure. Not only so, but there is language used in the 6th chapter of Exodus, which implies that they were to be especially careful in acquiring gifts of this sort.

"These are that Moses and Aaron to whom the Lord said, Bring out the children of Israel from the land of Egypt according to their *armies*," *i.e.*, in the manner of men *equipped for war*. And in Exodus xii. 51, the same idea is expressed, "The Lord did bring the children of Israel out of the land of Egypt by their armies."

It being then commanded from the first that they should go forth in this fashion, the idea to be entertained is, that while the women were collecting "the raiment and the jewels," the men were careful to possess themselves of weapons with which to fight the battles before them. Moses also, I again remind the reader, had, according to Josephus, at one time been the commander of the Egyptian army, and St. Stephen, in his address to the Sanhedrim, seems to allude to his " mighty deeds" in that capacity. His ability as a leader conspicuously appeared in the journeyings of the Israelites, and thus he was admirably fitted to counsel them in the acquisition of the arms that were necessary, and to superintend the whole matter of their military organization.

But Bishop Colenso asks again, How can we suppose that Pharaoh would allow the Israelites to possess such gifts ? The reply is, How could he hinder them ? His people are driven distracted by the judgments. "Egypt," they declare, " is destroyed." They are disposed to give anything, as has been said, if only the Israelites were well away from their land. It is expressly recorded that "Moses was very great in the sight of Pharaoh, of his servants, and in the sight of his people, and the Lord gave the people favour in the sight of the Egyptians" (Ex. xi. 3). The objection supposes that Pharaoh held the chosen people by force of arms up to the hour when he consents to let them go. It was far otherwise. Had the Divine Deliverer so pleased, the Exodus might have taken place long before, and Pharaoh, with his people, prostrate under the judgments, could have interposed no barrier. The delay was certainly not owing to the power of the Monarch, as if *that* were difficult to vanquish; but because it had been decreed that his pride should be thoroughly humbled, by his being forced to sanction publicly the Exodus of those whom he had so cruelly oppressed, and even to *supplicate* that they should be gone.

Before we leave this subject, we may for a moment glance at the objection taken on moral grounds to the whole transaction. It looks to many like a robbery—a fraud, an injustice. The Israelites are represented in our English translation as "borrowing" these gifts, and the Egyptians as "lending" them; and often enough are the expressions emphasised in the account of the matter by the Bishop of Natal. It had been a truer version of the real facts of the case, if the rendering had been simply, "the Israelites asked"—"the Egyptians gave." The usual translation implies, of course, an obligation of repayment. This could not be, unless they were to return. Now, the one question is, Was this expected or bargained for? When Pharaoh set out to pursue them, was it on the plea that they had broken a compact, and were refusing to come back? Not so. He had long been scheming to secure this, but no such pledge would be given him. He was anxious at first that only the men should go, and the families remain. This was refused; and he then proposed that the flocks should be detained. What was all this but an effort to bind them down to a return? But Moses insisted on going out altogether free: "Our little ones shall go with us, and not one hoof shall be left behind,"—a declaration as strong as it was possible to make, that their emigration was to be complete and for ever. As for the people of Egypt, when we think of all their terror and suffering under the judgments, it seems very certain that they would rather dread the return of the Israelites as a great calamity. "Egypt," says the Psalm, "was glad when they departed." The spoils, then, were not a loan, but a gift.

We must bear in mind that the bondage of the Israelites was in the highest degree *unjust*. They certainly were not an inferior race. They had not been defeated in battle, and led captive into Egypt. They had settled there on the faith of protection and safety. The breach of faith, therefore, was to be charged on their oppressors, who enslaved and aimed to exterminate them. The divine command to gather that spoil was equivalent to a decree that the Egyptians should make restitution for all their injustice and wrong. They must in this way pay up wages for work done amid bitter tears, and under a bondage that made the worker sick of existence. Thus there was preached, on a grand scale, the great lesson, that the gains of injustice do not endure, and that Heaven in its own time and way will bring the balance straight again.

III. The next point for consideration is the *Passover* in Egypt. Every one knows what difficulties Dr. Colenso has found here, and how strongly he attacks the account of it in the Pentateuch. Indeed, it is a subject on which many confess themselves perplexed. The following considerations seem to have been generally overlooked, and are, I believe, worthy of remark:—

1. The Passover was kept by the Israelites, not when dispersed in Goshen, or intermingled with the Egyptian households, but in their encampment in Rameses, when awaiting the signal for the Exodus. This, I believe (though not the general opinion), is the conclusion to be drawn from the hints and statements of the narrative, and Dr. Colenso's difficulty about informing "the two millions" scattered throughout a district "twenty-five miles square," as he computes it, is consequently altogether gratuitous.

Let us notice how the Israelites are separated from the Egyptians as the judgments continue. They were intermingled doubtless at one time, if only as tyrants and slaves. But a change takes place when the plagues continue to fall with such terrible effect. The task-master lays down his rod; the cry of oppression ceases to ascend. Terrified by the frown of avenging Heaven, the Egyptians seem to have abandoned Goshen; and to have left the people to the disposal of Moses and their chiefs, to manage and muster them as they may. How completely the two peoples became apart, appears from such passages as the following:—"I will sever in that day the land of Goshen, in which my people dwell, that no swarm of flies shall be there. I will put a division between my people and thy people" (Ex. viii. 22). Again, the cattle of the Israelites did not suffer from the storm of hail. And a proof still more decisive of such separation is, that when the awful darkness settled down upon the land of Egypt for three days, "the children of Israel had light in all their dwellings." How could this be, if they were interspersed as is generally supposed, and the destroying angel struck down the first-born in the adjacent households? The narrative, then, warrants our inferring that, the Egyptians having ceased to mingle with the Israelites, Moses and Aaron had the people at their disposal before the Exodus, and could thus assemble them so as best to accomplish the great object which was always kept in view.

If it should be objected that Pharaoh would forbid this, the answer must be an appeal to the incidents of the narrative. It is idle to suppose, that he is detaining this people by force of arms after the judgments of Heaven have interfered in their behalf. His listening to the bold rebukes of Moses, and his humble petitioning for the removal of the judgments, evince his dread of the Hebrew leader, and prove that he would not interfere forcibly with any arrangement of the people. He often, indeed, declares that if Moses will accept his terms, he will let them go at once; and Moses speaks to him as if they were quite ready to move.

The last expression quoted—"the children of Israel had light in all their dwellings"—warrants this additional inference, that they were by this time collected from the various villages of Goshen into a settled encampment. It is surely obvious that such a light must have been supernatural. It came from that cloud that now hovered near them, and which could have exhibited now, as afterwards, its double action of light and darkness, "a pillar of cloud—a pillar of fire." That they were already in their tents is confirmed by another consideration. The observance of the Passover here was the model for all after-times. Now it was a stringent command that they were not to celebrate such a feast in their usual dwellings. "Thou mayest not sacrifice the passover in any of thy gates, but in the place which the Lord thy God shall choose," etc. (Deut. xvi. 5-8.)

The narrative thus requires us to believe that the people were already by this time massed together in one large encampment at Rameses, whence they started. Moreover, their patriarchal traditions had given them a perfect organization, like that of families and clans under a chief. And thus the signal for slaying the Passover, about which so much difficulty has been made, could have been spread over the encampment within a single hour.

2. The narrative requires us to believe that Moses and Aaron are with their brethren on the night of the Passover. The common opinion is that Moses, on that occasion, is in the capital of Pharaoh, and is roused at midnight to appear in the royal presence. He has, consequently, to travel to the rendezvous of the Israelites; a circumstance, as we have seen, which induces many to reject Memphis as the capital, because it is so far away. But the great leader has no such journey to undertake; that message of Pharaoh is sent to him by swift couriers, and finds him among his own people, sharing their wonderful protection.

We are told, indeed, that Pharaoh called for Moses and Aaron by night, and said, "Rise you, and get you forth from among my people, both ye and the children of Israel; and go, serve the Lord as ye have said; and also take your flocks and herds, as ye have said, and be gone, and bless me also." This language, taken by itself, would certainly indicate a personal interview, and if so, the

Hebrew brothers *were* in the capital. But looking at the narrative in other parts, it cannot be so understood. Let us remember the strong language that had passed between Moses and Pharaoh on a previous occasion,— "Pharaoh said unto him, Get thee from me, take heed to thyself, see my face no more: for in that day thou seest my face thou shalt die. And Moses said, Thou hast spoken well, I will see thy face again no more" (Ex. x. 28). Language so peculiarly emphatic on both sides, seems to forbid the idea of a personal encounter afterwards, and therefore on the night of the destruction of the first born. It is true, Moses gave another warning; but we may infer from the narrative that the statement now quoted was nevertheless verified. He entered the palace, it is true, but his words seem to have been uttered only in the hearing of the courtiers. He expressly affirmed that the request to go out should be delivered by them. "All these thy servants shall come down unto me, and bow themselves unto me, saying, Get thee out, and all the people that follow thee: and after that I will go out." It is added, "He went out from Pharaoh in great anger." Why was this? There is no sign that Pharaoh at this time, as formerly, refused to let them go. The true explanation seems to be, that he would neither see Moses nor answer the message. "Let the messenger go as he came!"

Leaving the palace in the mood of mind indicated, where should Moses go but to his own people? Why, truly, should he linger in the capital? He has declared his warning, and now let Pharaoh look to it. He has no further request to make; the next time, Pharaoh shall be the suppliant and he the listener. Besides, the usual theory involves the inference, that the Israelites likewise were in the capital, for Moses is evidently with his own people at the solemn crisis. When the shadows of that evening are falling, the words are caught from his lips which spread through the encampment, "Draw out and kill the Passover : none of you shall go out of the door of his house until the morning" (Ex. xii. 21).

Would the great leader have been safe elsewhere? In the capital of Pharaoh? Its palaces, innermost chambers, bolts and bars, shall be of no avail against the destroyer. Like the meanest of his brethren, Moses needs the protection of the Passover, and on that night of death is sitting, reverent and awe-struck, within one of the blood-besprinkled tents of the children of the covenant.

3. We come now to consider what is with many, perhaps, the grand difficulty respecting the Scripture account of the Passover, the number of victims that required to be slain. Bishop Colenso calculates them at 150,000 at the lowest computation. It is questionable whether we get over serious difficulties really involved, by accepting the answers usually given, even though we reduce the numbers of the Exodus to half a million. A lamb was to be slain for "a household." The Bishop allows to each an average of fifteen or twenty persons (which is also Kurtz's estimate), and thinks that in doing so he is dealing very leniently with the narrative. He appeals to the numbers in the company that ate the Passover in the time of Josephus. But the usage then observed can be no guide for the estimate in "the households" of the Israelites in Egypt, for in their later history great changes had been introduced into their social life, and the observance of this feast especially had in many respects been

corrupted by the Rabbis, from its primitive simplicity. The grand point to settle is, what constituted a Jewish "household" in the Pentateuch sense of the term?

The Bishop interprets the word according to our modern ideas as denoting simply a family—the parents and their children. Herein lies the grand mistake, and it is a very common one. It ignores the most characteristic feature in the life of that ancient time. A "household," in the patriarchal sense of the word, meant all the lineal descendants of a living man,—his sons, his sons' sons,—who were born in his lifetime. This was the radical idea of the whole system. Clans (called "families" in Scripture) and tribes are but its wider and necessary development. And it was not by a mere figure of speech that all the descendants were thus regarded as forming but the "one house" of the patriarch at its head, for the authority he exercised was real and undisputed. Such a social organization is the most ancient, and has left traces of its presence all over the world. In the East it is still to be met with, and is in some cases carried out in the literal manner of ancient times; all the descendants living together in "a house of many mansions." Such was the case in the time of the Patriarchs. The family of Jacob are all around him in Canaan,—his sons and sons' sons; and all accompany him to Egypt. They form but one household. "All the souls of the house of Jacob which came into Egypt were threescore and ten" (Gen. xlvi. 26). It was not otherwise, we may believe, with "the households" of the Israelites in Egypt. Each was framed after the fashion of their "father Jacob." And so this patriarchal idea developed itself into a social organization, which Moses in nowise created, but only took advantage of, when he returned from the exile in the desert to Egypt. He found already existing "tribes," "the congregation," "the elders of the congregation," "the fathers' houses," "heads of the fathers' houses." When the census was taken in the wilderness, this formula occurs throughout, "by their generations, after their families, by the house of their fathers, according to the number of the names;" that is to say, the names were taken according to (1.) the tribe, (2.) the clan, (3.) the household; a state of things based on the patriarchal idea of social life.

Many of the laws of Leviticus were framed for a household in such a sense, not dispersed after the fashion of modern times, but living together. The idea likewise, I believe, lies at the root of the somewhat strange expression in the second commandment of the Decalogue, "Visiting the iniquity of the fathers upon the children unto *the third and fourth generation.*" It is here affirmed that the crime of idolatry was so heinous, that the penalty would fall on the entire household of the transgressor at its head.

Let us take three different statements of the narrative in further illustration of this point, one of the most important in the whole controversy. The first will be the account of the descent of "Jacob and his house" to Egypt, which Bishop Colenso regards as one of the most vulnerable points in the Pentateuch. If it is to be read in the light of our modern ideas of a family, then indeed the blunders are more numerous than he dreams of. According to our notions, Leah had only six sons, but the writer affirms five times this number. "These be the sons of Leah which she bare unto Jacob in Padanaram, with his daughter Dinah; all the souls of his sons and his daughters were thirty and three." Zilpah had two sons, Rachel two, and Bilhah two, according to our estimate. And yet the writer describes their offspring as follows:—" These are the sons of Zilpah whom Laban gave to Leah his daughter, and these she bare to Jacob, even sixteen souls." "These are the sons of Rachel which were born to Jacob; all the souls were fourteen." " These are the sons of Bilhah which Laban gave unto Rachel his daughter, and she bare these unto Jacob; all the souls were seven." Would any modern writer, I ask, have written of the genealogy in this manner? But while thus contradicting our notions, the language is true to the ideas of that ancient time, for all the descendants are as children of the Patriarch, and regarded as part of his household. Again, let us see what is said of Hezron and Hamul. Their father Pharez could not have been above three or four years old at the time of the descent to Egypt, and there, consequently, his two sons must have been born. And yet these are included in the sixty and six who came down from Canaan. Here, says Bishop Colenso, is a grave blunder,—a glaring contradiction. According to our modern ideas, we must admit that it is so, and, moreover, affirm that a still more unaccountable blunder follows. Joseph had two sons, Manasseh and Ephraim, who were born in Egypt. After expressly stating this, the narrative goes on to include them in the number that came into Egypt. "All the souls of the house of Jacob which came into Egypt were threescore and ten." What are we to make of this statement if the household of an Israelite was constituted as our own? We must pronounce it a palpable contradiction, and revealing, on the part of the writer, an amount of carelessness utterly unaccountable. But it is *we* who err by thrusting upon his language our modern ideas. This writer speaks of what he knows, and his language is true to the customs of an ancient time. He is mentioning the number of the household, and so he inserts every living descendant of the Patriarch's lifetime. And as not one such remained behind in Canaan, all are included in the statement, that "Jacob and all his seed with him came into Egypt,"—" all the souls of the house of Jacob which came into Egypt were threescore and ten." And yet several of them may have been born in Egypt. If Manasseh and Ephraim are included in the phrase "came down to Egypt," why should it not also be used respecting Hezron and Hamul, though they also were born there? It is enough that their fathers came, or rather that the Patriarch himself came. Several grandsons of Asher are mentioned, and, for aught we can tell, these also were born in Egypt. But why, the reader may ask, does not the writer go on adding the subsequent descendants of Jacob, and thus speak of a number as coming into Egypt far beyond threescore and ten? The answer is, that when the Patriarch dies, the household is broken up, and therefore the subsequent posterity cannot be included. Thus the language of the genealogical account, so far from being erroneous and absurd, is emphatically true to the spirit and ideas of the patriarchal age, and thereby tends to establish the contemporaneous character and genuineness of the whole narrative. The language of every people bears a reference to their manners and customs, and where these are forgotten, many words, phrases, and proverbs will be enigmas and appear to be blunders. How much learning and research have been expended in bringing to light the life of ancient Greece and Rome, for example, that we may the better appreciate the allusions and phraseology of their historians, and orators, and poets? How easy to point out errors and contradictions there also, if our modern ideas of things are to guide our consideration. The criticism of the Scripture narrative especially must eminently be historical, and if, in forgetfulness of this just principle, we judge of that vanished age, many of whose traditions and customs are so opposed to our own, we shall certainly come on blunders enough, only let us understand that the blunders are our own.

Our next illustration will be taken from the language of the narrative respecting the catastrophe that befell "the household" of Korah, Dathan, and Abiram. That these were patriarchs of venerable age, is obvious from their demeanour and claims, the prize they were aspiring to (the priesthood and general government of the people), and their powerful influence with the congregation of Israel. The narrative speaks of "their wives, their sons, and their little ones." And Josephus, in recording the speech of Korah, represents him as affirming, "I myself am equal to Moses by my family, and superior to him in riches and age." Had our customs then ruled, the families of their sons would have constituted separate households, and so have escaped the terrible catastrophe. But these customs were unknown, and in the language of the writer we see but a household to the third generation, and all that household living together. Hence we read, "The Lord spake unto Moses and unto Aaron, saying, Speak unto the congregation, saying, Get you up from about the tabernacle of Korah, Dathan, and Abiram. And he spake unto the congregation, saying, Depart, I pray you, from the tents of these wicked men, and touch nothing of theirs, lest you be consumed in all their sins. So they gat up from the tabernacle of Korah, Dathan, and Abiram, on every side: and Dathan and Abiram came out, and stood in the door of their tents, and their wives, and their sons, and their little ones. And the earth opened her mouth, and they and all that appertained to them went down alive into the pit, and the earth closed upon them, and they perished from among the congregation" (Numb. xvi. 24, 26, 27, 32). "The earth opened her mouth and swallowed them up, and their households and their tents, and all the substance that was in their possession in the midst of Israel" (Deut. xi. 6). All, therefore, perish, and the fact is to be explained only by the idea of a patriarchal household as now exhibited.

Let us take, as our last instance, the incident respecting Achan, who stole "the accursed thing." It was an easy matter to cast the lot among a people so organized. First, " the tribe of Judah is taken," then " the family," or " clan of Zarhi is taken." Then came its household, "and the household of Zabdi is taken." "And he brought his household, man by man, and Achan *the son of Carmi*, the son of Zabdi, is taken." The point to be observed is, that Achan was the *grandson*, and yet a member of the household. So long, then, as a patriarch lived, all his descendants formed " his house" in the Pentateuch sense of the term. If there be a single exception, it is yet to be produced. The point, as I have stated, is of the greatest importance, and will dispose of many objections which Dr. Colenso has pressed to such a decisive issue. But we must keep to those relating to our present inquiry.

Moses was commanded, in the following terms, to give injunctions respecting the Passover :—" Speak ye unto all the congregation of Israel, saying, In the tenth day of this month, they shall take to them every man a lamb according to the house of their fathers, a lamb for an house ; and if the household be too little for the lamb, let him and his neighbour next to his house take it, according to the number of the souls, every man according to his eating shall make your count for the lamb" (Ex. xii. 3, 4).

The view of a household, as now exhibited, explains the phrase here used for the first time, but often recurring in the narrative, " the congregation" of Israel. It has been usually assumed that this is just the same as " all the people." But in that case the frequent change from the one phrase to the other is unaccountable. Take the following verse :— " The congregation lifted up their voice and cried, and all the people wept that night" (Numb. xiv. 1, etc.) Can the language of Korah be understood if the terms are interchangeable ? " And they gathered themselves together against Moses and against Aaron, and said unto them, Ye take too much upon you, seeing all the congregation are holy, every one of them, and the Lord is among them ; wherefore then lift ye up yourselves above the congregation of the Lord ?" (Numb. xvi. 3.) Moses is often said to address "all the congregation" after an express summons,—a statement much more accurate and true to the fact than many suppose it to be. The Septuagint translates the phrase " the congregation" by the significant epithet συναγωγή, the synagogue, which only by the most loose translation can be identified with " all the people." In the idea of a patriarchal household lies the explanation of the term. It was the gathering of the patriarchs ; of the heads of each household, in whose power most of all lay the government of the people. They alone required to be instructed what the will of the Lord was in any case, for the obedience of the household certainly followed.

And we may here remark, keeping in view the grand distinction between the expressions in question, how true to nature is the manifestation of feeling in the verse that has been quoted. The congregation—men of age and authority—indulge in scorn and loud upbraiding ; but the people, on the other hand, including the women and children, break out into violent grief. "The congregation lifted up their voice and cried" (clamoured), " and the people *wept* that night."

And now comes the question, what was the number of the congregation ? The Bishop himself will aid in the calculation. On an average, he thinks, there were four sons in each family. Let us accept the estimate. These marry, and they and their children continue part of one household. In such a household, then, there are *five* first-born males (the eldest son and four of the grandchildren). (In Jacob's house there might have been thirteen.) But take the average of four in a patriarchal establishment (as we must allow for cases in which the eldest-born is a daughter). Now, we have a statement of all the first-born males ; they amount to 22,273 (Numb. xi. 43). Dividing this number by 4, which represents one household for the reason stated, we have as the result, *five thousand single households.* The head of each is one of the congregation: "all the congregation," then, meant 5000 patriarchs.

Here it is striking to notice that by the Bishop's own estimate the tabernacle suits "excellently well" for their accommodation. "It would hold," he says, "just about five thousand." He affirms the fact to be most damaging to the credibility of the writer; for how could the two millions of the people be crammed into the narrow space? Confounding thus things that differ, 'the congregation' and 'all the people,' he adduces as an objection what in reality we have endeavoured to show is a most striking confirmation of the ancient narrative. We can also understand how Moses could address "all the congregation," and through them the whole people. The elders of the congregation, seventy in number, were probably elected to superintend its interests.

It will now be seen how all this affects the question of the number of victims slain for the Passover. There would be but 5000, instead of 150,000. This estimate, of course, implies that one lamb was to serve for a very large average of inmates; so large, indeed, that many will think it quite insufficient. But we must bear in view—(1.) that the Passover was for the males only: "Thou shalt keep the feast of unleavened bread, all thy *males* shall appear before the Lord thy God" (Ex. xxiii. 17); see also Ex. xxxiv. 22; Deut. xvi. 16. In the injunctions about the Passover in Egypt respecting the mode of eating, with loins girt and staff in hand, the males are clearly singled out, as those by whom the institution was to be observed. Besides, it is expressly said, "every man according to his eating" (Ex. xii. 4). (2.) The Passover was not eaten to satisfy the cravings of hunger.

A little would suffice. There is special provision made if a household is too small (as all the lamb must be consumed), to join with "the neighbour next unto his house." But there is no additional victim commanded, however large the household; because a smaller portion would then be distributed to each, and would accomplish the object in view. Many indeed might have partaken of the Passover lamb, even as is done with the bread and wine of the "New Testament Passover," in the sacrament of the Supper.

On this wise, then, we believe, were transacted the solemnities of that awful crisis. The people have been already collected into their encampment at Rameses. Moses summons the congregation (the 5000 patriarchs), and tells them that on the tenth day they are to select "a lamb according to the house of their fathers—a lamb for a house." The command is obeyed; the victim is selected. The bunch of hyssop, too, is ready, and the basin for the blood. The lintel and the side-posts are well remarked and remembered. The eventful day arrives. Moses summons "the elders" (the seventy) of the congregation, and addresses to them the solemn words, "Draw out now and kill the passover." Each speeds with the message to his own company of expectant householders, and every one through the vast encampment slays the lamb for his house. He collects the blood in the basin, and besprinkles it on the lintel and door-posts of the entrance to the circle of tents where his large household dwell. They witness the strange and solemn transaction; and to any who may ask, What mean ye by this service? the answer is ready, "It is the Lord's Passover, for the Lord will pass through this night to smite the Egyptians, and when He seeth the blood on the lintel, and on the two side-posts, the Lord will pass over the door, and will not suffer the destroyer to come in unto your houses to smite you." And now they enter the consecrated shelter, with the solemn charge of the great leader ringing in their ears, "None of you shall go out until the morning." The service within is also very solemn and impressive. They eat the flesh roasted with fire, with bitter herbs, loins girded, shoes on their feet and staff in their hand, eating it in haste. When it is done, all await the issue. A deep awe creeps over the spirit, as we try to image the silence of that midnight hour, when "the Lord passed over them." "Be still and know that I am God; I will be exalted among the heathen; I will be exalted in the earth." Then rises the awful shriek of Egypt's smitten families, "that great cry throughout all the land, such as there was none like, nor shall be like it any more; for there was not a house where there was not one dead." Pharaoh, says the graphic narrative, rose up in the night, and all his servants, and all the Egyptians. "It was a night much to be remembered!"

The pride of the monarch can hold out no longer. With the cry of a fearful despairing man he calls for Moses and Aaron; and the message is, "Get thee forth from among my people, both ye and the children of Israel, and go serve the Lord as ye have said." Eagerly his servants catch up the sanction and hurry with it to Rameses. It is as Moses had foretold: "These thy servants shall come down unto me, and bow down themselves unto me, saying, 'Get thee out, and all the people that follow thee, and after that I will go out.'" Speedily they clear the intervening space of sixty miles from Memphis—the cry of the great city of Egypt ringing in their ears, and every village shrieking "haste, haste," as they passed. What a spectacle to the Israelites in their arrival and humiliation! They bow down to the great leader in humble entreaty, and soon thereafter the blood-besprinkled tents are struck, and the vast multitudes are on the move for Sinai.

IV. One question remains, How long did the Israelites take to pass from Rameses in Goshen, to the shores of the Red Sea? There are but two stations, named Succoth and Etham. The prevailing opinion, strengthened by the eminent names of Dr. Robinson and others, is that they were but one night at each; that they reached the encampment at the Red Sea in three days! The distance is thirty-five miles, so that this involves a march of twelve miles each day for three days in succession. Bishop Colenso asserts this to be impossible, and few who think of the encumbered state of the multitude, with their little ones and cattle, will deny that there is much force in his statement.

But does the narrative say that this march was accomplished in this short time? On the contrary, it rather excludes any such idea, and to entertain such is, I believe, to mistake remarkably the whole spirit of the Exodus.

Let us see what is said of the doings of the people at their first encampment, Succoth. "They baked unleavened cakes of the dough which they brought forth out of Egypt (for it was not leavened), because they were thrust out of Egypt and could not tarry, neither had they prepared for themselves any victual." Thus, then, a considerable time was occupied in furnishing the requisite supply of passover-bread for the vast multitude. In fact, they may have been quietly encamped *here* on the *third* day, when they are usually thought to be overcome by terror at the sight of the Egyptians on the shore of the Red Sea.

It is not unlikely they may have also remained several days at Etham, the second encampment; and that they so reached the shores of the Gulf in about three weeks after their departure from Rameses. Such an idea seems to harmonize well with a statement respecting the time of their journeyings mentioned in Exodus xvi. 1. We there read that on leaving Elim for their next encampment in the wilderness of Sin, they had been a whole month away from Egypt, counting from the first day of the Exodus. Now they could have reached that encampment, after crossing the Red Sea, easily in ten days; giving them time to stay at the intermediate localities (three days in the wilderness of Etham, two in Marah, five in Elim). Therefore they may have spent the three preceding weeks of the month before crossing the Red Sea at all, halting for a time at Succoth, Etham, and Pi-hahiroth.

Again, on the usual theory, we cannot understand the pursuit of the Egyptian army. In Numbers xxxiii. 4, it is said, "the Egyptians buried all their first-born which the Lord had smitten among them." Now, is Pharaoh not to be allowed time to bury his first-born? He is generally believed to have come with all his army on the Israelites two days after they left! But that awful blow struck low his own royal heir, and the first-born of his chief warriors too, bowing the most stubborn among them to the dust. Surely they could have but little spirit left to follow in the pursuit so soon as is supposed. A considerable interval must be presumed for recovery from this stupor, for the burial of the dead, so essential in Egypt, for the terrified human heart to harden itself once more, and for the feelings of kingly revenge to rise on the wild resolution of pursuit.

The feelings and conduct of Pharaoh may thus be at last identified with something like human nature. The monarch is still not humbled even in his misery and despair, and after the lapse of two or three weeks, the stunning effect of the blow has passed away, and is followed by a still more decided reaction of his habitual feelings. He has become frenzied with hatred and the desire of revenge. And these feelings are stimulated by the knowledge of the palpable fact of the Israelites lingering for such a time within his frontiers. He thinks it is not yet too late to recapture them. They make a strange movement from Etham, which brings the resolve to a head. Instead of going eastward to the Desert, they actually turn down by the western shore of the Red Sea, thus keeping within the boundaries of Egypt. As they had sought to go into the wilderness to sacrifice, this appears to him a strange diversion from their route. It indicates irresolution, confusion, as of a people who have lost their way and have no competent guide. They cannot get out of Egypt after all. "They are entangled in the land," he exclaims, "the wilderness hath shut them in!" So he resolves on their capture, and assembles his army for the pursuit.

Again we read, "God brought them out of Egypt." Surely we should think of their journey as calm and leisurely, under His omnipotent protection. That cloud the symbol of His presence—advanced with majestic calmness, and they followed in peace, their Exodus not the trembling flight of slaves, but rather resembling the march of a victorious army who had left the enemy defeated behind them.

In every way, therefore, the idea of three days' march to the Red Sea is to be rejected; and consequently all objections, founded on the supposition that it was otherwise, will fall to the ground.

Pharaoh's resolution to pursue with his army, was only to issue in his deeper ruin. The honour of Jehovah, the highest interests of humanity likewise, were imperilled and destroyed if the desperate attempt could be successful. After all the judgments inflicted, the attempt is seen to be an act of the most audacious impiety, and shall be signally punished. What avails a numerous and powerful army against the elements of an angry Heaven?

"The Lord overthrew the Egyptians in the midst of the sea."

CHAPTER III.

PASSAGE OF THE RED SEA.

As I have mentioned, while yet in Cairo some friends (who had left London with us, but remained behind at Paris) arrived, and proposed to join us in our expedition to Sinai. We gladly assented, and so, instead of three, became eight in number. We proceeded to the Consul's office, and with much formality had the contract with the Dragoman drawn up; one version was in Arabic, the other in English. It bargained for suitable tents, camels, provisions, escorts, etc. One of our number signed for the party; thereafter the Dragoman "set his seal" to it, and so it was made "firm and sure."

We were to travel at the rate of £1 sterling each a day; the half of the whole sum to be paid before starting, the other half to lie in deposit till our return, and to be forfeited in the event of the Dragoman playing false. We were to leave by the early train for Suez on Monday the 6th March, the camels to be sent forward over the desert three days before; and all was to be in readiness for a fair start from Suez to Sinai on the Tuesday morning.

On the morning of our leaving Cairo a heavy mist, which dropped like rain from the trees as we passed to the railway station, hung over the route for a considerable time, leaving us to imagine that houses, minarets, and gardens were still around us, long after we had left them behind. By and by it cleared away, and there, beneath a strong sun, lay the DESERT, in all its sternness and utter desolation.

A strong ridge of mountains rose on our right, running in a direction parallel to our own, and on to the shores of the Red Sea, where its termination is the "Ras Attakah." This formed, as will afterwards appear, the landward barrier to the escape of the Israelites.

As might be expected, we were anxiously watching for the first glimpse of the Red Sea, and at last one of our party exclaimed in high satisfaction, "There it is!" On looking out there appeared, sure enough, a blue expanse of water, strangely calm, and fading away in a haze into the azure of the sky. As we whirled along, its outline shifted; the yellow plain appeared where the blue had been, and so we had the mirage of the Desert. We soon, however, came in view of the gleaming waters of the Gulf, with the opposite shore clearly defined, and about two o'clock arrived at Suez.

We looked about for our Dragoman to guide us to our encampment, but for a long time he was nowhere to be seen. We had time to realize strongly the impression how dreary a place Suez is, and how travellers haste from it as speedily as possible. Only dire necessity would induce any one to make it a residence. The aspect of the town does not at all relieve the dreary desolation of the desert around; there is no tree, or garden, or trace of verdure to refresh the wearied eye; it seems only a mass of houses instead of rocks glaring in the sun. At the railway station were wagons with tanks of water brought from Cairo, and most carefully guarded. The well of Suez is on the other side of the Gulf, and the water is brought on camels, but so brackish as to be scarcely used by Europeans. And then, on that side, is "the great and terrible wilderness" of the Exodus, around which the mind has gathered such strong associations of drought and privation; so that the reader may conceive how unattractive the town looks to the traveller.

We sat down on our baggage waiting for our Dragoman, sheltering ourselves as we best could from the fierce sun, that now claimed us fairly as his victims, and strongly hinted how he meant to treat us when in the depths of the desert. A group of Arabs gathered round, and by gestures, exclamations, and two or three words of broken English, tried to find out what we wanted. We replied in monosyllables and broken English also, indicating the principal points of the case—Cairo! Bedawy! Gemmel! Mahmoud! Mahmoud! At last one had caught our meaning, and set off to the place of encampment. Mahmoud soon made his appearance with his dark Arab escort. They came up grinning their salaam, laid hold of our luggage, and marched us off to our tents, about half a mile north of the town.

It may be as well that the reader here make some acquaintance with our attendants and escort.

Mahmoud, the Dragoman, has the characteristics of many of his race and religion. He is a Mohammedan, silent, grave, imperturbable, with a quiet energy of will. He has admirable control over the Arabs, contrasting favourably in this respect with our Jewish dragoman in Palestine. He is very fond, like others, of his cigarette, which he freely uses, although it is the Mohammedan fast of Ramadan. As he lifts it to his lips, you mark the maimed forefinger of his right hand. He told me, with pathos, how his father sent him up the Nile to a relative when a mere boy ; and how the finger was then chopped off at the middle joint, in order that he might not be seized afterwards as a soldier. His description both of the amputation and the means of healing were sufficiently harrowing.

Here, too, is Baomi! who waits at our table, and makes himself generally useful ; short and square in his build, with dark broad face, snub nose, and strong dark eye. Our first impression of him is not very favourable, but the sturdy creature turns out so active and obliging, listens so respectfully to our moral lectures, is so frank in the confession of his evil and reckless ways, and makes such resolutions of amendment, that he gains on our interest. He has served in a hotel in Cairo, by his own account, and has thus learned his broken English. We will long remember his morning summons, " Six clock, gentlemen, *berry* fine morning ; want you oshen (washing) water—I come *thirectly!*"

Like Mahmoud, he has a story about the despotism of the country ; only he delivers his tale with much energy and gesture. He tells how, in boyhood, he was playing in his village on the banks of the Nile, when he and other playmates were suddenly seized for the Pasha's steamboat. His mother and sisters followed along the banks with outstretched hands, with clamour and bitter tears, but the vessel bore him remorselessly away. An orthodox Mohammedan would shake the head both at his creed and conduct. He owns to a heretical relish for wine and brandy ; and quietly confesses to me that he is troubled sometimes with intellectual doubts about the creed of Islam. He cannot well understand how money-power, railways, great ships, and terrible cannon should belong to the "infidel," and the Moslem be so poor and defenceless in comparison. He would sometimes say to me, "Why *my* country so poor? And why Christian country so rich? Why God do this if he like Mussulman religion better than Christian religion?" I confess I encouraged these difficulties, and our conversation would sometimes end by his saying, "I not see many things— if I see, I *too much* believe."

I may here remark, that questions and difficulties of this sort are working in many minds, both in Egypt and in other regions where the religion of Mohammed prevails. Railways, the electric telegraph, the manifest wealth and power of England, and the valour of her armies in the Crimea and India, of which many have heard, are telling with great force against the prejudices of the Moslem. They are sapping, perhaps, more than anything else just now, the foundations of his creed. In many cases the "infidel" is no longer regarded with contempt, but is rapidly becoming the object of respect and fear.

The Sheikh of the Arab escort was Nassar. He wore a loose flowing robe, by way of distinction from the rest. He also carried a small rod—emblem of office; as the rod of Moses was the recognised symbol of his authority. Nassar went on with the baggage; passing us generally where we halted for lunch in the middle of the day, and fixing the place of encampment for the night. We paid a visit, at his urgent request, to his tented village in the wady near Serabit-el Khadim, where we saw the sheep killed in haste for us, and in an hour thereafter served up for repast. The general appearance of the escort indicated great poverty and hardship. They were "black," but you scarcely add that they were "comely." They seem to suffer sometimes severely from the heat and privations of their nomadic life: and, indeed, such dried roasted skins, cleaving to the bones, we saw nowhere else. Throughout, we found them pleasant and obliging. They grinned when they did us any service; appealed to us whether it was now "taib" (good), and on our answering "taib," would go off repeating Taib! Howagee! grinning broader than before. They liked the English, as they often declared, but protested emphatically against the railway invasion. Once, as we were passing down to Wady Feiran, they became quite frantic when speaking of the railway to Suez. The engine—with its fires, its fearful scream, its snort and puff (which they imitated), and the perfect ease with which it dragged any quantity of their camel loads—was to them a fearful thing; and indeed they declared it to be none other than the black fiend himself. Poor fellows! the fact is, that it sadly cuts up their trade from Suez to Cairo.

We were especially interested in Selemma, a fine Arab boy of about fourteen years of age, his skin not yet blackened, only tawny, and his features still happy-looking. We enjoyed his merry ringing laugh; the song also with which, as the sun was stooping in the west, he would cheer the wearied camels,—a slow monotonous song improvised for the occasion, and in which, by Mahmoud's account, he was telling the camels what a fine rest and herbage they would have when their journey was done. Like other young bards, he was fond of "poetic license" in his descriptions.

When we arrived at our tents, about half a mile, as I

have said, from Suez, matters were heard of which tended to the impression, that this escort of ours was to be of very little use in our protection. We had bargained for three good tents, as there were eight of us, but found there were only two. We were startled to hear from Mahmoud that the third tent had been stolen on the way from Cairo; the escort attacked by a hostile tribe, and one of them killed. Here was a "nice sensation" incident with which to begin our tour in the desert. Incidents of a startling kind were not altogether unlooked for, were possible at any rate, but it seemed as if "robbery and murder" had commenced a little too soon. There was, we thought, great improbability in the statement. Such a thing could hardly have happened between Cairo and Suez, on a road comparatively so frequented and under the protection of the Pasha. The Tihayeh Arabs were hostile, we knew, to the Towerah who formed our escort, but surely they were far away from the district in the uplands and mountains of the Tih. We strongly declared the story to be incredible, but Mahmoud insisted in a favourite phrase that there were "lots" of bad Bedawy in the immediate neighbourhood that came down for plunder on the route. Baomi, as he had accompanied the baggage, was called in to confirm the tale. With impassioned gesture the fellow went through the terrors of the scene: "Much Bedawy! plenty Bedawy!—fight!—take our tent!—kill one man! —cry to me come, come!—but I 'fraid—I run away!" Mahmoud stood before us calm and depressed under the examination, and at last offered us a vile-looking small tent, which he said he had intended for himself, and which really turned out quite as bad as it looked.

We consulted in this "situation of affairs." We were unable to examine any of the Arab escort, as none of them could speak one word of English, and, except a word or two, we knew nothing of Arabic. How far they were implicated in the matter we could not tell. We could not get over the idea that a vile trick had been played us. This was the most probable alternative. On the whole, however, it were well, we thought, just to give some evidence that our fire-arms were not altogether for show, but could be used if necessary. One of our English friends had serious doubts about the Christianity of wearing fire-arms, and his pistol was innocently stowed away in his portmanteau. The incident, however, proved rather a shock to his peace principles, and he emphatically declared that if this was to be the "style of things, he should go and load his revolver."

We now began to fix in our minds the features of the locality around us, which, however unattractive in its natural aspect, was yet the scene of one of the sublimest of all the Scripture miracles—the crossing of the Red Sea. Somewhere on this splendid plain was the last encampment of the Israelites in Egypt. Somewhere along this shore within sight, the waters of the gulf were driven back that "the redeemed of the Lord might pass through." These wastes, now so silent, and where you hail with the joy of a discovery any appearance of a living object, were then alive with the bustle and hum of the many thousands of Israel. Here they experienced the strongest emotions with which the soul can be thrilled; the joy of a new-born freedom, the terror of a return to bondage, and yet again the amazement of an unlooked-for deliverance. Where was their encampment here? or rather,

Where was the scene of their crossing to the further side ? Let us drop the incidents of the personal narrative, and look at the interesting question. Here, on the plain of the encampment, is the fittest place for the discussion, when the reader has marked more distinctly the mountain ridge bounding it on the west and south.

Some fifteen miles southwards from Suez is that ridge, already referred to in our journey from Cairo, which terminates abruptly on the shore, and is called Ras Attakah. Words will not easily convey to those familiar only with pastoral hilly country, an idea of its grim and terrible aspect. It arises not so much from its sudden elevation, as from the precipitous chaos and endless confusion of the sand-heaps that lie along its slopes. From the confusions of a quarry, or the fantastic heaps of an enormous snow-drift, an idea, on a small scale, may be gained of these mountainous heaps on the ridge, where the whirlwinds of the Desert, as one might fancy, have it all their own wild way. We saw similar aspects of rugged desolation afterwards in the range of Jebel el Tih, and in other hills of the Desert, but at Jebel Attakah it appalled us with the force of a first impression.

You cannot but think that the Israelites, looking to these hills, would feel that escape was as hopeless as resistance was vain. The ridge circles round to the north, and as the enemy came down upon them from that direction, they were fairly imprisoned—the Egyptian army on the north, the hills on the west and to the south, and the sea on the east. It was as though they were pent up for the slaughter ; and at the only opening, the enemy was coming in to work his cruel will. They felt as a bird taken in the snare, and their descendants long afterwards entered into their mood, alike of despair and deliverance.

> "Ev'n as a bird
>   Out of the fowler's snare
> Escapes away,
>   So is our soul set free :
> Broke are their nets,
>   And thus escaped we,
> Therefore our help
>   Is in the Lord's great name,
> Who heav'n and earth
>   By his great power did frame.

We have already tracked their route from Goshen to Succoth and Etham. Thence they turned by way of the Red Sea, and encamped before Pi-hahiroth over against, or rather before Baal-zephon, between Migdol and the sea. These seem the four boundaries of their last encampment in Egypt. Where did they cross? Various localities have been fixed on; and it is desirable that the point be settled, if possible, with much more distinctness and precision.

Dr. Robinson, following Niebuhr and Burckhardt, would have it that they crossed near Suez, where indeed, at ebb-tide, the Arabs with their camels can pass without difficulty at the present day. The distance now is about two and a half miles. If this was the place of the crossing, then our tents were on the very ground of their encampment. The agency at work to clear a passage for the Israelites, in this case, was simply a north-east wind acting on the ebb-tide, and so blowing the water well off these shoals. Some will ask, Does Dr. Robinson, then, not admit a miracle? The answer shall be in his own words : " The miracle was mediate—not a direct suspension of the laws of nature, but a miraculous adaptation of these laws to produce a required result. The result was wrought by natural means supernaturally applied." The natural means were the wind and tide, and these acting under divine direction, as he believes, drove back the waters; this saved the Israelites. On the other hand, by the same natural action, the waters in due course returned again, and the Egyptians were overwhelmed.

Canon Stanley seems to acquiesce in the theory; and thus, if great names are sufficient to prove its correctness, it were dangerous to meddle with it. But the maxim must be remembered, *Amicus Plato, magis amica veritas.* He does not indeed argue the point, balancing the difficulties; but affirms that the narrative compels us to look for the passage near the head of the then Gulf, whose waters could be parted by a strong wind.[1]

Certain it is, however, that argument is needed, in order to demonstrate how these natural causes are sufficient to account for the stupendous phenomena and their results; for if better reasons cannot be brought forward than those advanced by Dr. Robinson, his theory, I believe, must be decisively rejected. The opinion is not one of mere abstract speculation. It is, as might be anticipated, in high favour with the Rationalists, who would regard the escape of the Israelites as a lucky accident, where there was no miracle at all, and such a consequence is easily reached if this locality be fixed upon. How natural to exclaim, It is only a fortunate combination of wind and tide, and what is there miraculous, strictly speaking, in

---

[1] *Jewish Church.*

this! Of course, Dr. Robinson, and some others who hold the theory, would repudiate the language, and far be it from us to imply that they have sympathy with the views of Rationalism. But still, in the most favourable aspect of the hypothesis, there is no room to suppose that any great miracle was wrought, certainly not that sublime miracle which the narrative implies, which the Song of Moses celebrates, and which rung prominent in the melodies of Israel long ages afterwards. It is evident that if the grand results were caused by the fortunate and conjunct action of wind and tide, then, as such a combination may have happened often both before and since, the alleged miracle turns out rather a poor and commonplace affair. The glorious Song of Moses, too, " with its waters standing upright as an heap"—" its depths congealed in the heart of the sea," is, in the light of this theory (to say it mildly), an exaggeration, which no plea of poetic license can excuse or explain. And when we remember the language of the Psalms, that the Red Sea was rebuked —" dried up," " that He turned the sea into *dry land*," " that they went through the flood on foot," are we to put down all this as little more than a grand flight of poetry? Are we to think that the event so glorified can be seen any day on a small scale in the crossing of the caravan at Suez, when the tide is fairly out? If these grave consequences are involved in the theory, the proof ought to be very strong before we adopt it.

Some inquirers, to avoid this locality, have gone far down the Gulf to the south of Jebel Attakah. Travellers on the Red Sea are generally pointed to the lower valley of the Tawarik as the route from Egypt; and the above named place, at the termination of that valley on the shore, was, according to such directions, the scene of the miracle. This is a route, however, which, as has been shown in discussing the locality of Goshen and the journey thence to the Red Sea, is in every way objectionable. It is opposed to the requirements of the case (since we cannot, as I have endeavoured to show, locate Goshen by the side of the capital, Memphis), to tradition and to the Scripture narrative, especially to that portion of it which mentions the Israelites as crossing on the second day from Rameses to Etham on the edge of the wilderness. This latter could be no other than the Wilderness of Arabia, for we are expressly told, that, after crossing, they wandered for three days in the Wilderness of Etham. The locality, therefore, at the foot of the valley Tawarik, may be dismissed from our consideration. To return, then, to the views expressed by Dr. Robinson.

The one question to be asked about this or any other theory regarding the crossing of the Israelites is, Will it answer the plain conditions of the simple narrative? Will it account for events? We know what happened on the occasion— the Israelites escaped, and the Egyptians were drowned. Now, the one necessity clearly is that we assign causes adequate to those results. Be it a great miracle, or a small miracle, or no miracle at all, —only let it be understood that the cause shall be sufficient for the production of the effect. It is because the theory in question utterly fails in this, and connects the grand results with causes greatly insufficient, that we reject it. Wind and tide are strong, it is true, but what was done here was far beyond them.

F

First of all, it is impossible to understand how wind and tide, acting conjointly, could part the waters for the space and in the manner which the narrative requires. The wind was north-east, says Dr. Robinson (it is east in the narrative), and this would tend to blow the waters down the Gulf. And he adds, it would do this for the space of half a mile. This "gives us pause." The waters are turned to dry land, and the space cleared for half a mile! How could this thing be? The Doctor says, it is "the largest supposition admissible." Really it seems so very large as to be quite *in*admissible, and threatens to upset his theory by pushing the whole matter at once into the realm of the miraculous.

2. Again, How had the Israelites a wall of water on each hand as they passed through, if wind and tide were thus acting? The waters would, one should think, be all on one side. The conjoint action of the forces are driving the waters down the Gulf, and so how are any remaining in its upper portion, so as to be a wall of waters on the left hand? Dr. Robinson appeals to the turn at the head of the Gulf, and argues that such a wind would cut through it, and keep the upper waters imprisoned. An inspection of a good map, he says, will make this obvious. One can only state his impressions, and there are many, I fully believe, who will at once declare from actual observation, that such a wind would rather drive the waters out of the head of the Gulf, and indeed on to the very shoals where the Israelites had to cross. Much more would this be the case if the tide, as is supposed, were strongly ebbing in that direction. Dr. Robinson seems to have forgotten this.

3. Again, on this theory we ask, How did the waters

return so quickly as to drown the Egyptians? The tide obeyed its natural laws all the while, though urged by the wind. Therefore it took some time to return, as by supposition it did to go out. It went out, on this theory, "all the night," and was driven back much farther than usual. How, therefore, did not some of the Egyptians manage to escape during the two or three hours, at the least, of its return? It is unfortunate to cite the instance of Bonaparte in somewhat similar circumstances, for he managed to escape.

This difficulty is greatly increased if we think of the immense size of the Egyptian army. If the Israelites were about three weeks before they crossed the Red Sea, Pharaoh would have time to collect a large force. He had with him "six hundred chariots," we are told. These, it has been rightly conjectured, were only his body-guard, for it is added, "and all the chariots of Egypt." And from the Song of Moses it is evident that the catastrophe was a death-blow, not to a section, but to the great body of the Egyptian army, and, in fact, an overwhelming national calamity. Indeed, the immense number of those they had come to capture, implies an army on this grand scale. We may conjecture something of its real size more nearly from estimates such as the following. Diodorus gives, as a part of the attending army of Sesostris, 26,000 chariots alone. Josephus gives the numbers on this very occasion as 50,000 horsemen and 200,000 footmen all armed. Kurtz (*History of the Covenant*) also mentions the statement of Ezekiel the Jewish tragedian, and referred to by Eusebius, estimating the army of Pharaoh at a million of men. Wilkinson has shown us that cavalry was an arm of warfare held in high estimation by the Egyptians, as well as the chariots of war. And that these were also present in the pursuit may be inferred from the language, "The horse and his rider hath he cast into the sea." Unquestionably, then, making all allowance for exaggeration, the Egyptian army was here in its strength, and must have been very large.

How, then, *all* should have been drowned—in a passage only two and a half miles from shore to shore, so narrow, so short, and with prominent shoals too, and only gradually covered by the returning tide,—is a mystery. There could be little difficulty in fancying this fate to overtake a detachment, or the advanced guard, but annihilation of the whole army at such a locality may be regarded as an impossibility.

Dr. Robinson estimates a thousand of the Israelites abreast passing in where the space was broadest, *i.e.* half a mile. Then in the same space, only about 300 (say) of the horses and chariots might be supposed to advance. What a long time must elapse, then, before all could enter! And the tide is on the turn; gradually narrowing the limits, and so, by reducing its breadth, extending the procession. How could the whole of such an army have been in the depths (or the shallows) of the passage at one and the same time? If the van was there, the rear-guard was only on the brink, and had not entered at all. The theory, then, does not account for the facts of the case, but threatens to *allow the Egyptians to escape.*

Suspecting this difficulty, Dr. Robinson assumes that the Gulf was here broader and deeper than it is now, and that it extended farther north. The assumption is arbitrary, and seems contradicted by positive evidence. But, admitting it for the sake of argument, we only get rid of one difficulty to fall into another. We have an awkward dilemma in either way for the theory in question. If the water was shallow and narrow as now, how were the Egyptians drowned? If broader and deeper than now, how then was its solid mass parted by the mere force of the wind? How, we ask, could it divide the waters at all, much less to the required extent of half-a-mile? There are indications, however, that the Gulf could not have reached much farther to the north than now, in the traces of the ancient canal found there. As Lepsius remarks: "No canal could be cut where there was sea;" and far as we can go back in history, we find nothing to indicate the supposed extension.

4. But, again, it is difficult to see, on this theory, why the Egyptians should have gone into the sea at all.

The Israelites being close to the head of the Gulf, as is here supposed, we must station the enemy a little north from it, and they need not in this case have done otherwise than have gone round to the opposite shore.

5. And finally, what of the *force of the wind* that is here supposed? And how did the Israelites make head against it? To have quite bared the shallows, and made them as dry ground, and parted the waters as required, we must have a force of wind, to which the hurricane is gentleness and calm. Fiercer than the beatings of the fiercest tempest that wind must have blown. And yet the multitudes of men, women, and children somehow get quietly and safely through! May we not say, that if at the outset this theory is likely to let the Egyptians escape (which is bad), it now, on deeper examination, threatens to drown the Israelites (which

is worse), and sweep them down with the storm-driven waters?

6. Besides the above objections, founded on the circumstances of the case, it is obvious from the narrative that the waters, both in the outflow and return, did not obey the natural laws of tidal force, but were influenced by the miraculous rod of Moses, stretched over them by the command of God. The wind, we may believe, was only the sensible emblem, indicating the Divine power at work.

For these reasons, I reject the hypothesis of crossing at Suez, however eminent some of the names that have adopted it.

The true locality from which the Israelites crossed the Red Sea may, as I believe, be fixed some distance south from Suez, and close to the ridge of Jebel-Attakah already referred to. It is thirteen miles in direct distance from the town, but about double that in travelling, as the Gulf runs considerably deep into the land.

I now submit the reasons for this opinion.

1. The distance across to the opposite shore at this place will suit the time allowed to the Israelites.

They passed through in the April night, which, at least, would give them eight or nine hours. And we must not forget the strange action of the Cloud, which would allow them longer time to escape unmolested. It moved back between them and the enemy, whom it enveloped in deepest gloom. The distance is not twelve miles, as Dr. Robinson has conjectured, but about seven, as Captain Moresby has ascertained, and marked in his chart.

2. It will be seen that here was a passage where the

Egyptian army could be tempted far within the depths, and so utterly overwhelmed.

3. This is the locality that best suits the names of their encampment, Pi-hahiroth, and Baal-Zephon, " Migdol and the sea."

Here, as has been already remarked, we seem to have the four boundaries of the encampment on the plain marked for us, and the minuteness of the description should help us to decide where it really was. The names of ancient Scripture localities are often found to linger with little change to the present day. And such seems to be the case with Pi-hahiroth and Migdol. Hahiroth corresponds to the modern Ajroud, and Migdol to Muktala; and since the names have thus continued, we may believe that in ancient times these were large and well-known districts: Migdol was the west, and the sea the east boundary; Pi-hahiroth the north, and Baal-Zephon the south. And the question now is, Can we determine this last or southern boundary? It has been sought for in the plain near Suez, but it has not been found. No trace of the name has been hitherto discovered; but it is of such a character as to show that we should fix it on a *mountain*—not look for it in a plain at all.

The prefix Baal is here to be well noted. It excludes the idea that the Egyptian god Typhon is meant, as many conjecture. And, as has been remarked, the word Typhon, being an imported word, would have been here so written, and not changed into Zephon (see Art. Smith's *Dict. of the Bible*). But, indeed, the prefix Baal points to the special idolatry here perpetrated, as the worship of the great Phœnician divinity. It should not surprise us to meet with the indications of such idolatry here, for Baal was the great object of worship in that wilderness, to the brink of which the Israelites had now come. Frequent were the warnings of Moses against this superstition, and they were specially commanded to destroy "the gods on high mountains and hills" (Deut. xii. 2). These were the high places of Baal. In the centre of the wilderness was the high mountain Serbal, Serbaal (Lord Baal),—a name indicating the character of the worship,—at whose base, in the rich valley of Paran, was the city of the Amalekites, the tribe who attacked Israel at Rephidim. On its eastern border, was *Baal Peor*, where were the high places of Baal, from which Balaam saw the tents of Israel "spread forth as the valleys, and as gardens by the river side." And so here, on its western frontier, is a Baal-Zephon in front of which they have encamped. Now, it ought to be observed, that where a word with the prefix Baal designates a locality, it refers to "a mountain or hill," and never a plain. This can be seen by glancing over the names of Scripture that have such a prefix. The places of Baal were "high places" invariably. And this arose from the very nature of the worship,—Baal being a celestial divinity, the god of the sun and planets. The name, therefore, Baal-Zephon, would point us to the ridge of Jebel Attakah as the southern frontier of the encampment. The Egyptian army coming in on them from the north, so as to prevent escape to the wilderness again, would make them retreat close to its precipitous ridge, until they could not move farther, and in the prospect of these inaccessible precipices were overwhelmed with despair.

4. It will be seen how strongly such a locality is indicated by the emphatic testimony of Josephus. He has gathered his information in many points from writings of authors now unknown. On the point before us, such testimony, we think, is important. The locality was not in the depths of the Desert, but was quite accessible, and would likely be frequently visited. The grand features would live, we may well suppose, in the traditions of the people, as of a place where their nation had well-nigh perished, and had been saved by one of the grandest miracles that ever impressed the human imagination. Now, nothing can be more emphatic than the testimony of Josephus to the fact, that they were here close to the ridge of precipitous mountains. "They were shut up," he says, "between the mountains and the sea—mountains that terminated at the sea, which were impassable by reason of their roughness, and obstructed their flight." He gives the speech of Moses to allay their terrors, which thus concludes, "God can make these mountains plain ground to you, if he so please, and we should hope that God will succour us, by whose operations we are now encompassed in this narrow place." He gives also the prayer of Moses, "We are in a helpless place, but thou canst make these mountains open for us, which now enclose us."

This language plainly shows that they were not in a plain, as would have been the case if they had crossed at Suez, but that they were close to the ridge, as we are contending for.

5. We may also regard as corroborative of this locality the traditional names attached to this and the opposite shore. Here is the Ras Attakah, or "mountain of de-

liverance," and opposite are the Ayoun Mousa, the wells of Moses.

6. I add finally, in support of such a locality, that it affords room for the display *of a great miracle*, such as is always implied, and such, moreover, as the distracted state of the Israelites absolutely required.

I know that with some this condition of such a miracle is just the strongest difficulty in their admitting this topography. I put the difficulty forward, however, as really an argument in its favour.

It is impossible, in our present inquiry, to ignore the controversy that has of late raged so keenly on the subject of miracles. It obviously has a direct bearing on the Scripture locality under consideration, and on many others mentioned in this narrative. It is very evident that if the miracles of Scripture are to be denied, as has been done by those who yet profess their faith in its doctrines, there will be an end to all such investigations as those in which we are engaged. The circumstance that specially fascinates the imagination of the traveller in these lands of the East, is surely that they were the scenes of miracles. If not so, then it is indifferent where the Israelites crossed the Red Sea; and Sinai is not worth searching for in these mountains of Arabia. As such a controversy, then, lies so directly in our way, the reader will allow a few words on the subject bearing on the discussion before us.

It is a mistake to suppose that the Bible can be read with fewer stumbling-blocks to "faith and reason" when the miracles of its narrative are set aside. Getting rid of one difficulty (as it is supposed) by denying these strange phenomena in the physical world, we are confronted with phenomena in the moral world all the more perplexing and unaccountable. The whole Jewish history becomes a puzzle. Ignore the miracles, and how comes it that a people, so terribly prone to idolatry, came to embrace such a religion, to possess such a law, to worship in such a temple, and to exhibit in their literature such prophecies and psalms?

The writer on Miracles in the *Essays and Reviews* characterizes them as "accidental accessories" of the Christian faith, and to be viewed in contrast with its "essential doctrines." The phraseology is unfortunate, for the fact is far otherwise. The miracles of the Bible are part of its deepest essence and spirit. You cannot drop them from the narrative, and quietly go on as before. They are pillars in the temple of its revealed truth, by removing which only a mass of shapeless ruin seems left, and the bewildered mind knows not well what to believe or where to worship.

The miracles of the Exodus and of the journeyings through the wilderness will, if we look into the matter, be found amongst the most essential influences that formed the peculiar character of the Jewish people. Their psalms tell how thrilling was the memory of them to the latest stage of their history. And they are absolutely necessary to explain to us the progress in their religious development, which, in the lapse of time, was very great; especially if we remember all along their tendencies to idolatry, and the contagious example of the nations around them.

Contrast the timid herd here gathered on the shores of the Red Sea, and the brave warrior nations of David and the kings! Contrast the bacchanalian crowd around the golden calf at Horeb, and the meeting of the solemn assemblies afterwards in the temple! Contrast their low ideas of God in the wilderness, and the sublime conception of his character in the national psalms! The transformation is immense! Put aside the miracles and what can we make of all this? It appears an effect without a cause; a puzzle in history which nothing can explain.

And all the while the nations around are sunk in the most degraded idolatries. Solomon, in his prayer at the dedication of the Temple, is surrounded by the princes and people of Israel, and alludes to them as those "whose fathers thou broughtest out of Egypt." We think of the contrast between *its* worship and this grand solemnity at Jerusalem. When the Holy of Holies is being thus dedicated, in a prayer of matchless sublimity, to the living Jehovah, "whom the heaven of heavens cannot contain," Egypt is prostrate still before her brute gods, adoring in his temple at Memphis "the ox that eateth grass," and burying the carcase with divine honours beneath the shadow of the pyramids. "The theory of development" will not suit here. The tendencies of that people as they came from Egypt had to be checked, not developed,—punished, indeed, at times with judgments that threatened their extermination. The progress will be found to be owing greatly to the miracles of their history, "making known," as the Scripture so graphically puts it, "the name," or character, of "the true God." We must cling to the belief of this, therefore, as a key to the explanation of what may be called the higher moral phenomena of the case, which otherwise would be the most incredible "miracle" of all.

These remarks bear directly on our argument for the

locality under consideration. We need a great miracle to explain, how, in the presence of such an enemy, that people could have ventured to make a forward movement like this. Indeed, we cannot otherwise understand how they would make any effort to escape at all, instead of surrendering without a shadow of resistance. It could not be in consequence of the authority and influence of Moses, for at this time they did not venerate him, but rather upbraided him as the author of their misfortunes. They turned on him with rage and bitterest sarcasm. "Because there were no graves in Egypt (a land of tombs), hast thou brought us out to die in the wilderness?" Their fear of the Egyptians will not explain their advance, for that was of such a nature as to incline them to an instant submission. They are here on the shore of the sea, a vast multitude of men, women, and children—confused, distracted, encumbered with flocks and herds; close on them is the terrible enemy who had crushed their spirit to the dust, equipped with swift horses and chariots, and eager to lead them back again to bondage. We cannot conceive of a people in their circumstances thinking of anything else than surrender, precisely as the narrative represents. Their terror, like that of the trembling victim beneath the swoop of the eagle, took from them all courage to advance, all hope of escape. This consideration of itself would dispose us to reject the theory "of the wind and ebb-tide," so objectionable, as we have seen, on other grounds. Such a theory might hold were this an army defeated and flying, but it was not for a multitude of trembling slaves, who had arms indeed, but could not use them, and who were accompanied by their families and flocks, to advance merely because the tide was well out. How could such a crowd be assured that they would cross safely, if the billows were to return by natural laws in three or four hours? And was there any guarantee that the Egyptians would perish and follow them no more? Surely it was of little use to take advantage of the ebbing tide, if the enemy is to be swift upon them on the opposite shore, and to be more vengeful when he comes.

We are driven, I believe, by the necessities of the case to the theory of a great miracle, unmistakable above all to them, as the true explanation of their advance and wonderful escape. In their terror and present ignorance of the divine character, they will take no promise of escape on trust. They must see the way open unmistakably, or they will not venture. They must "walk by sight," they cannot walk "by faith." As, therefore, they subdued their terror—gave up the idea of surrender, and passed through to the opposite shore with all their flocks and herds—we are forced to believe in a miracle of the most transcendent character, whose phenomena made even their dull minds take hold of the idea required, that the God of their fathers was still able to save them.

To sum up in a sentence, I have sought to vindicate this promontory of Attakah, as the point of the passage through the Red Sea, from a regard to the position of the last encampment of the Israelites in Egypt; the distance across to the opposite shore (six and a half miles); the present traditional names of "the mountain of deliverance" on the one side, and "the wells of Moses" on the other; the emphatic testimony of Josephus; and lastly, the scope here afforded for such a miracle as the emergency required.

In many respects it is probable the scene has greatly changed since that people were here. Traces of ancient villages or towns have wholly disappeared, their ruins buried deep by the sand-storms of the Desert. But two grand features remain—the sea and the mountains beside it, whose sterile and rugged precipices echoed to the cry of their frantic despair.

Their deliverance issued in results for the world far more sublime and lasting than may at first be adequately comprehended. In the narrative it is said, "The Egyptians were drowned;" "The Israelites were saved,"— expressions of far-reaching significance.

"The Egyptians were drowned;" the judgment was "a rod that broke in pieces the oppressor," struck a deadly blow at the idolatry of Egypt, and through it, at the idolatry of the world. For such, at this time, was the position of Egypt with its armies and temples, its science and wisdom, that idolatry was here smitten in its citadel and "pride of place," and far and wide would the echo of the blow resound. The song of Moses grandly anticipates the effect on the nations through which the Israelites were to pass :—

> "The people shall hear and be afraid :
> Sorrow shall take hold on the inhabitants of Palestina.
> Then the dukes of Edom shall be amazed ;
> The mighty men of Moab, trembling shall take hold on them :
> All the inhabitants of Canaan shall melt away.
> Fear and dread shall fall upon them ;
> By the greatness of thine arm they shall be still as a stone ;
> Till the people pass over, O Lord, till the people pass over,
> Which thou hast purchased."

"And the Israelites were saved." With them were saved the dearest interests of humanity and religion.

They had left Egypt for the world's sake as well as for their own. From them rose the great line of prophets and psalmists, apostles and martyrs, and of them "as concerning the flesh, Christ came, who is over all, God blessed for ever." The real question at stake was, Is the world to be enlightened and redeemed, or to sink helplessly in idolatry and spiritual death? Who that appreciates this as the grand issue, but must admit that the occasion was worthy of a transcendent miracle?

In the narrative, an end is expressly stated, as justifying the Divine interposition, involving all that has now been said. That end was the glory of God. "The Egyptians shall know that I am the Lord, when I have gotten me honour on Pharaoh, his chariots, and all his horsemen" (Ex. xiv. 18). "And Israel saw the great work which the Lord did upon the Egyptians, and the people feared the Lord, and believed the Lord and his servant Moses."

The glory of God! For this end the heaven and earth were made; for this end the waters of the Red Sea flowed at first, and these mountains on its shores were upreared; and when this requires it (as in the case before us), these ancient mountains shall shake; these waters shall dispart, and even in the lapse of time shall altogether pass away.

We may be allowed to linger for a little on the strange phenomena of an event which was to issue in such splendid results for the world, and which severed the last connexion of Israel with the land of their bondage. "The Egyptians," said Moses to the affrighted multitude, " whom ye have seen to-day, ye shall see no more for ever."

Marvellous, then, was the action of the Cloud that accompanied them in all their journey. Its shape and action were always as its mission. In the Temple its placid brightness in the Holy of Holies indicated that the Divine presence was at rest. In the Desert it hung calmly in the deep sky, visible to all, and fitted to awe that unruly host, to guide them, tempering it may be the fierce heat of the day, and, changing into "a pillar of fire," diffused a cheerful glow over the encampment of the night. Here, on the shore of the Red Sea, its form and influence were just what was required for the rescue of the people and the distraction of the enemy. It came "between the camp of the Egyptians and the camp of Israel, and it was a cloud and darkness to them, but it gave light by night to these, so that the one came not near the other all the night." "For the Lord God is a sun and shield."

And now they were to "see the salvation of God." A Divine power was at work, of which the strong wind was but the emblem, parting the waters, throwing them back on either side into massive heaps, until a broad and magnificent pathway was cleared through the depths, along which, to the farther shore, the flame of the guardian Cloud cast its wondrous gleam. The command is then given by their Divine Leader, "Go forward;" Moses, according to the Jewish historian, himself first obeying it, and leading the way.

The front advances with strange and mingled feelings, casting, we may well suppose, many an anxious glance at the piled-up waters, that chafe and fret like bridled steeds, yet are held in by the strong hand of God. And the flame of the Fire-Cloud, playing on the crest of the billows, would make the foam sparkle and flash; serving still more to increase the light of the way, and revealing the waters on either side as a wall of beauty no less than of strength. And so onward they pass; each tribe as they come up encouraged by the experience of those in advance, all deeply awed by the exhibition of the Divine power and goodness, until the last foot is lifted from the bed of the sea, and every heart is heaving with emotions of which the song of Moses is the needful outlet and expression.

And now, what of the Egyptians? Tired out with the urgent pursuit, and having at last gained sight of the Israelites, they rest for the night : on the morrow they are sure of their victims, thus imprisoned between the mountain and the sea. When made aware of their flight, we need not wonder at their determination to follow. How could they brook that the enemy should escape, when so nearly in their grasp? They think, no doubt, that where the Israelites go they can follow ; and if there be danger, they have great advantage in their horses and chariots. But that Egyptian army and its king are ripe for destruction. The previous judgments that befell should have warned them back from the awful fate that is now impending. But their hearts are "hardened," and they, doubtless, have some way of accounting for all that happened. It may have been chance ; some transient displeasure of their deities, now appeased ; or some superior magic on the part of Moses. And then they are mad at the thought that they should have had so much trouble and misery with slaves, whom at one time they could so easily trample under foot. Anyway, they have ventured into that sea-girt road in the hot pursuit, and so rush upon their doom.

"The Lord looked through the cloud, and troubled the Egyptians." A fearful sentence! Strange meteors of fire, awful glances of lightning, strike in amongst them, startling the chariot-steeds, driving them frantic, and at once spreading bewilderment in the marching host. The chariot-wheels sink in the mire; all is outcry and confusion; and then at the appointed signal, the released waters bound forward like lions on their prey, bringing "swift destruction."

What a spectacle for the Israelites to behold in the lurid dawn! "The sea returned to his strength," and "the Lord overthrew the Egyptians in the midst of the sea;"—"He sent out his arrows and scattered them, and shot out his lightnings and discomfited them!" The awful shriek of that drowning host is soon quelled, and there prevails the roar of the angry elements, that tells how truly they have avenged the insult offered to their God.

"The enemy said, I will pursue, I will overtake, I will divide the spoil; my lust shall be satisfied upon them; I will draw my sword, my hand shall destroy them. Thou didst blow with thy wind; the sea covered them; they sank as lead in the mighty waters. — Thy right hand, O Lord, is become glorious in power; thy right hand, O Lord, hath dashed in pieces the enemy."

CHAPTER IV.

ISRAEL IN THE WILDERNESS.

In our encampment at Suez, we were introduced to the novel experiences of camp life, its comforts, discomforts (especially as we were short of one tent), and its delightful freedom. On our arrival, some time was occupied in hearing the story of the robbery and murder, making various arrangements, discovering and inventing contrivances in the tent for the disposal of luggage (in which a good deal of ingenuity may be shown), and getting "all right" for the journey. There yet remained two hours until dinner, when we strolled over the sterile plain, surveying the locality, and with the strange feeling that our foot was now fairly on the Desert. We often glanced at those boundless wastes on the opposite shore, which we should traverse on the morrow, and which lying there under the glittering heat often recalled the Scripture expression: "the great and terrible wilderness." Baomi summoned us to dinner, and again we tried to make something of the mysterious tale, of which we were still incredulous. But it was the same story over and over again. Mahmoud now announced his intention of going to the town and getting another tent, which, however, never came. The encampment of our escort was close at hand, and was sheltered by no tent of any kind whatever. Sauntering out in the evening, we found the recumbent camels arranged in a circle around their owners, who were squatted about the fire in the centre, at their supper, consisting of roasted beans, which they picked from the ashes and tossed into the mouth with great rapidity.

They grinned a welcome, and rose as we approached. "Taib Ingles" was their salutation, and we replied, as our knowledge of the language allowed, Taib Bedawy! The night had fallen, and as we look up, what a glorious heaven of stars! They hang so deeply down, as it were, from the solemn concave firmament, and are so pure, lustrous, and large, as to make the night of the Desert for ever memorable. All around lay an impressive stillness, deepened by the murmur of the sea. Southwards, in the clear starlight, loomed the heights of Jebel Attakah, where, as we have endeavoured to prove, the Israelites crossed to the farther side. A dark mass of cloud now hung on its summit, from which the vivid lightnings were flashing every minute, a scene that helped still more forcibly to recall the solemn memories of the past.

There were three in our tent, and so the space, when we turned in for the night, was rather small. In the affair of bedding, we were not so well off as a party who preceded us. Though carried at the same rate, they had been provided with iron bedsteads,—a most wise precaution on the threshold of the rainy season : but as Mahmoud had furnished us with no such luxury, our beds were stretched on the sand ; and on one or two gusty nights, the sand was blown in, and the sleeper complained of being awakened by the cough and discomfort thereby occasioned. Fortunately the nights generally were calm, and moreover, we soon learned to pile the sand well up on the canvas, so as to free ourselves from this annoyance. In the deep calm of this first night at Suez, it was strange enough to lift the canvas at your pillow, and see the heads of the camels in the circle, the glancing of the stars, and the rapid flashings of the lightnings on the heights of Jebel Attakah.

On the mutual inquiries next morning how the night had passed, each had his own story about the attack of the fleas, as indeed we had anticipated. Our poor friends in Mahmoud's tent suffered greatly, and one of them provoked our pity and laughter by exhibiting his arm blistered nearly to the shoulder. We could not look forward to our journey without a shudder. Mahmoud tried to console us by saying, that we had slept on the usual site of the encampment, where, therefore, fleas were very abundant, but it "would be all right" when we got away into the Desert.

We now proposed to start. We approached to select our camels with a kindly interest, and with the charitable notion that they were, despite of vague rumours to the contrary, fine embodiments of meekness and patience. But our near presence was the signal for an astounding explosion of the most unearthly gurglings, groanings, and roarings conceivable. Clearly they did not relish the prospect of the journey at all. They would roll the head round most angrily, with a hideous roar, as if protesting that if you persisted in your intentions, they would not be responsible for the consequences. The choice made, we walked on over the fine sand for a few miles, as the morning was so delightful, leaving the baggage and camels to follow. We talked of the unexpected display of their fierceness, each remarking on the animal he had selected: "I don't like his eye; what a mouth he opened on me!" etc. Some one had read, too, of the dangers of the first mounting; how that a tumble is not uncommon, the collar-bone sometimes broken, and that you are squeamish with the first day's experience of the "ship of the desert." But the experiment, it was clear, must be made, limbs and stomach notwithstanding.

So at last we halted. The camels on coming up were ordered to kneel down by the attendant Arab. They obeyed, but again with a horrid gurgling remonstrative roar, the face anything but "a revelation of the beautiful." It made one somewhat indignant that the animal should thus cry out before he was hurt, and so quickened the resolution to lay aside fear and mount at once, that you and he might know the worst of it. The saddle, let the reader know, is a wooden apparatus, suited to the hump of the camel, having before and behind a strong peg of wood, by which the novice as he mounts holds on as for very life. Over it are thrown bed and bedding, and so it becomes a broad level eminence, allowing the rider to vary the attitude as the humour takes him. The attendant Arab keeps his foot firmly fixed on the bended knee of the recumbent camel until you are fairly seated. He then demands, "Taib Howagee?" "Are you right, sir?" when (with a frightened gasp) you respond, "Taib!" "all right!" clutching desperately the aforesaid prominences of the saddle. The animal then rises, first on his knees, then from behind, then entirely, giving you the three terrible jolts—backwards, forwards, backwards, and there you are!

Comical enough were the faces of the party as this first mounting was achieved.

No accidents happened in our case, the difficulties here, as often elsewhere, being less in reality than in anticipation. We by and by learned to make the animals kneel without help, when preparing to descend, but in the affair of mounting, the Arab required to be in attendance to the very last. One of our party once tried the getting on in the independent style, but the camel was too quick for him; and on the rider being raised aloft, moved off rapidly before his seat was secure, and in consequence he, his pillows, bed, and bedding, like snow from a house-top, came tumbling to the ground.

We soon had reason to remark how admirably fitted these animals were for the desert. The powerful eye strongly shaded from the sun; the nostril capable of firm contraction when the sand-storm is raging; the fine spread and energetic spring of the foot; the elevation at which it carries its rider above the burning sands; the unsightly hump even an advantage, helping, it is said, by being absorbed, to keep up the strength when food is unattainable; all these adaptations fit the camel wonderfully for such barren latitudes where other animals would fail, and distinguish it emphatically as the "ship of the desert."

In consequence of the tide, we required to go round by the head of the Gulf. There we saw the banks of the ancient canal that ran from this point northwards, forbidding the hypothesis that the Gulf, within at least the date of history, extended much beyond its present limits. By the time that we reached the opposite side, the heat became very intense, and we had occasion to learn another Arabic word often shouted on our journey: "Moi! Moi! Water! Water!" Before us now stretched to the far horizon the silent barrenness of the wilderness —the vacant air glittering and quivering with the intense heat; and as we moved on in silence, a solemn mood sometimes overshadowed the mind, for it seemed like taking a farewell of the living world for a time. Our travelling costume was now complete; and what with green spectacles and veils, sprouting beards, enormous wide-awakes wound with calico, the ample folds of which floated down behind for the protection of the neck, with *revolvers*, moreover, as "robbery and murder" had commenced, I daresay our friends at home would have been puzzled to know us.

We passed on to Ayoun Mousa, "the wells of Moses," opposite to Attakah, where there are a few gardens and some wells of brackish water, of which we could not drink. On this the outset of our journey, the place seemed scraggy and contemptible enough, but on our return it seemed a little paradise in contrast with the barren wilderness we were leaving behind. Here we halted for lunch, the baggage camels passing onwards with the Sheik Nassar, who always fixed the encampment for the night. After an interval we followed, and about six o'clock reached our tent, having started from Suez about seven in the morning.

Here is a slight jotting from a journal, made as dinner was getting ready, and which may finish this sketch of our first day in the Desert :—

"A glorious sunset to-night; golden fleecy clouds lying in long narrow parallels in the magnificent sky,

with larger clouds above. Far up reaches the ruddy tinge of the sunset. The Israelites as they passed would often see such a glory, but as the night darkened there would be a difference in their favour. Now, as the sun is sinking behind the hills of Egypt on the western shore, these clouds are losing their lustre; they become grey, sombre, dark as in other lands. But to that chosen people the light of one Cloud continued, brightening into clearer refulgence as the darkness fell, and at last shining out 'a pillar of fire by night.'"—
" What a life there is in the Desert after all! Most void of all life it seemed as we passed along to-day, the very flies refusing to follow on such a journey. But the candle is lighted in the tent, and, lo! insect life is here. Moths come in buzzing, and crackle in the flame. Horrid beetles too, black and hideous, struggle into sight, sometimes rising on the wing, and are soon busy dragging and kicking into their retreats the garbage of the encampment. Overhead is the night with its stars, calm and holy, and around a most grand and impressive silence."

Second day.—For a considerable time we were plodding over a comparatively level track, within view of the sea. The bright mirage would sometimes stretch up from the distant Gulf; its calm waters, scarce a mile distant, apparently wooing us in the oppressive heat to a luxurious bath. It is a strange delusion of the sense, and, mocking in this way the stern reality, makes the traveller feel all the more keenly " the heat and burden of the day." Our escort seemed content and joyous now that they were fairly in their Desert. They were impatient at Suez for the start, declaring their dislike to the noise and bustle of towns. They complained too of annoyance from the fleas that abound there, and from which they assert their Desert to be free. It was manifest, however, that they were afflicted with vermin of another sort—one of the plagues of Egypt! Rejoicing in the exhilarating freedom of the wild waste, they stepped along with vigorous limb. All of our escort were slim, spare, and muscular, wearing the look of men subject to many privations, but resolute to endure them. Their skin was black and parched, looking indeed as if roasted, the fat absorbed, and muscle only remaining. The dirty tattered costume, and indeed the aspect generally, indicated their poverty. Their sandals were of the rudest sort, said to be made of the skin of a fish caught on the shores of the Red Sea. Some had the turban with which to guard the head from the heat, others had only the fez. With matchlock, dagger, dangling flint and steel, they were equipped to satisfaction. At night in the encampment, they pulled from their baggage-camel a heavy cloak of goat's hair, which they threw over their scanty cotton dress to protect them from the chill. After a pipe and supper, they doubled themselves up in it, and heedless of a pillow, were off to sleep in a twinkling, snoring most profoundly. On several occasions they snatched a few minutes' repose during the day. The party wishing for this siesta, would trot away far in advance, and cast himself down by the track, trusting to the last that came up to arouse him.

To the north there ran parallel with our route the range of Jebel el Tih, that looked fearfully rugged and precipitous. In the clear atmosphere it seemed only about ten miles distant, but the Dragoman declared that it was nearer thirty, as was proved by the slowness with which we passed its prominences. One of these especially attracts the eye, the Cup of Sudr, apparently the shattered crater of an extinct volcano. We seemed to be abreast of it for hours together. Shall we never pass that Cup of Sudr? was a question often asked, and it was felt to be a real triumph when it lagged slowly in the rear.

Let the reader notice that the name of this track is Wady Sudr (Soodr), answering, I believe, to "the wilderness of Shur," into which the Israelites passed after crossing the Red Sea (Ex. xv. 22). Farther on, we came on another portion called Wady Aithi, in which we can recognise the "Wilderness of Etham," as first suggested by Lord Lindsay. By this name the Wilderness of Shur is mentioned in Numbers xxxiii. 8.

Throughout this part of the Desert the vegetation is very meagre. At intervals sometimes of ten or twenty yards, stunted shrubs pierce the surface. One of these is the Ghurkud, of which the camels are particularly fond. They will espy it a considerable distance and make for it, thus often rendering the course very devious and irregular. You do not like to check them in gathering what food they can, but find that this roving tendency is not favourable to prolonged talk with a friend. Ludicrous enough sometimes is one's plight in the midst of the interesting dialogue. You are seated comfortably on the broad saddle, sideways to the camel, and face to face with your companion. The talk proceeds, "Well, as I was saying,"—"All very true, but you forget that,"—when off at an angle goes the camel at a quickened pace after the ghurkud,—the other, probably, following the example, in view of a shrub on its own side; and so the discussion is interrupted, and "wastes its sweetness on the desert air."

Towards the afternoon we got quit of the dreary level, and entered upon long rolling hollows and prominences equally dismal. Casting the eye around, the scene could be compared to nothing so well as the tumultuous waves of an agitated sea. Over this expanse of sand the former winds have raged, as over the expanse of waters, whirling the loose particles into all manner of fantastic heaps. But then here all is so silent and fixed! This greatly deepens the feeling of the desolation and terror of the Desert. In the hollows the view is shut in, but on the summit of one of these prominences you see the sultry maze crowding and thickening to the horizon and the scarred ridges of Jebel el Tih. What confusion! what desolation! what a deathlike stillness! what a fate to be a lost wanderer here, straying among those "pathless wastes!" Before the Israelites moved the guiding Cloud high in air, and seen by all as they crowded along the winding hollows, or straggled through the bewildering rifts and ravines. It is a strange feeling to fall behind and realize something of this solitude and desolation. In a little while your party have disappeared, and you are in the Desert alone! Around on every hand are these boundless burning wastes, and no sight of bird in the air, or insect on the path, relieves this awful loneliness. It seems as a return from death to life when you rejoin the companionship and guidance of your friends.

When the day was well advanced, our Dragoman, casting his eye to the west, called out to "hasten the camels: hasten the camels." Their drivers first indulged in sundry energetic exclamations, and then one would commence a low, monotonous, plaintive song. It was peculiar in respect of its strange abrupt stops and spasmodic ejaculations, as if the singer had run short of breath. These were really part of the intended tune, duly interspersed throughout, and were peculiarly emphatic at the end of each line. The song amused us much, and the awkward attempt at imitation was relished by none more than by the Arabs themselves. About seven o'clock we hailed our tents, pitched in a little hollow, when, tired with a journey of twelve hours, we threw ourselves gladly on our couch on the sand.

Third day.—In the fine cool morning we took a walk for two hours, when we reached Howarah, the Marah of Scripture (Ex. xv. 23). A few scrubby palms here broke the monotony of the Desert, close beside which was a small green-mantled pool. When dipping the finger into the water just to taste it, the Arabs raised the cry, "Marr—Marah—Marah—bitter—bitter!" It was, indeed, most offensive. A poor camel who did not hear the cry, or did not understand it, ventured its lips to the pool, and thereafter made a face that was ludicrous to see. "Marah" was decidedly its verdict, as well as that of its owner, though they do drink of it, it is said, if very thirsty. The reader will see from the map, that near the spot is a wady, still bearing the name of Amarah.

In two hours more we reached Wady Gurundel, a valley which exhibits, for the Desert, abundant vegetation. Here a question of locality presents itself for our consideration. Is this the next encampment of the Israelites after Marah, "Elim," where there were seventy palm trees, and twelve wells of water? (Ex. xv. 27.)

Some would fix it in the Wady Useit, about six miles farther on. If the question is to be settled by a regard to the comparative fertility of these valleys, the preference must be given to Gurundel. This statement may startle some who have seen only that barren portion of Gurundel that is crossed in the direct route to Sinai, and who have in consequence judged it to contrast unfavourably with Wady Useit, through the entire length of which they had to pass. It so happened that we traversed both from end to end, and I can affirm that the vegetation of Gurundel is very great for the Desert, and that Useit is not to be named in comparison.

On our return from Sinai, we entered Gurundel from the sea. Here, to our great delight, we came on a fine little stream, bubbling merrily from an extensive palm-grove beyond. The rivulet can be traced upwards for more than a mile, and for five miles farther up the valley water can be obtained by digging in the sand. We saw here a large flock of camels, belonging, as the Dragoman told us, to one of the richest Arabs of the Desert. They found, even at this season, before "the latter rain," good and regular pasture, such as Useit could never supply. There cannot be a doubt, then, that this is Elim, if the present abundance of the vegetation is to settle the locality. But it may be questioned whether this test be the legitimate one.

1. If the testimony of Josephus is to weigh with us, Gurundel is to be rejected, from the very circumstance here urged in its favour. According to him the vegetation of Elim was inconsiderable. "The place," he says, "looked well at a distance, for there was a grove of palm-trees, but when they came near to it, it appeared

to be a bad place, for the palm-trees were no more than seventy." At the present day, in this valley, they might be counted by hundreds.

2. This locality seems too near the last encampment, Marah, the distance being only about six miles.

3. The encampment here, spreading down the valley, would touch on the sea-shore, whereas we read that "they removed from Elim, and encamped by the Red Sea."

It is therefore in the poorer valley of Useit that we are inclined to fix this Scripture locality. Besides presenting an appearance more in harmony with the language of the Jewish historian, it is much the broader and more level of the two, and so more suitable for the large multitude. Moreover, it is distant from Marah about ten miles, and thus marks with more probability the next advance. Again, from it they would have a march of about equal length to the foot of Wady Tayibeh, and so arrive at their next encampment by the sea (Numb. xxxiii. 10).[1]

To proceed with our journey. We lunched in Gurundel, by the side of a well dug by one of our escort, who had been sent forward in the morning for a supply of water. We found it very salt and brackish, and it was a wonder that our Arabs could use it at all. After an hour's rest we passed on. One of our companions had left us to take a sketch of the valley from a good point of view,

---

[1] There is, it will be seen, no resemblance in the words. And the name Elim, therefore, would seem to be lost, unless we may connect it with Zelimeh, the ancient harbour at the foot of the valley. Some, indeed, would ascribe to Elim a Hebrew derivation, and regard it as a place to which the Israelites had given a name. They sometimes, we are told, did so, but the narrative gives us no reason to doubt that in the present instance the name was already existing, and may yet linger in the district, as in the word Zelimeh.

and did not notice our departure. He shouted for a long time, but there was no response. We had crossed over a ridge and were out of the wady amid rugged ground bewildering enough to any one who did not know the path. As he did not appear, an Arab was sent back to look for him, and at last he came up covered with perspiration, and spoke of his sense of abandonment and desolation as the most painful he had ever felt.

Having emerged into higher ground, we had a splendid view of the sublime mountain scenery of the Desert, through the heart of which we were to pass all the way to Sinai. We now came on the wadys proper, which are just the valleys among those mountains, deep and rugged for the most part, and torn by the wild torrents of the winter rain. Flooded for a few days, the greater part of them lie thereafter sterile and desolate. Memorable was this first view of the mountain scenery, and strongly suggestive of the solemn associations of the past. Not in glad sunshine lay these Alpine masses before us, but overshadowed with clouds, solemn, full of gloom, "with the look that threatens the profane." In the far distance rose the towering cliffs of Serbal.

We here met some priests coming from the Convent of Sinai, attended by a party of Arabs. Our escort exchanged salutations. They touched the head, lips, and heart, and then firmly grasped the hand. One of the first inquiries, it seems, is, "How are all the camels?" What the reindeer is to the Laplander, the camel is to the Arab.

Wady Useit, through which we now held our way, is very broad, and could afford, as already remarked, ample space for the large encampment of the Israelites. I believe it to be one of those tracts in the wilderness which were more fertile in ancient times than now. Here water can be got by digging, and such, according to Josephus, was the way in which the Israelites obtained water at Elim. From the aspect of the remaining trees, it may be inferred that there might be still reproduced very considerable vegetation. Around on every side are the mounds of sand, the bare and blasted hills whose sides are covered with loose debris lying in inconceivable confusion. Among the loose masses the whirlwinds play, and many valleys anciently fertile have become utterly desolate, or yield, as here, a scanty and struggling vegetation. Two hours beyond Wady Useit, we arrived at our tents.

Fourth day.—Starting about seven o'clock, we passed down Wady Tayibeh, a deep, rugged defile. Here the traveller comes upon the strangely-coloured rocks which, afterwards repeated on a grander scale, make him think of the scenery of the Desert as the most wonderful and impressive he has ever beheld. We proceeded slowly down the ravine, lingering in view of its weird and rugged windings. The word was passed on from some one in advance that the sea was in sight. Our delight at the intelligence indicated how deeply the awful grandeur and solitude of the journey had impressed us. Those from behind hastened to enjoy the view, and there was in it a feeling of escape from a bewildering labyrinth in an unknown land, into the familiar world once more. We hailed the glittering waters as the face and laugh of an old friend, and were soon plunging amongst them, with a delightful experience of invigoration and refreshment.

The fine broad plain, on which the valley opens, seems

to have been "the encampment of the Israelites by the Red Sea" (Numb. xxxiii. 10).

Let me pause to remark that their arrival here was fitted to accomplish important moral ends, and aid in their religious discipline. The scene on which they now looked was eminently instructive. Murmurings and despondency had broken out, the Divine goodness had been forgotten, and they were again brought to the Red Sea, to be reminded of the great deliverance they had so lately experienced, and learn the lesson of unfailing trust in God. On the opposite shore loomed the mountains of Egypt, "the house of their bondage." Here it could be seen from a safe distance; the barrier between them and their enemies was for ever impassable. In that land was "lamentation, and mourning, and woe." Its families were prostrate under a double grief. They "mourned and were in bitterness for the first-born," and in some cases it might be, for a month had not elapsed, the tomb had not yet closed on the embalmed dead. By this time, too, intelligence had reached them of that other awful judgment, the destruction of Pharaoh and his army. Even now the mangled corpses were being lashed by the waters of this Gulf, or cast upon the beach a prey for the vulture and jackal of the Desert. Such was the suggestive scene before the eyes of the Israelites. It was one that brought out in strong contrast their position with that of their former oppressors. It was well fitted to rebuke their murmurings; to fill them with solemn and thankful feelings. We may believe that some, at least, with the spirit of a Joshua and a Caleb, broke forth once more into the song of praise, as these waters murmured at their feet : "Sing unto the Lord, for he hath triumphed gloriously : the horse and his rider hath he thrown into the sea. Thou didst blow with thy wind, the sea covered them : they sank as lead in the mighty waters."

Up to this time we read of no miraculous provision for the support of the people. If we may not take away from the miracles of the narrative, we are not, on the other hand, rashly to add to them, and are bound therefore to inquire, What natural means of subsistence had they thus far on their journey ? It had been well if such questions as these had received more attention from writers on the journeying of the Exodus.

1. They had brought large provision from Egypt. In any circumstances as venturing on a journey "into the wilderness to sacrifice to the Lord their God," we might have assumed that they would so far provide themselves with articles of food ; but we are assured that such was the case, inasmuch as they had entered on the feast of the Passover. They had prepared for it before they left ; but being urged by the Egyptians to go out in haste, "they took," we are told, "the dough before it was leavened ; their kneading-troughs being bound up in their clothes upon their shoulders." At Succoth, "they baked unleavened cakes of the dough which they brought forth out of Egypt." Josephus tells us that the provisions lasted a month, the time indicated in the Scripture narrative as the date of their entrance into the wilderness of Sin, where, for the first time, they cry for *bread*.

2. They had means of subsistence from the cattle they had brought with them. They left Egypt, we are told, "with flocks, and herds, and much cattle." They would thus in a great measure live on the milk of the

flock. Besides, at this stage, we are to understand that they were killing their cattle for food. They "lusted for flesh," and at various times passionately raised the cry, Who will give us flesh to eat? But we read of no clamour of this sort till they come into the Wilderness of Sin, so that previous to this, they could obtain their desire in the slaying of the cattle they had brought with them. Thus, when they have entered the Wilderness, their mode of living would not much differ from what they had been accustomed to in Egypt—a circumstance favourable to their more willing advance.

But admitting this, the reader will ask, How were the *cattle* sustained across this portion of the Desert, as it is now so waste and unproductive? The controversy of the day, I repeat, demands that such questions be no longer ignored.

1. By the time they had crossed the Red Sea to the wilderness, the original number of their flocks would be greatly reduced. It must be borne in mind that they were not in haste to pass the Egyptian frontier. They delayed at Succoth, and marched leisurely to Etham and Pi-hahiroth. So long, indeed, did they linger on the Egyptian side, that Pharaoh fancied them unable or unwilling to go forward into the Wilderness at all, and was tempted to make an attempt at their capture. About three weeks in all may have elapsed before they crossed. As they were slaying their cattle, and as for such demands the daily consumption would be great, we must conclude that the number would be reduced by several thousands, so that the Wilderness of Etham would not have to support the large flocks and herds that have been usually supposed.

2. There is reason to believe that this track was formerly more fertile than now. It has even yet a vegetation, though scanty, and we must allow for the results of the sand-storms which have swept across it during about four thousand years, and which have laid waste the adjoining frontier of Egypt, undoubtedly productive in former times.

3. In the time of the Exodus, the vegetation of the Desert would be at its best. It took place some weeks after the latter rain, when a transient flush of pasture covers many wadys, which at other times are utterly barren. In March, when we passed, our Arabs were eagerly expecting this rain, and for several days the sky looked so threatening as to make the Dragoman anxious about our return. The effect in April (the month of the Exodus) is to cover many barren districts for a few weeks with grass and various vegetation. For, all throughout, water is the grand condition of verdure, and however unpromising may be the appearance of the surface, palms and shrubs spring up, if water be near. Even at the present day, after the rain, the vegetation in the Wilderness of Etham is considerably increased, and many of the wadys about Sinai are actually green with pasture.[1]

The above considerations may help to explain the mode of subsistence of the Israelites with their flocks in their journey to the Wilderness of Sin. Here the provisions failed. Though they would still have some nourishment from the milk of their flock, *animal food* was no longer within their reach. Their clamour was that there was neither bread nor flesh to eat. "Would to God," they

---

[1] So our Dragoman and escort assured us.

cried, "that we had died by the hand of the Lord in the land of Egypt; when we sat by the *flesh*-pots, and when we did eat bread to the full; for ye have brought us forth into this wilderness to kill this whole assembly with hunger" (Ex. xvi. 3).

In a miraculous manner the bread and flesh were supplied. It was proved that "God could furnish a table in the wilderness." Quails were sent; but this provision was temporary. The manna was vouchsafed, falling as dew around their camp morning and evening, and was continued to them through all their journey. "This light food," it may be remarked, was the most healthful for them in the changed circumstances of their desert life; although, on a memorable occasion, in perverse humour, they expressed "a loathing" for it. Had their food continued as hitherto, had they been here plentifully provided with "the flesh-pots of Egypt," it is certain that plague and pestilence would never have been wanting. They would have perished from natural causes, or at least, revelling thus, would have been still more unfit for the religious teaching of their economy. Their simple fare—manna and the milk of the flock; also the privations that ever and again came on them with painful severity, formed part of a wise and elevating discipline. It nursed and developed manly qualities that would have lain utterly torpid amid the luxuries of Egypt, and helped to change the cowardly crowd of the Exodus into a nation conspicuous in history for valour and endurance.

I may remark that the milk of the flock, always a chief means of support to an Arab and his family, is sometimes his only one for weeks together. Various instances have been mentioned by travellers,[1] and one such is graphically described by the author of *Eöthen*. This, with the manna, sustained the Israelites from the Wilderness of Sin on to Rephidim. There, indeed, it seemed likely to fail altogether, for there was no water to be had. "Wherefore is this," cried the people, "that thou hast brought us out of Egypt to kill us, and our children, and our *cattle*, with thirst?" All were preserved by the water now miraculously brought from the adjacent rock of Horeb.

At this stage of their history occurred an event connected with the inquiry specially before us, and which helps to explain the difficulty so much dwelt on by some, viz., the support of the Israelites in the Desert for forty years. "Then came Amalek, and fought with Israel at Rephidim." The result was the total defeat of the Desert tribe. Josephus, in allusion to the event, says that the "Israelites took great spoil, and also *much cattle*." It could not fail to result in this, for they are now virtually masters of the peninsula, and would naturally seize the flocks and herds of the defeated tribe; the greater part of which might probably have been collected at their headquarters in the adjacent valley of Wady Feiran. The increase was a precious acquisition to the Israelites in their present circumstances. It greatly augmented their means of subsistence, and enabled them more easily to furnish the sacrifices enjoined in their economy, to the extent at least that was required.

Bishop Colenso, in his recent work, has argued that

---

[1] Dr. Robinson mentions that one of his guides managed to support himself and his children for a fortnight, exclusively on the milk of the camels, in the plain of Elkaa—the Wilderness of Sin.—*Biblical Researches*, vol. i. p. 150.

the sustenance of the people with their flocks was utterly out of the question, and for proof brings forward the emphatic statement of travellers as to the unexampled sterility of the Desert where they wandered. He pleads, of course, for the old conclusion, that the narrative of the Pentateuch is not trustworthy. And there is no doubt that to many minds the matter does present a serious difficulty, and is one not to be shirked, but fairly met. It is well enough known now, that the Desert of Arabia is indeed awful in its barrenness, a scene of mountains, of bare rocks, and stony wastes. The continued graphic description of all this by travellers only makes the above difficulty more pressing than ever. Shall we assert that the cattle, as well as the people, were supported by miracle? There is not a word of this in the narrative, and it cannot be assumed. The problem, I believe, finds its solution in the following considerations, which make for the two conclusions:—*first*, that the pasture of the wilderness was formerly much greater than now; and, *secondly*, that inasmuch as all the details of the Jewish economy were not carried out in the Desert, they did not require the immense number of cattle, for religious purposes, that is usually supposed.

I. As to the past abundant fertility of many tracts in the Desert. Doubtless in that ancient time, there were always vast districts of desolation answering to the graphic language of Scripture, "a land of drought, wherein there was no water." But that this was not, and could not be the case, with the whole peninsula, as the above-named writer so confidently asserts, may be inferred both from facts that meet the eye of the traveller at the present day, and also from the incidents and language of the inspired record itself.

At several parts of the usual route to Sinai, far inland, there remain the traces of ancient human industry to an amazing extent. There are deep quarries, for example, extending round Surabit el Khadim for many miles. On one occasion it occupied us for about four hours to pass through a section of this area. In other parts, deep mines are found in the rocks, and the smelting of ore has been carried on very extensively. Every new route opens up fresh discoveries of this kind. There must consequently have been many thousands of men at work for ages here, who required of course to be supported. How then was this managed? The question cannot be dismissed with the allegation that the provision was supplied from the Red Sea. There can be no doubt that to a considerable extent this would be the case. But to allege that this was the only or principal source is an incredible assumption, for the localities are inland and dispersed over the country. Again, it is well known that there are myriad inscriptions on rocks in the Desert. By whomsoever these were engraven (a point to be afterwards looked at), they lead to the conclusion that in the distant past there were multitudes sojourning, or, as I believe, dwelling in the Desert, to a far greater extent than could be possible now. Indeed, it may be affirmed that there is no locality in the whole East where the traveller is compelled to draw a wider and more marked contrast between the capabilities of the present and the past, as to the support of human life, than when he comes on these wide-spread traces of human industry and toil, in the now silent valleys of the peninsula of Sinai. We have further evidence of this in the fact, that even within the Christian era there was a population in the city of Pharan, which certainly could not subsist there now. The sterility of the Desert, I may add, is increasing more than ever, as the Arabs are deliberately cutting down the trees that remain, which they burn for charcoal and carry to Cairo.

Let us now consider what evidence on the point under consideration is furnished by the language and incidents of the Scripture narrative. Dr. Colenso, in dealing with that language, commits a strange blunder. Strong expressions are made use of in regard to certain scenes of the wanderings. "A land of drought —of deserts and pits—where there was no water." "A waste howling wilderness." This emphatic description he boldly applies to the Desert in all its length and breadth. Having, indeed, imagined a country, where hardly a mouse could live, he brings into it an imaginary multitude of cattle for the Israelites (upwards of two millions), and then triumphantly reaches his conclusion, that a book uttering such statements must be adjudged unhistorical. Nay, he asks, "How could there be any battle with the Amalekites, and how could such a tribe dwell in the Peninsula of Sinai at all ? Are we not told it was a land where no man passed through, and where no man dwelt ?" (Jer. ii. 6.)

Let the reader observe how the passages of Scripture depicting the desolation of the wilderness are to be restricted by the context. Moses, on two occasions, uses the expression, "the great and terrible wilderness," but in the following connexion : "When we departed from Horeb, we went through all that great and terrible wilderness which *we saw by the way of the mountain* of the Amorites (Deut i. 19). This is not a description of the whole Desert, but of the section of it after they left Horeb. The other quotation has to be limited in a similar way, indeed it refers to the same section of the country, when the Israelites are traversing it for the last time, and are about to enter the promised land. " Who led thee through that great and terrible wilderness, wherein were fiery serpents, and scorpions, and drought, where there was no water ; who brought thee forth water out of the rock of flint" (Deut. viii. 15). The experiences here alluded to are recorded in Numbers xx., xxi., and nowhere else. In a similar way we are to understand the passage from Jeremiah. The prophet does not mention Sinai, as the locality referred to ; and gathering as he did his idea from the Mosaic narrative, it is strange that his language should have been so misunderstood. It is not true that in that record the Israelites are described as always in want of water, or of food for their cattle, and the prophet could not have meant so. But there were tracts of country where the privations were terrible, where they were nigh perishing by famine and drought, and saved only by miracle ; and it is in reference to such alone that the language is applicable.

Such incidents as the following, point to a *fertility* in other parts of the Desert, which accords with the inferences already considered. Elim had its palm-trees and twelve wells of water. There is no complaint of want of pasture for the cattle in the Wilderness of Sin, or until they come to Rephidim. There was pasture in the plain before Sinai, and the people are commanded not to allow the cattle to feed before the Mount. Thither also Moses had led the flock of his father-in-law, when he was surprised by the spectacle of the burning bush. Besides, it was the country of the tribe of Amalek, the first of the Gentile nations. The Israelites took "much cattle" at Rephidim, and the spoil of sheep and oxen which Saul captured in his retaliatory invasion of that country was very great. There must, therefore, have been large tracts of pasture, on which, after the battle of Rephidim, the shepherd nation of Goshen were free to graze their herds and flocks while they roamed through the valleys of the peninsula in the long years of their sojourn.

On the whole, then, it appears that there is coincidence between the declarations and incidents of Scripture narrative, and the facts gathered from an actual survey of the Desert, leading to the conclusion that in ancient times it was far more fertile as a whole than now.

This position would not be affected, although we were unable to point out the cause which has produced such a mighty change since the Israelites were there, and issued in the wide-spread desolation that now appals the traveller in the peninsula of Sinai. But the cause is not difficult to discover. It is clearly found in the sand-storms that rage here with unexampled violence. These have extended their influence to many tracts of Egypt, so that barren wastes now appear, where formerly there was population and comparative fertility. Miss Martineau, a writer whose statements may be the more freely accepted as she is no advocate for the historical accuracy of the Pentateuch, speaking of her voyage up the Nile, says:—"If I were to have the choice of a fairy gift, it would be for a great winnowing-fan, such as would, without injury to human eyes and lungs, blow away the sand which buries the monuments of Egypt. What scenes would be laid open there! One statue and sarcophagus brought from Memphis was buried 130 feet below the mound surface. Who knows but the greater part of old Memphis and other glorious cities lie almost unharmed under the sand! What architectural stages might we not find for a thousand miles along the river, where now the orange sands lie so smooth and light as to show the clear foot-prints of every beetle that comes out to bask in the sun."[1]

Deep excavations were made around the Sphinx and the Pyramids so late as thirty years ago, but now these are filled up by the sand-drift. If such has been the effect on the border tracts of Egypt, what may we expect to have occurred within the valleys of the Desert of Arabia? As you pass into it at Suez, you see distinct traces of the old canal that joined the Red Sea to the Mediterranean. Here ships once floated, where now there is only a slight hollow depression, in some places not very distinguishable from the wastes around. We may instance again the country about Petra, where indeed there is vegetation still, but trifling to what must have been requisite in ancient times for the dwellers in " the city of the rock." In fact, the whole East supplies innumerable proofs of the fact that the grand cause of the present deterioration of its soil has been these sand whirlwinds, which of course have told with most effect on the valleys and fertile spots of the Desert itself.[2]

[1] *Eastern Life*, p. 38.

[2] Professor Stanley, describing a sand-storm—a phenomenon he thinks peculiar to these districts,—says, " Imagine all distant objects lost to view; the sheets of sand fleeting along the surface of the Desert like streams of water; the whole air filled though invisibly with a tempest of sand, driving in your face like sleet."—*Sinai and Palestine*, p. 68.

Only the skill and industry of man can keep this destroying agency in check. If from any cause the population should be reduced, and the storm allowed its own wild way, then of course during every year, the accumulation of sand would increase, and the tract become more sterile. Now we are told in the Scriptures that the ancient inhabitants of this Desert, the tribe of the Amalekites, were defeated and scattered by the Israelites, first at the battle of Rephidim, and then again under Saul, who was commanded to wage a war of extermination against them. "Amalek," said Balaam, " was the first of the nations, but the end is, that he shall be destroyed for ever." To those who are disposed to deal fairly by the Scripture narrative, and calculate the consequences of such a depopulation in this district, it will seem a natural consequence that the desolation of the Desert should spread, and that in the long centuries ruin and waste would cover and entomb in many valleys the pasture-ground which formerly afforded sustenance for this whole tribe, with their flocks and herds.

If the rains that now fall there could be better conserved and made use of by the poor ignorant Arabs, the productiveness of many valleys would re-appear. As it is, the effect in many of the wadys is a vigorous pasture for several weeks, showing a capacity in the soil beneath, of which its outward look gives no indication. You meet with strong trees scattered about, and can see no reason why these should not be multiplied a hundredfold. The one condition is care, and a more regular supply of water. At present the torrents of winter rush headlong to the sea, tearing for themselves wild channels, serving thus rather to increase the desolation. But it is easy to see that in many cases these could be taken advantage of (which seems indeed to have been done in ancient times by excavations and "pits"); and by thus securing for a longer time a constant supply of water to the soil, its barrenness would be greatly healed, and, in the words of the Scripture, "the solitary places would be made glad, and the desert would rejoice and blossom as the rose." Should the time ever come when modern enterprise shall direct its energy and skill to the vast mineral stores embedded in these rocky mountains, and toiling multitudes require to subsist there, it can hardly be doubted that a mighty transformation will ensue in the aspect of the Wilderness; and it will then appear how possible it was that the herds of the Israelites could be supported in their wanderings four thousand years ago.

II. Our next inquiry relates to the number of the cattle really needed by the Israelites. If Bishop Colenso has greatly erred in under-estimating the fertility of the Desert when the Israelites passed through it, he seems to have not less erred in over-calculating the number of their flocks requiring support. His estimate is about two millions,—an immense exaggeration. He is greatly at fault in supposing that the details of the Jewish economy were fulfilled in the Desert. Commenting on the Pentateuch, as if the injunctions about the turtle-doves, washings with water for leprosy, and the innumerable animal sacrifices, were all carried out in the wilderness, he asks, "Where were these obtained, and how were they supported?" The answer is, once more, *he misreads the narrative.*

Let us remark, that it was fitting that the whole laws of the Jewish economy should be established in the Desert instead of elsewhere and afterwards. There Jehovah declared the Decalogue, and this was the grand central fact. It behoved therefore that the whole system, whose great object was really to enshrine that covenant, guard and enforce its sanctions, should be established there also. The people were there formed into a nation. Moses was the appointed mediator, and therefore through him the whole series of injunctions was given. In short, *there* was established the *Theocracy;* and instead of the various laws being given forth at intervals extending over centuries, they were promulgated before the nation had passed to their inheritance in Canaan. But although this was the case, it is a great mistake to suppose that all the various *ceremonial* rites and sacrifices of the economy were necessarily observed here. There were physical hindrances, and moral ones as well, as that people had newly emerged from the base idolatries of Egypt. The narrative again and again speaks of these various rites as referring to "the land which the Lord thy God giveth thee." That much exception was allowed in the Desert appears from the language of Moses, when, referring to the settlement in Canaan, he says, "Ye shall not do after all the things that we do here this day, every man whatsoever is right in his own eyes. For ye are not as yet come to the rest and to the inheritance which the Lord your God giveth you" (Deut. xii. 8-9). In Leviticus there are laid down very minute regulations as to the treatment of leprosy, and various washings, repeated offerings of lambs and birds are enjoined. Now the case of Miriam is recorded as occurring in the Desert. Yet not one of the sacrifices is said to have been offered. There was simply removal from the camp for seven days, and "the people journeyed not till Miriam was brought in again." So, with the lepers mentioned in Numbers v. 2, on which occasion none of the victims was slain. Again, when the plague broke out among the people after the rebellion of Korah, Aaron made atonement, not by sacrifice according to the letter of the injunctions, but "took a censer, and put fire therein, from off the altar, and put on incense, and made an atonement for them" (Numb. xvi. 46). Still further, in the code of laws received at Sinai, the rite of circumcision was strictly enjoined, and various offerings at child-birth prescribed (Lev. xii.) Now, it is expressly stated that that important religious rite was *wholly omitted* during the Desert sojourn (Josh. v. 5); a fact which warrants the inference, that the accompanying sacrifices and offerings (which the Bishop laboriously calculates) were also dispensed with.

But further, the narrative is careful to mention what sacrifices were actually offered in the Wilderness, and these certainly would not be a heavy tax on the herds of the Israelites. There are some special occasions, as the consecration of Aaron and his sons, when a bullock and two rams are offered (Lev. viii. 2). There is the sin-offering in the next chapter, when only seven victims are offered. There is the consecration of the altar, the most important of all, when there are presented " twenty and four bullocks, the rams sixty, the he-goats sixty, the lambs of the first year sixty" (Numb. vii. 88). In other cases the victims were very few, and there only remains the usual morning and evening sacrifice, which surely could be supplied without difficulty. If all this be so, where is the necessity for supposing that the herds of the Israelites amounted to the millions which Bishop Colenso calculates on the assumption that the various laws respecting sacrifice were then fully carried out?

I must add before passing from the subject, that the slaughter of cattle in the Desert seems to have been prohibited for food, and permitted for sacrifice alone. It was expressly commanded that every animal slain should be brought to the tabernacle of the congregation and presented in sacrifice (Lev. xvii. 4). In the 11th chapter of Numbers, we read, the Children of Israel wept again, and said, "Who will give us flesh to eat?" And yet they had flocks and herds at that very time, for Moses asks, "Shall the flocks and herds be slain to suffice them?" But these might not be slain for food. This idea is further confirmed by the statement in Deuteronomy, that when they came to their inheritance in Canaan, they might kill and eat flesh in all their gates, whatsoever their soul lusteth after (Deut. xii. 15, 20). Such a promise for the future clearly implied a prohibition in the present, and we are thus led to the conclusion, that from the time of the proclamation of the Law, the cattle of the Israelites were slaughtered only for sacrifices, and these, at this stage of their history, being few, the number requiring support was what we might estimate as needful to yield milk for their nourishment. This milk, with the manna, we believe, was their principal sustenance.

On the important question then relating to the support of the Israelites in the Desert, our conclusions are these:—

They came from Egypt with numerous cattle, but their exodus took place in the season when the vegetation of the Desert was most abundant. They slaughtered them for food at their first stage of desert life, and only began to cry for "the flesh-pots" when they were a month away from Egypt, and had come into the Wilderness of Sin. The manna was then vouchsafed. They passed on to Rephidim, and there gained a victory over the Amalekites, whose cattle they secured. There was no foe left to dispute the pasture of the peninsula, which was anciently much more abundant, as is proved by the traces of a far more numerous population in the past than can possibly subsist now. The various typical sacrifices prescribed were indispensably carried out in the Desert; but those of a ceremonial kind very partially, the people not having yet come into the land of their inheritance. Moreover, as slaughter of animal life was not permitted after the promulgation of the law save for sacrifice alone, their cattle needed not to have been so numerous as is generally supposed. During the Desert sojourn, the daily manna and the milk of the flock sufficed them for food.

Recent speculations on the Pentateuch must be my apology for dwelling at such length on the points that have now been discussed. Unquestionably the subject has been one of serious difficulty to many, though they may not have ventured to push it to the extreme conclusion of Bishop Colenso; and my object will have been gained, if that difficulty be in any way removed. My belief is, that the more thorough and just the examination of the Pentateuch, it will be found not only that the record is true, but that its language is pre-eminently distinguished for accuracy and precision. To this, as to other inspired books, the encomium applies: "The words of the Lord are pure words; as silver tried in a furnace of earth, purified seven times."

CHAPTER V.

THE ROUTE OF THE ISRAELITES TO SINAI.

On the fourth day we continued our journey from the foot of Wady Tayibeh on to the plain of Murkah, usually regarded as the Wilderness of Sin. It is a wide open plain, bounded on one side by the sea, and on the other by a lofty mountain ridge, exhibiting on a large scale the colours of the Desert. The central mountain is very grand—a naked alp of red granite, rent by a wild and gloomy gorge, and high up on its slopes lie ridges of pure white sandstone. Here our party were threatened with scarcity of provisions. The camels are straying onwards, feeding on the comparatively abundant pasture, and the Dragoman is well in advance. Two Arabs are seen coming in haste from the opposite direction. They stop to address him with much gesticulation. The imperturbable Mahmoud is evidently excited, and it looks in the distance a scene of earnest remonstrance and debate. What had happened? Another tale of "robbery and murder?" On coming up to the Dragoman, he informed us that the great part of our provisions had been left behind: a serious matter in the depth of the Desert! "These are two Bedawy," he said, "going back to fetch them." "Have they to go far?" "Yes, they will not be back till the morning." "But what if we should never see our goods?" for a party of Arabs had passed us lately, who would be sure to find them on their track. Mahmoud told us that there would be no fear of their recovery. "Could we depend then on the honesty of the party passing? Would they not steal?" "No," he said, "not from their own Bedawy." "Then why make this fuss with them?" His answer was to the effect that he must rebuke them for their carelessness, and show his authority. Should a camel die, and its burden be left in the depths of the Desert, the owner has but to draw a circle round it, and it will lie untouched for months. And even without this express precaution, goods are safe if left behind by any of their tribe when hired as an escort to the stranger. Our provisions accordingly arrived all safe at our tents early the following morning. We had further evidence how much the Arabs trust each other in the careless guarding of the stores that are left in the rocky cells of Wady Feiran. There is often only a board at the entrance secured by a bar of wood easily enough removed; and the owner of the stores inside (poor indeed we would think them) moves away with his family to some other valley for a time. Inquiring, through the Dragoman, at one of the escort, if they had no fear of their property being stolen in the long absence, he shouted the decided "La! La!" No! no! as if the question were a little ridiculous. This mutual trustfulness is, in their circumstances, a strong necessity, as all are obliged to migrate for a time from the valley, which is more strictly their home. Theft is punished among them very severely, in some cases with expulsion from the tribe. Let them, however, have a chance of a stranger, and they will rob most mercilessly, and turn him adrift to his fate.

Wady Murkah extends along the sea-shore, until it merges into the great plain of El Kaa. Passing along for two hours, we struck into the mountain district by a magnificent pass, wild, narrow, and winding; each turn revealing aspects of grandeur and desolation strangely impressive. Those in advance heard the deep involuntary ejaculations of the rest of the party, as one aspect after another burst on their view. Approaching the end of the ravine you are confronted by a majestic dark mountain, rising as a haggard precipice from the plain; and across its scarred front lay broad bands of brightest colours. The plain widens at this part into a recess on one side at its base, and here are many small pyramidal hills of the same dark colour, flanked by ridges of the white sandstone. So different are these scenes from those of mountain grandeur to which one is accustomed, that there sometimes rises the feeling of the land being unexplored, and that you are "the first that ever burst" into these weird and uninhabited ravines. The whole scenery of this day stirred our sense of the marvellous in the highest degree, reaching its climax when viewed from the place of our encampment at night.

We turned from the pass into Wady Shellal, specially memorable for its inexpressible confusion of blasted hills of all shapes and colours. Passing through this labyrinth we ascended the rugged pass of the "Sword's Point," where we had to dismount, and then paused to look back upon the scene. What a tumultuous sea of hills! Or we may liken them to quarry heaps, of mountain size, exhibiting all colours, red, white, green, blue and black. The forces of nature seem here to have acted in the fiercest collision, the inner fires to have found for themselves a thousand openings. It was near sunset as we gazed, and, through the thin haze, the rays spread themselves fan-like on the chaos, while here and there a keener shaft of light would pierce into some abyss and chasm, slowly lighting up their gloomy grandeurs. And then all was so silent, so fearfully silent and dead. No life is there, hardly a trace of the slightest vegetation. In vain the sunlight played on those summits, and wandered through the intricate confusion of the scene; it rather seemed a more impressive revelation of death. If there had but appeared anywhere the sign of a human dwelling! Could we but have caught the sight of an Arab shepherd tending goats! The scream of a bird in flight was heard,—a hurried, harsh, startled scream. "All this," said one, "is like what I have read of the probable appearance of the mountains of the moon." "To be alone here," said another, "how dreadful!" Eastwards appeared something like a continuous mountain ridge, enclosing the wild confusion in that direction, but in keeping with it, as its strata were broken and deeply inclined. It looked as if molten waves of stone had been rolling before a fiery tempest, and then suddenly arrested. About six o'clock we arrived at our tents pitched on this plateau, and all around were numbers of petrified shells.

Fifth day.—Descending into Wady Sidra, we came into a narrow defile; high precipitous granite cliffs on one side, and rough sandstone on the other. The sandstone seemed in a state of great decay, frittered into thin broken layers. Large boulders of it seemed to be supported by feeble crumbling props, looking as though a very slight cause would loosen the whole mass, and bring down an avalanche of ruin. Getting into more open ground, we caught a glimpse of a flock of goats tended by a timid Arab shepherdess, indicating that an encampment was near. The rain that had threatened all the morning, now descended heavy as a thunder-shower. It seemed as if the wish of the Bedouin for it would be amply fulfilled, and that we should hear in the Desert "deep calling unto deep." But in an hour it had passed away, and the sun shone out as strong as ever.

We shortly afterwards arrived at the Wady Meghara, and paid a visit to the ancient ruins and mines existing there. The inscriptions of Egypt, the forms of their brute gods—as the ibis and serpent—covered several of the rocks. One opening seemed to extend a long way into the mountain, but was so filled with rocky debris, that we could not make extensive explorations. Portions of the rock were left to support the roof. This is but one of many similar that are found in this tract of the Desert, where of course multitudes must at one time have been toiling.

"Go anywhere," it is said, " and you will find a Scotchman," and here, to be sure, was one in the recesses of the Desert! We were hospitably entertained in his tent. He had been in the district for five months, for the sake of his son's health; who had well recovered, and, ere we left, returned with a party of Arabs from a shooting expedition, bringing in a gazelle. He was picking up also some precious stones that are found in this locality, especially specimens of Turquoise; some of which have fetched a large price. The likelihood is, that the enterprise will be richly rewarded which shall first seek to explore and take advantage of the mineral wealth of these mountains of Meghara and Mokatebb.

Bidding our host good-bye, we made for Wady Mokatebb, which we reached in an hour. On turning into it two of our party were seen suddenly to halt before a large rock, and point to it with interest. We all hurried forward, knowing that here was our first view of the far-famed inscriptions, whose origin and authorship we shall afterwards have to consider. Away up the broad ascent of the valley we found hundreds of these on the faces of the rocks. Some were on the outstanding crags, others on those more retired, and among the rocky debris also many stones were seen to bear them. Dr. Wilson of Bombay, on visiting the other side of the valley, found traces of most extensive operations in mining and smelting, to which, as he thinks, the book of Job seems to make plain allusion.

This afternoon, if a comparison is to be made, was the hottest in our journey. The flaming sun was overhead; a hot oppressive glare lay all around, very painful to the eye; the camels groaned, and the riders were indisposed for question or remark—the only shout heard was, "Water, water!" and each set himself to the journey up the burning plain, as to a stern duty, and strove to bear in silence the burden of the day. About three o'clock we passed from Mokatebb to the northern end of the great Wady Feiran. It was also very spacious, and closed in the distance by the cliffs of Serbal. It seemed as if some three hours would bring us to our tent behind them, but it turned out to be nearer eight. Mahmoud shouted with peculiar earnestness, "O Gemah, O Selemma, hasten the camels! hasten the camels!" The usual exclamations followed, and then the slow monotonous song. Selemma was to see his mother to-morrow, and this, according to Mahmoud's account, was the reason of his glee this afternoon, for he was in high spirits, and evidently thought himself in excellent voice. He was cutting a great dash too with his new turban, which was the usual strip of cotton cloth, but so wound as to sport in front a finely-ornamented trade ticket, naming the firm in Manchester where such articles were to be had. He gave his services gratuitously, and you would say proudly, to the said firm; a walking advertisement of their goods to all whom it might concern in the depths of the Desert. When he ceased singing, some of the party would try an imitation, which produced great laughter, the novice, indeed, intentionally exaggerating those abrupt spasmodic ejaculations, which were a genuine part of the air. Mahmoud's Mussulman gravity was often quite upset, and he bent as if he would fall from his camel. The Arabs also were highly amused at the bungling imitation. After some vain attempts to compose his features, Selemma would again strike in, and the plaintive monotony really seemed to be relished by the camels.

About six o'clock we were journeying in a narrow ravine that showed little trace of the vegetation we had expected to see in this celebrated valley. We were four hours yet from our tents. The night fell, and, between the black enclosing precipices, seemingly more than 1000 feet high, we wound our way, wondering at the beauty of the stars overhead. It was very dark, and we had to trust to the instinct of our camels amid the rocks and rugged banks of the dry torrent-beds. I happened to be in advance, and was urging my camel over what seemed a trifling barrier to a clearer path. He refused to stir, and I found afterwards that it was a high precipitous bank, venturing over which it is likely both the camel and his rider would have come to grief. It was found best for us all to move in single file, the Dragoman ahead with an attendant Arab. And now, trees of considerable size would stand out at intervals, and again vanish as ghosts in the darkness. And then—welcome music for the Desert!—a soft hushing sound was heard as of a murmuring brook, or of a grove of palm-trees stirred by a gentle breeze. We were soon caught by overhanging branches, and became merry with the struggle. Selemma shouted and sung in exuberant spirits, still it seemed in the glad prospect of being in his own village to-morrow with his family. He urged the camels with cries, and shouted, "*Sowah, sowah, howagee koolohoom, sowah!*"—" All together, Howagee, all together!"—till the echoes rang again. Lights now sparkled out of the hill-sides, and still pressing our way through what seemed a thick copse of trees and brushwood, we arrived at our destination; rejoicing to see the gleam of the tent-fires reflected from a glorious cluster of palms.

Next morning some of the party decided on ascending Serbal. Others were content to saunter up the Wady Aleiat that leads to its base. This valley is full of rocky debris, over which it is difficult to pick one's way. The ancient inscriptions are seen all around; also hundreds of cells used by hermits in the early ages of Christianity. There are the remains too of a large fort, for Feiran was anciently a town of note with a large population; a fact which we commend to the attention of Bishop Colenso, with his theory of the Desert as a place "where no man dwelt, and no man passed through." The palm-grove extended about three miles above our encampment. Wandering through it in the afternoon, we looked with interest at the Arab burial-place, and its rude stones at the head and foot of each grave.

Memorable to all of us was the social worship, the silent musings during this Sabbath-day in the Desert, beneath the grand shadow of Serbal. Our Arabs also had a day of rest after their own fashion, and were receiving numerous visits from friends. Before our tents we saw repeated the salutation and manners of patriarchal times; and were again and again reminded of the meeting of Moses and Jethro before Horeb— "the Mount of God." The natives of the valley entertained the escort with a musical festival. Not only was there the frequent song, but a rough sort of fiddle was brought into use, from which the performer drew some three or four quivering notes as an accompaniment to the nasal plaintive ballad. While the Arab circle smoked and listened with head to one side, as of gentlemen serenaded with the finest strains, the frequent gleam of the eye seemed to ask at the bystander, whether all this was not most exquisite and overpowering.

I may here fitly discuss two important questions. The one refers to the inscriptions first seen in the Valley of Mokatebb, and the other to the theory which pleads for Serbal as the Holy Mount Sinai.

I. First, as to the meaning and authorship of the mysterious writing on the rocks of the Desert. The reader may conceive of the astonishment of the traveller in coming on these myriad inscriptions in valleys now so utterly deserted and silent. The wastes become peopled in the mind's eye, and over these rocks are bent multitudes of living men writing their experience and thoughts, which have proved, however, hitherto only a puzzle to posterity, for the Layard or the Rawlinson is yet to appear who shall satisfactorily decipher their meaning. Professor Beer has indeed devoted much attention to the subject, but according to him the most of these records are simply proper names, with the ever-recurring phrases, "May he be blessed, May he have peace!" This theory is surely incredible. Can this be the paltry result of so much pains and so much pretension? It is too much like the cry, "In the name of the Prophet, figs!" These inscriptions, we may be sure, were not written in sport or for such vague ejaculations only, any more than those of Egypt or Nineveh. Those who can best judge of such studies are satisfied that the true alphabet and interpretation have yet to be discovered. Leaving this, then, to be yet determined, I confine myself to the question of their authorship, which I believe may be established on independent grounds.

They are scattered far and wide over the Desert. They are to be found in the far east of the peninsula as well as at Mokatebb; as far south as Wady Lega, near Jebel Mousa, and as far north as Petra; and it is only because of their numbers in Mokatebb that it is called, by way of emphasis, "the written valley."[1] They are written, I may add, on the sandstone equally with the granite. Strange to say, among these mys-

---

[1] Photographs have been taken of the Mokatebb rocks, and to these I must refer the reader who wishes to guess at words and sentences.

terious letters are interpolated Greek and Latin and Arabic words legible enough—Ιωβ (Job), Ιωσεφ μοναχος (monk Joseph), also the form of a cross (✝ ✣). Sometimes, too, the figures of dogs, ibexes with monstrous horns, curving serpents, are roughly portrayed.

Our interest at present relates to the undeciphered letters. Who wrote these? Some would answer, the Israelites. And who would not wish such a theory to be true? Who would not welcome this additional record of the experience of that people during their wanderings, penned with their own hands, and graven on the rocks for ever? But unfortunately there is little reason to believe that "the voice of Israel" is here. For questions will arise which on this theory have no solution. Thus, Why are these inscriptions so mysterious? and why should they be confined to the Desert? Why not find traces of them in Egypt, where they had previously lived, or still more on the rocks of Palestine, when it became their home? The same questions are to be urged against the theory that would set the inscriptions down as the work of any pilgrims and strangers whatsoever. Why do we not find similar writings on the rocks and monuments of those countries from which these pilgrims came? Diodorus Siculus, writing about the Christian era, making mention of these inscriptions, affirms that even in his day no one could find the key to their interpretation. There seems only the alternative, confirmed, I hope to show, by other proofs, that we look on these writings as the work of the ancient inhabitants of the Desert.

It seems somewhat strange, indeed, that this should ever have been a matter of doubt. The inscriptions in

Egypt are put down to the Egyptians, those of Assyria to the Assyrians. Why then do we change the theory when we come to the Desert, and impute its inscriptions to other than the inhabitants? The burden of proof is certainly on those who contend for this being an exception to the general rule. But that it is not such may be shown by the following considerations:—

1. It is in the highest degree improbable that the race proverbially jealous of their Desert from time immemorial would allow strangers from other lands to come into their territory, and inscribe on their rocks such records as these. The Amalekites who attacked Israel at Rephidim could not have been, and are not described, as a rude and feeble tribe. It is morally certain that they would not have allowed such an invasion as this. Their hand was against every man, and so they were perhaps the very last people that would permit such a liberty.

2. It has been too readily assumed that they could not have been the authors of them, as they were not acquainted with the art of writing. But where is the proof of this? Does the Bible account imply that they were rude and ignorant savages? On the contrary, they were brave, disciplined, and pronounced by Balaam "the first of the nations." Jethro, the father-in-law of Moses, was an inhabitant of this same desert, being the high priest of Midian, a town on the Red Sea. Their prevailing religion was Baal-worship, the religion of Phœnicia, the country from which letters first came. Philo expressly says that they were Phœnicians. The adjoining nation of Egypt, with whom they must have had some intercourse, were busy with their hieroglyphics

all over the land, and the Desert race may be believed to have observed this custom, which was indeed that of other nations of the age; and to have recorded on enduring stone such events as deeply impressed them. It is not improbable that when in this country as an exile, Moses received or committed to writing the patriarchal Book of Job, the allusions of which point obviously to the sights and incidents of a Desert life.[1] And if ever the inscriptions be deciphered, it is far more likely, I conjecture, that we may gain some part of the original of that noble poem of sacred antiquity than find the record of any experiences of an Israelite in the forty years of the wanderings.

3. This theory of their authorship obviously accounts for these inscriptions being discovered all over the Desert where the Amalekites dwelt, as well as for their individual character, which has so marked them off from the writings of other nations. The Amalekites were a people specially isolated, and must have had a language and writing peculiarly distinct. Their country was not invaded, conquered, and possessed as others were. No successive waves of populations passed over it. It held out no great temptations with its rocks and wastes and privations, being rather "sands for the pilgrim than fields for the conqueror." The language and writing of a people so isolated may well have taken a peculiar type.

4. The height at which they now appear upon the rocks seems to furnish a proof of their high antiquity. The theory that they were written by a rider on a camel, elevated in this way for the purpose, is surely very un-

[1] There seems a direct allusion to these rock-inscriptions in the well-known passage: "O that my words were graven with an iron pen and lead in the rock for ever" (Job xix. 23, 24).

satisfactory. As written at first they were probably much lower, but the torrents of ages upon ages may have washed down the sands of the plain by several feet, and hence their present height. Their extent, then, their mysterious character, and their antiquity, seem to point to the ancient inhabitants of the Desert as the authors of these far-famed inscriptions.

But some will ask, What of the Latin and Greek words which are here and there interspersed? These differ from the mass of characters as day from night, and have clearly a more modern origin. They are to be set down to the Christian hermits that swarmed in these valleys in the early centuries of Christianity. From them clearly came such expressions as Ιωβ, Ιοσεφ μοναχος (already quoted), $A + \Omega$ (Alpha and Omega), and the numerous marks of the cross. That sacred symbol had, in these early times, a deep significance, indicating something more than the writer's profession. It was thought to exorcise the spirit of evil, and consecrate profane and heathen localities for Christ. As for those grotesque figures of dogs, camels, serpents, etc., drawn in sport and caricature as many seem to have been, we may trace their origin to the Arab shepherd or hermit whiling away the tedium of his life in such employment. For, as is well known, the appearance of inscriptions on rock, tree, and wall is infectious. Human nature only requires the hint, and every kind of scribbling soon covers the space, often obliterating the original. A new era has lately dawned for the better understanding of the past in the deciphering of ancient writings on monuments and temples, and we may indulge the hope that patient study will yet discover a key to these hieroglyphics in the rocks of Arabia, which so many circumstances lead us to regard as among the most interesting and ancient in the world.

II. We come now to the second inquiry proposed, Whether Serbal is Sinai?

If majesty and rugged grandeur could decide the question, the advocates of Serbal would easily gain converts to their view. Dr. Lepsius has appeared of late as its most strenuous defender, and he is followed by Dr. Stewart. Professor Stanley leaves the question undecided between it and Jebel Mousa. The German writer argues strongly from the inherent probabilities of the case in the following fashion : "Is not this," he says, "the spot to which Moses would naturally strive to bring the people? It is the most fertile oasis in the Desert. There is plenty of water. There would be the only chance of supporting the large multitude, and as the head-quarters of the Amalekites, the securing of it would yield to him the undisturbed possession of the peninsula." All this proceeds on the assumption that Moses guided the enterprise of the Exodus by his own wisdom mainly. The guiding Cloud, which indicated the special divine direction, is ignored ; and without this Moses might never have secured the following of that people into the Wilderness at all. Moreover, it seems of little use to attempt a theory which would explain the support of the multitudes of the Exodus without miraculous intervention. Even in the groves of this Wady Feiran, the many thousands of Israel would soon have perished if left unassisted. Then again, in defiance of the drought which the narrative alleges to have been experienced at Rephidim, Lepsius fixes that very locality in a rich and well watered valley, a fact which makes his hypothesis questionable to Dr. Stanley. Even, however, supposing Rephidim were here, still the inference drawn in favour of Serbal could not be allowed. The general opinion indeed is, that Jethro met Moses at Rephidim, and since " the Mount of God" is spoken of as close at hand, Lepsius argues that Serbal alone can be meant. But it seems a mistake to imagine that Moses received the visit of his father-in-law during his stay at an encampment so transient as that must have been. Indeed, after the mention of the interview, it is recorded, that the Israelites "*were departed* from Rephidim, and *were come* to the Desert of Sinai, and had pitched in the wilderness; and there Israel camped before the Mount." Josephus, I may add, understands the interview as occurring after the people *had left* Rephidim, and indeed the whole scene of Moses giving judgment with the judicious advice of Jethro in reference to it, is in itself proof that the Israelites were not at such a temporary station, but at their settled resting-place under the shadow of *Horeb*, " *the Mount of God.*"

It were enough, I should have supposed, to see the nature of the ground to discard the hypothesis that Sinai is here. Neither mountain nor valley will suit the theory. Thus the Valley Aleiat, that leads to the base of Serbal, could not in any wise allow of an encampment before this mountain. The Israelites could not have been led up to the barrier at the foot of it, as the narrative requires us to understand; for it is full of rocks and debris to an unparalleled extent. It is nearly as fatiguing to walk up this valley as to climb Jebel Mousa: travellers therefore who wish to ascend Serbal, take their camels as far as possible up the rocky and arduous path. It is far too narrow besides, where it approaches the foot of the Mount by an abrupt turning, to have afforded room for the thousands of Israel listening to the proclamation of the Law. Altogether, in the whole Wilderness, it would not be easy to select a less likely place; accordingly, its advocates have suggested that only Moses and the elders were near at the giving of the Law, while the people remained afar off from the first. But this is contrary to the whole tenor of the narrative, being specially contradicted by the words, that "when *all* the people saw the thunderings and the lightnings they *removed afar* off." The theory is also beset with physical difficulties when the mountain is looked at. Moses, we know, often went up into it, and as we shall see, was always directed to come to Sinai, "the *top* of the Mount." On two occasions he descended with the tables of the testimony in his hands. But Serbal is remarkably difficult of ascent. Lepsius himself confesses it to have been one of the most arduous undertakings in his travels, and accompanied with no small danger. The experience of others is similar. Therefore it is somewhat amusing to read the account of some, who, after telling us how they slipped, and had to climb creeping on their hands and knees amid the steep loose debris to a more level platform, coolly declare that *this* may have been the spot to which the seventy elders came up. It is hardly possible to understand the frequent ascent and descent of Moses on such a mountain as this, and especially how he could climb its rugged summit, for he was always commanded to come up to "the top of the Mount."

There is another strong objection to this locality,

based on moral grounds. It was the chosen sanctuary of heathen idolatry. It was a mount consecrated to the worship of Baal. The name itself indicates as much, being (with some) Lord Baal, or (with others) the grove of Baal. All tradition points to this fact, which, so far from being disputed by Lepsius and others who hold his view, is affirmed to be an additional ground for the conclusion that Serbal is Sinai. It is impossible to admit this argument, whether we regard the character of Jehovah or the purpose of the Exodus. Its great design was to fix an impassable gulf between the religion of the chosen people and all idolatries, and more especially the worship of Baal, the prevailing idolatry of the Wilderness. Terrible were the judgments inflicted on the Israelites when they fell into it. "The Lord their God was a jealous God;" they were to be to him "a peculiar people." We can hardly conceive of anything more fitted to thwart the important end of all the divine dealings with them, than that their law should have been proclaimed from the mountain specially dedicated to the worship of this idol. Of all places, Sinai, one should infer, *à priori*, would be free from idolatrous associations, and solemnly consecrated in the imaginations of the Israelites, as exclusively the Mount of Him whose first words were, "Thou shalt have no other gods before me." They fell into idolatry there, it is true; but then it was the idolatry of *Egypt*, not of Baal, which would have been the case at Serbal, as it was afterwards at Baal-Peor.

But there remains the argument from tradition, which Lepsius is confident should of itself prove his theory beyond all dispute. Dr. Stanley affirms also that though Serbal has in later times lost its historical name, in earlier ages it enjoyed a larger support of tradition than Jebel Mousa. This deserves to be examined. First, we are referred to the ancient mysterious inscriptions whose authorship we have already discussed. But how do these prove Serbal to be Sinai? We may as well select a mountain in Mokatebb, or in other parts of the Desert where these inscriptions are found. If it be said that in Serbal they are the work of Jewish or other pilgrims visiting the mountain, because of its connexion with the giving of the Law, this is, of course, begging the whole question. Paran, it is again argued, was once an episcopal city, and surrounded by a numerous colony of hermits. But this admitted fact by no means establishes the inference in question. The inhabitants of Feiran embraced Christianity; hence it naturally became the seat of the bishop and the centre of the colony of hermits who, according to Chrysostom, flocked to the Desert, because "it was the land of the afflictions and patience of Job." The facts also quoted by Dr. Robinson show, that the monks about Mount Sinai were in circumstances vastly different from those of Feiran. While the latter enjoyed comparative abundance, tranquillity, and protection, the former clung to the rugged rocks of their hermitage amid austere privations, dangers, and death. Nilus describes a massacre of the monks of Sinai in the fourth century, when the remnant that escaped fled for safety *to their brethren in Feiran.* Such indeed was the influence of the church there, that they obtained retribution for the outrage from the king of the Saracens; a fact surely decisive of the distinction contended for. Lepsius quotes the language of Eusebius as supporting his view. But his words are not that Rephidim was *at*

Feiran, as he translates them, but *near* it (ἐγγὺς Φαράν). This may imply a distance of eight or ten miles, which is all that we contend for. The principal authority, however, is Cosmas Indicopleustes (A.D. 540), who says of the Israelites: "They encamped at Rephidim, now called Pharan, where they had no water. At the command of God, Moses, with the elders, taking the rod in his hand, went to Horeb, that is in Mount Sinai, near to Pharan by about a mile and a half" (ἐξ μίλιων), which Lepsius so translates. This passage is thought to be very decisive. But in so urging it, Lepsius assumes that the writer refers to the *city* of Pharan situated at the foot of Serbal. This cannot be granted, for, by his own evidence, the word was used with a wider latitude of meaning in that age, being applied to different portions of the western side of the Gulf of Suez, and sometimes also to localities near the Gulf of Akabah. Which Paran, therefore, does this writer refer to? Surely he could not mean the fertile oasis at present so called, seeing that he expressly mentions the privations which the Israelites endured. And if this writer locates Rephidim as only a mile and a half from Horeb before which they next encamped, how are the two encampments to be distinguished? They are confounded in the argument of Lepsius, who believes the Israelites lived throughout in this valley of Pharan. Besides, Serbal is *three* miles from the spot. This authority therefore is far from conclusive, or rather is irreconcilable with the theory. Lepsius is careful to remark, that this writer uttered the traditions of his age, and that he was the contemporary of Justinian. Now the one fact which decides that the ancient traditions opposed the theory under discussion is, that Justinian, in the sixth century, did *not* build the convent on Serbal. Why was this, if the tradition had pointed to this mountain? It is easy to *assert* a change of tradition, but in the absence of proof, it is incredible. Is it to be supposed that the flourishing episcopal church at Feiran, who had gathered round this hallowed spot and made it their glory, would have consented to surrender it in favour of Jebel Mousa, fifteen miles away, making no remonstrance, no complaint, but rather acquiescing in what was done, and taking the poor monks of the newly erected convent into their diocese and fellowship? And what motive could Justinian have had for violating the traditions of his age, and insulting the most cherished feelings of the whole Christian Church? I submit therefore that the ancient traditions of the early age are *not* in favour of Mount Serbal as Sinai.

What, then, are the scriptural associations of Feiran? In its fertile valley was situated the capital of the Desert tribe, known in Scripture as the Amalekites, who fought with Israel at Rephidim. Tradition has always marked it out as such; an opinion, moreover, warranted by its superior fertility compared with that of the valleys around. There is a wady in the vicinity called Amhalek to this day. Mount Serbal, looking down upon Feiran, was the "high place" where Baal was worshipped, and this is all that can be said of it. Amalek, aided, as Josephus tells us, by the other tribes, sallied out upon the Israelites at Rephidim. The attack is represented as having been fool-hardy and criminal in the extreme. They had heard of the wonders of the Exodus, and should have hesitated before they meddled with a people so remarkably guided, and whose unknown Protector manifested such incomparable power. But they were blind to obvious consequences, and trusting in the aid of Baal, they resolve to try the issue of battle. It is recorded as the grand sin of Amalek, that in attacking Israel, "*he feared not God*" (Deut. xxv. 18).

If the claims of Serbal can thus be disposed of, we are now in a position to consider whether the route to Sinai usually assigned—that marked on the map by a dotted line—is the true one. I believe it is *not*, for the following reasons :—

1. It is inconsistent with the language of the narrative in several points. The Israelites, according to the usual theory, had entered the strongholds of the hostile tribe, threatening the metropolis, their sanctuary, and their richest possessions. They would in that case have been represented as the *attacking* party, whereas, from the narrative, the blow came from Amalek, and was quite unprovoked. It is said, "Then came Amalek and fought with Israel at Rephidim." They came, too, as by a cowardly surprise, while on the part of the Israelites, the battle was clearly one of self-defence. "Remember," said Moses to the people, "what Amalek did unto thee; how he met thee by the way, and smote the *hindmost* of thee, even all that were feeble behind thee, when thou wast faint and weary, and he feared not God." It is not easy to understand this language if the Israelites had threatened Feiran in their route. It implies that they were attacked in rear, not provoking battle, not anticipating it, and must have made a detour in order to pass the valley where the enemy were stationed. Again, the narrative would have expressly mentioned "the Wilderness of Paran" (Feiran) if they had

come by this route. It tells us that they came into that wilderness when leaving Sinai; and so, if they had entered by it, a record of the fact would have been made. They came out, on this theory, by Rephidim also; in that case, why is it not so written?

2. The route is liable to the moral objection, that it brings them at this stage of their history into contact with the terrible temptations of Baal-worship. Surely those luxurious groves of Wady Feiran, with their heathenism (a heathenism which the subsequent history shows but too plainly could not be resisted), were of all places the worst for that people to pause at or pass through! Even after the thunders of Sinai, and the infliction of terrible judgments, they fell helplessly before the impure seductions of this idolatry. How, then, could they have resisted it now, when but newly emancipated from Egypt, and with all its sensualities so strongly besetting them? The probability seems to be, that if they had been conducted hither by this path, they would have fallen, as at Moab, into its congenial Baal-worship, and never have reached Mount Sinai at all.

3. It is difficult to understand how the Israelites could have been supplied with water along this route. For example, how did they escape utter privation in passing through Wady Shellal, already described. "Here," Miss Martineau says, "I now seemed to feel for the first time true pity for the wandering Hebrews. What a place was this for the Hebrew mothers with their sucking babes! As I thought of their fevered children imploring water, and their own failing limbs where there was no shade to rest, I could imagine the agony of the Hebrew fathers, and well excuse their despairing cry,

Give us water that we may drink." But in fact they raised *no* such murmuring cry at this stage; this was their cry only when they came to Rephidim, which, in any theory, was much farther on. How therefore they were supplied in passing this tract of utter desolation is a problem, which those should settle who contend for the route in question. And while, as I have sought to show, there were many valleys anciently much more fertile than now, it is difficult to believe that this particular section of the Desert could ever have been anything else than "a land of drought where there was no water."

4. I may add, that coming on to the Rephidim either of Lepsius or Robinson, the Israelites, if we may judge from present appearances, could have found plenty of water. And yet this was the very spot where the supply utterly failed them.

5. It seems impossible to fix, with any probability, the stations of Dophkah, Alush, Rephidim along such a route. The first two, if the conjectures respecting their locality had been at all near the truth, would have been represented by the narrative as "in the Wilderness of Paran." And since Rephidim has been usually placed beyond Wady Feiran, we are required to believe that the Amalekites allowed the Israelites to go unmolested through their most fertile valleys, neglecting to fight them when passing through the defiles most favourable for attack, and giving battle only when they had reached the more open ground of Wady Sheikh. This is far from probable in itself, and is not warranted by the account in the narrative.

For these reasons, I am unable to see how the modern

and prevailing view of the journey of the Israelites at this stage can be accepted. We must go back, I believe, to the more ancient traditions, which led them much farther south, along the great plain of the Wilderness of Sin, before they struck upwards to the mountain ridge of Sinai.

They would in this way escape the seductive temptations to the Baal-worship of Serbal in Wady Feiran already referred to. Such a route explains too the language of the narrative regarding the attack of the Amalekites. The Israelites had made a detour, avoiding the valley where the enemy's force is gathered. They were attacked in rear when "faint and weary," suffering from drought, and from the fatigue of the march up the mountains. They had not entered the Wilderness of Paran at all, and accordingly, there is no reference to it in this part of the narrative.

To reach this point of Wady Dughait, they must have *journeyed* for some time in the Wilderness of Sin. And that they were some time there seems evident from the 16th chapter of Exodus, which gives an account of their murmurings for food, and of the supply of the manna. By the other route they would have left it after one day's journey.

Moreover, we can better understand the supply of water for the people by this route. Their clamour was for food, and for that alone, but by the other route they would have murmured for want of water also. In respect of water, no plain in the Desert is so well supplied as that of El Kaa, through which they held their way. It receives a copious supply from the mountain range that bounds it on the east, and where rise the abundant springs of Jebel Mousa. Down near the sea there are several wells, and here too is situated the palm grove of Tor, by far the richest in the peninsula. The waters from the mountains do not flow rapidly off by deep valleys to the sea, but, arriving at the broad plain, disperse their fertilizing influence, which results in the (comparatively) abundant vegetation. The plain at the Gulf of Akabah is similarly situated with reference to a mountain range, where water can always be got by digging for it, and much more would this be the case here.

In answer to the cry, " Who will give us flesh to eat ?" quails were sent. On another occasion a similar supply is provided when they are far in the depths of the Desert, but in that instance *a strong* wind is said to have brought them up from the sea. Here no such agency was needed, for they were now on the sea-shore, and so we read simply, "It came to pass that at even the quails came up and covered the camp."

Lastly, we can trace their route to Sinai from the Wilderness of Sin by existing names. Here, I believe, the ancient theory was at fault, inasmuch as it led them up by Wady Hebran and over to Sinai by the Pass of the Winds. We read, "They took their journey out of the wilderness of Sin, and encamped in Dophkah" (Numb. xxxiii. 12). Accordingly, leading from this plain into the mountain district, is Wady Dugheit, or Dughadeh, or Docht, in some maps. The name corresponds as in the other cases mentioned, and the locality answers well for their *first* encampment after journeying out of the plain. This second resting-place is Alush. Now, winding up the wadys, in the direction of Sinai, we come on a mountain marked, "Ala." Here also the modern name approximates to the Scripture one, and the identification is so far confirmed by two circumstances mentioned by the Jewish chronicler, and referred to (under the word) in Kitto's *Cyclopædia*. One is, that Alush was a strong fort. This feature forbids the idea of its location on a plain (which the other route necessitates), but suits well such a locality as that on the map, where it might guard the advance into the interior from the harbour of Tur. The same chronicler adds, that the distance from Dophkah was twelve miles, which also seems to agree with our location. Moreover, at neither of these encampments, as I have already remarked, are the Israelites said to have suffered from want of water. Josephus mentions that they lighted on small fountains till they came to Rephidim. Now, it is to be remarked, that there are wells up among the mountains in this very direction at the present day. Lepsius himself found such when he reached the range on his journey from Tur. Niebuhr says, that the finest water is not from the plain, but brought by the Arabs from these hills. In fact, the pools and wells there are formed by the water from the upper mountains filtering its way to the plain below.

So far, then, we seem to be following the track indicated in the narrative. And now we come to Rephidim, a name which lingers, I believe, in the name Wady Rudhwan (see Map). But how should they have missed the water here, the reader will ask? I have to suggest that this resulted from its position on the watershed of the district. At such a place the water flows in different directions, part westward to the plain of El Kaa (in the direction we have followed), and part eastward from Jebel Mousa by the Wady es Sheikh. As the Israelites ascended higher and higher into the mountain district, the fountains would become more scarce, until at such a locality as Rudhwan they would disappear. Hence the miracle wrought to bring a supply from the adjacent rock of Horeb.

Such a location of Rephidim agrees well, it seems to me, with the most ancient traditions. Thus Eusebius declares Rephidim was near Feiran, but still *nearer* Horeb. It is beside Horeb : 'Ραφιδίμ, τόπος τῆς 'Ερήμου, παρὰ τὸ Χώρεβ ὄρος, ἐγγὺς Φαράν. (Euseb. *Onomast.*) It is also truer to the distance mentioned by the writer, Cosmas, (if we adopt the literal translation)—*six miles* (ἐξ μίλιων) from Horeb.

Coming by such a route, the Israelites would enter the plain of Rahah at the northern end, that *most distant* from "the Mount of God;" an entrance, it appears to me, much more likely than the other by the Wady Sheikh, in which case they would have passed close to it with all their flocks and herds. The narrative would lead us to believe that the mountain was consecrated from the very first; that the flocks were never in front of it, and that the people came near it for the *first* time when they heard the proclamation of the Law. They have entered, then, through the narrow ravine at the southern base of Nakby Howy, and the tent of their chiefs is pitched "before the Mount," probably about the watershed of the plain.

Thus, then, have we discussed another stage of the route of the Israelites, reaching from "the encampment at the Red Sea" to Sinai. This seems, as far as I can judge, the only track which the limits and incidents of the narrative will sanction. And here, as in the division of their journey already considered, the ancient names still linger. All their encampments (see map) after crossing the Red Sea, are as follows: Etham (Aithi), Shur (Sudr), Marah (Amarah, Howara), Elim (Zelimeh?) "encampment by the Red Sea," "Wilderness of Sin" (El Kaa), Dophkah (Dughait, Dughadeh, Docht), Alush (Ala), Rephidim (Rudhwan), Sinai.

As they have toiled up the mountain range to Rephidim they are "faint and weary," to use the expression of the narrative, and "have no water there." The forces of Amalek steal out from Feiran through Wady Solaf, attacking them in rear. They are signally defeated, and a heavy curse of extermination is pronounced, which took effect in the days of Saul and David. For Amalek has set the example to the other tribes of defying and injuring this heaven-protected people, and has virtually sought to place Baal above Jehovah.

Here then was fought the first of those battles of the Old Testament, which have been to many the theme of such wonder and adverse criticism. Humanitarian sceptics have murmured tenderly over them, and even Christian philanthropists have followed in this track, who fancy that the sins and idolatries of the world ought to be "*cured by rose-water.*" It is forgotten that the Israelites did not provoke this or the other contests on their way to Canaan, but would have passed peaceably through if they had been allowed. It is forgotten also that these nations were sunk in brutish idolatries, that a patient and holy Heaven had become weary of their cruelties and vices. It is forgotten that the inhabitants of Canaan were cast out because "their iniquity was full," and that the Israelites were warned of a similar fate if they forsook "the covenant of their God." The Israelites, moreover, were intrusted with most important interests of mankind, which must be protected at any cost, so that they had no alternative left but to clear a space amid the foul jungle of heathenism for their worship of the true God.

The Divine judgments, it may be added, are still abroad in the earth. With our own eyes we may see that Providence still employs methods of terrible rigour to punish the nations of whose sins it has become weary. And it must be maintained that much service has been done to the cause of truth and religion in the world by the record in Scripture of these "battles of the Lord." They represent a true phase of the great contest between good and evil ever going on; one most necessary in these rude and idolatrous ages of the past, nay, sometimes indeed requisite still. They have in a very stern way taught lessons respecting the infinite worth of moral goodness, purity, and truth in the eye of Heaven, lessons which man is slow to believe in. They have inspired Psalms that have summoned many to the defence of these at all hazards, cheerfully making every sacrifice of comfort and of life. In evil times, when the cause of truth, justice, conscience, and religion languished or was trodden under foot, God has again and again raised up men for its rescue and re-establishment, and these heroes have gone forth to the struggle, even of blood, all the more valiantly because they have heard pealing through the centuries the *war-cry* of the Desert, "Rise, Lord; let thine enemies be scattered; and let them that hate thee flee before thee!"

CHAPTER VI.

HOREB AND SINAI—THE ARGUMENT FROM TRADITION.

Our Arabs had enjoyed a day's rest in Feiran, while at the same time the camels obtained what Selemma had often promised them in his song—a peaceful pasturage in the shady groves. On Monday morning the cavalcade was early astir. As we passed we looked into some of the cells formerly used by the hermits, now the storehouses of the Bedouin in their wanderings; in which latter capacity, as I have already observed, they are but feebly guarded. Selemma had been away on a visit to his village; and in due time the sprightly little fellow was seen trotting over the valley to join us. We hailed his return with great laughter. He had been presented by one of our party with an article of dress to keep his legs warm among the cold uplands of Sinai, but he and his mother between them had managed to transform said article into a flannel jacket. The metamorphosis was sufficiently ludicrous. It was now my duty, in consequence of a conversation held with Baomi, to inform a section of our party of an important decision which he had announced. Often, after the fatigue of the day, we three Scotchmen had a pleasant banter during the dinner hour with our English friends, on the comparative merits of the Scotch and English. Baomi, in attendance at our table, overheard what passed, observing also that we were in a minority of one. He now confided to me that his preference was decidedly Scotch. He had enjoyed ample opportunities of forming an opinion on the subject under discussion during the period of his service in the hotel at Suez. In proof, he quoted the respective salutation of the two peoples. "De English say, How *aw* you? de Scotch, How *arr* you? De English say, Dis is a *reay waam* day; Scotch, Dis is a *verry warrm* day. I like de Scotch, it is *morr strrong.*" Whatever the discussion afterwards, on points political, historical, or philosophical, Baomi stood to his verdict, and thus the votes were equal.

Journeying onwards, many of the valleys seem to have been covered with a deposit of mud which the torrent had washed clean away, with the exception of an occasional mound at the side. The appearance of these lingering fragments confirms the argument for a greater fertility in the distant past.

About two o'clock in the afternoon we arrived in sight of the outer ridge of mountains, which enclose, as with a perpetual bulwark, the sanctuary of Sinai. The day had overcast, and the rugged scene lay enshrouded in solemn gloom. We descended into the wady that swept in from the west, and soon reached the foot of the pass of Nakh by Howy (Pass of the Winds), on the other side of which we should behold the object of our far pilgrimage. The pass is one of singular grandeur. Great mountains, as wild as ever met the eye of man, rise steeply on either side, their inaccessible peaks erected in clear outline against the sky. The traveller has here to dismount, and as he scrambles upwards, sees piled above him, in awful and perilous confusion, gigantic masses of loose granite, from which have fallen the rugged debris along the path, and where frequently it seems as though at any moment another avalanche may come thundering down. The narrow defile is as a solemn colonnade "not made with hands," that fitly leads to the great temple beyond. For two hours we toiled up the pass, finding the path somewhat freer and more level at the farther end. Pressing eagerly forwards, we reached this point; and there, rising at the southern termination of the plain of Rahah, as "a mount that might be touched," venerable, silent, holy, was "Horeb, the Mount of God!"

In many of these eastern localities the mind does not feel their sacred associations until after a time, and as the result of meditation. But few travellers, I imagine, if any, ever came in sight of this mount without experiencing at once, and powerfully, the solemn associations of the past. Instinctively an ejaculation of awe and wonder arises, and then ensues a deep prolonged silence! You seem to have come upon it with irreverent haste. The thought is, "How dreadful is this place!" "The place is holy ground!" "Come let us worship and bow down, let us kneel before the Lord our Maker." The Arabs, it is said, always come in view of the scene with feelings of solemnity, and certainly those of our party did exhibit a peculiarly quiet and subdued demeanour, ceasing to shout or sing or talk, with the vehement loudness so common to them.

What deepened the impression in our case, was the appearance of a dark massive thunder-cloud hanging over the mount, and casting its shadow far into the plain. On either side of this plain rise mountains of most stern and rugged aspect, as if the lightnings of heaven had often struck here, making wildest havoc, splintering their summits into a thousand peaks and rending the mass into chasms, to whose edge no human foot can ever attain. What a scene was this for the Israelites to be in, amid "the lightnings, the thunder, and the earthquake, the sound of trumpet, and the voice of words!" Shall we hear the thunder also? was a question that passed through our minds as we looked at the threatening sky. Dr. Stewart was privileged in this respect, and he declared it to be worth the whole journey. But in our case, though the night was tempestuous, no thunder followed; and next morning there was a calm sky, as "the body of heaven in its clearness." For about two miles we journeyed among the rugged hollows of the plain, where I think it probable the Israelites "moved afar off," when appalled by the terrors of the scene. We then came to the watershed, from which, on to the front cliffs of the mountain, all was beautifully smooth and clean. It had become very cold; and the strong gusts of wind that swept down the valley of the Convent, occasioned great difficulty in fixing the tents. Indeed, we were beaten off from the first place selected, but at last we managed to fix ourselves under the lee of a remarkable mound that sweeps round the face of the mountain. If the traveller should conjecture that the original substratum of this may have been the precautionary barrier raised when the Israelites were here, I believe it would be difficult indeed to disprove it. During their long stay, such a safeguard, between the holy mountain on the one hand, and themselves with their flocks on the other, must have been of a strong and permanent character. Nothing at least can better answer than the form of the mound to the probable sweep of the barrier in question.

Next morning, as I have intimated, was calm and peaceful. The prominent feeling was that of the deep seclusion of the place. The clamour and confusion of the world are far, far away. "If," says Sir Frederick Henricker, "I were to take a model of the end of the world, it should be taken from the valley of the Convent of Mount Sinai." The aspect of that venerable convent, clinging to the steep cliffs, with its battlements and narrow windows, to which you may often look without seeing the trace of any human life within, together with the solemn cypress-trees of its garden, deepen rather than disturb the sense of the stillness and seclusion of the scene. This convent was built by Justinian in the sixth century, and has been spared for 1200 years the destruction that has overtaken elsewhere these sacred memorials of the past.

Having presented our letter of introduction from the bishop in Cairo, we secured a guide for the day's explorations. I need not dwell at any length on the ascent, which has been often described. My aim shall be to call special attention to those features in the mountain, which, as may afterward appear, clearly mark it out as "the mount of the law."

Toiling upwards, then, from the Convent valley for more than 1000 feet, the traveller comes to a lengthened hollow, where stands the Chapel of Elijah. Here is a beautiful cypress-tree, and a fine pool of water. Behind the southern end is the summit of Jebel Mousa, "the top of the mount." The hollow runs lengthwise to the other extremity of the mountain, where it terminates in the cliff of Sufsafeh, immediately overhanging the plain. We first proceeded to the summit of Jebel Mousa, the height of which is about another 1000 feet from this spot, or about 2000 from the plain below. Very grand was the view from that summit; hills and valleys lying around in bewildering confusion. But let the reader notice, that from this point nothing whatever can be seen of the plain of Rahah. You would not suspect the existence of such a plain within many miles of the spot. You see, however, very distinctly, the valley Sebayeh immediately at the base, which is very rugged and broken up by the torrents of the rainy season. We descended after an hour's stay, and on reaching the Chapel of Elijah, proceeded northwards, along the hollow spoken of above, in the direction of the front summit Sufsafeh. Throughout we came on traces of water, sometimes in little pools; and indeed the general configuration of the place is that of a natural reservoir gathering in the rains from the rugged steeps on every side. The water finds its way to the plain below by a deep gorge in the centre of this northern precipice. We managed by great exertion to clamber up to its western division; as for the eastern and higher summit, probably no traveller ever reached it. From the eminence on which we were thus perched, there was the plain of Rahah clearly visible below; also our tents, pitched as has been said immediately under the mountain. We descended now with considerable difficulty to the hollow, and instead of returning by way of the Convent, scrambled down by the gorge to the plain. The streamlet in its course forms pools, some of which are three and four feet deep. About

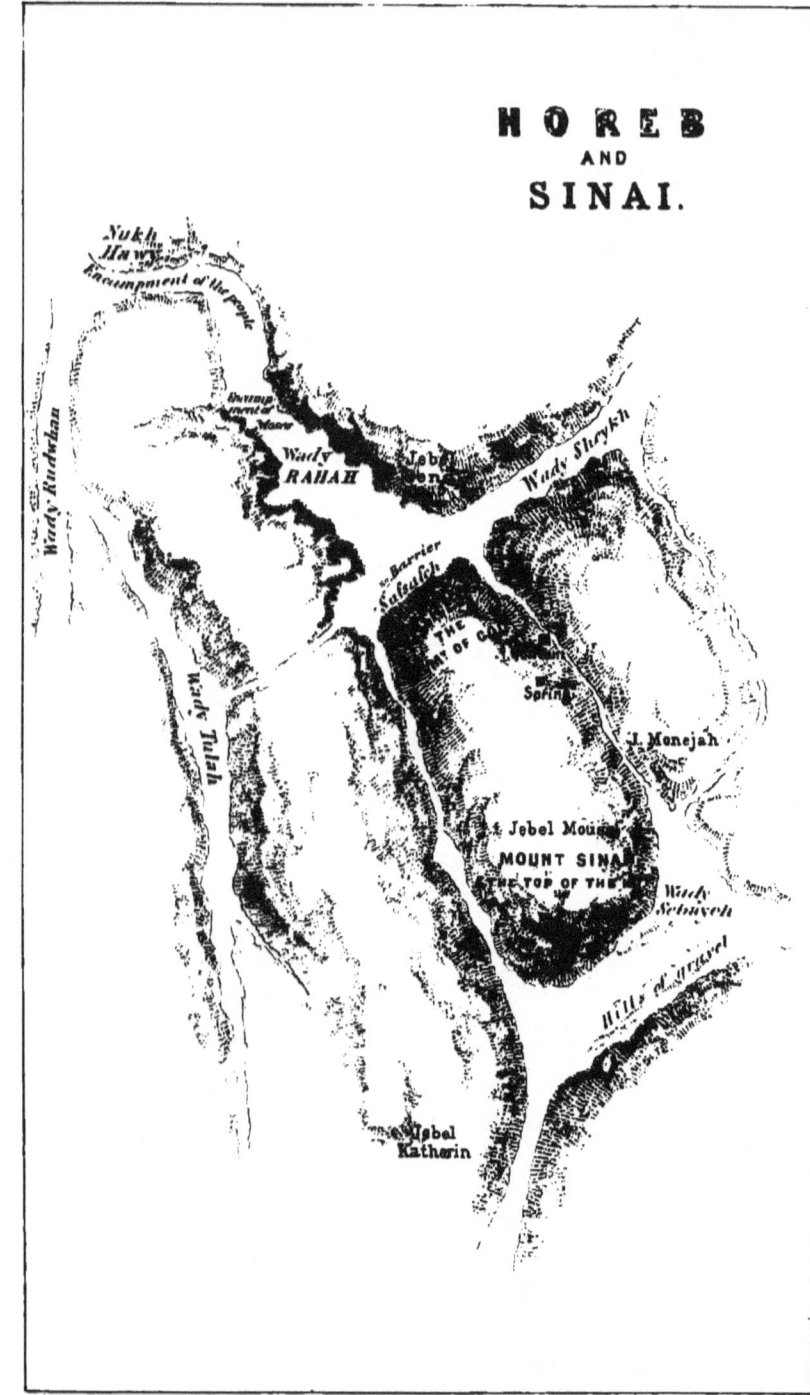

five o'clock we reached our tents, feeling that we had spent a day of hard toil, yet of surpassing enjoyment.

This brief description, illustrated by the accompanying sketch, will enable the reader to judge of the evidence now to be produced, by which this mountain of the Convent is identified with the Sinai and Horeb of Scripture. There are two points to which I solicit attention :—

I. There has been the unvarying testimony of tradition to this mountain.

II. Its features clearly explain and illustrate the description and incidents of the sacred narrative.

In these two respects this locality has a claim to our regard far beyond any other that can be named, and which, if I mistake not, leaves nothing to be desired by those who believe in the giving of the Law as an actual historical event. The remainder of the present chapter will be devoted to the consideration of the argument from tradition.

I admit that such an argument in favour of holy places is often untrustworthy, and in some cases obviously absurd. But it is clear, judging merely from the probabilities of the case, that the knowledge of this locality had a chance of being preserved that few others could possess. The event was one of unparalleled sublimity, and was felt to be so at the time of its occurrence by the whole Jewish nation. It was not here as in other cases where the importance of the incident disclosed itself after long years, and where a late posterity, becoming gradually alive to its significance, proceed to inquire for the place where it happened. The record of the scene at Sinai was taken on the spot, where all witnessed its solemnity and terror. Again, this is not a locality liable to be swept away by the decay of time, or the ruthless tread of the conqueror. It is not a tomb, or a house, or a village, of whose site we aim to form a vague conjecture amid heaps of ruin. The scene here is in a land where the conqueror did not come; where his steps would indeed have left little trace. It is, moreover, a mountain which, " being girded with strength, is not removed, but standeth fast for ever."

But proceeding to more positive evidence, let us notice, that the traditions of the Christian era point to this mountain, and this alone. It has been alleged by some, as formerly stated, that Serbal should in this respect have the preference. If correct in our criticisms on the views of Lepsius, this is a great mistake. It cannot be, I remind the reader, that the inscriptions on that mountain indicate any connexion with Sinai; they might prove this much of a hundred others, for they are scattered far and wide among the rocks of the Desert. The decisive fact is, that Justinian built the convent on Jebel Mousa about the year 560, obeying the settled tradition of the time, inasmuch as the monks of Serbal never dream of questioning it, or offering any opposition. So far from this, there appeared such acquiescence and co-operation, that the newly-established church of Sinai was placed under the protection of the episcopate at Feiran. This, surely, was the last thing that would have taken place if the tradition had previously pointed elsewhere, and especially to the locality of Feiran itself. The fathers and hermits would have protested, would have fought to the death, before consenting to be robbed of their consecrated mount. Other and more detailed evidence might be mentioned, but, I repeat, it is enough to indicate the real tradition of the early time—that on Jebel Mousa the orthodox Emperor built this convent, not only unchallenged, but with the consent of the whole Christian world. He erected it as at once a sanctuary and a citadel, to protect the monks in their worship from the plundering and massacre that had hitherto been their fate.

But now comes another question for our consideration. What evidence have we that an interest was taken in the locality during the centuries that preceded these early ages of Christianity? May not the traditions have been lost during the Jewish era? The strange opinion seems to prevail that the Jews felt little interest in such a spot, and did not visit it!

First of all, then, let us notice that the Israelites encamped before the mount for about twelve months, and wandered in its vicinity for nearly forty years. They reached Sinai on the fifteenth day of the third month of the first year, as stated in Ex. xix. 1 (*i.e.*, two months after they left Egypt), and left it on the twentieth day of the second month of the second year (Numb. x. 11). And what events had happened during this long stay? The Ten Commandments are proclaimed by the voice of God; the Tabernacle is erected; their whole religious economy is established. There was no place surely whose features would be so photographed in their minds and in those of their children often wandering in the valleys around.

Again, after the encampment broke up, the people moved north to Kadesh, where they were defeated by the Canaanites, and the command was given to go back to the Desert. The direction of their return is indicated

—"Turn you, and get you into the wilderness, by the way of the Red sea" (Numb. xiv. 25). The question is, Which arm of the Red Sea is here referred to? It seems to be assumed on all sides that it was the Gulf of Suez in the direction of Egypt, and the extensive uplands of the Tîh are usually represented as the scene of the wanderings. But the incidents and expressions of the narrative appear to forbid the assumption. We read, that on hearing the report of the spies, "they said one to another, Let us make a captain, and let us return to Egypt" (Numb. xiv. 4). Is it likely then that a people in such a mood, and indulging in such yearnings and repinings as the narrative records, are directed at this very time to go to the frontiers of Egypt, and thus imperil the whole purposes of the Exodus? After their second advance to Kadesh when refused a passage through Edom, we read that they "journeyed by way of the Red Sea to compass the land of Edom" (Numb. xxi. 4). Here unquestionably is meant the eastern arm or the Gulf of Akabah, and in the parallel passage (Deut. ii. 8) the stations of Elath and Eziongeber on that Gulf are mentioned. The inference consequently that ought to have been drawn is, that by "the way of the Red Sea" was indicated this eastern gulf on their *first* return likewise. This is confirmed by the fact, that one of their last encampments, as they went north for the second time, was Eziongeber on this same gulf, where Solomon afterwards built his fleet for the commerce of the East.[1] Now this

---

[1] During the period of their wanderings "by the way of the Red Sea," the rebellion of Korah took place. Tradition locates the scene at Sinai itself, which certainly is very strange, if it happened somewhere among the uplands of the Tîh.

gulf adjoined the district of Sinai, so that the bearings of it must often have been taken from different directions during the wanderings. In the view of this fact, we can understand the strain of the exhortations of Moses that pervades the book of Deuteronomy, and which abounds in references to the transactions of Horeb, not only presupposing but tending to maintain a correct knowledge of the locality.

But it may be thought that the Jews ceased to care for these Desert localities, Sinai among the number, after they were settled in Palestine. I have now to submit the proof that it was far otherwise.

Let us premise that the whole Desert now known as Arabia Petrea was the territory of but one tribe, Amalek. It extended south as far as Rephidim, and north as far as the southern frontier of Palestine, since we read of the Israelites again coming into conflict with them on their first attempt to enter (Numb. xiv. 45). As regards their eastern and western boundaries, they are said to have dwelt "from Havilah to Shur;" which seems to correspond to the country embraced by the two arms of the Red Sea. The name Havilah is thought by Niebuhr and others to be still lingering in that eastern district; and Shur is clearly the tract to the west, into which the Israelites entered after crossing the Red Sea. No other tribe is said to have shared this extensive tract with them; hence they were strong and numerous, and according to Balaam's description, the "first of nations."

While their defeat at Rephidim was so signal as to prevent them meddling with the Israelites during all their sojourn, they readily allied themselves with the other nations in battle against the common enemy, after the conquest of Canaan. During the period of the Judges, the Israelites had many conflicts with the surrounding idolatrous tribes, by whom they were often conquered and led away captive. In those conflicts Amalek took part. Doubtless they obtained a share of the captives, who were thus led once more into the Desert where their ancestors had wandered, and would gaze on the grand scenes of Sinai, of which their "fathers had told them." Of the very first attack on the Israelites it is said, that Moab "gathered unto him the children of Ammon and *Amalek*, and went and smote Israel, and possessed the city of palm-trees" (Judg. iii. 13). A hundred years had not elapsed since the Israelites left the Desert, coming from the encampment of Eziongeber adjacent to Sinai. There may thus have been, among the captives of the tribe whose head-quarters were in Feiran, the grandsons of those who had heard the thunders of the Law. In the song of Deborah, Amalek is again mentioned as the enemy that is smitten. The frequency of the attack from the same quarter appears from such language as the following: "The children of Israel cried unto the Lord, saying, We have sinned against thee, both because we have forsaken our God, and also served Baalim. The Lord said, Did not I deliver you from the Egyptians? The Zidonians also, and the *Amalekites*, and the Maonites, did oppress you; and ye cried to me, and I delivered you out of their hand" (Judg. x. 10-12). Indeed, if we had no other evidence, the sublime opening of the song of Deborah, "The mountains melted before the Lord, even *that Sinai*, before the Lord of Israel," would indicate how well the events were remembered in connexion with the locality.

But it is to the wars of Saul and David with this very tribe, that I have to direct the special attention of the reader. Both were led by these wars to the district in question; and if I mistake not, "the singer of Israel" has celebrated the event in one of the grandest of his Psalms. For a long time it seemed as if the threat against Amalek for his attempt on Israel at Rephidim —that God would "utterly put out the remembrance of Amalek from under heaven"—had been forgotten. But in the time of Saul it began to take effect: "Thus saith the Lord of hosts, I remember that which Amalek did to Israel, how he laid wait for him in the way, when he came up from Egypt. Now go and smite Amalek, and utterly destroy all" (1 Sam. xv. 2, 3). In obeying this command, the army of Saul are brought necessarily into the vicinity of Sinai. *There*, in the adjacent Rephidim, had been the attack for which retribution was exacted; *there* were the head-quarters of the tribe whose king was captured. And another fact confirms this opinion. The descendants of Jethro, according to Josephus, had their dwelling at Midian on the Red Sea. In that case they were near Mount Sinai, a fact confirmed by the wandering of Moses to the spot, when keeping the flock of his father-in-law. These "Kenites," as the Scripture narrative calls them, Saul was commanded to spare, a fact implying that his army was to march to the Sinai district. Indeed it swept the whole country, for he smote them from "Havilah to Shur that is over against Egypt," *i.e.*, from the Gulf of Akabah to the Gulf of Suez (1 Sam. xv. 7).

And now let us look at the exploit of David "the anointed one," who is drawn by a strange course of events to take a terrible vengeance on the tribe, completing the work of destruction in which Saul had failed. He had made a raid into their country frequently before (1 Sam. xxvii. 8). In retaliation of which, and taking advantage of the opportunity afforded by Saul's war with the Philistines, the Desert tribe attacked and plundered the city allotted by the Philistines to David and his followers. "The Amalekites invaded the south, and Ziklag, and had smitten Ziklag, and burnt it with fire; and had taken the women captives that were therein: they slew not any, great or small, but carried them away, and went on their way." David resolved to pursue, and he came of necessity into the immediate vicinity of Sinai. The Amalekites had returned to their resting-place, for David came on them feasting, and making merry over their spoil. He naturally seeks them at the head-quarters of the tribe at Wady Feiran, and there is here a stream which may explain for us the allusion to the brook Besor, where two hundred men are left behind. Some have conjectured that this was a stream near Gaza. But Gaza was not in the Amalekite country at all. Besides, it was but a short way from Ziklag, so that it is impossible to understand how such a number of hardy freebooters have been utterly exhausted and left behind. But such a fact is accounted for, if we suppose that they have undergone a hurried march for several days in the Desert to Wady Feiran.

However, David does not find the enemy in this valley, and this is not to be wondered at, if we remember that Saul with his army had lately been in this locality, laying it waste and carrying off all its cattle. He comes upon a sick "Egyptian in the field," and by him is guided to their haunts. He steals upon them unawares, and utterly exterminates them, with the exception of "four hundred young men who rode upon camels and fled." Now, I cannot help thinking that he came upon them making merry in the plains of the great Wady Sheikh that leads up to Sinai; the scene, let me add, of the merry-making of the descendants of the tribe to this day.

I put forward this hypothesis all the more confidently because of the remarkable coincidence between the incidents of this pursuit and the strain of the 68th Psalm, where "the hill of God," and Mount Sinai, are referred to in rapturous recollection.

It may be permitted to dwell on this point for a little. Most various, it is well known, have been the suggestions offered to explain the allusions and origin of this "the grandest and most splendid of the Psalms."[1] The great difficulty is to point out those incidents in the poet's life that most easily and naturally account for the ideas introduced, and to exhibit their connexion. I have to submit, that in the consideration of *this* event—one of the most critical in his chequered life—we find those features which meet the conditions required. Doubtless the *immediate* occasion of the Psalm was the building of the temple of Jerusalem. It is strange that this occasion should have been rather thought to be the bringing up of the ark, inasmuch as the strain uttered on that festive occasion—a strain altogether different from that in present view—is expressly recorded in 1 Chron. xvi. 8-36. The Psalm, I repeat, is suggested by the glad anticipation of the house of the Lord that was to be erected, for which in his later

---

[1] Ewald.

years David made such earnest preparation, and in which, to his great joy, the people exhibited hearty sympathy and co-operation (1 Chron. xxix. 6-20). To all this there is a plain reference in the Psalm. And that such was its immediate occasion, is confirmed by the language of another stanza: "Because of thy *temple* of Jerusalem shall kings bring presents unto thee" (Ps. lxviii. 29).

But now let us remark how fittingly at such a time, the Psalmist surveying his past life, crowded as it is with instances of the Divine mercy, selects the event alluded to for special commemoration.

1. He purposed to build the Temple in gratitude for the Divine favours bestowed on him, and *this* was in some respects the most memorable of all. It is not so much to the recovery of his wives and children that we here refer—a great and unexpected mercy, which he deeply felt: but let us think how critical was his position in relation to his followers. They shared his fate at other times willingly and courageously, shedding their blood in his defence. But the terrible calamity that had now befallen produced on these followers an appalling change. *They threatened his life.* The language of the narrative is singularly graphic: "David and his men came to the city (Ziklag), and, behold, it was burnt with fire; and their wives, and their sons, and their daughters, were taken captives. Then David and the people that were with him lifted up their voice and wept, until they had no more power to weep. And David was greatly distressed: for the people *spake of stoning him;* because the soul of all the people was grieved, every man for his sons and for his daughters: but David encouraged himself in the Lord his God" (1 Sam. xxx. 3, 4, 6). Never,

then, were his fortunes so low, never was his future so utterly dark; nothing left for him but simple trust in God. By divine aid he pursues the enemy and recovers all: his followers become more attached to him than ever. Presents of rich spoil are sent to his friends in different parts, which tended to gain affection for him, and secure their choice of him as their future king. The transition was as from midnight to noonday, and therefore the memory of this marvellous deliverance might well be associated in the joyous mood of mind excited by the prospect of a temple reared in Jerusalem to the God of all his mercies.

2. There was another strong link of association between the two events. The Temple was to enshrine the ark of the Covenant wherein were the tables of stone put in at Horeb (1 Kings viii. 9). How natural, then, if David, at such a time as that referred to, had visited the scenes, and stood on the sacred spot where these tables were first given to Moses, that this event should have here special commemoration?

3. But let the reader notice more particularly how the various incidents of the narrative underlie and give connexion to the utterance of the Psalm![1]

(1.) *The enemy.*—The Amalekites are regarded as "the enemies of God" in a sense more emphatic than any other tribe, and are so characterized in the language of the narrative: "Behold a present for you of the spoil of *the enemies of the Lord*" (1 Sam. xxx. 26).

---

[1] It is not necessary to allege that David excludes from his view other battles in his eventful life, where, by Divine help, he gained the victory. All that is contended for is, that the figurative language and allusions of the Psalm directly refer to *this* event, and that its whole strain derives therefrom a sequence and unity.

Again, we read, "David inquired at the Lord, saying, Shall I pursue after this troop? shall I overtake them? and he answered him, Pursue, for thou shalt surely overtake them, and without fail recover all" (ver. 8). How natural, then, that he should enter the Desert with the animating war-cry which his forefathers were wont to shout here, and with which the Psalm opens : " Let God arise, let his enemies be scattered ; let them also that hate him flee before him" (Ps. lxviii. 1).

(2.) *The defeat.*-- It was overwhelming. " David," we read, "smote them from the twilight, even unto the evening of the next day ; and there escaped not a man of them, save four hundred young men, which rode upon camels, and fled" (ver. 17). He also affirms, " The Lord hath delivered this company into our hand" (ver. 23).

The memory of all this prompts the strain of the second verse in the psalm : " As smoke is driven, so drive thou them away ; as wax melteth before the fire, so let the wicked perish at the presence of God. But let the righteous be glad : let them rejoice before God. Sing unto God ; extol him that rideth through the heavens," or, as some commentators have it, " that rideth through the Desert."

(3.) *The recovery of the captives.*—The Amalekites had carried away their wives and sons and daughters (ver. 3); but "David recovered all :"—" there was nothing lacking, neither small nor great, neither sons nor daughters" (ver. 19). Hence the strain of the next verse : " A father of the *fatherless*, a judge of the *widows*, is God in his holy habitation." The sixth verse speaks of the enemy as " the rebellious dwelling in a dry land."

(4.) *The past mercy of which the Desert had been the*

scene.—As David had experienced such a signal display of the divine mercy, he is led to speak of that bestowed on their forefathers as they travelled through these wastes centuries before : " O God, when thou wentest forth before thy people, when thou didst march through the wilderness : the earth shook, the heavens also dropped at the presence of God : even Sinai itself was moved at the presence of God, the God of Israel. Thou, O God, didst send a plentiful rain, whereby thou didst confirm thine inheritance, when it was weary. Thy congregation hath dwelt therein : thou, O God, hast prepared of thy goodness for the poor" (ver. 7-11).

(5.) *The divine sanction for the pursuit.*—Reverting to his own experience, he alludes to the express sanction of God for undertaking the expedition, inciting his followers to cling to him, and accompany him in the pursuit. Hence the Psalm continues, " The Lord gave the word ; great was the company of those that published it" (ver. 11).

(6.) *Statute about dividing the spoil.*—Then reference is made to a statute in Israel, adopted for the *first* time on this occasion : " As his part is that goeth down to the battle, so shall his part be that tarrieth by the stuff : they shall part alike. And it was so from that day forward, that he made it a statute and an ordinance for Israel unto this day" (1 Sam. xxx. 24, 25). In accordance with this is the sentiment of the Psalm, " Kings of armies did flee apace, and she that tarried at home divided the spoil" (ver. 12).

(7.) *Scene of battle.*—Then follows the description of the battle. It is described as beneath the shadow of Sinai itself. The description is a graphic one of the grand rugged hills by which it is surrounded. "When the Almighty scattered kings in it, it was white as snow in Salmon. The hill of God is as the hill of Bashan; an high hill, as the hill of Bashan. Why leap ye, ye high hills?" The answer: "This is the hill which God desireth to dwell in; yea, the Lord will dwell in it for ever. The chariots of God are twenty thousand, even thousands of angels; the Lord is among them, in Sinai, in the holy place" (Ps. lxviii. 14-17). To me it appears one of the most forced interpretations ever given, to apply this to Zion—the Temple hill—which is not high, and where no such battle was fought.[1] But it applies perfectly to Mount Sinai. Along with Horeb it was still nationally, as well as religiously, sacred to the Jewish mind, and still thought to be the dwelling-place of Deity. Hence the language, "Elijah went to Horeb, the Mount of God."

(8.) *Captivity captive.*—As we read "that David recovered all, and there was nothing lacking that was taken away," the sentiment of the Psalm appropriately follows, "Thou hast ascended on high, thou hast led captivity captive."

(9.) *Escape from death.*—The result elevated David to greater prosperity, and gathered around him more attached followers, instead of its resulting, as seemed imminent at one time, in his disgrace and death. How fitly then he adds, "Blessed be the Lord, who daily loadeth us with benefits; unto God the Lord belong the issues from death."

(10.) *Fit association with building of temple.*—The

---

[1] When David fought the battle with the Philistines in the valley of Rephaim (2 Sam. v. 22), Zion was *not* "the hill of God," nor was the Ark yet brought to Jerusalem.

God of Sinai was to inhabit the Temple of Jerusalem; and the rest of the Psalm is a glowing anticipation of the joy of its consecration, and the height of glory to which Jehovah would advance the nation among the kingdoms of the earth. Having thus referred to the grandeur of the divine manifestation in Sinai and Zion, the Psalm fitly concludes, " O God, thou art terrible out of thy holy places. Blessed be God."

The correspondence between the narrative and the poetry would have appeared still more clearly if the renderings of some of our best commentators had been adopted, but our own version is sufficient to indicate what were the events glowing in the memory of the Psalmist when he penned this, " one of the most able and powerful of his Psalms."[1] Instead of appearing a collection of disjointed utterances, it is pervaded by a marked and intelligible unity, and is proved, moreover, to *be* a Psalm of David—a point often disputed by many who fail to give any more probable explanation of its origin and authorship. If then our theory be correct, David has visited Sinai, and the tradition of the locality is correctly handed down.

Another fact bearing on the point is the subjugation of the Edomites by David (2 Sam. viii. 14),—an event fulfilling the prophecy: "The elder shall serve the younger" (Gen. xxv. 23). As the Edomites were the tribe adjoining that of Amalek, their conquest gave to the kings of Judah the complete sway of the entire country of Arabia, with its sacred district of Sinai.

Then, proceeding with the events of Jewish history, we

---

[1] Olshausen.

find that Solomon builds a fleet at Eziongeber, on the Red Sea (the Gulf of Akabah), adjoining the district of Sinai. Josephus, mentioning the fact, says, that "the country belonged to the Jews." It was at this epoch that the Temple was built, enshrining in the Holy of Holies the Ark containing " the tables of stone put in at Horeb." Is it credible then, I ask, that of the numbers necessarily attracted to the district, all were intent on commercial interests exclusively, and that no devout pilgrims turned aside to gaze on the holy mount?

The fleet of Jehoshaphat was also stationed at this same Gulf, and the whole country remained under the dominion of the Jews till the revolt of the Edomites under Joram (2 Kings viii. 20), that is, for about 150 years.

We now come to an important fact in the centre of the Jewish history directly proving our conclusion. "Elijah," it is said, "went unto Horeb, the mount of God" (1 Kings xix. 8). And he found his way to it from the northern parts of Palestine,—a fact altogether unaccountable if the sacred locality had been dropped from remembrance and regard.

It has been too hastily assumed that no other pilgrims visited the scene, inasmuch as the tendency of the events recorded in the Pentateuch was to fix the attention of the Jews on the Law itself, and not on the locality. Of course, the events are by far the most important, but is it the fact that these are so stated as to make the reader indifferent about visiting that locality? Let us ask ourselves whether *we*, had we lived in that age, would not have experienced the spirit of pilgrimage, and have gone thither if opportunity offered? We read the marvellous records which describe the miraculou manifestation of Jehovah on Sinai, how there he descended in the sight of our forefathers, and with his own voice proclaimed his Law; we are taught to regard this as the most astonishing token of the divine goodness ever vouchsafed to the world, and which distinguished the Jewish people far above other nations; we worship in the Temple, the glory of which was its possession of the Ark of the covenant, containing the tables of stone written by the finger of God himself; we chant in its courts the psalms which stir the heart to the deepest adoration and gratitude in memory of the divine goodness. Meanwhile, the locality that has been the scene of all this, the holy Mount Sinai, is hardly 200 miles distant, situated in a country over which our kings bear rule, and where they have built their fleets for the commerce of the East. I ask, is it credible in these circumstances that no desire should have arisen in the mind to visit the spot? Assuredly, if the reading of the Pentateuch *now* can attract Christians hither from the uttermost ends of the earth, there is no reason to suspect that the Jewish mind (so prone to be influenced by local considerations) could be a stranger to the spirit of pilgrimage. We may rather conjecture that many of the pious-minded found their way thither, and that Elijah travelled by a *beaten* path to "Horeb, the mount of God." He is said to have dwelt there in "the cave," which Ewald understands to mean the usual pilgrim's abode.

It is said, "God came from Sinai, and the Holy One from Mount Paran," and the passage is quoted as if implying that the attention of the Jew had been withdrawn from Sinai, and fixed on the divine manifestation in the Temple on Zion. This appears an undue straining of the language; and moreover, it cannot be held as proving that there were no pilgrims to the spot. For a pilgrim is one to whom *the past* is holy, and who is attracted to places that *have been* the scenes of momentous events.

From the expression in the narrative, which records the visit of Elijah, we are warranted to infer that it was still a place sacred and venerable to the Jewish mind: "Elijah went to Horeb, the mount of God." And it is evident that he retreats thither not only because it was an asylum from danger and persecution, but because it was a haunt for solemn religious meditation, amid the corruptions of an evil time. He could there, if not forgetting the hideous aspect of the present, yet muse with a deeper abstraction on the holy past. Sick at heart of the nation's idolatry, he would gaze on that awful mount from which these words were spoken: "Thou shalt have no other gods before me." He can no longer live in a land where "the covenant" had been so fearfully despised and trampled under foot, but will hide himself in these mountains of the Desert, amidst which its awful sanctions were thundered, and its words uttered by the voice of Jehovah himself. Welcome the solitude! Better the companionship of these dumb rocks and granite cliffs, fellow-witnesses to the everlasting obligations of this law, than the living faces and companionship of men who have rejected God and followed Baal. And when in the mount, the prophet witnesses such a scene as may well lead us to the conclusion, that the Divine presence still clung to the spot, in some special sense accounting for the appellation still given to it in the history "the mount of God." Before the awe-struck pilgrim on the mount, the same phenomena occurred as accompanied the giving of the Law. There was the earthquake, the tempest, the fire, and then came "the voice of words,"—"a still small voice." "And it was so when Elijah heard it, that he wrapped his face in his mantle, and went out, and stood in the entering of the cave. And behold there came a voice to him, What doest thou here, Elijah? And he said, I have been very jealous for the Lord God of hosts, because the children of Israel have forsaken thy covenant, thrown down thine altars, and slain thy prophets with the sword, and I, even I only am left, and they seek my life to take it away." This language at all events indicates that this pilgrim views the spot as most holy, and the fittest for nursing the faith which he is striving to retain amid the universal idolatry. And unless we ignore that characteristic of the Jewish mind, which so directly associated holy feelings with particular localities, one may well believe that such pilgrimages to the spot were not unfrequent. To describe the visits of pilgrims was not the object of Bible history, and very probably that of Elijah would never have been heard of, but for its high significance and lessons. At all events, the fact remains, that in the time of Elijah the locality of Sinai was not lost sight of.

Onward from this to the Christian era, we have glimpses of events that would still maintain the tradition. The Edomites recovered their independence after a subjection of 150 years. "In the days of Joram, Edom revolted from under the hand of Judah, and made a king over themselves" (2 Kings viii. 20). But this did not imply that the access to Sinai was closed (for it was in the country of the Amalekites); and we are told that in the reign of Ahaziah, "Elath" (on the Gulf of Akabah, which gave entrance to the district), was built and restored to Judah. In the course of time the Edomites themselves came to adopt the Jewish religion, the central facts of which were associated with this locality. Josephus asserts the fact frequently,[1] and it was illustrated in the after fortunes of the Jewish people. Some of the governors were of Idumean extraction, and in the siege of the Temple, thousands of Idumeans flocked to its defence at the call of the Jews themselves. Having thus adopted the Jewish religion, this people also became interested in the great events of the giving of the Law, and the traditional spot adjacent to their own territory would be still more secure of ultimate identification.

Finally, in the Christian era, pilgrims of the new dispensation visited the locality in numbers. One of the first was the great Apostle of the Gentiles. In his Epistle to the Galatians, he refers to it as "Sinai in Arabia;" and in the same epistle he tells us that he went "into Arabia," remaining there for three years to study more profoundly the genius of the Christian dispensation. It is no argument against our conclusion, that as he was then at Damascus, some other Arabia must be meant. For Elijah, when at Sinai, was commanded to "return to the wilderness of Damascus;" and in all likelihood by the same route the Apostle goes from Damascus to Sinai. Most fitting was the scene for the severer studies that then occupied him, and for making him welcome more deeply the grace and mercy of the gospel! Thus, during the very period of his preparation

[1] Josephus, *Antiquities*, xiii. 9.

for apostolic work, he saw "the mount that might be touched," in "blackness, and darkness, and tempest," and as the terrific thunder crashed along these awful crags, he would hear the echo of his own profound conviction, "By the deeds of the law shall no flesh living be justified."

Numbers of Jews also frequented Arabia in the early ages of Christianity, who exerted their great influence, says Neander, to oppose the introduction of the gospel. But this very fanaticism would rather tend to maintain their hold of the tradition of Sinai, to which God had so marvellously led their fathers, and where he had spoken with them face to face. Thus closely was the tradition handed down to the Christian hermits who, in the fourth century, settled round the locality and stained its crags with martyrs' blood.

In dealing with this subject we must not overlook the evidence furnished by the superstitions of the Arabs in reference to this mountain. They have a reverence for it such as they bear to none other. They believe the monks of the Convent (who for their own purposes foster the superstition) to possess the magic book that has power with heaven to obtain the necessary rains. It cannot be said that such feelings are due to the influence of the monks themselves, whom they suspect and dislike, sometimes even attempting their life. Its origin seems to lie in the traditional and deeply-cherished superstition in regard to this locality. Josephus mentions that the mountain from of old was surrounded by portents warning away the Arab shepherds from the spot. "There was a widely-believed rumour," he says, "that God dwelt there." And certainly the Scripture account is not inconsistent with this; for Moses, even on his first arrival here, saw the strange symbol of the Divine presence, and was told to take off the shoes from off his feet, for the place on which he stood was holy ground. And it is a remarkable fact that these mysterious inscriptions—the writings of the ancient inhabitants of the Desert—are not found on this mountain of Jebel Mousa. This circumstance, which has been quoted as telling against its being the actual Sinai, would rather seem to be an argument in its favour.

Certain it is that Josephus refers to Sinai as a mount regarded with deepest reverence by the inhabitants of the Desert in the days of the Exodus, and it is no less certain that Jebel Mousa, and it alone, is regarded by their descendants with such a feeling now.

From the above statements the reader may judge how far the tradition is likely to be correct, carried though it has been through long ages. Remembering the transcendent sublimity of the events of Sinai, and how long the generations of the Exodus settled beneath its shadow and wandered in its vicinity; how that, at the third generation and afterwards, their descendants are led captive here; how they afterwards became the conquerors of the country, and in the interests of commerce must have visited the neighbourhood in considerable numbers, it seems in the highest degree improbable, although particular pilgrimages are not specified, to suppose that the locality was forgotten or disregarded.

As if to make our decision sure, there are noted the visits of three greater than all others to the sacred mount. David, Elijah, and Paul were here gazing reverently on the scene, each finding in it the lesson appropriate to his circumstances and mood of mind. To the first, it was "the holy place" of the God of Israel, who there proved " a judge of the widow, and father of the fatherless," and scattered, as in the days of old, his enemies like smoke; to the second it was the mount where dwells the jealous God, "who will not give his glory to another, nor his praise to graven images," and who assures the desponding prophet that he has seven thousand who have not bowed the knee to Baal; to the third, it was the scene where the Law which man has broken was given, perfect in its precepts, awful in its sanctions, the thought of which makes him welcome for himself, and passionately proclaim to others, the necessity of seeking salvation through the pardoning blood of Christ. From amongst the unrecorded numbers who visited the spot, these three emerge into view, visibly bearing at wide intervals the chain of tradition across the centuries, until it is taken up by Christian hermits, who grasp it firmly, and amid privations, perils, and death, refuse to let it go.

CHAPTER VII.

HOREB AND SINAI—THE PROCLAMATION OF THE LAW.

I now propose to show that this mountain, which tradition has so long consecrated as the holy Mount Sinai, most remarkably answers to all the conditions of the narrative. Thus, if we ask for a plain of encampment,—" a mount that might be touched,"—an elevation from which the thousands of Israel could well hear the Ten Commandments,—a summit also where Moses was when he could neither see nor hear the revelries beneath,—a stream descending from the mount to the plain,—all are here in such fitness as they appear nowhere else, and throw a proportionately clearer light on the incidents recorded in the sacred history.

This mountain then has two summits, to be conceived of by the reader thus—

1. Sufsafeh (Horeb) overhanging the plain, about 1000 feet in height, and very difficult of ascent.

2. Jebel Mousa (Sinai of Old Testament) back from the plain about three miles, about 2000 feet in height. This is the top of the mount, invisible from the plain, and very easily ascended from the valley of the Convent.

The grand mistake hitherto in dealing with this mountain, as connected with the sacred record, has been in limiting the incidents of that narrative to either the one or the other of these summits. Dr. Robinson pleads for the front and lower peak Sufsafeh, and for it alone. With the other summit he thinks Moses "had nothing to do." Now Sufsafeh answers well, as will afterwards be seen, for the proclamation of the Law, but not at all for the place to which Moses was summoned for forty days and forty nights. For it is *not* "the top of the mount;" it is *very* difficult of ascent; and moreover, from such a summit Moses could have heard very distinctly the revelries at the base. He could have *seen* these likewise before he had moved downwards, and more and more distinctly at every step of the descent. But the narrative implies that everything was hid from his view till he came to the *foot* of the mount, where he cast the tables from his hands (Ex. xxxii. 19).

Dr. Wilson, again, would confine all the events to the other summit, Jebel Mousa. The great objection to this theory is, that it is unsuitable as a place for the proclamation of the Law. It is back from the plain three miles, and is moreover above 2000 feet in height. How then in this case could the people be said to be "near God," gathered to him "face to face," as the narrative tells us they were? Or how could they *hear* the words of the Law? If the narrative is emphatic on any point, it is, that it was not a confused noise, but "the voice of words" that thrilled the multitude on that solemn occasion.

It does not mend matters in the least, if we shift the plain where the people stood, from Rahah in the north to Sebayeh in the south. This with some is the grand solution of the difficulty. Several commentators of high research have spoken much in preference of this latter wady, and Dr. Kitto, in his *Daily Readings*, hails it as a great help to the settlement of the question. It is wonderful to him that Dr. Robinson has not taken it into account, and he devotes a special chapter to its description. Now, it is a mistake to suppose that any traveller who has been at the top of Jebel Mousa could fail to observe Wady Sebayeh. It lies beneath him clearly in view. The likelihood is, that Dr. Robinson did not mention it, because the first glance showed it to be in every way unsuitable for the purpose required: for, looking from the summit, it is seen to be a narrow rugged winding valley. And the mountain, instead of rising from it sheer and precipitous, as a "mount that might be touched," throws out from its base a number of spurs and rocky undulations far into the plain. What is further decisive against its claims is, that Moses descending with the two tables of stone, must have seen the revelries of the people at every step.

But instead of discussing further the various theories advanced on the subject, I proceed to show, that, provided we take into account both summits of the mountain, the entire locality not only accords with, but explains and enforces the statements of the Scripture narrative.

I. At the base of the mountain there is the plain of Rahah, suitable in every way for the encampment of the Israelites. This plain is, beyond every other named, broad, beautiful, and unobstructed. It is not cut up, as others are, by water-courses, but is remarkably level, and moreover sweeps in grand breadth right onwards to the precipitous cliffs of the mountain. It is incomparably the fittest plain that has yet been suggested in the whole Desert for the purpose required. Any one coming suddenly on it from the pass of Nukhby Howy can sympathize with the burst of admiration felt by Dr. Robinson, "Here is room enough for a large encampment!" The Israelites could be assembled well "under the mount," as the cliff rises with sheer abruptness. They could also, as the narrative represents, remove "afar off" in view of the appalling phenomena, when the voice ceased. Its length is five miles, and amid the rugged hollows and ravines at the farther end, we can well imagine the multitude seeking for shelter from the immediate terrors of the scene.

On the mountain itself were exhibited two distinct Divine manifestations. The first was displayed in the proclamation of the Law to the people; the second in the delivering it to Moses on the tables of stone, and in the communing with him in regard to the details of the Jewish ritual. The language of the narrative, it will be seen, requires us to assign to these events two distinct localities; one summit will not suffice, choose which mountain we may. From many indications, we can infer that the localities must have differed, *first*, in their elevation, and *secondly*, in their distance from the plain where the people had assembled.[1]

1. Let us fix attention on the locality where Moses received the tables of stone, and where he remained forty days and forty nights, obtaining the needful instruction in the various regulations of the Jewish economy. It is defined in the narrative invariably as the "*top of the mount.*" This appears from the account of his ascent at different times.

Before the proclamation of the Law he was summoned to speak with Jehovah: "The Lord came down upon

---

[1] The ancient tradition, be it understood, indicates two such summits. The peculiarity of the present view is, that it seeks to establish the hypothesis by an appeal to the incidents of the narrative,—in opposition to the present universal opinion that only *one* summit must be supposed.

mount Sinai, on the top of the mount, and the Lord called Moses up to the *top of the mount*, and Moses went up." Of his second ascent we read, "The sight of the glory of the Lord was like devouring fire on the *top of the mount* in the eyes of the children of Israel; and Moses went into the midst of the cloud, and got him up into the mount" (Ex. xxiv. 16, 17). And the account of the third ascent makes the point still more manifest when he went up to receive the new tables of the Law. "Be ready in the morning and come up in the morning into *mount Sinai*, and present thyself there to me in the *top of the mount*" (Ex. xxxiv. 2). Moreover, that he was then on a summit of high elevation, is to be inferred from the fact that he heard nothing of the revelries that had burst forth from the plain below. Along with his minister Joshua, he is far down in the descent before he can correctly interpret the meaning of the sounds. The tradition of Josephus, I may add, speaks of Sinai where Moses ascended as "the highest mountain in the country."

Again, that it was at *a distance from the plain* is evident from the fact that Moses saw nothing of the idolatry that had broken out, until he had quite descended to its base. The plain was not in his view as he came down. He cast the Tables from his hands on first sight of the revelries, and we are expressly told that these were broken *beneath the mount*.

Now Jebel Mousa, the southern summit of the mountain of the Convent, admirably satisfies the conditions of this Scripture locality in its elevation (2000 feet), easy access, and distance from the plain (three miles). Consequently, the songs of the bacchanalia around the golden calf were not audible there. After a considerable descent Moses identifies them, and, correcting the surmise of

Joshua, exclaims, " It is not the voice of them that shout for mastery, neither is it the voice of them that cry for being overcome, but the voice of them that sing do I hear." Still nothing is seen. Reaching the end of the valley (of the Convent), and then turning round by the abrupt cliffs of Sufsafeh, he beholds on the plain " the calf and the dancing!" I know no other mountain named as Sinai, where such could be the case in the descent of Moses: not Serbal, nor Jebel Katherin, nor Jebel Monejah. In all such cases the spectacle would have lain full in his view long before he reached the plain, and therefore he would have cast the Tables *on* the mountain instead of beneath it.

II. But we must look elsewhere on the mountain for the scene of the other and still grander divine manifestation in the proclamation of the Law.

(1.) In perusing the narrative, we are led to think of *this* summit as one *quite close* to the plain. The people are brought up, we are told, to " the nether part of the mount." " They came near and stood under the mount" (Deut. iv. 11). " Thou stoodest," said Moses, "*before* the Lord thy God in Horeb." The Divine presence was so near that it is said, God talked "face to face with you in the mount" (Deut. v. 4). These and similar expressions imply the Divine presence on a summit adjoining the plain where the people stood, and rising direct from it. And it is only by conceiving of such a precipitous eminence that we can understand the injunction to make a barrier round the mount, so that no one might touch it. And thus because of its proximity to the plain, this summit cannot be identical with the distant " top of the mount" from which Moses descended.

As Jebel Mousa answers for the one event, so Sufsafeh, the front summit, answers for the other. It rises grandly from the plain and overhangs it. It is the " mount that might be touched," and looking at it we see the necessity for the construction of a barrier.

(2.) The locality now under consideration required to be a summit of lower elevation than the other. Many readers have been accustomed to think of the precepts of the law as uttered in tones very loud and even wrathful and terrible. Each command, it is fancied, rolled like a thunder-peal from the high summit of the mountain. The Law, it is often said, " was thundered from Sinai," and the expression is used not only to indicate the terror of the sanctions (where it is appropriate enough), but also to describe the dread emphasis of the tones in which its everlasting precepts were proclaimed. And with this idea, a high summit of 2000 feet, 3000 feet, and even 4000 feet, has been argued for ; the higher, indeed, some seem to think, the better. But as the narrative makes no such assertion, it is competent for us to ask, Could the people have distinguished the language uttered from such a distant and elevated height ? Mere sounds, a thunder peal, the noise of a trumpet,—all this could be imagined easily enough ; but the hearing of words articulate and distinct, depends on some other conditions besides the loudness of the voice. That this is not a point of trifling importance is evident from the confident assertion of some that the Israelites heard no words at all, but only thunder, emphatically "the voice of God." Many feel a doubt on the subject, which gains additional weight from these descriptions of the high and distant summits from which the Law was proclaimed.

It behoves us therefore to consider how far the narrative sanctions the idea of a lower elevation.

(*a.*) The words of the law were to the people distinctly audible. Nothing seems clearer from the record than this, that the voice they heard was the "voice of *words.*" "God spake all these words, saying" (Ex. xx. 1). "Ye have seen that I have talked with you from heaven" (Ex. xx. 22). "The Lord talked with you face to face in the mount out of the midst of the fire.... Who of all flesh hath heard the voice of the living God speaking out of the midst of the fire as we have, and lived?" etc. etc. (Deut. v. 4, 26.) But to suppose that these *words* were uttered from Jebel Mousa, still more from Jebel Katherin or Serbal, seems to necessitate the assumption of a *second* miracle that the people might hear distinctly. It is no answer to say that the voice was divine, and so able to reach the mass, for it is just the tremendous loudness that causes the difficulty as to the utterance being distinct and intelligible. The imagination cannot but think that such a proclamation pealing from the distant height must have crashed along the cliffs like thunder—the distinctness destroyed by its own echo—and the people, indeed, so thunderstruck as to be prevented listening at all.

(*b.*) The people were summoned close to the mount, just that they might hear the voice of God. But this seems hardly necessary, and indeed not advisable, if they were addressed from the lofty summit that is commonly supposed. And, indeed, those who have contended for Serbal do not attempt to bring all the people near it. Yet that all were present is obvious from such language as the following: "Thou stoodest before the Lord thy

God in Horeb, when the Lord said unto me, Gather me the people together, and I will make them hear my words." Moses addresses Israel, as if all had been listeners, and therefore direct parties to the covenant.

(c.) It is important, as bearing on this point, to remember the spirit in which, according to the narrative, the Law was given. The spirit and tones of a proclamation are closely allied. If the Law had been uttered in wrath, the idea of loud terror in its tones might be admitted, but not if it was given as an act of favour and grace, as is always represented. It is very true that the Law is spoken of in the Epistles of the Apostle Paul as having an aspect of terror and vengeance; but in all such cases, he speaks to those who are abusing it by seeking in it the means of their justification before God. For this it made no provision, either in the Jewish or Christian dispensation. In sacrifice alone could such a blessing be obtained. But as a covenant and a rule of life the Law was an unspeakable privilege and blessing, and as such the historians, prophets, and psalmists of the Old Testament invariably represent it. The Lawgiver was not angry when he spoke to the people, and the tones must not be thought of surely as wrathful and condemnatory. Let us observe the terms of the message which Moses was to convey to the people, to prepare them for hearing its holy precepts: "Ye have seen what I did unto the Egyptians, and how I bare you on eagles' wings, and brought you unto myself. Now therefore, if ye will obey my voice indeed, and keep my covenant, then ye shall be a peculiar treasure unto me above all people" (Ex. xix. 4, 5). Again, after it was uttered, "Ye have seen that I have talked with you from heaven. In all places where I record my name I will come unto thee, and I will bless thee" (Ex. xx. 22, 24). Still further, the touching language in reference exclusively to the Decalogue, "O that there were such a heart in them, that they would fear me, and keep all my commandments always, that it might be well with them and their children for ever" (Deut. v. 29). There is an infinite pity and pathos in such language which makes us conceive of the divine voice as authoritative indeed, but withal distinct, tranquil, and uttered from a summit close at hand.

But some will ask, Did not the people in their fear remove afar off? True; and the fact is quite consistent with the view here presented. The voice might be solemn and quiet, and yet awe-inspiring, for it was the voice of God. And the narrative points out that they were especially terror-struck by the appalling sanctions with which the proclamation was followed. The distinction is important; for a law may be announced in comparatively quiet tones, while yet the language of the threatening may be very terrible. In the case before us there were tremendous phenomena when the Divine voice ceased, which drove the people backward in dismay. "And when all the people saw the thunderings, and the lightnings, and the noise of the trumpet, and the mountain smoking, they removed, and stood afar off" (Ex. xx. 18). We are therefore still to infer that only the sanctions were terrible, while it becomes us to believe that the proclamation was in tones harmonizing with the divine condescension and favour indicated by the passages quoted. It is not otherwise, indeed, with the gospel, "the law of faith," whose accents are at once calm and tender, while yet the language of its threatening to the despisers of it is unspeakably tremendous. The laws of nature too are gentle enough in the announcement of their presence, while each is followed by severe penalties if unheeded and transgressed. When Elijah was at Horeb, then too was he the witness of appalling phenomena. But did that indicate loudness and terror in the *voice* that addressed him? On the contrary, we are told that the Lord was not in the wind, nor in the earthquake, nor in the fire, but in the "still small voice" (1 Kings xix. 12). The language of Philo is remarkable: "The law," he says, "was uttered with such calmness and distinctness, that the people rather seemed to be seeing than hearing it."

Our conclusion then is, that the divine voice, with calm authority, spoke to the assembled thousands of Israel from behind the barrier which guarded the overhanging cliffs of Sufsafeh.

(*d*.) This conviction is strengthened by another circumstance mentioned in the narrative, viz., that although Jehovah continued to proclaim to Moses from the *same place* other statutes, yet nothing of this was heard in the encampment to which the people had retired. On witnessing the awful phenomena that followed the announcement of the moral law, Moses removed with the people afar off, for even Moses said, "I exceedingly fear and quake." But before the Divine presence retires, other statutes and judgments have to be addressed to them, which are contained in the 21st, 22d, and 23d chapters of Exodus. These do not relate to the sacrifices, or to any other portion of the Jewish ritual (which was not yet established), but are regulations carrying out the grand principles of the moral law into various complicated details of Jewish social life. The people urge Moses to go near and listen in their behalf, and be to them as a mediator: "Speak thou with us, and we will hear; but let not God speak with us, lest we die." And it is added, "The people stood afar off: and Moses drew near unto the thick darkness where God was" (Ex. xx. 19, 21). Or to take the fuller account in Deuteronomy. The people urge, "Go thou near, and hear all that the Lord our God shall say; and speak thou unto us all that the Lord our God shall speak unto thee, and we will hear it and do it. And the Lord heard the voice of your words, when ye spake unto me; and the Lord said unto me, I have heard the voice of the words of this people, which they have spoken unto thee; they have well said all that they have spoken. O that there were such an heart in them, that they would fear me, and keep all my commandments always, that it might be well with them, and with their children for ever! Go say to them, Get you into your tents again. But as for thee, stand thou here by me, and I will speak unto thee all the commandments, and the statutes, and the judgments, which thou shalt teach them, that they may do them in the land which I give them to possess it" (Deut. v. 27-32). Now Moses received these detailed injunctions on the plain close to the barrier from which the people had retired,—intimation being made to him at the close that he is *afterwards* to come up into the mount (Ex. xxiv. 1-3). It is to be observed, that in the tents of the people the divine voice is then no longer audible (for their request has been granted); and this is not conceivable if the words had been spoken all along from a high and distant elevation. The people in that case could not have *failed to hear* its tones, even although they had retired to the encampment, and their terror would have continued with its awful echo.

We require then, I believe, to modify the prevailing conceptions respecting the voice of Jehovah in the giving of the Law. The question is not, Were the accompanying or ensuing thunders loud?—for this is admitted. Or, Could not the divine voice have been loud and terrible also?—this also is indubitable, but away from the point. The question (bearing on topographical correctness alone) is, Was it of such a character in the present instance, and heard from a distance? Our answer, I believe, must be in the negative, from a view of those expressions and incidents of the inspired record which have now been noticed.

But how, it may incidentally be asked, can we understand the people hearing the voice of words even from the front summit, or, it may be, from the barrier at its base?

I have now to direct attention to the distinctness with which words are heard in this locality, which, in this respect, renders it perhaps the most remarkable in the world. If a stone be rolled down the mountain, it strikes with a hollow reverberation, as if awakening the echoes of a cavern beneath, and such as are heard nowhere else. Let a pistol be fired, and the echo is prolonged among the cliffs like mimic thunder. Shouts, of course, can be heard to a great distance; indeed, Niebuhr was told by his Arabs that their cry from Jebel Mousa could be heard across to the Gulf of Akabah (say thirty miles). This is, of course, an absurd exaggeration, but "one that arises," as Canon Stanley has remarked, "from the great distance to which sounds can actually be carried." To cite our own experience,—the chanting of two of our party on the top of Jebel Sena was heard about three miles away in the plain of Rahah by one of our companions, who inquired as to the fact when we met in the tent. But the special point of interest in connexion with the argument, is the distinctness with which words —*articulate sounds*—can be heard a long way off. There are many other places where a remote shout can be well heard; but the plain of Rahah is surely unrivalled in the world for the distinctness with which words spoken at a distance fall on the ear of the listener.

Thus, in descending from Jebel Sena, and proceeding across the plain for about half a mile, I overheard distinctly some words in the conversation of two of the party who were still at its base. The pitch of the voice was only that of earnest talk. On another occasion, in descending the gorge of Sufsafeh, those of us who had reached the plain were startled to hear so distinctly the voices of the others more than half-way up the gorge.

A thunderstorm, as the reader may well imagine, in this locality must be very appalling; and the following is the account of a recent traveller: "During the night," says Dr. Stewart, "we had a high wind, accompanied by torrents of rain and thunder, and the rain continued till the morning was far advanced. The solemn stillness that pervades this wilderness, and the distance at which man's voice may be heard, has not failed to be remarked by every one who has travelled it. I have already noticed the extraordinary reverberations produced by the blastings near Jebel Tinch by night. Some conception may therefore be formed of how majestic and awful a thunderstorm in such circumstances must be, but words are too feeble to describe the reality. Every bolt, as it burst with the roar of a cannon, seemed to awaken a series of distinct echoes on every side, and you heard them bandied from crag to crag as they roared along the wadys, while they swept like a whirlwind among the higher mountains, becoming faint as some mighty peak intervened, and bursting again with undiminished volume through some yawning cleft, till the very ground trembled with the concussion. Such sounds it is impossible ever to forget; it seemed as if the whole mountains of the peninsula were answering one another in a chorus of deepest bass. Ever and anon a flash of lightning dispelled the pitchy darkness, and lit up the tent as if it had been day, then after the interval of a few seconds came the peal of thunder, bursting like a shell to scatter its echoes to the four quarters of the heavens, and overpowering for a moment the loud howlings of the wind. I would not have lost that storm in such a place for all the rest of the journey."

The sum of the preceding discussion thus is, that the Law was proclaimed from the lower summit overhanging the plain, and that the precepts specially connected with the Jewish economy were given to Moses on the higher and more distant summit, that is now appropriately named Jebel Mousa.

Let me now proceed to notice some other considerations confirming such a distinction.

III. In view of two such summits we can understand why a fresh warning was given to the assembled people *after* Jehovah had descended. "The Lord came down upon mount Sinai on the top of the mount : and the Lord called Moses up to the top of the mount : and Moses went up. And the Lord said unto Moses, Go down, charge the people, lest they break through unto the Lord to gaze, and many of them perish" (Ex. xix. 20). Now, wherefore is this caution at such a time, if the Divine presence is as *near* the people as it will yet be ? If they had been yet in their tents preparing to leave the encampment, we could understand this repetition of the charge. But how account for it when they are already at the barrier ? On a due regard to the two distinct summits of the mount, our difficulty is removed. For, where the Divine Presence had now descended, there is an intermediate separation from the people, not only of the barrier, but of the entire length of the mountain. Over this interval Jehovah shall yet come, *i.e.*, from the summit of Sinai to that of Horeb ; and then He shall be "face to face" with the waiting multitude, nothing intervening but the barrier. Hence Moses is bidden once more to charge them to respect it, "lest the Lord break forth upon them, and they perish."

IV. Two such summits enable us to understand how the Israelites fell into the sin of idolatry at Horeb. "They made a calf at Horeb," we are told ; that is, at the very mount where the law had been proclaimed amid lightnings and thunders. There the elders had remained ; there Moses saw the idolatrous outrage after his descent to the plain, when he cast the tables from his hands. This conduct of the Israelites seems strange to many. Were they not afraid of the avenging thunder ?

How did they dare this blasphemy before the flaming symbol of the Divine Presence? But the pillar of fire, the symbol of that Presence, by this time had retired to the summit farther back—" Mount Sinai, the top of the mount." Moses was there " in the cloud," too far away to hear the outburst of the revelry. But over the front summit of Horeb no special portent hovered to overawe the people from the idolatrous deed. Accustomed by this time to the flaming symbol, and seeing it gleaming away back from them on Jebel Mousa—while around the grey crags of Sufsafeh all was calm, their idolatrous passions rose unchecked, and at its base "they change their glory into the similitude of an ox that eateth grass."

V. Two such summits explain satisfactorily the names of Horeb and Sinai applied to the Mount of the Law. Any one who is at all familiar with the literature of the subject knows how perplexed has been the discussion on these two distinct epithets, and how unsatisfactory the result that has been reached. Some have attempted to show that the one name is general, indicating a large district, whereas the other specially designates the Mount of the Law. Whether Horeb or Sinai be the general name is as yet unsettled. Now, there is not in the Old Testament a tittle of evidence sanctioning the idea of a wide district in connexion with either epithet, but all the passages where Sinai and Horeb occur rather point to one definite locality, treating of events which befell only when the Israelites were in the vicinity of a single mountain. Others regard the two words as synonymous, derived from different languages. But neither will this theory suit, for both are used in the same books, Exodus, Deuteronomy, and the Psalms. I now ask the reader's attention to the evidence of the fact that these epithets, while referring to one mountain, are used in the Old Testament with a very broad distinction of meaning; that the events occurring at the one locality are very different from those at the other, and indeed that the narrative can be understood only by supposing a mountain with two such summits as those of Sufsafeh and Jebel Mousa.

1. First of all, Horeb alone is called "the mount of God." Moses tending the flock "came to the mountain of God, even to Horeb" (Ex. iii. 1). Elijah came unto "Horeb the mount of God" (1 Kings xix. 8). This phrase, so emphatic, and indicating a special sanctity, is never conjoined with Sinai. It occurs frequently in Exodus, and is to be referred to Horeb, not only because of its conjunction with it in the instances cited, but also because Sinai is not yet mentioned. Thus it is said, "Aaron met Moses at the mount of God" (Ex. iv. 27). Let the reader remember, that when addressed from the burning bush, Moses had exhibited a sinful reluctance in accepting the office to which Jehovah was now so solemnly calling him. He was accordingly addressed in the language of rebuke and encouragement: "The anger of the Lord was kindled against Moses, and he said, Is not Aaron the Levite thy brother? I know that he can speak well, and also behold he came forth to meet thee, and when he seeth thee he will be glad in his heart." Aaron is thus already on his way and arrives at Horeb, there meeting Moses, who has returned from Jethro in Midian. It was fitting that beneath the shadow of the

sacred mount, the future high priest should learn for the first time the prominent part assigned to him in the great enterprise, and that there, under the overshadowing presence of Jehovah, the brothers should hold free and earnest conference on its wonderful character and issues. Then with assured heart they return to Egypt, and demand from its proud monarch that he should let their brethren go. Again, we read that "Jethro came unto Moses into the wilderness, where he encamped at the *mount of God* (Ex. xviii. 5). This also is Horeb, for not yet is Mount Sinai named.

Still further, we read that Moses went up into the mount of God (Ex. xxiv. 13). At first sight it may seem that this was Mount Sinai, as Moses is now going there to receive the tables of the Law. But here also the reference is to Horeb, and the whole description of the ascent answers well to the localities as we have viewed them. Jebel Mousa, the top of the mount, is reached by climbing the eastern steep of Sufsafeh; that is to say, Moses required to pass into Horeb on his way to the scene of fellowship with Jehovah. And after he has gone into the mount of God, he receives a summons which proves that his destination, Mount Sinai, was farther on and higher up: "The glory of the Lord abode on mount Sinai, and the cloud covered it six days: and the seventh day he called unto Moses out of the midst of the cloud. And the sight of the glory of the Lord was like devouring fire on the top of the mount in the eyes of the children of Israel. And Moses went into the midst of the cloud." Inasmuch as he had already crossed the barrier into "the mount of God," this fresh summons confirms the distinction contended for, showing the whole passage to be well illustrated by the present features of the mountain and the plain.

2. Let us now notice how the expression Mount Sinai is introduced into the narrative. We do not read of it until the 19th chapter of Exodus, which is very strange, if the writer has meant it all along. Its abrupt introduction in the 11th verse of that chapter seems to indicate a difference from the usual locality hitherto named as Horeb, "the mount of God," or simply "the mount;" and the repetition of it afterwards confirms this. We read in the 11th verse, "Be ready against the third day, for, the third day, the Lord will come down in the sight of all the people upon *mount Sinai*." The writer resumes the usual expression—the mount—in the subsequent verses; but when again speaking of the descent of Jehovah, he reverts to the expression, "and the Lord came down on mount Sinai, the top of the mount" (ver. 18. 20). Speaking of a summit only once before referred to, namely, that of Jebel Mousa, his language in this passage is most precise. I may remark, too, that we can now understand how the people were standing at the barrier near "the mount," although "the smoke on Sinai ascended as the smoke of a furnace."

3. Look also at the answer of Moses to Jehovah, when summoned to *Sinai* to warn the people not to come near the Lord. Reference has been already made to the warning itself, as explained by this theory; and now let us notice its bearing on the *answer* returned by Moses. "Moses said to the Lord, The people cannot come up to mount Sinai: for thou chargedst us, saying, Set bounds about *the mount*, and sanctify it" (verse 23). The meaning surely is not that the mount (Horeb) was

safe because guarded by its own barrier (for that is plain enough), but that *Mount Sinai*, where Jehovah now had descended, was likewise guarded by that same barrier, inasmuch as it could only be reached by Horeb.

VI. But now let us consider the events that happened respectively at Horeb and Sinai, and the distinction between them will more convincingly appear. The usual opinion is, that the same events are represented as taking place at either, and that the historian seems indifferent which name occurs in his narrative. From the following three considerations the reader will judge of the difference :—

(*a*.) The Israelites are represented as in the immediate presence of God at Horeb alone. " Thou stoodest before the Lord thy God in Horeb ;" " Ye came near, and stood under the mountain" (Deut. iv. 10, 11). " The Lord spake to you in Horeb out of the midst of the fire;" " The Lord our God made a covenant with us in Horeb;" " The Lord talked with you face to face in the mount, out of the midst of the fire" (Deut. v. 2, 4). But there is no passage that indicates such a nearness on their part to the Divine presence on Mount Sinai. This is rather a place where only Moses is said to be near God, having been invariably summoned to Sinai, " the top of the mount."

(*b*.) Still further, the narrative invariably represents the direct address of Jehovah to the people as from Horeb, not from Sinai. The passages already quoted indicate not only the near presence of Jehovah to the people, but his direct address to them. In the fourth and fifth chapters of Deuteronomy, Moses seeks with impassioned earnestness to impress on their minds the amazing truth that God himself had spoken to them, declaring his Covenant. This to him was the cardinal fact in their history. "Did ever people," he asks, "hear the voice of God speaking out of the midst of the fire, as thou hast heard, and live?" In such chapters Horeb alone is named. We shall search in vain for a single passage in which they are said to be directly addressed from Sinai. All the commandments given there are said to be brought to the Israelites through the *mediation* of Moses. Thus, "all the children of Israel came nigh, and he gave them in commandment all that the Lord had spoken with him on mount Sinai" (Ex. xxxiv. 32; Lev. vii. 38; xxv. 1; and xxvi. 46). The book of Leviticus closes with the statement: "These are the commandments, which the Lord commanded Moses, for the children of Israel in mount Sinai."

(*c.*) Again, Jehovah is said to have made the *Covenant* with the people at Horeb alone; on the other hand, what are called *statutes, judgments,* are represented invariably as given from Sinai. The distinction is important.

The following passages (taken as a specimen) will show the care with which the sacred writer restricts the emphatic epithet—"the Covenant"—to the Ten Commandments alone.

"God wrote on the tables the words of the covenant, the ten commandments" (Ex. xxxiv. 28). "He declared to you the covenant which he commanded you to perform, even the ten commandments" (Deut. iv. 13). "The Lord made a covenant with us in Horeb," and thereafter he rehearses the Ten Commandments, and adds, "These words the Lord spake, and added no more, and he wrote them on two tables of stone and delivered them to me," etc. These tables were in consequence called "the tables of the covenant" (Ex. xxxii. 15 ; Deut. ix. 11). The Ark that contained them was "the ark of the covenant" (Ex. xxv. 16-23 ; Numb. x. 33 ; Deut. xxxi. 25).

It is not enough to say, that the Decalogue was so characterized because of its special importance, but the phrase may be also applied to other precepts in a more general way. There is no proof of any wider application of this word in the Pentateuch as a covenant of *Jehovah with the people*. In the 4th chapter of Deuteronomy, after speaking of "the covenant, the ten commandments," Moses adds, "The Lord commanded *me* to teach you *statutes* and *judgments*," etc. The very same distinction is observed in the next chapter after the rehearsal of the Decalogue, called in the 2d verse "the covenant of Horeb." "Stand thou here by me, and I will speak unto thee all the *commandments*, and the *statutes*, and the *judgments*, which thou shalt teach them, that they may do them in the land which I give them to possess it" (Deut. v. 31). This at once refers us to Exod. xxi. 1, where Moses received "the judgments" that follow, having "drawn near to the thick darkness where God was." True also to this distinction is the language of Exodus xxiv., descriptive of the solemn assent of the people to the covenant. "Moses came and told the people all the *words* of the Lord, and the *judgments;*" that is, he repeated the Ten Commandments, emphatically called *the words of God*,[1] because uttered by his voice

---

[1] Such a distinction is clearly maintained in the original : "He wrote the

and distinctly audible. He also informed them of "the judgments" (Ex. xxi. 1). "Moses," it is added, "wrote *all the words* of the Lord." It is not said that he now wrote "the judgments;" and the book thus containing the precepts of the Decalogue alone, is called the *book of the covenant*, which he reads again in the audience of the people. They solemnly pledged their acquiescence and obedience, and the blood then sprinkled on them was called "the blood of the covenant." It is not necessary to multiply proof that "the covenant" of God with the Israelites is an expression applied to the Decalogue alone.[1] And indeed it lay in the nature of the case. For the people were not *direct* parties at any other precepts given, and did not hear these as "the words" of God.

Now, from Horeb alone is "the covenant" said to be given, as the passages frequently quoted show. Those, again, referring to Sinai are in the following strain: "These are the statutes, and judgments, and laws, which the Lord made between him and the children of Israel, in mount Sinai by the hand of Moses." "These are the commandments which the Lord commanded Moses for the children of Israel in mount Sinai" (Lev. xxvi. 46; xxvii. 34).

The two names then are not used indiscriminately, inasmuch as the events connected with them are widely different. The truth is, that which was permanent and universal in the Jewish dispensation was enjoined from

words of the covenant—the *Ten Words*." "He declared to you his Covenant which he commanded you to perform—the *Ten Words*." "He wrote on the Tables, according to the first writing, the *Ten Words*" (Ex. xxxiv. 18; Deut. iv. 13, and xvi. 4). The other judgments and commandments are never so named.

[1] The Covenant mentioned in Deut. xxix. 1, is one between *Moses* and *the people*,—an expression never applied to the Decalogue.

Horeb, that which was limited and fleeting was given from Sinai. The Commandments of Sinai have passed away, the Covenant of Horeb endures and ever will. For the Gospel enshrines that Covenant, surrounding it with higher sanctions, and stimulating obedience to it by more persuasive motives. From Sinai, Jehovah spoke as the King of Israel; from Horeb he spoke as the Lawgiver of the universe. And thus as being the scene of the *highest* Divine manifestation, Horeb was fitly characterized by the distinctive appellation---the Mount of God.

VII. Let us glance at a few other passages proving the correctness of the locality as now exhibited, and the precision in the language of the sacred writer. "Thou shalt smite the rock in Horeb, and there shall come water out of it that the people may drink" (Ex. xvii. 6). Now Sufsafeh fronts the *north*, the direction from which the people were then advancing. Also, as overlooking the plain where they are gathered, it suits the following references to Horeb: "They made a calf at Horeb" (Deut. ix. 8 ; Ps. cvi. 19). The tables of the Law received on Sinai are "put into the ark at *Horeb*" (1 Kings viii. 9 ; 2 Chron. v. 10). Again, we read that "the people stripped themselves of their garments for the tabernacle by the Mount Horeb" (Ex. xxxiii. 6). Not one of these events are anywhere represented as taking place at Sinai, the reason of which we can see at once if this locality be Jebel Mousa, the summit comparatively remote from the scene of revelry and the plain of the encampment.

I have only to add that in the lapse of time the name Horeb was dropped, so that in the New Testament and in Josephus, Sinai alone is used. The name of the highest summit thus came to be applied (as is often the case) to the whole mountain.

VIII. There is yet another incident in the narrative which receives here a fitting illustration. We read of a stream which descended out of "the mount" (Horeb); and so, in the centre of the mass of Sufsafeh there is a rugged gorge deeply worn by the action of a water-torrent descending to the plain. There are no springs in the whole peninsula comparable to those of this mountain. It is here that the Arabs resort in the scorching heats of the summer, when the supply is plentiful and unfailing, while most of the other sources are dried up. The deep lengthened depression between Sufsafeh and Jebel Mousa, as already remarked, is an immense reservoir, which, finding its natural outlet in the gorge referred to, goes right down into the plain, and so corresponds to "the stream descending out of the mount." A streamlet is seen there now all the way to the base, forming in some places pools from two to three feet in depth. It is small as compared with what it has once been. This is accounted for partly from the fact that the Convent has drawn off its supply (which is very abundant) from the reservoir above; and as you ascend from the Convent to Jebel Mousa you come to a little pool of delightful water (most grateful in the toil of the ascent), which marks the course by which it has been led off for the use of the monks. There is no other mountain suggested—not Serbal, or Jebel Katherin, or Jebel Monehah—where the stream comes so directly to the plain as to answer the language of the narrative. There is none, moreover, so likely to yield that copious supply which the Israelites enjoyed. Josephus mentions that among the phenomena attendant on the giving of the Law were violent tempests of rain, and this indeed might be inferred from the phenomena of the Scripture narrative. This would necessarily increase the supply during their stay, and swell the stream into which Moses cast the powdered ashes of the golden calf, and from which thereafter he made the people to drink.

Such, then, is the result of our examination. The discussion has been lengthened because it was necessary to call attention to several statements of the narrative which, I believe, have been generally overlooked or misapprehended. The aim has been to show, that as on the mount of the Law there were two summits, each the scene of a separate Divine manifestation, so the pilgrim thither may say of Jebel Mousa with more than usual confidence in such cases, "This is Mount Sinai;" and looking at the overhanging cliff of Sufsafeh, "This is Horeb, the mount of God." And inasmuch as legend-writers cannot mould the features of a mountain and plain which they have never visited, so as to make them suit the emanations of their fancy, the close agreement between the locality and the description of the events by the writer of the Pentateuch leads to the conclusion that the scene was drawn by Moses as an eye-witness, and provokes our contempt at the poor legend-theory of Bishop Colenso.

I have not endeavoured, in the discussion of the localities in the mountain, to fix the place to which "the elders went up," because I believe the language of the narrative forbids the idea that they were in the mount at all. The common opinion on this subject has no doubt been suggested by the language of the summons: "And he said to Moses, Come up to the Lord, thou and Aaron, Nadab and Abihu, and seventy of the elders of Israel" (Ex. xxiv. 1). "Then," it is said, "went up Moses and Aaron, Nadab and Abihu, and seventy of the elders of Israel" (verse 9). But to this has been added in the imagination of many, "into the mount," an expression which is not in the narrative, and is inadmissible. For the same phraseology is applied to the movement of the people: "When the trumpet soundeth long they shall *come up* to the mount... to meet with God" (Ex. xix. 13, 17). In so far as the language is concerned we are only to infer that the elders made a similar advance, *i.e.*, to the foot of the mount; and the following considerations confirm this view of their position :—

1. The language of the summons to the elders when fully read: "And he said to Moses, Come up unto the Lord, thou and Aaron, Nadab and Abihu, and seventy of the elders of Israel, and worship you *afar off*. And Moses alone shall come near the Lord, but they shall not come nigh" (Ex. xxiv. 1, 2). None therefore were to cross the barrier at the base, which consecrated the entire mount to the presence of Jehovah.

2. The language addressed to Moses when with the elders in the position assigned them: "The Lord said unto Moses, Come up to me into the mount, and be there;" "Moses went into the mount of God" (Ex. xxiv. 12, 13). Hitherto, therefore, all were outside the barrier, and there the elders were to remain, while Moses and his minister Joshua went into the mount.

3. The people have access to Aaron and the elders in

the absence of Moses, and under their superintendence construct the golden calf. Moses said to the elders as he left them, "Tarry ye here for us, until we come again to you; and behold Aaron and Hur are with you; if any man have any matter to do, let him come to them." During his long absence the people were weary of waiting; and we are told "They gathered themselves together unto Aaron, and said unto him, Up, make us gods which shall go before us, for as for this Moses, the man that brought us up out of the land of Egypt, we wot not what is become of him" (Ex. xxxii. 1). Aaron, then, could not have been in the mount, for the people could not have crossed the barrier seeking for him there, as the awful sanctions relating to it were not removed, and the avenging lightnings were ready to "break forth" upon the transgressor. Aaron was at the foot of Horeb, where the golden calf was afterwards made, and the elders were there with him. In thus fixing their position we have a locality much more in keeping with the meaning and purpose of this approach to Jehovah. They went from their encampment to this fellowship as representatives of the people, and thus the position most appropriate for them was that where the people had heard the words of the Covenant, now to be solemnly ratified through the partaking of the covenant meal.

For those who believe in the historical character of the Pentateuch, and the veracity of its description of the stupendous events connected with the giving of the Law, the question, as to which among those rugged mountains of Arabia is really Mount Sinai, will always offer the deepest interest. It is in vain to argue down this investigation into the holy places of Scripture. We are prompted to such inquiries by the profoundest instincts and holiest associations of our nature. If the events that so stir our awe and wonder had transpired in cloud-land or in some planet of the distant universe, then this interest and speculation might cease. But as they did really take place on this solid earth of ours, then in proportion as we are affected by them we are anxious to know the scene of their occurrence. The distinct knowledge of it makes the earth all the holier to us, while undoubtedly strengthening our impressions of Scripture truth.

To Bishop Colenso and his school, no doubt, all such investigations will seem profitless, if not ludicrous and contemptible. The whole affair is a legend!—with some kernel of fact, but the most of it is "such stuff as dreams are made of." He would admit, no doubt, that it refers to *some* event of *some* kind, among *some* people, in *some* age, and doubtless in *some* locality. But that locality could hardly be in his view anywhere in the present peninsula, "for is it not a place where no man dwelt, and no man passed through?" It might be anywhere; the hill Ramah in Palestine, the birthplace of Samuel (the author of the Pentateuch!!); or, if we like, we may imagine it somewhere among the mountains of Natal!

It is for those who are verily assured that the writer in the Pentateuch of the scenes at Sinai, was no dreamer, but spake of what he knew, and testified to what he had seen, that the preceding discussion has been entered on, which would fix the locality of their occurrence, whose unchanged features remain to this day.

Read in the light of the conclusions to which we have

come, the following brief summary of events, in the order of the narrative, will attest the careful precision of that writer's language.

At the summons of the trumpet, the people move from their encampment to the barrier, and stand "at the nether part of the mount." "And the Lord came down on mount Sinai, on the top of the mount, and the Lord called Moses to the top of the mount, and Moses went up." The charge being once more given that the people respect the barrier, the Divine presence moves forward from the summit of Sinai to that of Horeb, and, "face to face" with them, delivers "the Ten Words." "The Lord our God made a covenant with us at Horeb." At the close of the proclamation, there followed "the thunderings and the lightnings, and the noise of the trumpet; and the people removed, and stood afar off." Other detailed injunctions are yet to be given before the Divine presence retires, which refer to the application of the grand precepts thus announced to the institutions and customs of their social life. The terrified people implore Moses to go near and listen on their behalf : "And Moses drew near to the darkness where God was," and received "the judgments which he was to set before them." Returning to the encampment, "he told the people all the words of the Lord, and all the judgments ; and he wrote all the *words* of the Lord," *i.e.*, the Decalogue. Having built an altar of sacrifice under the mount, he sprinkled on it "half of the blood ;" the other half he "put in basins." "And he took the book of the covenant, and read in the audience of the people : and they said, All that the Lord hath said will we do, and be obedient. And Moses took the blood, and sprinkled it on the people, and said,

Behold the blood of the covenant, which the Lord hath made with you concerning all these words." Along with Aaron and the elders he goes up to the foot of the mount to partake of the Covenant meal. "And the Lord said unto Moses, Come up to me unto the mount. And Moses rose up, and his minister Joshua, and (crossing the barrier) went unto the mount of God" (Horeb). The Divine presence is back on Mount Sinai, and thither on the seventh day, he receives a further summons to come. "The glory of the Lord abode on mount Sinai, and on the seventh day he called unto Moses out of the midst of the cloud. And Moses went into the midst of the cloud." The people, tired at his absence, come to Aaron, who, with the elders, is tarrying at the barrier, as Moses had enjoined. Their request is, "Up, make us gods, which shall go before us." So "they made a calf at Horeb." Moses, in his descent by the valley, hears their shouts, but only on turning round at the base can he see what has been done. "He cast the tables out of his hands, and brake them beneath the mount;" and afterwards compels them to drink of the burnt ashes of the idol "cast into the stream that descended out of the mount." "He returned unto the Lord," and implores forgiveness for the great sin. In token of their penitence "the children of Israel stripped themselves of their ornaments by the Mount of Horeb." "And Moses took the Tabernacle, and removed it without the camp, afar off from the camp." Afterwards he is commanded to come up to Mount Sinai, the top of the mount, and there receive "the tables of stone, like unto the first." These were carried down to be deposited in the Ark of the Tabernacle, and consequently are said "to be put in at Horeb."

I know not how the language of the Old Testament narrative could be more exact than it is, or where it is possible to find a locality in more thorough agreement in all its details.

Our party remained at Sinai four days—a time which deepened the impressions of awe and wonder with which the spot was first viewed. The nights were cold, especially the last, and in the morning the shivering Dragoman entered the tent to declare that there was "skin on the water,"—handing in for our inspection a large piece of ice. But there rose over the scene which we were this day to leave, a day of wonderful beauty, calm and cloudless, "the body of heaven in its clearness." By a simultaneous discharge of fire-arms, we tried to elicit once more the deep prolonged reverberations among the hills. A solitary monk looked out for a moment from the battlements of the convent, which more than ever seemed the image of deep eternal repose. We moved away into the crescent of Wady Sheikh, paused at its first turning to take a last lingering look of the bold outstanding cliffs, and then with many feelings bade our farewell to Sinai.

CHAPTER VIII.

WILDERNESS OF THE WANDERINGS.

I HAVE already ventured to suggest that the broad valley of the Wady Sheikh may have been the scene of David's battle with the Amalekites, the success of which is celebrated in the 68th Psalm. "He came upon them eating and drinking, and dancing, because of all the great spoil that they had taken" (1 Sam. xxx. 16). This same valley is used for the annual conference and festival of their descendants at this day. The victory was thus won under the shadow of Sinai, "where God was terrible from his holy place," "led captivity captive," and proved himself "a father of the fatherless, and judge of the widow, in his holy habitation." In this wady is the tomb of Sheikh Saleh, said to have been a companion of Mohammed, and whose memory the Towarah specially venerate.

The Israelites on leaving Sinai moved down this valley to the Wilderness of Paran, where, after three days' journey, "the Cloud rested" (Numb. x. 12, 33). Hazeroth was one of their encampments, and its name has been recognised in the present Huderah. They had come to it from Kibroth-hattaavah, "the graves of lust" (Dr. Stewart believes that this place also may be identified), where the quails were sent. Professor Stanley tells us that "when near Wady Huderah, both on the morning and evening of our encampment, the sky was literally darkened by the flight of innumerable birds, which proved to be the same large red-legged cranes, three feet high, with black and white wings, measuring seven feet from tip to tip, which we had seen in like numbers at the first cataract of the Nile." From Hazeroth they seem again to have pitched their tents in the Wilderness of Paran (Numb. xii. 16). They then journeyed northwards by this same wilderness up to Kadesh, on the south frontier of Palestine. It was thus a tract of very large extent, receiving its name probably from Paran, the head-quarters of the Desert tribe. It is thus described by Moses in his address to the people: " When we departed from Horeb, we went through all that great and terrible wilderness which ye saw by the way of the mountain of the Amorites, as the Lord our God commanded us ; and we came to Kadesh-Barnea." Beyond the town or district of Kadesh lay the Wilderness of Zin, which bounded on the south the territory afterwards assigned to Judah. From Kadesh (or it may be travelling towards it), the spies were sent " who searched the land from the Wilderness of Zin," and passed upwards by Hebron into the heart of the country. After an absence of forty days they returned to Kadesh. Their report is given in the graphic language of the narrative : " We came unto the land whither thou sentest us, and surely it floweth with milk and honey ; and this is the fruit of it. Nevertheless the people be strong that dwell in the land, and the cities are walled, and very great : and moreover, we saw the children of Anak there. And we were in our own sight as grasshoppers, and so we were in their sight" (Numb. xiii. 27, 28, 33).

The people murmured at the tidings. The promises of Jehovah, the urgent persuasion of Moses, the entreaties of Joshua and Caleb, failed to urge their advance. At last the command was given, stern and inflexible, despite of their after penitence and tears, "Turn you, and get you into the wilderness, by the way of the Red Sea." I have endeavoured to show that the Gulf of Akabah is here referred to, and that it was in the south-eastern district of the peninsula, adjacent to Sinai, where the Israelites dwelt and wandered for thirty-eight years. The time was not lost, and indeed they entered the promised land as soon as they proved themselves fit to accomplish the mission intrusted to them. If we reflect on the matter for a little, we shall recognise the wisdom and love of the Keeper of Israel, who "led them by a right way to the city of habitation."

In many respects the Desert was a fit theatre for the training which that people required. The impressive grandeur of its scenery, of its naked alps standing out in strong contrast with the plains of Egypt, was fitted to brace up their long-enervated and sluggish disposition, to confirm solemn and elevating thought, and aid in the production of that stern intensity of soul, which afterwards marked their character, and which was essentially requisite for their holding fast the truth committed to them, that they might become the fit instruments of the world's renovation. It is clear from the language of Moses in his review of their journey, and also from the allusions in the Psalms, that they really profited in their sojourn by all this external grandeur, this physical terror, as well as moral awe, and that they transmitted the most impressive memories of it to their children. No traveller can wonder that it should be so. It is impossible to pass such scenes unheeded; they confront you, and challenge attention most remarkably. And the pillar of cloud hovering over the camp, the manna scattered around them every morning, and the appalling phenomena of Sinai, would tend to make the Israelites connect these aspects of the great and terrible wilderness with the greatness and majesty of Him who was so strangely leading them. And thus in the Desert may have been the first kindlings of that earnest glance into the mingled grandeur and beauty of the material universe, which their inspired seers afterwards so strikingly exhibited, and here may well have been nourished that adoring wonder whose holy utterances in their sublime Psalms render them still the chosen language of Christian worship.

The Desert was clearly of advantage for their further training, as the sole region left comparatively free from the usages and scenes of heathenism. How much harder must the discipline have been had their route lain through countries thickly peopled, and strewn with temples of Pagan worship in its full activity! How much harder to establish in such circumstances the pure religion which they were to guard for the world?

In the deep recesses of the Wilderness of Sinai this could best be done. No heathen temple is there seen in the background of the tabernacle; no idolatrous orgies of other tribes invade the sublime stillness of the encampment. The smoke from their own altar alone is seen ascending, at which their own priests are ministering, and the divinely-appointed sacrifices are being slain; while ever and again, as they move on their circuitous and seemingly endless journey, the deep echoes of the Desert prolong their thrilling shout, "Rise, Lord, let thine enemies be scattered, and let them that hate thee flee before thee."

The privations also which they experienced were needful for them. These grim and scorching wastes made little provision for the lusts of the flesh. The plenty of Goshen was not here, nor the river of Egypt. "For thirst and hunger their soul often fainted in them." Such discipline was healthful alike for their physical and moral nature. After settling down amid the abundance of the goodly land, even with the apparently stronger motive of possession and property to sustain them, they often succumbed to the enemies that had fallen before them after the rough ordeal of their wanderings. The present inhabitants of the Desert are a sinewy, courageous, and much enduring race.

Again, the Israelites had time in their desert sojourn to prepare for the inevitable conflicts before them. Most cowardly and abject was the spirit displayed as they emerged from the bondage of Egypt. They were not led by the nearer way of the Philistines, "lest they should see war;" they were saved at the Red Sea without requiring to lift their hand against the enemy. But in future their own energy must be conjoined with the miraculous help of Heaven, and at the close of their wanderings it was brought more and more prominently into action. During the forty years when they dwelt unmolested, they were in training for the inevitable struggles of the future.

When the due time arrived for taking possession of their inheritance, the cowardly slaves of Egypt had become an army of heroes; they went in like lions among the fierce idolaters of Canaan. Courage, intensity, and steadfast endurance have been wrought into the character of that people, and continue in one form or other to the present day. Their fiery valour in battle became conspicuous; they were the fiercest enemy the Romans ever encountered; their inextinguishable endurance is still the wonder of the world. As for the religious observances, which at first they felt so grievous—greatly preferring idolatry and "the flesh-pots of Egypt"—they have learned to cling to them with unparalleled tenacity, through the most barbarous oppressions and martyrdoms that ever fell to the lot of any nation.

Finally, the *miracles* that marked this stage of their history were of vast importance for their moral and religious advancement.

The theory which some in these days would have us believe is, that the miracles of Scripture were the offspring and embodiment of the religious opinions of their age. An event, says the writer in the *Essays and Reviews*, was settled to be "a miracle in consequence of a *previous* belief in divine goodness and power;" "the ideas of it depended on prepossessions *previous* to the event;" "belief in divine interposition depended on what was previously admitted respecting the divine attributes." The same idea has been confidently asserted in the more recent work of M. Renan. "All observation teaches us that miracles occur only in the age and country where they are believed in, and before the people disposed to believe in them."[1] If such a theory had been propounded to account for the legends of the middle ages, there might have been little to object, inas

---

[1] *Vie de Jésus.* Introduction, p. 50.

much as the spiritual ideas of Revelation had then become the creed of the nations. But the theory is one in utter variance with the incidents of the Scripture narrative and with the conclusion we are compelled to draw respecting the moral and religious condition of the Israelites as they emerged from the idolatries of Egypt. Is it a fact that at *that* time they possessed ideas of the character of Jehovah, such as answered to and were capable of "inventing" the miracles of their history? Did that timid despairing crowd on the shore of the Red Sea know that their Protector had supreme power over sea and land? They were *taught* this rather by the miracle that followed, and on the opposite shore, were as "men that dreamed." In the Wilderness of Sinai had they lofty spiritual conceptions of their Lawgiver? "*They made a calf at Horeb.*" Alas! *here* was the outcome and embodiment of their "ideas and preconceptions:" *this* they were capable of inventing; the splendid miracles of the Exodus never! In fact, so far were they from being imbued with the religious views and feelings which the theory in question assumes, that they obstinately refused to entertain them even when presented. They were "a stiff-necked and rebellious people;" and because they persisted in their sensualism, darkness, and unbelief, they were visited by the most alarming judgments, and "the carcases of a whole generation fell in the wilderness."

The miracles of their history, instead of being the effect, were the *origin* of the lofty spiritual ideas which afterwards distinguished the creed of the nation. They not only proved the doctrine, but embodied and proclaimed it, enforcing it sometimes as with thunder and flame upon hearts which no mere didactic utterances could have convinced. We ignore the highest purpose of such phenomena when this is forgotten ; when we deal with them merely as physical events, and discuss them exclusively in relation to physical laws. Their highest test must be the *moral* laws of the universe, for they had their origin in the moral emergency of the world, and aimed to inculcate moral and spiritual truth. They " made known " Jehovah to the Israelites, not only as a God of power, but as a God of holiness, justice, goodness, and truth. And if the purpose of the universe be after all a *moral* one,—the advancement in truth, purity, and love, of the creature whom God has made in his image, then the miracles of Scripture can be shown to be in harmony with its mightiest force and highest law. By them that nation, who, like others, were sinking into idolatry and spiritual death, were " brought out of darkness into marvellous light," and made to learn for themselves and preach to the world the unity and spirituality of the Infinite One. Their prophets and teachers continually go back on the miracles of the Exodus for the illustration and enforcement of their spiritual conceptions. It was *their* memory especially that kindled the devotion of the Psalmist ; interpreted for him the " open secret" of nature ; filled heaven and earth with a holy joyous solemnity, and made him recognise the providence of a living God among the affairs of men. Thus there issued from his rapt soul tones of the " eternal melodies" which can never cease, but will pass on with thousandfold symphony from the devout hearts of all generations to the end of time.

The purpose of their sojourn in the Wilderness being accomplished, and a new generation having risen with something of the character requisite for the task before them, they again moved northwards to take possession of Canaan. As one of their last encampments was Eziongeber, we are to infer that this time they went up the valley of the Arabah. Passing on till they came to the Wilderness of Zin, they once more encamped at Kadesh on its frontier. That it was the same Kadesh is evident. It is situated on the borders of Edom (Numb. xx. 16), which agrees with the reference to Seir in Deut. i. 44; Hormah was the place of their defeat the first time, and at the second time of their victory (Numb. xxi. 3). Denied a passage through the territory of Edom, they were obliged to retrace their steps along the Arabah, " the plain from Elath and Eziongeber" (Deut. ii. 8), until they compassed Edom, and then entered Palestine.

The district where they had wandered for thirty-eight years was bounded by the mountains Sinai, Paran, and Seir.[1] Throughout, they had experienced miraculous manifestations of the Divine favour and guardianship, the manna and the pillar of fire continuing to the close. In this fact, I submit, lies the true explanation of the language of Moses in the blessing wherewith he blessed the children of Israel before his death. "And he said, The Lord came from Sinai, and rose up from Seir unto them: he shined forth from Mount Paran (Serbal), and he came with ten thousands of his saints; from his right hand went a fiery law (pillar of fire) for them, yea, he loved the people" (Deut. xxxiii. 2).

It was not our good fortune to travel in any part of this northern route, as the majority of our party had resolved before starting to return from Sinai to Cairo.

---

[1] Kadesh adjoined Seir (Deut. i. 44, ii. 4; Numb. xx. 16).

On the incidents of our return I shall not dwell. We visited the wonderful ruins of Surabit el Khadem, where are remains of pillars and temples of the Egyptian type. It is the centre of a large district where quarries have been excavated, in which multitudes must have worked: a fact from which inferences of importance have been already drawn. Some hours distant was the tented village of our Sheikh, and he pressed earnestly and courteously that we should dine with him. Accepting the invitation, we passed through a district which appeared full of the slag and debris of extensive smelting operations, and where are two large isolated rocks shaped like the Sphinx and Pyramid of Gizeh. Our Dragoman accompanying us as interpreter, mentioned that the Arabs do not like to hear their children too highly praised or much looked at. They dread the evil eye. Ask how many children they have, you cannot depend, it seems, on the answer. The Sheikh, in reply to this inquiry, mentioned that he had a family of two, whereas Mahmoud asserted that he had four. As we journeyed onwards we saw the footsteps of a beast of prey, which, by Mahmoud's account, had lately passed. About midday, on turning an abrupt spur of a grand mountain, we found ourselves at the village. Some came out to meet us, headed by Nassar and his little boy, into whose hands he put the rein of the leading camel, the rest following in single file. One party were busy skinning a sheep which seemed hardly to have expired. We pulled up at the largest tent of the row, and with the help of our saddle-cushions, a comfortable divan was prepared, so that we were soon solaced with the pipe and coffee. The Sheikh, with one or two villagers, was in the tent; the others, old and young, squatted around the door.

"The Towarah Arabs are very good," we said, "and have taken good care of us and our baggage." The Sheikh acknowledged the compliment, spoke of their liking for English travellers, and added, that we might leave plenty of money in Wady Sheikh one year, and come back to find it all safe the next!

"Why do you not grow more corn and trees in the Desert?" we asked. "We do as our fathers; we get corn from Cairo, and take charcoal there; we like this best." "But if you go on in this way, the trees of the Desert will be all cut down; what will come of you then?" "God will take care of that."

Their religious ideas seemed very few and indistinct. Even Baomi and Mahmoud expressed their pity on this subject. "These Bedawy," they would say, "know nothing; never pray!" a statement true as far as we could see, with the one exception at the tomb of Sheikh Saleh, on our leaving Sinai.

As we were talking in the tent, a poor African slave, his wrinkled skin and haggard features telling of sickness and age, crawled into the circle. "Give me," he said, "medicine to make me young. I want to work and get food." We told him we had no medicines that could make him young. "Did he fear to die?" "No." "How?" we asked. "Why, after death me like dog (a poor starved dog was near, gnawing a bone that had been tossed to it); no father, no mother, no dress, all over." We tried to convey, by what images and words we best could, some idea of a Divine friend in the skies, who loved the poor and pitied the sorrowful and the helpless. "Good," he said, "very good," and shrugging his shoulders, resigned himself to his fate.

Here also, and at other opportunities, we endeavoured to convey some religious ideas to the Arabs, and awaken a desire for instruction, Baomi and Mahmoud being our interpreters. On one occasion the Sheikh got quite interested in the matter; he professed a great anxiety to have his people taught to read. I asked, "Would you be kind to a teacher sent to you?" "How," he inquired in reply, "could we have a teacher, and we so poor?" "But if the kind English would send one to you free, would you treat him well?" "Yes," he said, "and I will give him eight piastres (about 1s. 6d. !) ; we will take care of him, he shall live with us, and if he cannot sit in our tents, we will put him on our *heads!*" It is sad to think that the interests of a whole race, and occupying a region of the world marked by *such* associations, should have been so long utterly neglected. In respect of this, what can be said of the Convent of Sinai? "It is hard," says Canon Stanley, "to recall another institution with such opportunities so signally wasted. It is a colony of Christian pastors planted among heathens, who wait on them for their daily bread, and for their rain from heaven; and hardly a spark of civilisation or of Christianity, as far as history records, has been imparted to a single tribe or family in that wide wilderness. It is a colony of Greeks, of Europeans, of ecclesiastics, in one of the most interesting and most sacred regions of the earth, and hardly a fact from the time of their first foundation to the present time has been contributed by them to the geography, the geology, or the history of a country, which in all its aspects has been submitted to their investigation for thirteen centuries." The monks there are doing no good, as far as one could judge, to themselves or others. Such insipid, blank, wasted faces! They show in the charnel-house the skulls of their brethren gathered for the last thousand years: but when you think of the neglected barbarism and ignorance of the Arabs outside, you are tempted to wonder whether there is much difference between the skulls of the dead and the skulls of the living. The Arabs have had no chance of civilisation and Christianity,—the grand experiment has yet to be tried. May it be soon!

On Thursday evening the 24th March, we hailed the oasis of Ayoun Mousa. The sunset flooded the whole scene with rich and varied colouring, steeping the Egyptian hills in deep blue, covering with a bright-yellow the desert expanse, while a dark rich purple mantled the uplands of the Tih. Next morning we rode our camels to the shore, where a boat was waiting to convey us across the Gulf.

We now, not without regret, took farewell of the Desert life, of the camels, and our Arab escort, who had been throughout civil, attentive, and honest. Arriving at Suez, one of our party talked to Baomi about the loss of the tent on our outset, and, affirming that we must make some inquiry about the fact on reaching Cairo, appealed to him once more to say whether the story was true. "Look here," said the fellow with emphatic gesture, "I not say two word, I say one word, it was one *lie*." A terrible quarrel which he had with Mahmoud two days before may have helped this confession. Subsequent examination in Cairo confirmed our conviction that a trick which might have had serious consequences had been played us, and although Mahmoud, after asking forgiveness, and kissing our hands all round, received the full sum bargained for, we decided, to his great disappointment, to withhold from him a certificate. Poor Mahmoud! he never dreamt of such an investigation, but made merry on the railway journey from Suez, often exclaiming, "All back gentle'em, and all sat'sfied!"

So our Desert tour was ended. We felt that there was much cause for thankfulness in the retrospect; for without accident, in the full enjoyment of health, our party had been permitted to gather instructive lessons of travel in the region which, next to Palestine, is the most sacred on earth, and which to the end of time will attract its pilgrims from the most distant lands. We had enjoyed the great privilege of reading the Bible narrative of the scenes of the Exodus, by the shore of the Red Sea, in "the great and terrible wilderness," and under the shadow of Horeb and of Sinai.

CHAPTER IX.

ALEXANDRIA TO JERUSALEM.

We arrived in Alexandria on the Saturday evening, and on Monday afternoon were steaming out of its harbour for Jaffa, *en route* for Jerusalem.

The night looked stormy, and we had a rough passage, against the consequences of which our experience of "the Ship of the Desert" in no way fortified us. The steamer tumbled about all next day and next night, and though opposite Jaffa on the second morning, it was doubtful whether we should be able to make the shore. When the ship's boat was lowered for the postmaster, a huge wave heaved it up nearly to the bulwarks, which made the alarmed Frenchman skip up the gangway again, double quick, somewhat to the amusement of the onlookers. Two large boats at last came alongside; our luggage being deposited, we toiled through the billows, and amid the cries and shouting of the oarsmen, managed to shoot the narrow entrance of a dangerous line of reefs, over which huge breakers went tumbling to the shore.

After visiting the so-called house of "Simon the tanner," we went out to the model farm of Dr. Philip, and were greatly struck with the productive capabilities of the soil. The Doctor pressed me to stay over the night, and accompany him next day to Jerusalem. Enforcing his request by the promise of a good horse, I consented, and my friends went on to Ramleh for the night.

From the elevated position of his mansion, a magnificent view was obtained of the plain of Sharon and the hills of Judah. I gazed long on the scene by sunset and moonlight, and shall not soon forget the mood of dreamy, wondering, grateful enjoyment which marked that first evening in the Holy Land.

The journey to Jerusalem usually takes about fourteen hours, travellers halting at Ramleh for the first night. It was one o'clock next day before we started, and by a desperate push the Doctor thought we might manage it in the six hours that were at our disposal. So off we went at a continuous canter across the plain; stopped for three minutes at Ramleh for a cup of coffee, and then away to the foot of the hills. We reached them about half-past four o'clock. So far we had kept our time well, but our pace afterwards was comparatively slow. The path was often in the dry bed of a mountain torrent, full of rocks and debris; but we seized every opportunity of pushing on rapidly. By and by the last rays of the sunset were dying away from the mountain tops, black clouds rose in the sky, and it was evident that we were to be shut out from the benefit of the much-needed moonlight. Lights were sparkling as we passed, in the village of the great Sheikh, who commands the hill-country. Two miles farther on was a part of the road where my companion had once before lost his way; after that, he thought we might get along easily enough, dark as it was. We reached and passed the spot, mounted the hill to the summit, and there were obliged to pull up. The Doctor exclaimed, "We have lost our way. Here is something like a pond or a lake, which I never saw before; that castle is too near us; we must go back and find the road." The attempt to do so ended in still further bewilderment. Our horses strangely got up on ledges of rock, and could hardly get down again. Peering through the darkness, we might sometimes see a grey speck, as if indicating a trace of the path, but it often turned out a rock or a dry bed of a mountain stream. There was nothing for it but to sit down and watch for the morning. It was very dark and "eerie," and the jackals howled around. At last the tramp of a horse was heard, and the Doctor hailed the rider. A ring of arms was heard in response, but it turned out to be a friend, the Jaffa postman, a fierce enough looking fellow, armed to the teeth. It was singular how his steed tripped along over the rough way, and under his guidance we got back to a tent for the refreshment of pilgrims, which we had long passed. A strange-looking company of Arabs and camel-drivers were huddled within the rude caravanserai, and we deemed it prudent to keep watch alternately, giving each the chance of two hours' sleep.

Next morning we passed leisurely on, and I must say that the aspect of the rough precipitous path for the after journey made me thankful that we had been compelled to pause.

About seven o'clock we came in sight of Jerusalem, a view which no pilgrim can ever forget! We entered by the Jaffa gate into the stir of the market-place, and were soon at our quarters in the Mediterranean Hotel.

After service in the Episcopalian Church (for it was Good-Friday) I set off with one of my friends for a view of the Kedron and the Mount of Olives. We entered a large gateway leading apparently in the right direction, and suddenly discovered that we were in the sacred enclosure of the Haram es Sheriff! We were recognised; soldiers, boys, and men shouted, gesticulated, cursed, and lifted up stones, which caused us to make a speedy retreat. At last we found St. Stephen's Gate, and there the valley of the Kedron! Gethsemane! the Mount of Olives! lay before us. While my companion went to the Mount of Olives to take a sketch of the city, I passed along the walls by the golden gateway, and round the south-east corner of the Haram. Turning in by the gate of the central valley, the visitor beholds the western wall of the ancient Temple, from which projects a fragment of one arch of the splendid bridge that formerly led from its courts to the upper city. Passing up, a low hum as of voices, rapidly muttering, fell on the ear; I knew that I was in the vicinity of "the Wailing-place." There were about a hundred Jews collected, for it was the afternoon of the day of preparation for their Sabbath, when they resort here in large numbers.

The bright-eyed boy came with book under his arm; the aged Jew tottered in, leaning on his staff. Some were with great rapidity reading their prayers seated, yet always swinging the body; others were standing repeating them at the Temple wall; some were calm, others as if overwhelmed with grief. The women were generally in groups, listening to one reading from the Scriptures or the Talmud, and all were weeping most bitterly.

Several of the more patriarchal worshippers would bury their head as much as possible in the rents of the wall, as if imploring,—now with a subdued voice, now with a wild cry,—an answer from some presence within. It seemed the despairing remonstrance and grief of those on whom "the door was shut;" while others were seen leaning their heads against the wall, "dumb, not opening their mouth," or as if in silent prayer. Altogether it was an affecting scene, however you might be disposed to question the sincerity of some, and one which every Christian must solemnly connect with the crime of the nation committed 1800 years ago.

In the evening we went to the Church of the Holy Sepulchre. No lights were here visible, save the candles carried by the monks in their procession round the different sacred localities of the building. At every such stage the procession paused, when a sermon was preached ; they then moved on to the next, uplifting the thrilling strains of the *Stabat Mater*. After a time the service became a weariness ; the bishop yawned, the monks shifted uneasily from one foot to the other ; the French officers giggled and whispered, and the most solemn-looking of the spectators were the Turkish guard, who, on these festivals especially, keep peace among the Christians. The scene became doubly wearisome to any who had no faith in the locality ; and such was my own position, with the strong arguments of Robinson and Fergusson in mind. Before the display was over, I left for my hotel, and, after the fatigue and want of rest the previous night, slept soundly.

It is not my intention to detain the reader here with an account of the so-called holy places in Jerusalem.

Almost every point of interest in the topography of the city has been the theme of endless discussion, in the perusal of which many a reader has exclaimed, "No one seems to know anything about the matter." Assuredly it is a remarkable circumstance that so much difficulty has been felt in settling the sacred localities, which the Jew first, and afterwards the Christian, might be expected faithfully to conserve. The city was never very large, and moreover was marked by strong natural features, which no amount of rubbish (the usual explanation attempted to account for the discrepancy between existing theories and present appearances of the city) has obliterated. Here is the Valley of Hinnom on the west, the Kedron or Valley of Jehoshaphat on the east; a central valley in the city, from Damascus gate down to Siloam; and one also from the present Herod's gate, bending away to the Kedron at the gate of St. Stephen. Hardly another city can be named, that is more strongly marked by its natural features; and—considering the language and allusions of the Bible, with the history of Josephus, who has devoted so many pages to its especial description—the difficulties and disputes that have arisen regarding its ancient features are very surprising. I will only say here, that a theory has been started, which, if found to be correct, accounts somewhat for the anomaly. Mr. Fergusson, some years ago, endeavoured to show that the Church of the Holy Sepulchre was originally on the eastern hill, and is identical with the building now known as the "Mosque of Omar." It was afterwards (eleventh century), he contends, shifted to the western hill where it now stands. If this be true, then it is probable that other localities on the eastern hill were shifted along with it; hence a later confused topography has been established. To recover the knowledge of the correct topography, we must, I apprehend, direct special attention to the ancient form and features of the hill on which the Temple stood. The important inquiry, I consider, is the following: Did the Temple stand on a separate hill, or was its site a continuation of the present eastern ridge? In other words, was the ground enclosed by the Haram es Sheriff a level plateau as now, or was it formerly divided by a deep ravine running across its breadth, i.e., running from the central valley of the city across to Kedron? Adopting this latter alternative there rises before us, I believe, a view of Jerusalem answering to the language of Scripture, and of Josephus, —the grand test for the correctness of any theory. We shall be enabled to understand the Jewish historian's description of the hills of the city, the site and size of the Temple and the difficulty of building it: we shall be able to fix precisely the meaning of Zion, with its two distinct applications in Scripture,—" the stronghold of Zion, which is the city of David," and "the holy hill of Zion," or " the mountain of the Lord's house." Light will also be thrown upon the Sepulchres of the Kings; and above all, on the holy places of Calvary and the Sepulchre. As the peculiar feature, then, in the topographical theory now to be submitted is the recognition of a ravine running through the present Haram es Sheriff (between the site of the " Mosque of Omar" and that of the ancient Temple), I may fitly conclude these introductory observations with a brief account of our visit to that area which now, as is well known, presents the appearance of an unbroken plateau.

On our return from a tour to Jericho, the Jordan, and the Convent of Marsaba, we found a note from the Consulate at our hotel, requesting to know how many of our party might wish to visit the Mosque of Omar. We all availed ourselves of the opportunity, by paying the entrance fee of £1. I was perhaps particularly glad of the facilities offered, having examined somewhat Mr. Fergusson's theory, which, if true, renders its Sakrah the most sacred on earth. While there were some difficulties I could not get over, the fact remained that the *architectural* argument had never been answered. I had spoken on the point to an authority on such matters, resident at the time in Jerusalem, and who had written on the topography; but all the reply I could get, was to the effect, that the said theory looked exceedingly plausible; that the inquiry was most able, etc.; that, in fact, there was no one whom he would not rather answer than Mr. Fergusson. The consequence of this was a strengthening of my persuasion that the theory might be true. We assembled at the Consul's house before six o'clock, then proceeded with a considerable party to visit that enclosure into which, for many hundred years, no Christian until lately had been permitted to enter—the few that ventured incurring a deadly risk. We were received at the north-west entrance by the Sheikh of the grand Mosque, and on passing within were surrounded by the guard appointed for our protection. The enclosed ground is an area of thirty-six acres, according to the measurement of Dr. Barclay. We passed down to the spacious elevated platform, which may be roughly estimated as a square of 500 feet, nearly in the centre of which rises the magnificent "Dome of the Rock." Arriving at the steps of this platform, we were requested to "take off our shoes;" and as none of our party had prepared himself with the usual slippers, the marble pavement felt very chill to the tread in the early morning. The Dome of the Rock is an *octagonal* building,—a fact which Mr. Fergusson contends is fatal to the idea of its having been originally built as a *mosque*. Some thirty years ago Mr. Catherwood succeeded in taking drawings of the interior, its pillars, arches, and other features of its architecture; the examination of which originated the theory referred to, that this was the original church built by Constantine over the sepulchre of Christ. As you enter, you see a massive rock, rising about five feet above the marble floor, and, according to Dr. Barclay, sixty-five feet long by fifty-five feet broad. It is enclosed by a railing, and over it is suspended a curtain of rich purple colour, while the light streams in from above through coloured windows. We went down into its inner cavity, a space about fifteen feet square, as measured by that explorer. Near the centre is a slab of marble, on which the Sheikh emphatically struck his foot, when its hollow sound distinctly indicated the existence of the large excavation below. This is the Bir Annah, or "Well of Souls," which however was found to contain no water when examined by Mr. Pierrotti. If this rock be indeed the Sepulchre, it is (though in the keeping of the Mohammedans) a satisfaction to see it left in austere simplicity, and free from the tawdry frippery and scandalous "pious frauds" with which the rival site on the western hill is so disagreeably associated.

We passed out of the building by the southern entrance, where, having got clear of the platform, we were allowed to resume the portion of dress so opposed to Oriental ideas of reverence, and proceeded to inspect the Mosque el Aksa. It is clearly a Mohammedan structure; and is correctly described by a pilgrim of the seventh century as "a place of prayer of the Saracens, capable of holding 3000 people, and had its pillars connected with beams." This Mosque stands over the site of the ancient Temple, of which there are undoubted and precious remains in the foundations and substructure generally. Passing down the steps adjacent to the porch, we reach a broad covered entrance that formerly led to the Temple from the south. It is divided by a series of pillars; from the manner in which the one avenue is closed at the northern end, it seems probable that it admitted only to the court of the Gentiles; while the other was the entrance of the priests, and led onwards to the foot of the altar.[1] At the southern end stands a noble monolithic column, six feet six inches in diameter, which was thus well fitted to support the splendid Stoa Basilica of Herod, that stretched along the southern side of the Temple. Beyond is the double gateway, now closed up; answering well, from its position and ancient architectural style, to the description of Josephus. On our ascending to the area, we asked the Sheikh to show us the subterranean lake or excavated sea, discovered some time before by Dr. Barclay, and a representation of which is given in his book. To our surprise, he denied all knowledge of its existence, and was supported by an official of the Consulate, who boasted of having been often in the Haram, and could assure us there was no

[1] Fergusson's *Ancient Jerusalem*.

such thing. However, as Dr. Barclay, during a conversation the previous evening, had given us some idea of its precise entrance, I along with a friend got permission to linger behind for a little, to see if we could find the spot. We were successful, and after working our way down a rough, broken entrance, came to a splendid flight of steps, cut out of the solid rock, and greatly worn. At the foot was the strange underground receptacle in question, with its magnificent sheet of clear, chill, delicious water; parts of the rock had been left standing as pillars to support the roof; the slightest noise, our talking even, evoked a deep prolonged echo. When we got out, we summoned our friends, among others the gentleman who had ridiculed the idea of such a place, and who for the first time examined the surprising excavation. From this lake the half of Jerusalem is still supplied with water; the pool of Siloam is an overflow from it, and here unquestionably was the grand source of supply for the ancient Temple-service. Three centuries before Christ, Aristeas went on a special mission to the High Priest of the Jews from Ptolemy, King of Egypt, and thus speaks of the water-resources of the Temple: "There is a continual supply of water, as if there had sprung an abundant fountain underneath, and there are wonderful reservoirs underground, and openings in the pavement, not to be seen at all but by those that officiated. Through these the water, gushing out with force, washes away all the blood of the numerous victims." This unfailing supply of water may be referred to in the words of the Psalm: "There is a river whose streams make glad the city of God, the holy place of the tabernacle of the Most High."

We also visited the remarkable substructures at the south-eastern corner of the area, generally known as Solomon's Stables. These consist of a number of arches of varying width, extending northwards, and built for the purpose of elevating the ground to the level of the area. We then examined the interior of the gate in the eastern wall, known as the Golden Gateway, of which Mr. Catherwood took drawings, and to which Mr. Fergusson appeals for additional proof of his theory. After an exploration of two hours in the area, we were escorted to the gate by the guard; and any further venture near its precincts during our stay was sure to expose us to menace and insult.

CHAPTER X.

HILLS OF THE CITY.

In proceeding to discuss the topography of ancient Jerusalem, I shall not venture on the endless and wearisome task of presenting all the different theories that have been put forward, or estimating the value of the innumerable explanations, conjectures, and discussions, of which almost every local feature in it has been the subject. While it is due to the great names that have advocated other views than those now presented, to state the principal objections which render these untenable, the tone of my remarks will be as little controversial as possible. The candid reader will be left to judge how far the topography, as here adopted, explains and is demanded by the language and incidents of Scripture, with the commentary supplied by the Jewish historian. These data, in connexion with the present appearance of the ground, must be the grand test for the correctness of any theory on the subject.

The most important passage of Josephus, first claiming our consideration, is that relating to the *hills* on which the city was built.

"Jerusalem, fortified by three walls—except where it was encompassed by its impassable ravines, for there it had but one rampart—was built, the one division fronting the other, on two hills, separated by an intervening valley, at which the rows of houses terminated. Of these hills, that on which the upper town is situated is much the higher and straighter in its length. Accordingly it was called a Fortress (φρούριον, not ἄκρα) by King David, the father of Solomon, by whom the Temple was originally built, but by us the Upper Market-place. The other, which bears the name of Akra, and supports the lower town, slopes on both sides (ἀμφίκυρτος). Opposite to this was a third hill, naturally lower than Akra, and formerly separated from it by another broad ravine. Afterwards, however, the Maccabees, during their reign, filled up the ravine, with the intention of uniting the city to the Temple, and levelling the summit of the Akra, they reduced its elevation, so that the Temple might be conspicuous above the objects in this quarter also. The valley of the Cheesemongers (Tyropœon), as it was designated, which divided, as we have said, the hill of the upper town from that of the lower, extended as far as Siloam, so we call it, a fountain whose waters are at once sweet and copious. On the exterior, the two hills on which the city stood were skirted by deep ravines, so precipitous on either side that the town was nowhere accessible."[1]

The accompanying sketch will aid the reader in forming a conception of the manner in which the above passage of Josephus has been generally understood. It is presented as being the view which is usually exhibited, and because Dr. Robinson is its distinguished advocate. It has of late, however, been challenged and denied by various writers, as Fergusson, Thrupp, and Lewin. I

[1] Josephus, *Bell. Jud.*, v. 4. 1.

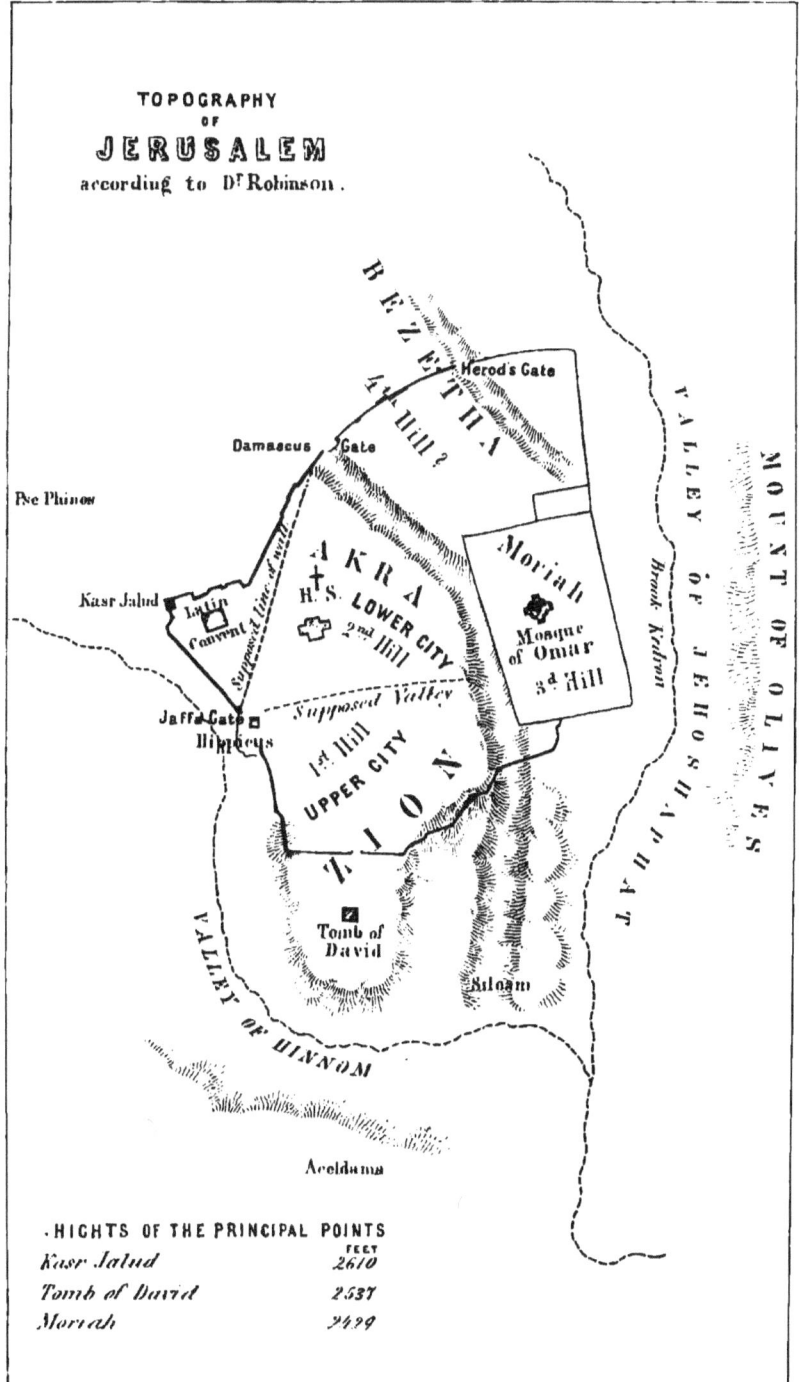

confess myself unable to see how it accords with the description in one single particular.

1. There is not, on this theory, the slightest trace of any such central valley as Josephus indicates, and it is consequently marked on the map "supposed valley." It is supposed to have stretched from the Jaffa gate to the Temple enclosure. Certainly as you ride in by that gate you would never in the least suspect its existence, nor, when the hint is given, are you able to find any traces of it whatever. Mr. Williams, who lived on the spot for eighteen months, persists that there could have been no such valley at all; my companion from Jaffa, who had been in Jerusalem frequently, looked for it in vain. It must have been, according to Josephus, a deep valley edged by crags, for his language implies that the houses ended on the brink at either side. Despite, then, of the hypothesis of rubbish filling it up (which may be pushed too far), some token of its existence would surely have survived; but there is none.

2. There are no such hills of the city, on this plan of it, as Josephus indicates. In fact, the relative elevations are reversed. What is marked on the map as the upper city, is *actually the lower* of the two; its southern end (at the so-called tomb of David) being lower than the northern end of the other hill by about seventy feet (see elevations as marked). True, indeed, Dr. Robinson would exclude this northern corner of Kasr Jalud from the city altogether, and so draws his wall where the sketch indicates "supposed wall." But such a line of wall is in itself a grave objection to his view, for this leaves outside a point of advantage for the besiegers, such as we know from the history of Jerusalem was never so neglected.

If such an eminence had been left for the attack of an enemy, the whole history of the siege of Jerusalem would have been changed. But supposing the wall had gone in the direction indicated, it is still impossible to understand the language of Josephus, who asserts the hill of the upper city "to be *much the higher*" of the two; they would, on the contrary, be nearly level after all, if indeed the northern section is not still the more elevated. However, Mr. Fergusson has shown that the famous tower, Hippicus, from which the wall started, was at this corner of Kasr Jalud; and hence its great strategic importance and vast munimental strength.

3. Again, on this theory, the description of Akra is unintelligible. Akra was, says Josephus, ἀμφίκυρτος, which Dr. Robinson translates by the phrase, "Curved on both sides like a gibbous moon." Accepting the translation, it is at the same time impossible to conjecture how this hill could have had such a shape; certainly the outline of the valley from the Damascus gate, to which Dr. Robinson refers, seems rather to contradict any such supposition.

4. Josephus goes on to say, "that there was a *third* hill (the site of the Temple) by nature lower than the Akra, and formerly separated by a broad ravine. The Maccabees (Asmoneans) filled up the valley, worked down the height of the Akra, so that the Temple might appear the higher." Now it is certain that the height of Dr. Robinson's Akra has *not* been worked down. It stood and still stands higher than the site of the Temple by a hundred feet. Again, the Book of the Maccabees indicates that the citadel which they demolished was in "*the city of David.*" "They also that were in *the city of*

David in Jerusalem had made themselves a tower (ἄκρα), out of which they issued and polluted all about the sanctuary, and did much hurt in the holy place" (1 Macc. xiv. 36). According to the plan, the city of David, or Zion hill, was altogether different from the Akra district, and thus the statements of Josephus as to the site of this citadel are in direct contradiction to those in the Book of Maccabees. Also, in the same book we read that it was a citadel adjoining the Temple, which was not the case with any stronghold in the Akra portion of the city as here defined.[1] It was immediately north of the Temple, and on the same spot rose the great castle of Antonia.[2] The citadel here alluded to could not be on the western hill, either in its northern or southern section.

5. Josephus adds : "The Temple was *opposite* the hill Akra." According to Dr. Robinson himself, it is opposite "at the *eastern point* only." "Moriah (the Temple hill) was apparently at first an elevated mound of rock rising by itself upon the ridge of Bezetha *over against the eastern point of Akra.*"[3] The language of Josephus is surely very different from this.

These remarks, I trust, are sufficient to show that this usual theory of the topography of Jerusalem cannot be correct. If thus at fault on the position of the Temple hill and the hills of the city, with the deep intervening valley going down to Siloam, the whole hypothesis loses its basis, and therefore its minor matters of detail need not concern us.

The following objections, however, tell further against it, and are applicable equally to another theory, which

---

[1] "The hill of the Temple that was near (παρὰ) the Akra."—1 Macc. xiii. 52.
[2] See Sketch, p. 257.   [3] *Biblical Researches*, vol. i. p. 267.

locates, correctly enough, "the lower city" Akra, to the north of the Temple. But the *ravine* between it and the Temple hill is omitted, and so the language of Josephus is still unintelligible. It is of no use to point to *other* ravines round the temple. Josephus asserts one to have existed "*between* it and the Akra." Instead of this, they are generally treated of as one continuous ridge.

Again, from the Akra the Temple appeared as a *hill*, "the *third* hill." The usual theory, while representing it as a hill from Kedron on the east, from Siloam on the south, and from the Tyropœon on the west, yet fails to exhibit it as such from the very direction of which the historian speaks. Here the hill disappears, and we have in its stead, to use the language of Robinson, an "elevated mound of rock on the *ridge* of Bezetha," or, as the theory under review would express it, "on the unbroken ridge of the Akra."

Still further, Josephus has hitherto spoken of *three* hills, and then he mentions, in the same chapter, "a fourth hill called Bezetha." The usual theory regarding the Temple site as only a part of the eastern ridge cannot indicate how there should be a fourth hill; there are but *three*, viz., the upper city, the lower city, and Bezetha.

To my mind the accompanying sketches exhibit the view required by the historian's language on this subject, and throughout his history. The names of Scripture are marked in the one, in the other those of Josephus. The various hills and ravines here noted, are so seen by the traveller at the present day, with one important exception, "the valley of Maccabees." The ground there is nearly quite level now, and is indeed part of the in-

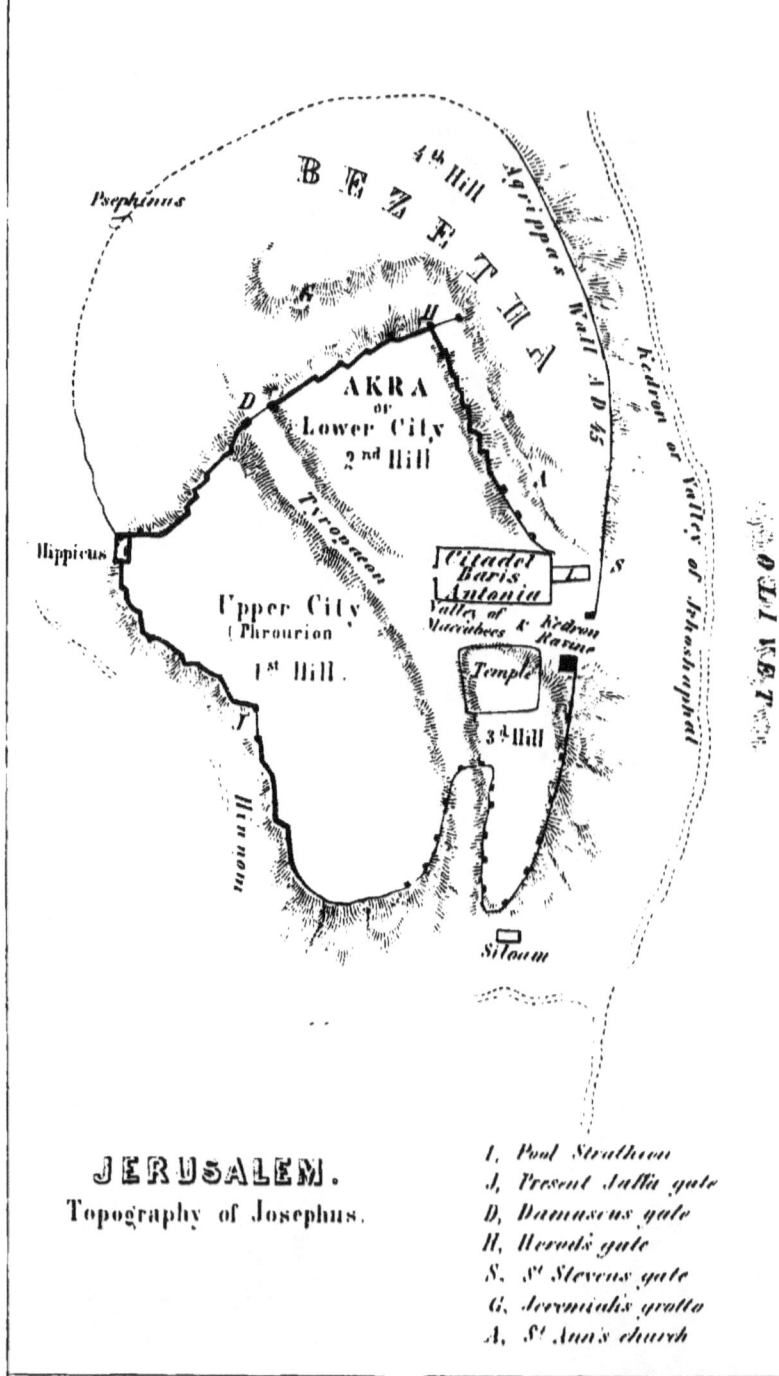

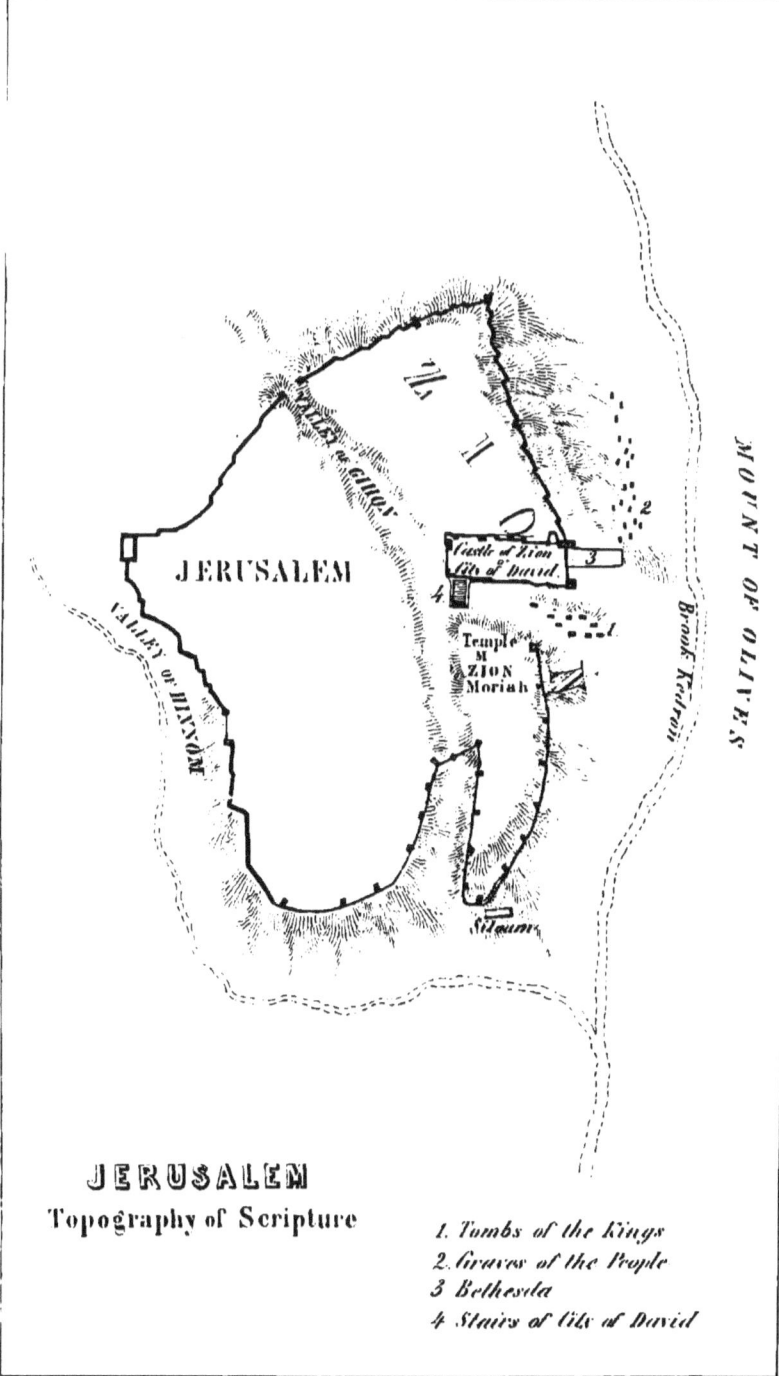

closure of the Haram es Sheriff; but I hope to convince the reader afterwards that it was not "a supposed valley" like the other. Meanwhile the traveller to Jerusalem will see two valleys proceeding southwards, such as are here marked, the one from the Damascus Gate, and the other from Herod's Gate. The first strikes the most careless observer as clearly dividing the city, the second also is visible enough, although its bearing on the language of Josephus has not been hitherto clearly exhibited. Referring to it, Dr. Robinson says: "A small valley or depression comes from the north, and entering the city east of Herod's Gate, passes down in a south-easterly direction; traces of it are found extending through the eastern wall of the city, where it forms a depression outside, just south of St. Stephen's Gate."[1] Dr. Barclay, who resided several years in Jerusalem, describing the intermediate ground, says: "A narrow *ridge* separates the valley of Damascus Gate from that on the east in which Herod's Gate is placed."[2] Both valleys then are clearly defined, although the rubbish now accumulated is very great. Thus the church of St. Ann, situated in the latter, is buried among the debris to its roof, the result of changes in the city in times comparatively modern. If we reflect what previous effects of change must have accumulated there in the more ancient history of Jerusalem, we may conclude that this valley at the time referred to by Josephus, exhibited the rugged depth which his language implies.

Let us now read his description in the light of these conclusions and appearances: "The city was built, one division fronting the other, on two hills, separated by an

[1] *Biblical Researches*, iii. 178.   [2] *City of Great King*, p. 86.

intervening valley, at which the rows of houses terminated. Of these hills, that on which the upper town is situated, is much the higher and straighter in its length. The valley of the Tyropœon, as it is now designated, which divided the upper town from the lower, extended as far as Siloam." Let the traveller then station himself at the Damascus Gate, and he will recognise this as the best description of the city now. Before him is just such a valley running down to Siloam. On the right hand is an unbroken hill bearing the upper city; on the left is another of lower elevation (about one hundred feet on the average), on which stood the lower city. Not more clearly does the visitor to the Scottish metropolis see its central valley, with an upper and lower town rising on each side, than the traveller to Jerusalem when taking his stand at the place indicated.

2. "On the outside," adds Josephus, "each city was skirted by a deep ravine." Accordingly we can on this view of localities point to the ravine of Hinnom on the outside of the upper city, and to that from Herod's Gate on the outside of the lower city.

3. Josephus adds a distinctive feature in the appearance of the lower city, which can also be verified: "The lower city is ἀμφίκυρτος, sloping down on both sides." The ground between the valley at the Damascus Gate and that at Herod's Gate necessarily had the form of a ridge. As such Dr. Barclay speaks of it, and as such it is represented in his pictorial illustration of Jerusalem from the North. Dr. Robinson says: "The northern wall of this portion of the city rises by a steep ascent from the Damascus Gate, is carried over the top of the hill upon the rock; then the ridge drops off on the east (to Herod's Gate). There are at present no traces of an outer fosse

underneath the highest part of the ridge; none certainly was needed, the rock alone is sufficiently elevated for the security of a wall without a trench."[1] The ground of the lower city having thus the shape of a *ridge*, the language of Josephus affirms that the houses on it covered *both the sides*, and was thus distinguished from the upper city, which lay only on *one* slope.

4. We can understand on such a topography why this lower city was named Akra. At its southern extremity lay the strong citadel, which played an important part in the history of Jerusalem from its capture by David to its overthrow by Titus. It is called "Akra" (Castle Rock) at the time of which the historian speaks (that erected by Herod was named Antonia), and thus gave the name to the hill on which the lower town stood. We still name a locality the Castle Hill in a similar way.

The consideration of the next passage in the paragraph under review, and of some other statements in the chapter of which it is the commencement,[2] directs our attention to the *transverse valley* immediately under the north wall of the Temple, marked in the sketch as "the valley of the Maccabees" or "the Kedron ravine." The recognition of such a valley is the special characteristic of the view of ancient Jerusalem as now presented. To prove its existence, and develop the bearing of it on some of the most important localities mentioned in Scripture, is the great aim I have in view; and I may be here allowed to mention the circumstance which first led me to its recognition. Beginning afresh on my return from the East the study of Josephus, my attention was specially arrested by his statement of the circumstance that hampered Pompey in his siege of the Temple. Twice over,—

---

[1] *Biblical Researches*, iii. 190, 191.   [2] Josephus, *Bell. Jud.* v. 4.

once in his *Antiquities*, and again in the *Wars of the Jews*, —he affirms that the great obstacle to its capture was a *ravine on the northern side*. The Roman general had got within the walls, and "stationed garrisons both in the city and in the King's palace."[1] When close to the Temple on the north he had to pause, and only after great toil was the valley filled up so as to admit of the prosecution of the siege. Dr. Robinson and other writers indeed would represent this merely as an artificial *trench* that had been dug to strengthen the defence; but the Jewish historian on both occasions, affirms the existence of a ravine (φάραγγι) as well as of a fosse (τάφρος). "On the north side of the Temple a *deep fosse* had been dug, and a deep *ravine* begirt it round about."[2] The Roman commander filled up the fosse and the whole of the *ravine* which lay on the north quarter. "It was a work of difficulty," he adds, "because of its prodigious depth" (διὰ βάθος ἄπειρον).[3] Endeavouring to read other portions of his history in the light of the important fact thus repeatedly asserted, much light seemed thrown on some other statements which had hitherto appeared confused and unintelligible. Several months after I had submitted the substance of the views now about to be presented to two of the ablest writers on the history and topography of ancient Jerusalem, I accidentally fell in with the map of Dr. Schultz. Somewhat farther north than the place indicated in the present plan, he had marked such a transverse valley. "Traces of a valley," says Mr. Thrupp, in reference to this point, "debouching into the valley of the Kedron, near the middle of the eastern wall of the Haram es Sheriff, and which seemed to have been artificially filled up, were

---

[1] Josephus, *Antiquities*, xiv. 4. 2.   [2] *Ibid*   [3] *Bell. Jud.* i. 7. 3.

detected by the late Dr. Schultz. He expresses himself indeed but doubtfully on the subject ('traces of an artificial filling up may *perhaps* still be recognised'); but his testimony is all the more valuable, because the historical point of view in which he treated his own discovery is entirely different from that in which, if the traces really exist, they ought to be regarded."[1] If during his residence as Prussian Consul at Jerusalem, it had been in the power of Dr. Schultz to visit the enclosure of the Haram, he would not have indicated this supposed valley on the *north* of the rock of the Mosque of Omar, as there can be detected the obstruction of the solid rock. Still, the idea of this German author, that a valley had formerly crossed the present enclosure, confirmed the impressions I had previously formed; and I have now to adduce some facts from this chapter of the Jewish historian on the hills of the city, which prove its existence as exhibited in the sketch.

1. In the paragraph already quoted, it is said that "opposite to the hill of the lower city, and formerly *separated from it by a broad ravine,* was a third hill. Afterwards, however, the Maccabees, during their reign, filled up the ravine, wishing to unite the city to the Temple, and by earnest toil[2] they reduced the elevation of the Ἄκρα, so that the Temple appeared higher than *it* (ταύτης)." This third hill is here shown to be the site of the Temple, and Dr. Robinson tries to reconcile the statement by his view of Akra on the western hill. As has been shown by his own admission, the Temple was opposite to that

---

[1] *Ancient Jerusalem,* p. 320.

[2] Κατεργασάμενοι. Robinson and Traill translate this word *to work down, to level.* But this seems an unnecessary repetition of the idea in the same clause. It seems rather an emphatic expression for the toil of three years, which the demolition of the fortress required.

locality only at *one* point, "the eastern" (or rather south-eastern),—a different idea surely from what the language would convey. But if Akra was on the *eastern* ridge, as several writers now admit, then this language distinctly affirms its separation from the Temple enclosure by a ravine (φάραγγι). Again, the Book of Maccabees speaks of "THE HILL OF THE TEMPLE that was near the Akra" (τὸ ὄρος τοῦ ἱεροῦ τὸ παρὰ τὴν "Ακραν),[1] language altogether inappropriate if the intermediate ground had been a level plateau then as now. Until the time of the Maccabees, therefore, the present enclosure was severed by a cross valley extending from the Tyropœon to the Valley of Jehoshaphat, and at its north-west corner can still be seen the traces of their toil in the destruction of the fortress, with the materials of which they "filled up," or rather perhaps made an embankment across the ravine (φάραγγα ἔχωσαν).

2. Such a ravine alone accounts for the statement, that after the suburb of Bezetha was included, the city with its Temple stood on *four* hills. In the language now quoted Josephus speaks of the Temple as on a *third* hill, and he afterwards adds " a *fourth* hill, which is called Bezetha, was also surrounded with habitations."[2] The usual topography cannot show how Bezetha could have been a *fourth* hill;[3] it is the third, bearing on its southern extremity the site of the Temple. According to the plan here proposed, the number can be easily made out : (1.) the hill of the upper city ; (2.) the hill of the lower ; (3.) the Temple hill; (4.) the hill Bezetha. The recognition of this Temple ravine, therefore, gives to the language of the historian its just and obvious interpretation.

[1] 1 Maccabees xiii. 52. [2] Josephus, *Bell. Jud.* v. 4. 2.
[3] See Robinson's *Topography*, p. 253.

3. Such a ravine accounts for the termination of the defending wall that girt the city on the north. It terminated at the citadel of the Akra, afterwards called Antonia.[1] This citadel (the fact is admitted by Lewin and Thrupp, after being pointed out by Fergusson), it can be shown on other grounds, did not stretch along the breadth of the Temple, but lay at its north-west corner. Moreover, it did not, and could not have *adjoined* it, if only because the Jews would never have tolerated the barracks of the Roman soldiery close to their Temple. On the contrary, it stood at some distance; and yet, it is true, the wall terminated there. Why was this? it may be asked. Why did not the rampart stretch across the northern side of the Temple, and shield it completely from attack? Considering, indeed, that the sieges of the city were invariably from the north, bearing right down on the Temple, the most cherished possession of the Jews, this was precisely the place where such a defence would have been regarded as most necessary, yet there was in reality nothing of the kind. The reason lay in the fact, that the Temple did not need it, since there the deep rugged ravine was of itself sufficient.

4. Such a ravine explains the junction of Agrippa's wall, A.D. 45, with the southern wall of the city that swept up from Siloam by Ophel, joining there the eastern portico of the Temple. Speaking of the wall of Agrippa, Josephus says, "connecting itself with the old wall, it terminated at the ravine called the Kedron."[2] Josephus does not here mean, as the reader may at first suppose, the valley of the brook Kedron, or what is commonly called the Valley of Jehoshaphat.

Mr. Lewin has clearly pointed out, that when the his-

---

[1] Josephus, *Bell. Jud.* v. 4. 2.   [2] *Ibid.* v. 4. 2.

torian speaks of this latter, he simply calls it the Kedron, but there is another spot he calls "the ravine (φάραγγον) named from the Kedron."[1] The proof of such a distinction will be afterwards more fully considered; let it suffice at present to remark, that no one has attempted to represent either wall as descending into *the Valley of Jehoshaphat*, and effecting their junction in its hollow.

The present wall from the north by St. Stephen's Gate indicates the track of the wall of Agrippa, as is proved by the old stones found there. The ravine of the sketch explains how the two walls joined "at the Kedron ravine," though neither of them touched the Valley of Jehoshaphat.

Passing from Josephus, I may here add two proofs of the point contended for, which are furnished by the present appearance of the ground.

5. The space could not have been *level* as at present but for the existence of such a ravine. It has been calculated that there were here nearly a million cubic feet of materials in the Temple, the ruins of which were hurled all around. These have filled up the valley of the Tyropœon on the west: they lie in deep masses on the slopes of Ophel on the south; and in the Valley of Jehoshaphat on the east. Indeed there is some reason for believing that the waters of the Kedron still run there, only they are covered from sight by the inconceivable heaps of rubbish that were rolled into the valley. While these ruins thus fell on the west, south, and east, are we to suppose

---

[1] While Mr. Lewin has clearly pointed out this distinction of the historian (p. 441), it is not easy to see how "the Kedron ravine" could be appropriate for the ground to which he applies the epithet. It was in his view "the tract upon the slope toward the Kedron valley," "the intramural space shut in between the Temple and the old wall, the outer peribolus of the Temple platform." I am unable to see how it can be seriously maintained that ground of this nature should be described as a *ravine*, and that the historian applied the epithet to a gentle slope instead of to a *bona fide* valley.

that none fell on the *north* of the Temple? But if so, then as the ground is level in that direction now, *there* likewise must have been a ravine to receive them.

6. Still further, as the traveller passes down the Valley of Jehoshaphat, he sees an immense mound protruding in this very direction, and this is referred to by Dr. Schultz. So much is this the case, that that valley is narrowed here to a few feet. It has the exact appearance as if a *cross ravine* at this point had debouched into it, and was now filled with the accumulated rubbish of ages.

Regarding, then, "the Temple hill" as disparted on every side, the following incidents of the Scripture narrative are explained :—

1. The sacrifice of Abraham on Mount Moriah. Some would shift the locality away from Jerusalem altogether, and locate the place at Gerizim. But it is not easy to see how Abraham could have travelled to Gerizim from Beersheba[1] in two days. Again it is said, "On the third day he lifted up his eyes, and saw the place afar off;" and leaving the servants behind, he with his son advance to the mountain. Since Gerizim is seen some fifteen or twenty miles off, in the plain of Sharon, we should have to believe that Abraham and Isaac travelled all this distance on foot, carrying with them the materials of sacrifice. This is hardly credible. Moreover, both Josephus and the Scripture identify Moriah with the place on which the Temple was subsequently built. But in that case the whole transaction is unintelligible if the place was only "an elevated mound of rock," and moreover, joined on to the rest of the city, as at the present day.

---

[1] The place was in the extreme south of Palestine, as the well-known expression implies, "from Dan to Beersheba."

It is obvious that in that case the walls, following the ravines, would have enclosed the spot, just as they do now. Accordingly the scene of the sacrifice must have been enacted *within* the city. But let this ground be viewed as a clearly separate outlying hill, and the narrative can be understood. As Abraham advanced from the south, he came in view of the appointed eminence from the opposite side of the Valley of Hinnom, or he may have seen it (as Dr. Barclay has shown that it can be seen) from a promontory in the valley of the Kedron, several miles south, where the name Kirbet Ibrahim is still in use.[1] But there may be an undue straining of the meaning in the expression, "saw it afar off." It may mean only two or three miles, the rather as Isaac bore the wood, and Abraham carried the knife and the fire. Together they descended into the winding Valley of Hinnom, and climbed the long ascent of Ophel to the summit. We may suppose it to have been early morning, when the population of the adjoining city were not yet astir. Mount Moriah is detached on every side by a deep and broad ravine; so that the preparations could be better accomplished without notice or molestation. "They came to the place which God had told him of; and Abraham built an altar there, and laid the wood in order, and bound Isaac his son, and laid him on the altar upon the wood. And Abraham stretched forth his hand, and took the knife to slay his son." The weapon was arrested by the heavenly voice, and on the smoking altar a ram was substituted, caught, it is probable, on the slopes of Ophel, proverbially rich in pasturage.

2. In after centuries David selected this height for

---

[1] *City of the Great King*, p. 58.

building the Temple, purchasing it from his friend, Araunah the Jebusite. It is difficult to understand, on the ordinary topography, how the spot failed to become part and parcel of the city, necessarily falling into the hands of the victor after the siege, and becoming his by right of conquest. And still further, if the locality was only "an elevated mound of rock," this was a paltry possession for a prince of the Jebusites, for which David could have paid so large a price! On the other hand, if we view it as a detached hill, lying quite outside the city, then it did not necessarily fall into the hands of David at the conquest. It was possessed by Araunah, and as a friend of the king, he kept unquestioned possession. On the rich slopes of Ophel he reaped his crops, and the summit of the hill was his thrashing-floor. David saw the angel on that summit, with the sword pointing not to Zion, his own residence, but to Jerusalem. Crossing the ravine from his castle of Zion, he "went up" (if there had been no intercepting ravine, it would have been a going down) to the thrashing-floor of Araunah. He expressed a wish to purchase the spot, refusing to take it as a gift, and "serve God with that which cost him nought." He then bought the thrashing-floor for fifty shekels of silver,[1] and the entire hill for 600 shekels of gold.[2] On its sides he accumulated the vast materials for the building of the Temple, in reference to which he utters his last prayer: "Give unto Solomon my son a perfect heart, to keep thy commandments, thy testimonies, and thy statutes, and to do all these things, and to build the palace, for the which I have made provision."[3]

[1] 2 Sam. xxiv. 24. [2] 1 Chron. xx. 25. [3] 1 Chron. xxix. 19.

CHAPTER XI.

ZION.

Our first inquiry in this chapter relates to the situation of Zion in the ancient city. Prophets and psalmists were wont to refer to Zion in terms of special eulogy and rapture, and the word has passed with many hallowed associations into the language of the Christian Church.

To the view of the cursory reader this is only another epithet for Jerusalem. But we meet with such passages as the following: "The daughter of Zion hath despised thee; the daughter of Jerusalem hath shaken her head at thee;" "to declare the name of the Lord in Zion, and his praise in Jerusalem;" "they build up Zion with blood, and Jerusalem with iniquity," etc. It is not easy to believe that epithets thus employed are identical; the Hebrew parallelism did not mean trifling repetition and unmeaning tautology. With others, Zion means the "City of David;" but again, the latter is expressly called "the *Castle*," "the *stronghold* of Zion;" it was therefore only a portion of the locality embraced by the word in question, as the Acropolis is of Athens, or the Castle rock of the Scottish metropolis. Others, again, restrict the epithet to the Temple hill. It is true that it came at last to be thus restricted (as in the Book of the Maccabees it is used for the Temple hill exclusively), but if it embraced the "City of David," it must at one time obviously have had a much wider application. The truth is, it was the name for a separate *district* of the city, and hence in Scripture we read of "the daughters of Zion," "the sons of Zion," "the people dwelling in Zion," "the king, princes, and prophets of Zion." It is sometimes employed figuratively for the whole city, in the same way as Jerusalem,—the name, strictly speaking, of the other and larger district. Josephus tells us that the city was built on two hills, separated by the valley that went down to Siloam; and this fact, I believe, satisfactorily explains to us how there came to be applied to it two epithets so widely different.

The first time we meet with the word *Zion* in Scripture, is in the account of the siege by David. We are apt to suppose that the newly-elected king needed to capture the entire city from the enemy: but the language of Josephus and Scripture warrants a different idea; it was only the Zion district, occupied by the Jebusites, that required to be subdued. In his detailed account of the various sieges of Jerusalem, the Jewish historian narrates how it fared with the upper and lower city respectively. But it is worthy of notice that in describing the attack of David, he makes *no mention* of the upper city at all, and leaves us to infer that his whole efforts were directed to the lower city with its fortress. And in the Scripture accounts we do not read that he took the entire city, but that he took from the Jebusites the stronghold of Zion, which is "the city of David."

A glance into the previous history of the city may help us

to understand how matters stood at the time of this siege. On entering Canaan, the Israelites attempted to secure entire possession of Jerusalem, but failed. We read that "the children of Judah could not drive out the Jebusites, but the Jebusites dwell with the children of Judah to this day." Again, "The children of Benjamin did not drive out the Jebusites that inhabited Jerusalem, but the Jebusites dwell with the children of Benjamin in Jerusalem unto this day." As the city lay on the frontier of both these tribes, we can understand how they should thus unite in the attempt to expel "the inhabitants of the land." They failed, however, and a compromise was agreed upon, of which Josephus thus speaks: "The Benjamites, to whom belonged Jerusalem, permitted its inhabitants to pay tribute; so they left off, the one to kill, the other to expose themselves to danger, and had time to cultivate the ground. The rest of the tribes imitated that of Benjamin, and did the same; and, contenting themselves with the tributes that were paid them, permitted the Canaanites to live in peace."[1]

Thus in many parts of the country there would prevail a state of things such as is still seen in the East, with its various races and its hostile religions. The Canaanites and Israelites would in some cases inhabit separate villages after the manner of the Druses and Maronites in the slopes of Lebanon; if in the same city, they would select different districts. Accordingly, as at Jerusalem there are now the Christian, the Jewish, and the Mohammedan quarters, so in the time of David there would be the Benjamite and Jebusite quarters. And as the city was divided by a central valley, we may presume that on

[1] Josephus, *Antiquities*, v. 2. 5.

either side of it would be the respective dwellings of its two classes of inhabitants.

The question now is, On which side of the central valley was the hill of the Jebusites? This is simply to ask which was the Zion district, inasmuch as the fortress from which David expelled them was "the stronghold of Zion."

The usual theory locates it on the western hill. I shall now endeavour to show that it was the *eastern* hill, and vindicate this position by the concurrent testimony of Scripture, of Josephus, and of the Book of the Maccabees.

Arguing from the language of Scripture, let us notice —(1.) That on the eastern hill was the possession of Araunah, a prince of the Jebusites. About this there cannot be a doubt, for it became the site of the Temple. Now it is a fair presumption that his possessions lay on *the same side* of the central valley with that of his race. Indeed, it afterwards received the name of the "holy hill of Zion." So that the district embraced by the name must have been as the sketch represents. (2.) Only on the eastern hill was there a rocky fortress corresponding to the Scripture expression, "the stronghold of Zion." The original word (Metsud) is of emphatic import. It is applied to a fastness or castle on a rock, such as the "stronghold on the mountains" to which the Israelites betook themselves when under the oppression of the Midianites; the fastness of Ziph, where David hid himself from Saul; to the munitions of rocks (Isa. xxxiii. 16).[1] Moreover, there was a fortress called by this very name (Mesada) in the vicinity of the Dead Sea, which is de-

[1] See Gesenius' *Lexicon*.

scribed by Josephus as "a rock lofty throughout its entire length, and encompassed on every side by unfathomable ravines."[1] Thus the term is used to define *a castle on a rock*. Now on the western ridge there was no such fortress, as far as we can learn. But there was one on the eastern hill to which the term might be fitly applied, and which afterwards it took the Maccabees three years to destroy. At the northern boundary of the enclosure of the "Mosque of Omar," the traveller can see traces of their toil at the present day.

We now turn to the testimony of Josephus. There is one passage indeed that seems to contradict our locality, and has been thought decisive in favour of the western hill. Speaking of the upper city, he says: "On account of its strength it was called the fortress of King David, but by us the upper market-place." The usual conclusion is, the upper city must be understood as "the stronghold of Zion, the city of David." I will here remark that the precipitous character of the upper city on every side (except the north) will account for its being here called "a fortress," and the difficulty of capturing it was experienced from the first attack on the city by the tribe of Judah onward to the siege of Titus. But the question is, Does Josephus regard it as the stronghold of the Jebusites captured by David, and to which the Scripture epithet is applied? In answer to this I remark: (1.) That Josephus, in his description of the siege, applies to the fortress so captured a different name. He calls it the Akra (Mesada, the rock-castle); whereas in this passage about the upper city the word used is *phrourion* (φρούριον). (2.) He affirms that David,

[1] See representations in Traill's *Josephus*.

after capturing the citadel, filled up the fosse and united it to the lower city. Now, the upper city was never so joined to the lower, but remained divided by the central ravine up to the time of the siege of Titus. His language, therefore, in the passage quoted, where alone he speaks of the upper city as a fortress, does not warrant the inference usually drawn from it. (3.) His account defines the range of the capture :—" David took the *lower city* by force, but the citadel (Akra) held out still. He promised that he that should go over the ditches that were beneath the citadel, and should ascend to the citadel itself and take it, should have the command of the entire people conferred upon him. So they were all ambitious to ascend, and thought no pains too great in order to ascend thither, out of their desire of the chief command. However, Joab, the son of Zeruiah, prevented the rest, and as soon as he got up to the citadel cried out to the king, and claimed the chief command. David made buildings about the lower city ; he also joined the citadel (Akra) to it and *made it one body*."[1] In the whole account he says not a word of the capture of the upper city, and the last phrase of itself renders the idea inadmissible.[2]

When driven from the lower city itself, the Jebusites betake themselves to its rocky fortress, and thence offer the most insulting defiance. In view of what Josephus tells us respecting its strength, we can hardly wonder at their confidence and scorn. For example, in the time of the Maccabees a heathen garrison held this fortress for many months against the most strenuous efforts of the

---

[1] Josephus, *Antiquities*, vii. 3. 1, 2.
[2] Καὶ τὴν ἄκραν συνάψας αὐτῇ ἐποίησεν ἕν σῶμα.

Jews to expel them. They were at last reduced by starvation; and as indicating the importance of the prize, we read that the Maccabean chief "took possession of the citadel with thanksgiving and branches of palm-trees, and with harps and cymbals, and with viols and hymns and songs." The anniversary of this event was observed by the Jews as a day of solemn thanksgiving, and to prevent any recurrence of the danger, the rock was levelled with the ground. "In that work," says Josephus, "they spent three whole years working day and night without intermission."[1] Around this stronghold originally was a fosse, and so the Jebusites scorned their besiegers, and placed in their view the weakest and most insulting defence. They shouted derisively, "Except thou take away the blind and the lame, thou shalt not come in hither." The spirit of the warrior-king chafed under the insult. "David said on that day, Whosoever getteth up to the gutter (fosse), and smiteth the Jebusites, and the lame and the blind, hated of David's soul, shall be chief and captain. So Joab the son of Zeruiah went first up, and was chief. David dwelt in the fort, and called it, the city of David" (2 Sam. v. 6, 8, 9). Thus the stronghold of Zion, or the city of David, is identified with the citadel of the Akra on the eastern hill.

Further proof is found in what is said respecting the work of Hezekiah and Manasseh.

In the reign of Hezekiah the city was invaded by the Assyrians, and the king endeavoured to deprive the besiegers of water as far as possible. The overflow of the springs was stopped, and the water brought into the city by a subterranean channel. "Hezekiah," says the

---

[1] Josephus, *Antiquities*, xiii. 6. 7.

narrative, "stopped the upper water-course of Gihon, and brought it straight down to the west side of the city of David" (2 Chron. xxxii. 30). Now, if we suppose Zion to be the southern section of the western hill, and Gihon to be the upper part of the Valley of Hinnom, we may well ask, why was not the water brought into the city at the northern section, which was nearest? why lengthen the subterranean channel outside the walls of the city until it came to the west side of the city of David? Besides, it is questionable whether the levels of the ground would have permitted it. But the description can well be understood if the Valley of Gihon be the central valley, and the city of David placed on the eastern hill. One fact strongly confirmatory is, that recent explorations have discovered conduits bored through the solid rock, indicating a work with precisely such a purpose as the king contemplated.[1] The language employed respecting the work of Manasseh points to the same locality. "He built a wall without the city of David, on the west side of Gihon, in the valley." It is impossible to suppose that he did this in any part of the valley of Hinnom, which the usual location of Zion on the western hill would necessitate. A wall there could not have served for defence, as it would have been commanded by the overhanging cliffs. We find at once an explanation of the language in supposing Gihon to have been the central valley, and the city of David in the position contended for.

In the Book of the Maccabees (B.C. 150), dealing with events 800 years after the siege of David, we still find mention of a locality in Jerusalem called "the city of

[1] Barclay, pp. 310, 538.

David." Antiochus Epiphanes, the Macedonian King, enraged at the leaning of the Jews towards the Ptolemies of Egypt, insulted their religion, offering swine's flesh on their altar, and on his departure left a garrison to overawe them. That garrison, it is said, "built the city of David with a great and strong wall, and with mighty towers, and made it a stronghold for them. It was a place to lie in wait against the sanctuary, and an evil adversary to Israel" (1 Macc. xiii. 36). "A tower from which they issued and polluted all about the sanctuary, and did much hurt in the holy place" (chap. xiv. 36). Turning to Josephus, we shall find in the account of these events that this fortress of the enemy was the Acra or eastern hill. "At this time it was, that the garrison in the citadel (Akra) at Jerusalem did a great deal of harm to the Jews, for the soldiers that were in that garrison rushed out upon the sudden, and destroyed such as were going up to the temple in order to offer their sacrifices, for this citadel adjoined to and overlooked the temple."[1]

Deciding thus as to the situation of Zion, we can appreciate the various usages of the word in Scripture. We can understand that as a distinct district it could be employed for the entire city, and can see how, when used along with Jerusalem (properly, the town on the *west* side of the central valley), there is expressed a parallelism of beauty and force. We can also see how it came to be associated in the Jewish mind, with a peculiar reverence and joy, inasmuch as on one portion of it was the palace of their king, while another was consecrated by the temple of their God.

[1] Josephus, *Antiquities*, xii. 9. 3.

The remainder of the chapter will be devoted to the consideration of the proofs of a transverse valley on this eastern hill, which are furnished by the expressions applied to Zion and the city of David.

1. (*a*) In the Book of Maccabees, the Temple site is called "*the hill Zion*"[1] *in relation to the citadel* (Akra). In one place it is spoken of as "the *hill* of the Temple that was near the citadel"[2] (1 Macc. xiii. 52). But how, I ask, could it be so described, if there were no separating ravine? In that case, it was not a hill at all, but merely a ledge of rock on the same unbroken ridge, as is indeed commonly supposed. (*b*) We read of fierce and protracted contests between the garrison in that citadel (or city of David, as it is there called) and the Maccabees in the Temple. How are we to explain all this, since, on the usual theory, the Temple could be only an artificial building lying at the foot of the terrible stronghold, with no special advantages for attack or defence? The strong temple of Herod, let the reader remember, was not then built. Without at present dwelling on the point, I will only remark that the account of the Book of Maccabees becomes intelligible and credible, if we think of the Temple as protected by a ravine in the direction where the enemy threatened it, and its defenders as thus placed on equal vantage-ground with their assailants.

2. Passing to the Scripture evidence, let it be remarked (*a*) that there are epithets employed to describe *two* different portions of Zion, which find an explanation only on such a view of the locality. The one is the "Castle of Zion, which is the city of David" (*Mazoudoth Zion*),

---

[1] Τὸ ὄρος Ζιών.   [2] Τὸ ὄρος τοῦ ἱεροῦ τὸ παρὰ τὴν Ἄκραν.

and the other is "the holy hill of Zion" (*Har Zion*). This last was the Temple site, as appears from the whole strain of Scripture. But how should portions of the same district be so distinguished, unless the ridge where they stood was thus divided? (*b*) Let us note the language descriptive of the transference of the ark to the Holy of holies in the Temple. "Solomon assembled the elders of Israel, to *bring up* the ark of the covenant of the Lord out of the city of David." "The Levites *took up* the ark" (2 Chron. v. 2, 4). Had there been no valley, it would have been a bringing of it *down*, for until the time of the Maccabees the citadel so named was higher than the Temple. Moreover, throughout the Scripture the worshipper is said to "*go up* to the house of the Lord," whereas it must have been really a descent "to the people dwelling in Zion," if the valley be ignored and the usual theory accepted. (*c*) In the 48th Psalm, Zion is described as a *mountain* in relation to this very section of the city. "Beautiful for situation is Mount Zion, the joy of the whole earth, on the sides of the north is the city of the great king."[1] The language seems exactly to correspond to that of Josephus, who speaks of the Temple "as a third hill opposite to the Akra, and separated (till the time of the Maccabees) by a broad ravine." The psalmist refers not

---

[1] This expression I take to be identical with the special locality of the city of David. It seems impossible to apply it to the city as a whole. (1.) In the first verse the Temple is named the "city of God," and it is unlikely that the writer would apply a similar phrase to the city itself, if indeed any sense can be made out of the passage when so rendered. (2.) "The city," in verse 2, is properly a fortified place (Gesenius), which "the city of David" was. (3.) If the epithet "the great king" had referred to Jehovah, it would have had the article, which the original wants. (4.) The city, as a whole, lay to the west and north-west of the Temple, so that if here referred to, the description is unaccountable.

to the city, as is generally supposed, but to the Temple, "the city of God, the mountain of his holiness." He celebrates its beauty and the commanding strength of its position, the fitting abode of the great and mighty God, whose "praise was unto the ends of the earth." "Kings saw it, and so they marvelled; they were troubled, and hasted away." Conceiving of it as situated on a steep eminence girt round by deep ravines, we can understand this description, and also the exulting appeal at the close: "Walk about Zion (the Temple), and go round about her; tell the towers thereof. Mark ye well her bulwarks, consider her palaces: that ye may tell it to the generation following. For this God is our God for ever and ever: he will be our guide even unto death."

3. Let us now turn our attention to another point of special interest as relating to the locality under consideration, the *sepulchres of the kings of Judah*. Where are these, and how is it that they have never been discovered?

If they had been situated in any portion of the present (so-called) city of David, or indeed in any part of the city now inhabited, it is a mystery how, in searching for foundations, they should have escaped all observation.

The burial of the kings in the ancient times was very splendid. Immense chambers of a highly ornamental character were cut into the rocky sides of a ravine, and in the innermost of these was the body deposited. Such are the tombs of the kings in the ravine at Thebes, which exhibit the custom of the age in highest splendour. The Hebrew patriarchs were buried in the rocky "cave of Machpelah." Josephus tells us that "David was buried with great magnificence, and with the funeral pomp that kings used to be buried with." This leads at once to the conclusion that it was some large sepulchral excavation in the rock of a *ravine;* an idea further confirmed by his adding, that in its chambers were deposited vast wealth. One of these, he mentions, was entered by Hyrcanus the high priest, and three hundred talents taken away. "Another chamber" was entered by Herod the Great, "who opened the sepulchre by night, and went into it, and endeavoured that it should not be at all known in the city, but took only his most faithful friends with him. As for money, he found none as Hyrcanus had done, but that furniture of gold and those precious goods that were laid up there — all which he took away. However, he had a great desire to make diligent search and to go *farther* in, even as far as the two bodies of David and Solomon, when two of his guards were slain by a flame[1] that burst out upon those that went in, as the report was. So he was terribly affrighted, and went out and built a propitiatory monument of that fright he had been in, and this of white stone at the mouth of the sepulchre, and at a great expense also."[2]

When we reflect that in the same locality were buried many other kings (doubtless in each case with royal splendour), we are perplexed in trying to imagine how the requisite space could be obtained unless in a ravine. Now in our topography there was one under the city of David, and precisely such as was used for interments in that ancient time. While the bad and unworthy kings were buried in their own gardens, or in the city of Jeru-

---

[1] An explosion of fire-damp?
[2] Josephus, *Antiquities,* vii. 15, 3 ; xvi. 7, 1.

salem, the good were buried with splendour " in the city of David,"[1] and in the adjacent Valley of Jehoshaphat were " the graves of the children of the people."

There is a remarkable passage in Ezekiel that becomes invested with striking significance in this view of the topography. " He said unto me, Son of man, the place of my throne, and the place of the soles of my feet, where I will dwell in the midst of the children of Israel for ever, and my holy name, shall the house of Israel no more defile, neither they, nor their kings, by their whoredom, nor by the *carcases of their kings* in their high places. In their setting of their threshold by my thresholds, and their post by my posts, for there is but a wall between me and them (marginal reading), they have even defiled my holy name by their abominations that they have committed: wherefore I have consumed them in mine anger. Now let them put away their whoredom, and the carcases of their kings, far from me, and I will dwell in the midst of them for ever" (Ezek. xliii. 7-9).

The prophet is referring to the acts of daring impiety that had marked a previous period of Jewish history, and which ultimately brought about the captivity in Babylon. By " the whoredoms" here, he most probably refers to the idolatrous orgies enacted in this valley, as well as in others around Jerusalem. But the passage is important because of its allusion to the sepulchre of the kings as *encroaching on the Temple threshold.* The partition between was but a wall, and this proximity of the dead to the house of God is declared to be an insult and a sacrilege. With the above view of the sepulchres, the

[1] See *Jerusalem in Time of the Kings*, p. 278.

language can be well understood. They were at first on the *citadel side* of the ravine, which the Temple overlooked, but we can well suppose that, in the impious spirit of the time, the foundations of the holy house might be so approached in the excavations for the royal sepulchres as to provoke the censure of the prophet. He therefore calls on them to put away the carcases of their kings, for "the limit round about the mountain is most holy." This was "the law of the house" (Ezek. xliii. 12).

Again, as adjacent to the Temple and the castle of Antonia (on the site of the ancient citadel), we can understand how Hyrcanus and Herod managed to enter the tomb of David secretly, and carry off immense treasure. By way of atonement for his intrusion, Herod erected a splendid monument over its entrance, to which it is probable the apostle alludes in his sermon on the day of Pentecost.

4. Let us notice further a passage in Nehemiah, which finds a fitting illustration in view of this locality. The building of the walls of the city having commenced from the Sheep-gate, were carried forward to the "pool of Siloah by the king's garden, and unto the stairs that go down from the city of David." We are then told that "Nehemiah, the son of Azbuk, the ruler of the half part of Bethzur, repaired unto the place over against the sepulchres of David, and to the pool that was made, and unto the house of the mighty" (Neh. iii. 16).

Bethzur (the house of rock) was a strong fortress in the south of Palestine, and, as the name implies, of a nature similar to the Akra. To its ruler therefore was fittingly intrusted the repairing of the great fortress of the city of David. The outer enclosing rampart seems to be here described, and it swept "from the stairs of the city of David round even to before[1] (*ad negeth*) the sepulchres of the kings, and to the pool that was made." Now, on the eastern side of the platform, there is a pool of elaborate construction—the Struthion of Josephus, the traditional Bethesda of Scripture. It is called a pool by the Sheep-market (John v. 2), and here, consequently, was the Sheep-gate, as is indeed usually allowed. Be it observed then, that the circumvallation *began* from the Sheep-gate (Neh. iii. 1), so that when the ruler of Bethzur had done his work to "the pool that was made," the circle of defence would be complete. And such a conclusion is warranted by the subsequent verses of the chapter; inasmuch as the further repairs are carried on by the Levites, and are connected with the precincts of the Temple. But I ask, How could the wall of the ruler of Bethzur, sweeping from "the stairs of the city of David" on to this eastern pool at the Sheep-gate, have *passed near the sepulchres* of the kings, if these were anywhere else than is now maintained?

I shall afterwards refer in detail to the arguments of Mr. Fergusson, by which, on architectural grounds, he contends that the "Mosque of Omar" is the church which Constantine built over the sepulchre of Christ. I may here then be allowed a closing reflection :—

If Constantine was right, if the cavern there be really the tomb of Joseph, then the Messiah of the Jews had his grave near the Sepulchres of the Kings. For centuries indeed no royal burial had been there; and the

---

[1] This is a truer translation than "over against," as in the English version.—Gesenius' *Lexicon*.

ravine had been greatly filled up, as has been already observed, by the labours of the Maccabees and the efforts of Pompey. But this massive rock lay cropping out at the surface, and was bought by Joseph for his own tomb. A rich man, and a friend both of Jews and Romans, he could without difficulty purchase this grave, although lying between the Temple and the fortress. Thither Jesus of Nazareth was carried from the adjacent Calvary; and so, in the vicinity of David's tomb, rested David's Son and David's Lord. The effect of the address on Pentecost can be conceived of as much more stirring if the tombs were thus adjacent,—the former conspicuous by the white expiatory pillar which Herod the Great had erected after his sacrilegious attempt. While the grave of Joseph was then really empty, as all might see for themselves, on the other hand, no disturbance whatever was apparent in the adjoining sepulchral chamber of David, and the monument testifying to that fact was still entire for the view of that audience.

Thus, after Providence had conspicuously overruled the events of the crucifixion, securing that "a bone of him should not be broken," that he should "be with the rich (the noble) in his death," and that there should appear on his cross this title written, "Jesus of Nazareth *the King of the Jews*,"—the same irresistible care had appointed for Him a temporary resting-place in a rock of the ancient city of David, whose deeper chambers held the ancestral "sepulchres of the kings of Judah." The dust of the royal Psalmist still "rested in hope" near by; and we may well conceive how this fact aided the impression produced by the apostle as he proceeded to quote David's words, prophetic of the resurrection of Jesus of Nazareth, "whereof we all are witnesses." He adds a comment on the quotation which was irresistible, "For David is not ascended into the heavens: but he saith himself, Jehovah said unto my Lord, Sit thou on my right hand, until I make thine enemies thy footstool. Therefore let all the house of Israel know assuredly, that God hath made that same Jesus, whom ye have crucified, both Lord and Christ." It was then that the assembly were "pricked in their hearts, and said, Men and brethren, What shall we do?" On the testimony of those witnesses, under the power of the descending Spirit, there were "added about three thousand souls," while "the Lord added to the Church *daily* such as should be saved." The locality of this wondrous meeting, not far from the very scenes of ocular demonstration on the great point at issue, thus appears to our view to have been not without its prominent use in the founding of the infant Church.[1]

[1] The early traditions identify the place where the Spirit descended with such manifest power on the apostles on the day of Pentecost, with "the upper room" where they had observed the Passover with their Lord. If I mistake not, the language of the sacred narrative confirms the idea. In Acts ii. 1 it is said, they were assembled "*in the same place*," ἐπιτοαυτό, which refers us back to "the upper room" in the thirteenth verse of the first chapter; and while it is merely "an upper room" in our translation, the original has the article ("*the* upper room"), which connects it with the "large upper room" in which the Passover was held. The Pentecostal room must also have been "large," which further proves the identification. I shall afterwards aim to show that tradition locates this spot on the slope of the Temple hill near Siloam, and that this also agrees with Scripture.

CHAPTER XII.

THE TEMPLE—THE CASTLE OF ANTONIA.

The Jewish historian, it must be confessed, has received but scant justice at the hands of those who advocate the usual theory regarding the size of the Temple. All are agreed indeed that he oftentimes is disposed to exaggerate, and that we require to take with considerable qualification many of his statements, such as those referring to the population of the city, the height of the mountains, and the depth of its ravines. But we may well pause before consenting to the opinion, that on two of the most important points he has fallen into the opposite extreme, so as greatly to have understated the real dimensions of the Temple and those of the great fortress Antonia. With regard to the former, it might be reasonably supposed that he would fall into no mistake either on one side or the other, inasmuch as its real size could be ascertained by all who took an interest in its worship; and moreover Josephus was himself a priest. If however he did err in statement, it is morally certain that it would be on the side of exaggeration; for was not this the building which a Jew thought of with highest pride, and regarding which he was most anxious that a stranger should entertain the most exalted conceptions? Yet, according to the current hypothesis, he has not only shown great carelessness in that portion of his history which refers to the Temple and to Antonia, but has greatly disparaged their dimensions. He affirms that each side of the Temple was a stadium (600 feet) in length. Instead of this, we are told he should have said a stadium and a half, for does not the southern side measure 927 feet at this day? Again, he says the Temple was a square, as indeed resulted from the fact that the sides were of equal length. This also, it is alleged, is an error. Further, he is understood to affirm that the space covered by Antonia, when united to that of the Temple, was a circuit of six stadia. Here too his calculation has been greatly defective, for the present measurement gives eight stadia.

It was thus assumed that Josephus greatly blundered on these points, until Mr. Fergusson directed attention to the subject. He contends that the historian was right and his commentators are wrong. He appeals in his argument to the construction of the southern wall itself. Advancing from the western corner, for the space mentioned by the Jewish authority (600 feet), the foundations are found to be solid and strong, and altogether such as were necessary for the superincumbent structure. But beyond that point we come on the series of arches (commonly called Solomon's Stables) supporting the present plateau, and which are far too feeble to have borne the pillars and colonnades of the Temple. Along this southern side stretched the famous Stoa Basilica of Herod, whose massive pillars Josephus describes. Their size is *double* that of the pillars underneath, and moreover, Mr. Fergusson has shown that some must have stood on the very crown of those arches.[1] The portico therefore could

[1] *Dictionary of the Bible*: Jerusalem.

not have stretched so far, or indeed extended beyond the point indicated by the language of Josephus. There are other features in the present enclosure which lend confirmation to his statements about the other three sides of the Temple, and the theory of Mr. Fergusson on the subject has been adopted by Messrs. Thrupp and Lewin, two of the most recent writers on the subject.

Understanding then that the Temple was a square of 600 feet, we have now to inquire into the original aspect of the ground on which it was built. I hope to show that here also the statements of the historian imply the existence of a ravine in the present enclosure of the Haram es Sheriff. If the recognition of it has helped us to understand better the description of the hills of the city—has thrown any light on the Scripture allusions to Zion and the sepulchres of the kings—it will be found, I believe, of still greater service when we deal with the language regarding the building of the Temple, and with the expressions of Scripture as to its site and appearance in the time of the Jewish monarchy.

For the clearer elucidation of this subject, let us first test the following language of Josephus by the theory that there was *no* such valley. Let us suppose the space to have been that of an unbroken plateau as at the present day.

1. Josephus invariably speaks of the Temple as placed on a *hill:* "The Temple was situated on a strong hill;" "It was the hill which Solomon encompassed;" "It was the third hill" which the Maccabees joined to the city. From no quarter does he represent it as on a plateau. And yet most assuredly this should have been the description of it if the current assumption be correct. It

stood, in that case, exactly like the "Mosque of Omar," many indeed believing that this is the identical spot. But no one would think of describing that mosque as on a *hill* in reference to the part of the city directly on the north. It is on part of the same ridge (to use Robinson's phrase about the site of the Temple), and on a *lower* elevation, so that from the northern wall you go *down* to it. How then, I ask, can we understand the historian's language unless that ridge had been intersected by a valley at the place where the Temple stood? It may be said that his description is to be taken in a general way, and refers to its appearance on every side except the north. Now, it so happens that this is just the direction where its aspect as a hill is mentioned, and where consequently the existence of a valley is implied. "It was a hill *opposite to the Akra*, and formerly separated from it by a broad ravine." And I remind the reader of the parallel expression in the Book of Maccabees: "The *hill* of the Temple that was adjacent to the *Akra*."

2. The historian further tells us, it was a hill with a very narrow summit. "Originally the level space on the summit scarcely sufficed for the sanctuary (the *Naos* or shrine) and the altar; the circumjacent ground being abrupt and steep."

· This language intimates, let the general reader understand, that there was no room at first for the courts and porticos of the Temple; these were erected long afterwards on embankments artificially formed. The original level space, affirmed here to have scarcely sufficed at first for the Naos Altar, could not have been much more than an area of 150 feet. Here, again, is a most unaccountable statement, if the plateau was not at that time divided by a valley. The dimensions of it could not have differed much from those of the present enclosure, for we can tell where the rock crops out at various points, and if continued all through it is difficult to see why Solomon had not abundant space for a temple of far grander proportions.

There is rock on the south at the place where an excavated subterranean sea is to be found; rock on the north at the distance of 1200 feet; there is rock at the extreme west of the Mosque of Omar, and also at its eastern side near the Golden gateway. If this ridge, then, was not cut in two before the original founding of the Temple, how comes it that Solomon was so straitened for space? What should have prevented him from building a Temple of the size of Herod's, 600 feet each way, nay, erecting it twice over on the unbroken plateau?

3. Josephus affirms that the ground on which the Temple was built was steep and abrupt on all sides.[1] There is the steepness of the Valley of Jehoshaphat on the east, the slope of Ophel on the south, the Tyropœon on the west; but how can such language be descriptive of the northern side if such a valley be ignored?

4. He also repeatedly speaks of immense valleys filled up with earth to make the hill broader on the summit.[2] Where could these have been? Not on the east nor on the west of the Temple, for the rock is there, and his language expressly excludes the south side. Once more, then, the hypothesis renders the description unintelligible. The hill of the Temple turns out to be "a mound of rock" on a spacious plateau!

---

[1] Πέριξ ἀπόκρημνος ἦν καὶ κατάντης.
[2] Josephus, *Bell. Jud.* v. 5. 1; *Antiquities*, viii. 3. 9; and xv. 11. 3.

But admit a previous ravine at the place indicated, and all these statements in reference to the site of the Temple can be well understood. It is thus on every side "a hill." It is "the third hill," which was united to the city; a hill "opposite to the Akra," and "severed from it by a ravine." David, crossing such a ravine, is said to have "gone up" to the thrashing-floor of Araunah; and Solomon, for the same reason, is said to have "brought *up*" the Ark out of the city of David. Into this ravine on the north Solomon built, in order to obtain the space requisite for the Temple, and as it debouched into the Kedron, it must have been of *great* depth; hence, consequently, the language (no doubt exaggerated) that the ground was raised from a depth of 400 cubits.[1]

Solomon's Temple, continues Josephus, had but one colonnade, that on the eastern side. "On the other sides, the Sanctuary (the Ναος) stood exposed. But in process of time the people were constantly adding to the embankments, and so the hill became level and broad." In our view, this means that more space was gained on the north, and the next sentence, it is evident, corroborates the idea: "Having then thrown down[2] the *northern* wall, they enclosed as much ground as the Temple at large subsequently occupied." The whole passage indicates that it was the work of centuries. Some progress appears to have been made in the days of Jehoshaphat, as a *new* court is mentioned in 2 Chron. xx. 5. But the grand result appeared in the size of the Temple of Herod, who had also the debris of the previous structures to help the expansion. "He breasted

---

[1] Josephus, *Antiquities*, viii. 3. 9; or 300, as stated in *Bell. Jud.* v. 5. 1.
[2] Διακόψαντες δὲ καὶ τὸ προσάρκτιον τεῖχος.

up with a wall the area around it, so as to enlarge it to twice its former extent.[1] The plain thus formed by embankments, the accumulated toil of ages, could not have supported the buildings of the Temple unless by strong artificial support; and hence we read, "that the hill was surrounded from the base with a triple wall, and the lowest part was built up from a depth of 300 cubits, and in some places more."[2]

Thus the difficulty and long delay had been caused by the existence of the original valley on the north, the filling up of which was the work of ages, and which ultimately furnished the requisite expansion, finally allowing the Temple to become a square, with each side 600 feet in extent.

The language of Scripture is in harmony with that of Josephus. The site of the Temple is "the mountain of the Lord's house," "the holy mountain," "the mountain of Zion," "the holy hill of Zion," "the house on the top of the mountain," "the mountain of his holiness," "the mountain of the Lord of Hosts." Let the worshipper approach from any quarter, he "went *up*" to the house of the Lord. This language surely points to an eminence begirt it on all sides by a ravine.

Thus set apart by its natural position, the Temple at Jerusalem strikingly answered to the ideas of the age, as a holy and consecrated spot. In every case a locality where was the shrine of a nation's worship was cut off (τέμνω, *templum*) from all profane and common uses. This separation was effected, when necessary, by artificial barriers, but, as in this case, the natural division of a ravine symbolized the consecration in a much more

[1] Josephus, *Bell. Jud.* i. 21. 1. [2] *Ibid.* v. 5. 1.

significant and impressive manner. It tended to deepen the impression of its solemn associations, and enforced the precept, "Keep thy foot when thou goest to the house of God." The awe and reverence so earnestly enjoined were felt all the more deeply, because "the house of the Lord" was separated by so distinct and wide an interval from the common dwellings of men. It was thus in thorough accordance with the whole system of Jewish worship, wherein the ideas of holiness were so impressively taught by sensible signs of remoteness and separation.

Moreover, thus reared on the summit of a strong hill, we can better appreciate the high enthusiasm in the description of its glory. A most impressive spectacle it must have been to the multitudes that thronged from all parts to the holy day and festival! As they came in view of it from "the mountains round about Jerusalem," it appeared to them "beautiful for situation." Their inspired poets furnished them with graphic expressions and appropriate psalms wherewith to express their feelings of veneration and joy. It was "the perfection of beauty," "the house of the Lord," "the Holy One was in the midst of her;" "this is the Mount Zion which he loved," "a glorious high throne was the place of his sanctuary." "Walk about Zion and go round about her, tell the towers thereof: mark ye well her bulwarks, and consider her palaces." When the worshipper entered to tread its courts, every sense was appealed to, in order that his deepest awe and loftiest devotion should be evoked. In the centre was the Altar, with its most significant service; beyond was the Holy of holies, shrouded by the waving veil, mysterious, unapproachable, containing "the tables of stone put in at Horeb." What a scene for *silent* worship! How sublime also the impression when, in those crowded courts, the people are told to "shout to God with the voice of triumph." The stirring memories of their past history are chanted; the miracles of mercy that marked their Exodus are enumerated; and the grand chorus ever and anon bursts forth, loud as the sound of many waters, with the refrain, "For his mercy endureth for ever." Thus wisely adapted was the whole service for the religious development of human nature in that era of the world's history, which so intensely craved for symbolism and sensuous splendour; and the impressive effect, I believe, was greatly owing to the natural position of the "holy hill," standing apart, begirt with deep ravines, confronting the mass of the city with battlements and pinnacles exclusively its own.

About five hundred years after its erection by Solomon, the Temple, along with the city, was sacked at the Babylonian captivity. The horrors of that awful time are portrayed in the most vivid colouring by the pen of Jeremiah. A graphic picture is often sketched in a single sentence. The straitness of the siege! "The hands of the pitiful women have sodden their own children." How complete the captivity! "The city sits solitary that was full of people!" And so in a single verse we have a picture of the utter ruin and desolation of the Temple hill, where he alone was left to lament, "The *mountain of Zion* is desolate; foxes walk on it."

After an interval of about fifty years, the second temple was built by Zerubbabel. The opinion is not uncommon that it was double the size of the former one, but we have no direct statement to that effect either in Scripture or Josephus. It can only be inferred by assuming that Herod's temple covered precisely the same ground; for that edifice, Josephus tells us, comprised twice the area of the first. There seems little doubt, however, that the temple of Zerubbabel (though inferior in height)[1] was somewhat larger than that of Solomon ; and this was owing, it is likely, to the widening of the space on the summit by the artificial embankments before referred to,—an expansion the more easily accomplished because of the ruins of the former temple that had been thrown into the ravine. In the language of Zechariah, a contemporary (who aimed to stimulate the Jews to the work of building it), the Temple site is spoken of as "Zion, the *mountain* of the Lord of hosts, the *holy mountain*" (Zech. viii. 3).

And now let us pass over an interval of three hundred years, and view the aspect of the locality in the time of the Maccabees. The one name for the Temple site is still Mount Zion ; and, as in Josephus, the language of this book specially marks a valley between it and the Akra. The "hill of the Temple that was *near* the Akra he fortified," etc., Τὸ ὄρος τοῦ ἱεροῦ τὸ παρὰ τὴν Ἄκραν (1 Macc. xiii. 52). Nicanor, coming from the city of David, where the Akra was, "*went up* to Mount Zion," ἀνέβη εἰς τὸ ὄρος Ζιών" (1 Macc. vii. 33). He therefore crossed the valley for which we contend ; and we shall find further evidence of its existence in noticing the protracted contests between the Jews in the Temple on the one side, and the heathen in the Akra on the other. Each party was then besieged in turn for months to-

---

[1] Josephus, *Antiquities*, xv. 11. 1.

gether, and the whole account seems fabulous, unless we are to believe that the Temple was defended by a precipice on the quarter where it was threatened. We read that the army of Antiochus "pitched against Mount Zion," and "besieged it many days." "They set their artillery, with engines and instruments to cast fire and stones, and pieces to cast darts and slings; whereupon they" (the defenders in the Sanctuary) "also made engines against their engines, and held them battle for a long season. There were but few left in the Sanctuary, because the famine did so prevail against them, that they were fain to disperse themselves every man to his own place" (1 Macc. vi. 48, 51, 52, 54). But few as the defenders were, they held their ground, so that the king came to terms, promising the Jews all liberty to observe their laws. In the faith of this they admitted "the king and princes into the stronghold of the Temple." "Then the king entered into Mount Zion, but when he saw the strength of the place, he brake his oath that he had made, and gave commandment to pull down the wall round about" (1 Macc. vi. 62). It is not possible, I submit, to believe that the Temple could have stood such a protracted siege unless for this intermediate valley. If situated on the level ground, it is not easy to understand how defence on the part of the scanty garrison should have been attempted at all, far less how it should have been successful. In fact, lying at the foot of the impending stronghold of the city of David, held by an enemy so fierce and vigilant, we are perplexed to discover how Judas and his followers could have got access to it at the first, and managed to purify its courts for the purposes of worship.

Ultimately, however, the garrison of the citadel were, after a long period of siege, compelled to capitulate to Simon, the brother of Judas. He enclosed the place with a wall; he cut off all means of their obtaining provisions. "They also of the tower in Jerusalem were kept so strait, that they could neither come forth nor go into the country, nor buy nor sell; wherefore they were in great distress for want of victuals, and a great number of them perished through famine. Then cried they to Simon, beseeching him to be at one with them, which thing he granted them, and when he had put them out from thence, he cleansed the tower from pollutions" (1 Macc. xiii. 49, 50). The joy of the people at the possession of "the tower" was immense, and it was ordained that the day should be kept every year with gladness (vers. 51, 52).

We have now arrived at another stage of the evidence in support of the view we are seeking to establish. Hitherto the argument has aimed to show that such a transverse valley did exist in this eastern ridge. It is a natural inquiry, How came it to be so entirely filled up? We have a better answer than that rubbish and ruins in some inexplicable way obliterated all traces of it. We shall find the explanation in what is recorded by Josephus of the doings of the Maccabees, and Pompey, and also of Titus at the final overthrow of the city and its temple.

Having suffered so much from the enemy in the citadel, Simon persuaded the Jews utterly to demolish it, and so prevent against a similar calamity in all time to come. The rock, he resolved, must be razed to the foundation. "He thought it for their advantage to level the very mountain on which the citadel happened to stand, that so the Temple might be higher than it. They all set themselves to level the mountain, and in that work spent day and night without intermission, which cost them three whole years before it was removed, so as to effect there an entire level with the plain of the rest of the city. After which the Temple was the highest of all the buildings, now that the citadel, as well as the eminence on which it stood, were demolished."[1] This is the more lengthened account of the event referred to by Josephus in the passage already quoted on the hills of the city. "The Maccabees, working continuously on the Akra, reduced its elevation, so that the Temple might be conspicuous above it also."[2] The question then is, How did the Maccabees dispose of the materials of the rock thus demolished after the toil of three years? The answer shall be in the words of Josephus: "The Maccabees during their reign *filled up* the ravine (which is affirmed in the preceding sentence to have existed between the third hill and the Akra) with the intention of uniting the city to the Temple." Thus then the valley began to be raised to the level.

That it was but the commencement, or rather the filling up only of a part of it, is evident from what we find narrated in the account of the siege of Pompey about eighty years afterwards. Indeed, a little reflection will convince us, that it would have been a suicidal act for the Maccabees to have filled up the entire length, even if they had the materials for doing so, which they had not. For, by such an act, they would have deprived the Temple of the best defence on the north. The defending wall, I remind the reader, did not extend across the

---

[1] Josephus, *Antiquities*, xiii. 6. 7.   [2] *Bell. Jud.* v. 4. 1.

northern side of the Temple, but, stopping short of it, terminated at Antonia (then "the city of David"), for the simple reason, that the Temple, secure on the steep which it overhung in that direction, did not need any artificial defence. If then the Maccabees had filled up the valley throughout, they would have destroyed the strongest safeguard of their adored Temple, and exposed it more than ever to the designs of the enemy. The inference warranted by the language of Josephus, and confirmed by his subsequent narrative relating to this district, is, that the Maccabees constructed, out of the materials of the citadel, an *embankment* across the valley. Dr. Robinson admits that the phrases, "filled up the valley," and "joining the city to the Temple," may be thus understood, and does not believe that the valley was so filled up as to obliterate all traces of it.[1]

Pompey (B.C. 65) having laid siege to Jerusalem, gained admission to the city by the connivance of one of the rival parties, and proceeded to attack the Temple, resolutely defended by the other. He took up his position on the north side. And what was the grand obstacle to its capture? In the different portions of his narrative, Josephus affirms that it was a deep ravine lying under the northern wall. "Pompey pitched his camp within the wall (of the city), on the north part of the Temple, where it was most practicable, but even on that side there were great towers, and a fosse had been dug, and a deep valley begirt it round about."[2] "A fosse and ravine lay on the north quarter,"—"a prodigious depth of ravine."[3] The statement is thus most explicit.

---

[1] *Bib. Researches*, iii. 209. [2] Τάφρος δὲ ὀρώρυκτο καὶ βαθείᾳ περιείχετο φάραγγι
[3] Josephus, *Bell. Jud.* i. 7. 3.

It may be asked, How should the historian speak of a fosse as well as a ravine? This can be well explained by the view taken above of the work of the Maccabees. It meant the *cutting off* the communication with the Temple by the artificial pathway—a measure obviously necessary on the approach of an enemy.

Pompey was arrested for many days by this obstacle, and would not have been able to overcome it, but for the circumstance which the historian records with evident pride. Observing that on the seventh day the Jews desisted from fighting unless when absolutely compelled by self-defence, he took this opportunity of filling up the fosse and valley, and securing a basis for his engines and battering-rams, which were afterwards worked with deadly effect. Did Pompey then fill up the ravine to its eastern extremity where it enters the Valley of Jehoshaphat? The answer must be in the negative. It is a fair presumption, that he would care to raise it only so far along as was necessary for his purpose—the capture of the Temple. We are led to this conclusion all the more clearly from the language of Josephus: "It was a work of vast labour, and the ravine was filled up but *poorly*, because of its immense depth."

The following facts, afterwards mentioned by the historian, show that at its *eastern* end the valley was untouched. It formed there the Kedron ravine to be distinguished from Kedron simply, or the Valley of Jehoshaphat.

1. The new wall of Agrippa, A.D. 45, coming down from the north, met the old wall that stretched up from Siloam at the eastern cloister of the Temple at the

Kedron ravine. None can allege that either the northern or southern portion of that wall touched at any part the Valley of Jehoshaphat; the northern lay along the ridge. From their directions, the new wall could have met the old one only at some transverse valley, as represented in the sketch, if we attach any meaning at all to the language employed.

2. In the account of the siege by Titus, A.D. 80, we are informed that "Simon occupied the upper town, and the great wall (of Agrippa), as far as the Kedron." John occupied the Antonia, "the Temple, and the parts about it to a considerable distance, with Ophla and *the Kedron ravine*," or rather "the ravine named from the Kedron." These chiefs are in utter hostility to each other, and their followers engage in deadly feud whenever the siege of the Romans outside may happen to pause. They hold no ground in common, and so "the Kedron ravine" is quite a different place from "the Kedron." The position of the Temple, Ophla, and Antonia, mark its locality, and the language used confirms our conclusion, that at its eastern termination it was still a *ravine*.

3. The Romans on coming close to the Temple "fired the northern colonnade as far as the eastern, the connecting angle of which was built over the Kedron ravine. The depth at that point was terrific."[1]

Our conclusion then is, that notwithstanding the labours of the Maccabees and of Pompey, the transverse valley was still apparent at the eastern extremity, as the illustrations represent.[2]

About forty years after Pompey (B.C. 37), Herod the

---

[1] Josephus, *Bell. Jud.* vi. 3. 2.
[2] See "*Jerusalem in the time of Christ*," and "*The Crucifixion*."

Great laid siege to Jerusalem, encamped on the north of the city, aiming like his predecessors at the capture of the Temple. After a siege of forty days he took the first wall.[1] In fifteen days more he gained possession of the second. This was none other than the outer wall of the Temple itself, inasmuch as the burning of the outer cloisters immediately followed. Here seems to have been a comparatively easy and speedy capture, for which, as I view it, Herod was mainly indebted to the previous toil of Pompey's troops, in filling the outer ravine to a great extent, and thereby affording more advantageous ground of attack. The siege was not yet at an end, for the Jews retreated to the inner courts of the Temple, which were of commanding elevation, and to the upper city. As their appointed king, Herod desired to spare the people as much as possible; but on the obstinate refusal to submit, he directed the Roman general to carry the inner Temple and city by storm. The attack succeeded, and a dreadful massacre ensued; the Roman troops exulting in the work of blood with a savage joy. Herod remonstrated, and demanded of the general Sosius, "Whether he was to be left king of a desert instead of a city?" He aimed also to preserve the *Naos* as much as possible, and standing before the avenue to it with a drawn sword, threatened to cut down the first man that should dare to enter. The siege had lasted in all five months.[2] While his reign throughout was very stern and cruel, he yet studied the religious prejudices of the people, perhaps as much from necessity as from choice, and especially sought that they should think of him as the most zealous protector of their wor-

---

[1] Josephus, *Antiquities*, xiv. 16. 2.   [2] *Bell. Jud.* i. 18. 2.

ship. With this view he proposed to rebuild the Temple for them, alleging that the present structure was unworthy of their former traditions, as being lower by sixty cubits than the Temple of Solomon. Our forefathers, he told the multitude, were not to be blamed for this, inasmuch as they were then under subjection to Cyrus and Darius of Persia. But now that in him they had a governor of their own, "the defect ought to be repaired, and he would endeavour to render the Temple as complete as he was able." Suspecting his sincerity and ability to accomplish his project, the Jews would not for a time allow the old Temple to be touched. But on his gathering all the necessary materials before taking down any of the existing structure, they consented; and in eight years there rose the famous third Temple, the same which existed in the time of our Lord, surveyed with fond pride by his disciples on Olivet, but by him with sadness as he foreshadowed its doom.

While thus consulting the interests of the Jews, Herod was mindful of his own. He built the great citadel of Antonia. It had been otherwise a dangerous thing to have erected the Temple in such splendour and strength, capable as it was of being used as a citadel from its natural position; indeed Tacitus remarks, that the Temple itself was a strong fortress of the nature of a citadel, while Josephus speaks of it as "the citadel of the city." But Herod managed to construct this fortress of vast size, and so to connect it with the Temple as to secure his own power, while apparently pandering to the prejudices and pride of the Jews.

The position of Antonia, and its situation relative to the Temple, must now receive our attention. It occupied the site of the demolished stronghold of Zion, the city of David, replacing another structure (the *Baris*), which the Maccabees had erected there. To secure the Antonia was the first ambition of the general who sought to capture the city. And not only on these accounts does it claim our interest, but it was also the residence of Pilate in the time of our Lord,[1] and as may afterwards appear adjoined the place of the crucifixion.

Let us mark the description by Josephus of this tower of Antonia. " It was erected on a strong rock fifty cubits high, and on every side precipitous. The interior resembled a palace in extent and arrangements, being distributed into apartments of every description, and for every use, with cloistered courts and baths, and spacious barracks for the accommodation of troops; so that its various conveniences gave it the semblance of a town, its magnificence that of a palace. The general appearance of the whole was that of a huge tower, with other towers at each of the four corners; three of which latter were fifty cubits high, while that at the south-east angle rose to an elevation of seventy cubits, so that from thence there was a complete view of the Temple. Where it adjoined the Temple colonnades, it had passages leading down to both, through which the guards (for in the fortress there always lay a Roman legion) descended in arms at the festivals, and dispersed themselves about the colonnades, to watch the people and repress any insur-

---

[1] Mr. Lewin has endeavoured to show that the residence of the governor must have been on the other hill at the north-west of the city, in Herod's palace, with the view of confirming the locality of the present Church of the Holy Sepulchre. He cites the case of Florus, who had his "judgment-seat" there. But the reason was, that he could not get into the Antonia. The apparent exception confirms the tradition that Antonia was the residence of the governor in military command of the city.

rectionary movement. For the Temple lay as a fortress over the city, and Antonia over the Temple; the guards of all the three being stationed in the Antonia, while the upper town had its own fortress, Herod's palace. The hill Bezetha was detached from the Antonia; it was the highest of *all*, and was joined to part of the new town, forming northward the only obstruction to the view of the Temple."[1]

What then was the position of this remarkable citadel in relation to the Temple? The general opinion (advocated by Dr. Robinson) is, that it was close to it, and moreover, that it lay along its whole northern wall; in fact, that the present enclosure of the Haram es Sheriff was divided into two portions nearly equal, the southern that of the Temple, and the northern that of Antonia. Mr. Fergusson has shown, from the two following facts in the siege of Titus, that this extension of the fortress along the Temple wall was impossible. In a review of the Roman army, which Titus held after he had obtained possession of Bezetha, the Jews are said to have looked on "from the *north wall* of the Temple." Again, they managed to resist an attack of the enemy from Antonia and the *north wall* of the Temple at one and the same time. Neither of these things, it is obvious, would have been possible, if Antonia had been joined along the entire length of that wall, as is usually represented. Mr. Fergusson would adjoin it therefore only at a limited portion of the Temple—the north-west corner.[2]

---

[1] Josephus, *Bell. Jud.* v. 5. 8.
Both Traill and Whitsius strangely enough translate, "It was the highest of the *three*," in opposition to the Greek πάντων, and to the statement elsewhere of Josephus, that Bezetha was a *fourth* hill.
[2] See *Dictionary of the Bible*: Jerusalem.

I have now to submit the following evidence, to prove that Antonia could not have *adjoined the Temple at all*. Passing over the considerations which have been adduced, that a valley had at one time existed at this point (although now greatly filled up), and therefore that there could have been here no such *rock* as that on which Josephus expressly says the citadel was built, I remark—

1. That any such junction is contradicted by what we read of the religious spirit of the age. At no period of their history did the Jews manifest a more intense temper of bigotry and fanaticism—a more sensitive jealousy connected with the services of their Temple. However strong the measures of civil oppression on which their ruler might venture, it behoved him to beware how he meddled with their religious services. Any insult of this sort roused them to ungovernable fury. Is it credible then that they should have endured, side by side with their own Temple, and *as part of it*, a fortress such as this, filled with Roman troops, and one of whose towers at least (the south-eastern) was of such elevation that the heathen soldiers could have looked down on the sacred service immediately below? A menace and insult so undisguised would have been the source of endless tumult; and of all their rulers Herod was the most unlikely to have ventured on such a provocation.

2. On this theory, Antonia could not have been of the *size* that Josephus asserts. According to the usual interpretation of the historian's language, it was a circumference of *six* stadia along with the Temple. Deducting the size of the latter enclosure (four stadia), there are two left (1200 feet) for the fortress; and as it was

"a *square*," we must think of its dimensions as 300 feet on each side. But how then could Josephus have described it as having "the appearance of a *town*," " with spacious barracks for the accommodation of troops." How in such a space could there be room for "a whole Roman legion ;" 4000 men on the average?

3. A fortress so situated did *not adjoin* Bezetha, and was *not* "separate from it by a fosse," as Josephus represents.

4. The proposed idea is further shown to be inadmissible by what is recorded of the siege of Titus. We may assume it as probable that the Romans, having captured a fortress of such altitude and strength, would have made an immediate conquest of the *outer* Temple at least, whose walls (by this hypothesis) joined on to it. But the Temple held out for a considerable time, and was not taken till after the adoption of additional measures. Titus indeed had to *demolish Antonia* before he could effectively besiege it; and not only so, but he erected other towers close to its wall, which therefore must have been raised on the very spot where the fortress had stood! If its position had been as represented, it is very evident that all this labour of the besiegers was utterly thrown away. The fact is, nothing would have suited the purpose of Titus better than such a fortress, if it had been so closely adjacent to the Temple; and after gaining possession of it, further resistance on the part of the Jews would have been out of the question.

The following considerations are intended to vindicate the location of Antonia as represented in the pictorial illustration. It was apart from the Temple, lying north from it about 200 yards, on the rock at the north-west of the present enclosure. It was connected with the Temple by *colonnades*.

I need not dwell on the fact, that as being thus apart, these events referred to as occurring in the siege of Titus can be explained, inasmuch as the possession of the citadel did *not* involve the easy capture of the Temple. But further, let us specially notice—

1. That this location is identical with that of "the stronghold of Zion" which Antonia replaced. Here are to be seen the traces of that earnest labour which, after three years, levelled the ancient rocky fortress, whence the enemy had so long continued to defy the efforts of the Maccabean chiefs, Judas and Simon. On this spot the Maccabees had erected a fortress called Baris, where the priestly vestments might be safely kept, and this came to be replaced by the Antonia of Herod.

2. This position accords with the language of Josephus, that "Antonia adjoined Bezetha, and was separated from it by a deep fosse." The valley came down from Herod's Gate, and though deep at first, we may conceive that it was gradually being filled up, while the town was rising on that eastern hill. We can thus understand then how Herod should here "dig a deep trench (elsewhere was rock) so as to strengthen the defence of the stronghold, and make its towers look more elevated." While this was the eastern boundary, its *western* side overhung the Tyropœan, the central valley of the city. It covered the breadth of the ancient stronghold of Zion, as has been said, and with such a view of its position, we can understand another expression of Josephus, "that it stood on rock fifty cubits high."

3. We may conceive of it as stretching up the ridge

of the Akra, and so having a size which accords with the description already quoted. It may be objected that this idea overlooks the statement, that the circuit of Antonia was only two stadia, being a circuit of six stadia including the Temple. The objection will have our consideration in looking at the next point, that it was connected with the Temple by *colonnades*.

First of all, Josephus, in two passages, affirms that the connexion was of this kind. "Antonia," he says, "lay at an angle formed by two colonnades, the western and the northern, of the outer court of the Temple."[1] Such language proves that the colonnades must have stretched up to it, if it was apart from the Temple as has been shown. If any should appeal to this language as proving that there was no interval between the buildings, I may, in addition to the foregoing considerations, notice that Josephus in that case would have remarked that it adjoined the north-west corner of the outer Temple itself, without speaking of colonnades at all. Again he says : "Where Antonia adjoined *the colonnades of the Temple*, it had passages leading down to both, through which the guards descended," etc., to the sacred festivals.

Again, the colonnades are distinguished by special names and phrases. They are τὰ μέλη (the *limbs* of the Temple) ; αἱ συνεχεῖς στοαί (the connecting colonnades) ; στοὰς τὸ συνεχὲς, πρὸς τὴν Ἀντωνίαν (the colonnades that reached onwards to Antonia).[2] Of the colonnades of the Temple proper such expressions are never used.

There are other incidents mentioned by the historian which have an explanation only in view of this relative situation of the buildings. Florus, the governor of

---

[1] Josephus, *Bell. Jud.* v. 5. 8.   [2] *Ibid.* ii. 15. 6 ; vi. 2. 9.

Jerusalem, whose residence was in the palace of Herod in the upper city, endeavoured by a stratagem to get possession of Antonia, and, through it, of the Temple; his object being to plunder its treasury. "He used all his efforts to approach the fortress, but was foiled in the attempt, and the troops retired to the encampment at the palace. The Jews, fearing lest he should return, and, pushing forward through the Antonia, possess himself of the Temple, instantly mounted the colonnades which connected the two buildings, and cut off the communication." As we never read of the colonnades of the *Temple proper* being damaged till the siege of Titus, this interruption could only refer to those running north to Antonia. Agrippa, we further read, reprimanded the Jews for this act on his return from Egypt. He warns them against insurrection, alleging that no people was a match for the Roman power, and that "even the Britons, girded by the ocean and occupying an island, not less than the country we inhabit, the Romans sailed to and subdued; and extensive as that island is, four legions keep it." The Jews reply, that "they have not taken up arms against the Romans, but to avenge themselves on Florus." To which the answer is, "But your actions are those of men already at war with the Romans, for you have not given the tribute to Cæsar, and *you have cut away* the colonnades from Antonia." Now, had these been simply the colonnades of the Temple itself, the Roman governor would have cared little, if at all, for the damage that had been done. It mattered little to him how they altered or destroyed portions of their religious buildings. And certainly this could be no ground for the charge of *in-*

surrection. But he had a pretext for that charge, if he could regard the buildings in question as belonging to Antonia also, whose destruction therefore impaired the ability of the Roman power to quell any tumult that might arise in the Temple,—the great purpose indeed for which Herod at first constructed them.

Further, the view here presented of the distance of the two buildings, and of their means of communication, will explain to us the language of Josephus with regard to a prediction that was current before the siege of Titus, in reference to the fall of the city. "The Jews, after the demolition of Antonia (by Titus), reduced their Temple to a *square*, though they had it recorded in their oracles that the city and the Sanctuary would be taken when the Temple should become square." Recurring to a former point I may here observe, that if the citadel itself had *joined on* to the Temple, then Titus with his army would have been represented as fulfilling this prediction, inasmuch as by them the work of its demolition was effected; whereas the reducing of the Temple to the dimensions stated, is affirmed to have been the act of *the Jews themselves*. When we turn to the full account of the matter, we find that the deed refers to the setting on fire by the Jews of the colonnade " connected with the Antonia, and that they subsequently broke off about twenty cubits, thus with their own hands commencing the conflagration of the holy places. The Romans, two days after, set fire to the adjoining colonnade,"[1]—these being double, as in the case of the Temple. The point to be remarked is, that in this act the Jews could not have touched the colonnades of the Temple proper, for then its dimensions would

[1] Josephus, *Bell. Jud.* vi. 2. 9.

have *ceased* to be those of a square. Moreover, the destruction of these is distinctly mentioned in a *subsequent* part of the siege. Further on we read, that the Jews retired from the *western* colonnade, allured the Romans (who by this time had their mounds erected close to the Temple walls) on to the ascent, and then, having set fire to it, caused vast numbers to perish in the flames ; and that the besiegers, who had now a free entrance to the colonnades of the Temple, "on the following day fired the whole of the *northern* colonnade as far as the eastern, the connecting angle of which was built over the Kedron ravine."[1] I submit that the view as exhibited in the picture, fully explains these facts of the Jewish historian.

Lastly, with this idea we can explain the language : "The colonnades of the Temple were thirty cubits broad, and their entire circuit, including the Antonia, measured six stadia," *i.e.*, two stadia in addition to the circuit of the Temple. This passage, taken by itself, would evidently sanction the idea that the historian is here referring to the dimensions of the fortress itself. As such, indeed, it has been generally understood, and on it have been based the different opinions which the preceding considerations have aimed to controvert. But if this had been the true interpretation, then, I remind the reader, we are forced to set down this fortress, which had "the aspect of a town," "spacious accommodation for troops," and "capable of holding a whole Roman legion," as an insignificant tower 300 feet square. And besides, how shall we account for the fact that Josephus, in a passage of his history which aims to celebrate the magnitude of the Temple alone, conjoins in his description this citadel

[1] Josephus, *Bell. Jud.* vi. 3. 1, 2.

occupied by the heathen soldiers of a foreign power? There is little need for further argument, as, in the view of other statements in his history, it has been shown that the fortress did *not* adjoin the Temple, and could not have been thus included. Let the reader remark that Josephus, in this passage, is speaking of *colonnades*. In our view, the colonnades at the north-west corner of the Temple were prolonged up to the Antonia. The Jews were thus free to enjoy their circuit; they were a splendid addition to the colonnades of the Temple proper, and hence the historian includes them. Moreover, the addition would be just such as he represents, viz., two stadia. The rock is distant from the Temple space between five and six hundred feet, and the breadth of the colonnades was thirty cubits. As these were double, the entire breadth was sixty cubits, or ninety feet. Let us think, then, of the colonnades reaching to the Antonia as about 600 (555) feet long by ninety feet broad, and the circuit of them would be two stadia (1200 feet), precisely as the historian represents.[1]

A glance at the Illustration of the scene of the crucifixion will enable the reader to understand why these discussions on the situation of the Temple in reference to Antonia have been so protracted. Not only is it one of the most important points in the topography of ancient Jerusalem, but, in our view, it has a direct bearing on that portion of it which was the theatre of the most impressive events in the history of the world.

The final destruction of the city and temple was accomplished in the siege of Titus, A.D. 70, when, as Jose-

---

[1] The southern side from which the colonnades started is not to be included in this calculation, because it is part of the dimensions of the Temple.

phus informs us, "the whole was so thoroughly levelled and dug up that no one visiting it would believe it had ever been inhabited." This is by far the most detailed history of any siege which he records, in which, indeed, he was an eye-witness and actor, and has been especially studied by the various theorists on the features of the ancient city. I shall now present his account of some events that bear on the localities that have occupied our attention. The language shall be his own, with a brief comment occasionally inserted, and if it be found to harmonize easily with the views of Antonia and the Temple now advanced, then it will establish still further their truth, and enable the reader better to judge of the arguments which aim to fix the true position of Calvary and the Holy Sepulchre.

At this period, let the general reader understand, the third wall of Agrippa, which encircled the suburb of Bezetha, had been built, and at its southern termination "met the old wall at the Kedron ravine." The city was held by Simon and John. Their followers are at deadly feud, and the warfare pauses only when they are engaged in defending themselves from the common enemy without. "Simon," it is said, "occupied the great wall of Agrippa as far as Kedron,"—the Valley of Jehoshaphat. Besides Antonia, "John occupied the Temple and the parts about it to a considerable extent, with Ophel and *the Kedron ravine;*" *i.e.*, the eastern termination of the transverse valley as yet untouched. As Titus makes the attack on the north, the brunt of the onset falls on Simon and his party. Though assisted by the partisans of John, the defence is unavailing, and after fifteen days, Titus gains possession of the first wall, "occupying the entire interval as far as the Kedron."[1] The platform between Antonia and the Temple could then be reached; but on making an attack in that quarter, the enemy was repelled by "John and his party, fighting from the Antonia and the north colonnade of the Temple." The Roman general now resolves to concentrate his efforts on the capture of Antonia, which lay at the termination of the second and yet uncaptured wall. Two mounds are erected, "one opposite to the middle of the reservoir Struthion, and the other at the distance of twenty cubits."[2] This reservoir was the pool Bethesda, and is the termination of the valley from Herod's gate. Opposite to it, and against the citadel which stretched up the ridge, the mounds are erected, on *the Bezetha* side of which the Romans had now possession.[3] The Jews endeavour to undermine these mounds, and at last they "fell in with a tremendous crash." Damage, however, had been done by these mines to the wall of the Antonia itself, and it afterwards gave way to the strokes of the battering-ram from the second mounds that were raised. "But the unhoped-for joy of the Romans at this event was speedily extinguished by the appearance of another wall, which John and his party had built inside. The assault of this seemed likely to be attended with less difficulty than that of the former, as the ruins of the outer wall facilitated the ascent to it." Titus harangued his troops, urging them to the assault. "Sabinus, a Syrian, in whose attenuated frame, little proportioned to its native prowess, dwelt a heroic soul," was the first to respond. "I cheerfully devote myself to you, Caesar,"

---

[1] Josephus, *Bell. Jud.* v. 7. 3.   [2] *Ibid.* v. 11. 4.
[3] See p. 257—Topography of Jerusalem.

he exclaimed; "I am the first to scale the wall, and I pray that your fortune may second my strength and resolution." He was followed by eleven others, but was slain, with three of his comrades, and the Jews remained masters of the fortress. Two days afterwards it came into the possession of the Romans in the simplest way. "Twenty of the guards, who formed an outpost, assembled, and inviting the standard-bearer of the fifth legion to join them, with two horsemen from the lines and a trumpeter, advanced at the ninth hour of night without noise to the ruins of Antonia. The sentinels whom they first fell in with, they killed in their sleep, and having gained possession of the wall, ordered the trumpeter to sound. On this the other guards suddenly started to their feet and fled, before any one had observed what number had ascended, and the peal of the trumpet led them to suppose that the enemy had mounted in great force. Titus, on hearing the signal, immediately ordered the troops to arms, and with the generals and his detachment of picked men, was the first to mount the ramparts. The Jews fled into the Temple; the Romans also making their way (into the Antonia) through the mines which John had excavated under their mounds."[1]

Thus easily at last was captured the great stronghold of Antonia.

But *the Temple* was not taken until after a fierce and protracted struggle. The Romans following up their success, aimed at that time to enter, but were resisted, and "a desperate conflict ensued around the approaches" (the connecting colonnades). "Drawing their swords, they engaged hand-to-hand, and in the narrowness of

[1] Josephus, *Bell. Jud.* vi. 1. 7.

the place, the men were mixed with one another and interchanged; their battle-cries, so loud was the din, struck confusedly on the ear." The engagement continued till the seventh hour of the day, when the Romans had " to be satisfied with the possession of Antonia." On another occasion, the capture of the Temple was attempted through these narrow colonnades, but with no better result. Titus then resolves to *demolish* the Antonia, "prepare a broad ascent to the Temple," and erect the towers close to its walls. These were four in number; two against the *inner* Temple, and two against the colonnades of the *outer* court.[1] The commanding elevation of the inner Temple, rising above the outer to an elevation of forty feet, required that it should be attacked from special mounds of corresponding height. Two (one of each kind) are on the western side (and therefore in the central valley), and the other two are on the northern side of the Temple. Since these strong mounds are rising, it is vain for the Jews to endeavour to keep possession of the colonnades that reached to Antonia, which was now demolished, except the south-eastern tower, retained by Titus, that he might the better superintend the progress of the siege. The direct attack on the Temple itself demands all their vigilance and concentration, and accordingly they " set fire to part of the north-western colonnade connected with the Antonia, and subsequently broke off about twenty cubits." Thus they began to reduce the Temple to the form of a square, and so fulfil the conditions of the prediction respecting its doom. " The Romans two days after set fire to the adjoining colonnade (it was double, like those of the

[1] Josephus, *Bell. Jud.* vi. 2. 7.

Temple), and the flame advancing fifteen cubits farther, the Jews cut away the roof, destroying the whole communication between them and the Antonia."[1]

Shortly afterwards commenced the destruction of the *Temple* colonnades. The first that fell was the western one. Retiring from it as if defeated, and thereby inducing many of the besiegers to ascend, the Jews set fire to it, having previously accumulated pitch, bitumen, and dry wood. "Encircled by the flames, some precipitated themselves backward into the city (part of which lay in that central valley), and some into the midst of the enemy." "The gallery was burnt down as far as the tower which John had erected above the gate that led out beyond the Xystus."[2]

The Romans had now entrance to the colonnades of the Temple, and so we read that "on the following day they fired the northern colonnade as far as the eastern, the connecting angle of which was built over the Kedron ravine, whence the depth at that point is terrific. Such was the state of affairs in the Temple."

In the next chapter the historian goes on to describe the fortunes of the siege in the *inner* Temple, which rose high above the enclosing courts as a central citadel. Its construction was a masterpiece of art, and the efforts of the Romans on its western wing from the one mound, and those directed against its northern gate from the other, were for a long time ineffective. "Giving up in despair all attempts with engines and levers, they applied the scaling ladders to the galleries," only, however, to encounter an unflinching and deadly repulse. "Titus seeing that his forbearance towards a foreign temple was

[1] Josephus, *Bell Jud.* vi. 2. 9. [2] *Ibid.* vi. 3. 2.

attended with slaughter and injury to his own troops, ordered its gates to be set on fire. The silver melting around quickly admitted the flames to its wood-work, whence they spread in a continuous volume, and seized on the galleries." Notwithstanding their bitter miseries and the obvious triumph of the besiegers, the Jews had desperately clung to the belief that the Sanctuary enclosing the shrine of their worship could never be taken or destroyed, and now when the leaping flames have seized on it, they are as men that dream. They "seeing the fire encircling them lost all energy alike of mind and body, and such was their consternation that they made no attempt either to ward off or extinguish the devouring element; they stood motionless spectators during that day, and the succeeding night the fire continued to rage, for they could only apply it to the galleries in detached places, and not to the whole range at once." Next day, in a conflict with the Jews, who had rallied from their stupor, the Romans penetrated to the holy shrine itself :—" And at this moment, a soldier, neither waiting for orders nor awed by so dread a deed, but hurried on by some supernatural impulse, snatched a brand from the blazing timber, and being lifted up by one of his comrades, threw in the fire through a small golden door which was the entrance on the north side into the apartments round the Sanctuary. As the flames ascended, a cry, commensurate with the calamity, was raised by the Jews, who flocked to the rescue, no longer sparing life, nor husbanding their strength, now that that was perishing for the sake of which hitherto they had been so vigilant."

In vain did the Roman commander seek to extinguish

the flames, and "prodigious was the slaughter of those found there." "To no age was pity shown, to no rank respect, but children and old men, secular persons and priests, were overwhelmed in one common ruin. The flames, borne far and wide, united their roar with the groans of their falling; than the din of that moment nothing could be conceived louder or more fearful. There was the exulting war-cry of the Roman legions as they moved in mass, the shrieks of the insurgents encircled by fire and sword, and the wailing of the people over their calamities as, deserted on the high ground, they turned in consternation toward the enemy. The multitude in the city blended their cries with the cries of those upon the hill, and now many, emaciated by famine, and whose lips had closed when they beheld the Sanctuary in a blaze, again gathered strength for lamentations and cries. The city beyond returned the echo, as did the mountains around, deepening the uproar. Yet were the sufferings still more fearful than the confusion. You would indeed have thought that the hill on which the sacred edifice stood was boiling up from its base, and that the stream of blood was ampler still than the fire, and the slaughtered more numerous than the slaughterers."

Thus fell the Temple of Jerusalem. We need not continue the account of the dreadful siege. The scene of desolation, over which Jeremiah wept, was but a faint image of the horrors that now befell the city and its inhabitants. "Wrath came on Jerusalem to the uttermost." The tears of the "Son of Man" fell fast in the prospect of it. "When he beheld the city, he wept over it." Once on Olivet the disciples were admiring the grandeur of the Temple, but he gazed sadly on its glory, and uttered the prediction now so terribly fulfilled: "Not one stone shall be left on another." And even when on the way to the cross, the fearfulness of that coming doom rose to his view amid the darkness of his own great sorrow: "Daughters of Jerusalem, weep not for me, but weep for yourselves."

The massive buildings of the Temple were hurled into the slopes and valleys around. Thus was "the Kedron ravine," the greater part of which had been obliterated long previously by the Maccabees and Pompey, still further filled up. The ground was greatly raised to the level, and the tumbled ruins formed the remarkable mound which falls at this point into the Valley of Jehoshaphat, and is visible to the traveller at the present day.

CHAPTER XIII.

THE HOLY SEPULCHRE—THE TRADITIONAL ARGUMENT.

Considering the prevailing opinions on this subject, I may be allowed a few introductory remarks. It is one of the strongest, and, if rightly guided, one of the healthiest instincts of our nature, to desire a knowledge of the locality of any event that has deeply moved our feelings. In many forms such a desire manifests its power in the life of men; and in consequence they become pilgrims to ancient cities, to battle-fields, to the homes of poets, to the graves of martyrs and the pious dead. It would be strange if Christianity were at variance with such an instinct of our nature; but the contrary appears from the tenor of the Scripture narrative, which so often gives the name of the locality in connexion with the incident. So far as the Gospel narrative goes, no satisfactory reason has been assigned why the "Rock of the Sepulchre" should be deemed an exception. The spot is described with a minuteness of detail which is highly significant. And yet, any remarks on this portion of the ancient topography of Jerusalem are often perused in a somewhat sceptical mood of mind. It seems indeed taken for granted that the place is not known, and never will be known, and what is more, *ought not* to be known! Sometimes there are quoted on this point (surely inappropriately enough) the words applied to the tomb of Moses: "No man knoweth of his sepulchre unto this day." It is not consolatory to be told that whatever be the chance of finding out the site and size of the Temple, the stronghold of Zion, the City of David, the Mount of Olives, and Siloam,—the holiest spot of all, the tomb of Christ, is delivered over to utter oblivion. Of course it settles the question, if such be the design of Providence; but we may well ask for a little more proof of the opinion than is usually assigned. Until this be furnished, the task is not to be given up as hopeless, especially after the definite topographical hints of the Scripture narrative.

Doubtless there have been scandalous abuses in the present Church of the Holy Sepulchre, sufficient to make any one blush that bears the name of Christian, the memory of which may induce us to welcome the conclusion that *that* site is fictitious. But it has yet to be proved that these are the legitimate consequences of the local influence, and not rather perversions of a feeling with which the most devout and intelligent may well sympathize. Unquestionably it is a great evil where the worship of holy places is reckoned a substitute for the religion of the heart, that living spirit of devotion which fits all times and all places, viewing as sacred the whole earth which the Saviour died to redeem, even as the heavens into which he has ascended. The investigation now proposed will doubtless be condemned by all who fancy that this disastrous change of feeling is inevitable, if the real locality were discovered. But it must possess a high charm for those who trust to avoid the error in question, and who are unable to admit its connexion with the knowledge they desire, in reference to what was a familiar locality to many hundred converts in the primitive age. For can there be any rational doubt that then, at all events, the sepulchre of Christ was widely known? It was near Calvary, the scene of public execution. Romans, Priests, Pharisees, and vast crowds from different parts of Palestine gazed on the spectacle of the cross. His tomb was watched; and the strange event of the disappearance of his body, while affecting different minds with different impressions, fixed the spot distinctly in the memories of all. The women were at his grave on the morning of the third day, and so were his disciples.

It may be thought, perhaps, that the disciples became indifferent to such a locality, and allowed it to slip from their remembrance. They were occupied, it is said, in thinking of the living Christ of heaven, not of the scenes of his death and burial. To which the answer is, that Christ was not thus "divided" in their conceptions; their rejoicing was that they could think of their Lord in heaven as none other than He who had lain for three days in the tomb of Joseph.

The Gospel they preached was based on the facts of his earthly life, each of which had a locality, and from that locality, in a certain sense, it could not be dissociated, unless by violence done to our common nature. It is evident that when the apostle Peter wrote his Epistle, although "about to put off his earthly tabernacle," he had not forgotten "the holy mount," which was the scene of the transfiguration. In his sermon on the day of Pentecost, likewise, a knowledge of the place of the Holy Sepulchre is presumed on the part of his audience. He interprets and develops the consequences from the admitted fact that the tomb had been disturbed, the tenant having risen; it stood thus in contrast with the sepulchre of David, which remained to that day. Or we may appeal to the language of John, the beloved disciple, who exhibits a lofty spiritual tone in his epistles, which all will admit to be free from the superstitious feelings only elicited by particular times and places. Even he cherished in his later life the memory of the sacred locality, as the minute descriptions of his Gospel abundantly show. Nay, did not the risen Lord tenderly touch the memories of Calvary and the Sepulchre in his august manifestation on the Isle of Patmos? The disciple was terror-struck by the vision. "Fear not," said the voice, "I am he that liveth and *was dead.*"

Although the way to judge whether the apostles cherished the memory of the locality is to inspect the Gospels rather than the Epistles, which are occupied with the doctrines of Christianity, yet, even in these, local allusions to such points was made when required. "Jesus, that he might sanctify the people with his own blood, suffered *without the gate*. Let us go forth, therefore, unto him without the camp, bearing his reproach" (Heb. xii. 11). Hundreds of Christian converts in the first century must have known of the locality, and to many, in these times of persecution and martyrdom, the memory of it would be most welcome. The doctrine most obviously peculiar to the new faith, most strikingly opposed to Pagan, Gnostic, or even old Jewish ideas—transcending even that of the soul's immortality—was intimately associated with the spot and its circumstantial evidences: it was the scene of an event that surpassed all others in its wonder and significance, the crowning evidence of the truth of the Christian religion. Thus the precise situation might be expected to take deeper hold than that of any other on the hearts of Christian converts; and from its nature, it could survive the shocks that obliterated others. The ravages of time, if not the desolations of war, that swept the towns and villages of Palestine, might destroy the home of Nazareth, of Capernaum, and of Bethany, at a period when none might care to rescue them from oblivion; but we may be permitted to believe that *the rock* of the Sepulchre escaped such a fate.

I venture to add, that if this "Holiest Place" were clearly discovered, the allowable emotion of the soul is in its deepest sense satisfied, although doubt might still attach to all the rest. For all the events connected with the Gospel history crowd to this spot, and are here hallowed and glorified by the sacredness of death. At the grave, the memories of any life that has kindled our interest come up with a strange significance, transfigured in a light such as can be associated with no other locality. There may or may not be doubt, then, as to the manger of Bethlehem, the home of toil in Nazareth, the Garden of Gethsemane, the exact spot of the cross; but if we know of "the Rock of the Sepulchre," if we can enter, "*and see the place where the Lord lay*," is not the Incarnation itself viewed with the deepest wonder *there*; are not the toil, the agony, the cross, revealed *there* in their most solemn and holy significance? Indeed, if *it* be known, might we not be content to feel that the other "Holy Places" also are sufficiently known and realized?

The genuineness of the present site of the Holy Sepulchre has been long denied by many competent judges. To the question what objection there is to the spot, the answer must be, Much every way. First of all, its situation answers in no wise to the conditions of the Scripture narrative. It could not have been *without* the gate. Adjacent is the large pool of Hezekiah, which certainly would not be left outside for the advantage of the enemy when he came to besiege the city; but if that reservoir was included, so likewise must have been the site of the present church. Of course it is possible to draw the line of wall in such a fashion as to make one of its angles leave this church outside; but one has only to see the strange zigzag which is necessarily produced, to be persuaded of its glaring improbability. Dr. Robinson has clearly stated the objections to the present site, to which I further refer the reader, but it must have been deeper within the city than he supposes. The wall started from a great tower called Hippicus, whose dimensions Josephus gives. It is a mistake to identify it with the existing tower at the Jaffa Gate, for this reason, among others, that the dimensions of the latter are about half as large again as those of Hippicus, and Josephus would not have fallen into the error of so diminishing it. At the northern corner of the present city was the site of the famous tower, and the wall starting thence took its present direction (for remains of it are found at the Damascus Gate); therefore the present site of the Holy Sepulchre was far within the city at the time of the crucifixion.

Again, if we enter the church and look for the traces of the Sepulchre, there is utter disappointment. There is no rock; no cave; all that appears is a sarcophagus built of blocks of marble—enclosing what? none are permitted to see. Some have a curious theory on this subject. It is said, the place has been often destroyed by the savage Mohammedans, who levelled and removed the ancient rock; still, they have left a little fragment, the *loculus* that contained the body. Very singular, truly! Then the Christian pilgrim might be allowed to gaze upon it.

Until Mr. Fergusson announced his theory, none seemed to doubt that this was really the place where Constantine built his church, about A.D. 320. Dr. Robinson, assuming it was so, tries to account for it by saying that Constantine had no guide in the matter but his own impulses, which he mistook for a "supernatural intimation," and in that early time fell into this mistake. His error was a glaring one, which a little reflection, one may suppose, would have prevented; but I believe that the language of Eusebius on this point by no means bears out the inference drawn from it, and that Constantine never professed to be guided to the Sepulchre by any miracle at all.

We now turn to the theory of Mr. Fergusson. He affirms that Constantine had nothing whatever to do with the present locality,—that it is comparatively a modern affair. As his church was very splendid, with numerous pillars and adjuncts, bearing of course the stamp of the architecture of his time, so it has been justly argued that if it had stood on the present site some fragments of that architecture would have been discovered. But there are none. One explorer indeed, Comte de Vogue, declared that he had found such a relic, but "he unfortunately published his drawing," and the result is, that it is marked by a style such as did not exist for many centuries after the age of Constantine.[1]

The position of Mr. Fergusson is, that the church now called "the Mosque of Omar" or rather "the Dome of the Rock" is the real church of Constantine over the Sepulchre, and was so regarded in the earlier centuries. Directly east from it, and overlooking the Valley of Jehoshaphat, was "the place called Calvary," where another church was built; *that*, however, the Mohammedans have destroyed. The grand entrance to the two churches was what is now known as "the Golden gateway." The principal argument is drawn from the fact, that on the "Mosque of Omar" and "the Golden Gateway" is stamped the unmistakable style of architecture that distinguished the age of Constantine. For details the reader must be referred to Mr. Fergusson's own works on the subject.[2] But I shall endeavour in a few words to indicate the line of his argument.

In any age then, previous to the seventeenth century, it is possible to frame a scale that will indicate the position of any building between those that precede and those that follow. This has been done for the Gothic style, and it can be done for the Corinthian, to which the building in question belongs. The history of that style is well known. "It was suggested by the Egyptians, perfected by the Greeks, enriched by the Romans, and corrupted by the Byzantines." The building of Constantine will necessarily exhibit the traces of this Byzan-

---

[1] Fergusson, *Notes on the Holy Sepulchre*, p. 37.
[2] *Essay on the Ancient Topography of Jerusalem*; *Notes on the Holy Sepulchre*; *Dictionary of the Bible*, Art. Jerusalem.

tine corruption. Such a feature, it is alleged, characterizes the architecture of the "Dome of the Rock," and also that of the Golden Gateway. In proving the date of the *latter*, the author refers to the buildings of Palmyra and Baalbec, A.D. 272, as "obviously of earlier origin, because they do not exhibit so much discrepancy from the pure classic examples." He then takes the buildings of Justinian in the date A.D. 527, and these he affirms to be too modern, deviating too far from the classical standard, and wanting the horizontal cornice found in the Gateway. Between the two dates must the architecture of the Golden Gateway lie. He then takes the date, A.D. 300, and compares the buildings of Diocletian at that period, but finds them still too early, though "the scent is evidently getting hot." Then there are instanced the Latin Baptistery and the Tomb of St. Constantia at Rome, which are of the time of Constantine; these are found to be of the same age with the architecture of the Gateway. He therefore concludes, "I assert most unhesitatingly, and defy contradiction to the fact, that it is a building of the first half of the fourth century, and it was built by Constantine himself." "If," he again asserts, "I had stumbled on this Gateway in any part of the Roman world, I should never have hesitated two minutes in making up my mind that it was a festal gate of the age of Constantine."[1]

Such are his assertions, and if any one is able to answer them, let it be done by all means, but the reply dealing fairly with these architectural data has yet to appear.

[1] This gateway is built up from the fear of the Mohammedans, that on the Christians entering through it, their power is gone. Such fear may have arisen from its being at one time their principal gateway to the Church of the Holy Sepulchre.

Not less unmistakably does the so-called "Mosque of Omar" bear the stamp of the architecture of the period. The dome itself is comparatively modern, built by the Mohammedan Emperor in 1566-1573, but the construction of the *main building* is of an earlier age. "The walls of the octagon remain untouched in their lower parts, the circle of the columns and piers which divide the two aisles, with the entablatures, discharging arches, and cornices still remain entirely unchanged and untouched; the pier arches of the dome, the triforium belt, the clerestory, are all parts of the unaltered construction of the age of Constantine." Thus all that is necessary to give character to the building, and decide the age of its erection, remains to this day, and Mr. Fergusson challenges all who are capable of judging of the style of ancient architecture, to say at what period this building was constructed, other than that which he has determined.

The assertion has been hazarded that the building may be Mohammedan, notwithstanding the presence in it of pillars used at first in Christian edifices, as it was not uncommon for the Mohammedans to take and use existing materials in the construction of the mosques. Such a hypothesis Mr. Fergusson declares to be untenable, and appeals to the plate representing the interior of the building.[1] "Not only the details of the pillars and their entablatures belong to the ancient style, but those of the eight piers between them, which are very complicated in form, and could not have been found and transferred from any other building. Round all the sinuosities of those piers this entablature runs, and both below it

[1] Frontispiece to "Essay on Jerusalem."

down to the ground, and upwards to the roof, the detail is all of the same age, all fitting exactly to the place where it is applied, and complete and appropriate in every part. The cornices under the roof too, on both sides, with the roof itself, are all parts of the same design. Besides, at the time when the Mohammedans could have built it, the Christian edifices were not yet destroyed, from which these rich materials could have been taken." The theory then of its being a patchwork structure is one of the most improbable that can possibly be conceived.

He challenges those who contend that the building is Mohammedan in any respect to specify its meaning and purpose. Is it a Mohammedan *mosque*? Then it is unique in all its construction, and has not its parallel in the world. It is a round octagonal building, whereas all mosques are so placed as to have the niche pointing to Mecca. "I feel quite certain that in no Mohammedan country, from the mouth of the Ganges to Guadalquivir, and in no age, did any Mohammedan erect a mosque of this form: the thing is an anomaly, an absurdity; it is to my mind like talking of a perpendicular pyramid, or a square circle." The Mohammedans themselves do not call the building the Mosque of Omar, but "the Dome of the Rock." If any should surmise that it may be an octagonal building over a *tomb*, such as are found in India, the reply of this author is, that in all their traditions there is not "the slightest hint that any Moslem saint or sinner was ever buried here."

Thus untenable is any theory of its Mohammedan origin, and I again appeal to the writings of Mr. Fergusson on the subject, that it may be seen with what a crushing force he shatters the commonly-received opinion on the subject. He has challenged any to assign to these buildings a different age, and for fourteen years the challenge has not been met. Dr. Stanley has said, "It is much to be wished that some competent opponent would seriously consider the architectural argument on which Mr. Fergusson relies, and which undoubtedly is calculated to produce a great impression." This competent opponent has yet to appear. I close with one other quotation: "The moment that I saw Mr. Catherwood's drawings, it was as if he had laid before me a clearly copied inscription, in a language I was perfectly familiar with, and which said, 'This is the church which I, Constantine, erected over the holy cave in which the body of our blessed Lord was laid.' If it should prove otherwise, I can only say that the studies of my life have been in vain, and all that I have learned during the last thirty years is a delusion and a snare."[1]

Such language, from one admitted on all hands to be a master in his knowledge of ancient architecture, cannot fail to produce this impression, that if his arguments are not answered, it must be because they are *unanswerable*. And thus, amid the sad confusion in which, from whatever cause, the question of the holy places in Jerusalem has become involved, this building, like a rock in a troubled sea, rises in calm strength, refusing to lie or to equivocate; "its stones crying out" that the venerated cave beneath was held, in the age of Constantine at least, to be none other than the Sepulchre of Christ.

We have now to inquire what light is thrown on this

[1] *Notes on the Holy Sepulchre*, p. 14.

subject by the testimony of the early pilgrims to Jerusalem?

The architectural argument of Mr. Fergusson has never been grappled with, but it has been held by many sufficient to appeal to the testimony of Christian pilgrims, and to say, "The early traditions forbid such a theory." The challenge, I believe, may be willingly accepted; the testimony being, I take it, triumphant in favour of the eastern site, and utterly irreconcilable with that of the present church. Keeping well aloof from the personalities raised by the discussion, I submit the following evidence, gathered from the statements of early Christian fathers and pilgrims, of whom let the general reader take this brief notice:—

1. Eusebius and Socrates, writers of ecclesiastical history. Eusebius was the contemporary of Constantine, and the chronicler of his doings in the building of the Church of the Sepulchre, A.D. 325. As Bishop of Cæsarea, he took part in its consecration. Socrates wrote his history about a hundred years after, A.D. 420.

2. The Bordeaux pilgrim (A.D. 330), who visited Jerusalem when the church was building.

3. Antoninus Martyr or Placentinus, about A.D. 610, or at least after the reign of Justinian, the name of whose Empress he mentions.

4. Arculf, a French Bishop, about A.D. 695. Shortly before his pilgrimage, the Mohammedans had taken Jerusalem, and built a mosque (Mosque el Aksa) on the site of the old Temple, but leaving to the Christians undisturbed possession of the Holy Sepulchre. On his homeward voyage, Arculf was cast away on the island of Iona, and furnished to Adamnan, the abbot of that

monastery, a description of the holy places. He also drew for him a plan of the Holy Sepulchre, marking the sites of the adjoining churches. Adamnan wrote down the information he had thus obtained in a tract; giving sometimes the *ipsissima verba* of Arculf, which with its accompanying plan was widely circulated.

5. St. Willibald, about A.D. 765. The account of his pilgrimage to Jerusalem is contained in the narrative of his life, written by a relative after his death.

6. The monk Bernard, who visited Jerusalem about A.D. 870.

The Holy Sepulchre, I hope to show, was, in the view of these early pilgrims, on the *eastern* hill, in the cave under the so-called Mosque of Omar, or rather, as the Mohammedans themselves better name it, "the Dome of the Rock."

I. *The Sepulchre is represented as* opposite *the old city*.—In the opinion of Eusebius, the Holy Sepulchre was the foundation of "the new and second Jerusalem" spoken of in the predictions of the prophets (Rev. xxi. 2), and he twice asserts in the same paragraph that it was on the opposite side from the old Jerusalem. His words are: "Accordingly, on the very spot which witnessed the Saviour's sufferings, 'a *new Jerusalem*' was constructed *over against* the one so celebrated of old, which, since the foul stain of guilt brought upon it by the murder of the Lord, had experienced the last extremity of desolation; the effect of Divine judgment on its imperious people. It was *opposite* the city that the Emperor now began to rear a monument to the Saviour's victory over death, with rich and lavish magnificence."

Socrates likewise affirms that "the New Jerusalem," as he also calls it, "was opposite the old deserted city." Now, this description *can* be understood, if it applies to the Dome of the Rock on the eastern hill. It was on the same side as the Temple, which Josephus describes as "over against the city." To the site on the western hill the historian's language cannot apply, for that was *in* the old city.

II. *Its distance from the Temple.*—About forty years after the reign of Constantine, the Emperor Julian sought to rebuild the Temple. The workmen, it is said, were scared by balls of fire bursting from the foundations, and took refuge in a *neighbouring* church, or, as Sozomen has it, *in the* church. This could be, as Mr. Fergusson has pointed out, no other than the church of the Sepulchre, for we have no record of any other that was built at that time. That church, then, is here described as *near* the Temple, and so corresponds to the situation of the Dome of the Rock.

III. *The structure of the Church.*—Besides the description of Eusebius, we have that of Arculf, on which Mr. Fergusson remarks: "In describing the church, Arculf says, it is supported by twelve stone pillars of great size; this is *exactly* the number we find surrounding the rock of the Sakrah, omitting the four great piers of the angles, which I think any one would naturally do. It is true he omits in the text to mention the outer range altogether, but they are carefully marked in the *plan*, which in this respect perfectly accords with the Dome of the Rock, while there is no trace of a second range in the present church (on the *western* hill).[1]

IV. *The Appearance of the Tomb.*—Eusebius calls it a cavern (ἄντρον). Arculf, more specific, says: "It is a cave cut out of one and the same rock, its height being about seven and a half feet." Now, according to the measurement of Dr. Barclay, the height of the cave of the Sakrah is about eight feet.[2] Arculf also mentions that in it nine men could stand to pray. According to Dr. Barclay the area is about fifteen feet square. If the reader fancies that on this point there is a discrepancy, let him understand that in the time of the pilgrim there was an altar here and twelve lamps (according to the number of the apostles), which would of course narrow the space that is now quite empty.

This description then, I believe, tallies well with this cave of the Sakrah. In the church on the western hill there is *no cave* at all!

The above evidence has been adduced by Mr. Fergusson, and is strengthened by recent explorations of Dr. Barclay. I now proceed to adduce other proofs strongly confirmatory.

V. *Colour of the Rock.*—Antoninus says it "was like a millstone;" Arculf says "its colour is not uniform, but a mixture of white and red." Dr. Barclay describes the Sakrah as "fine limestone, or coarse marble, somewhat mottled."[3] A Mohammedan writer, Ali Bey, speaking of it, says: "From what I could discern, particularly

---

[1] *Essay on Topography of Jerusalem.*
[2] *City of the Great King*, p. 497.   [3] *Ibid.* p. 497.

in the inside of the cave, the rock seemed to be composed of *reddish-white* marble."[1] Such, I may add, is my own recollection of the aspect of the cave. I repeat that no rock of any sort is seen in the church on the western hill.

VI. *The position of Golgotha relatively to Mount Zion.*—In his *Onomasticon*, a dictionary of Scripture localities, Eusebius affirms that Calvary (and consequently the Sepulchre near it) was *north* of Mount Zion. If then it can be proved that in these early times Mount Zion was the eastern or Temple hill, and not the western one (marked on the map as pseudo-Zion—the Zion of modern times), then the above description of Eusebius confirms the locality for which I contend.

To prove, then, that the Mount Zion of our sketch is correct, I remark—

1. The Temple hill was the *ancient* Mount Zion, and there is no proof whatever of any change in the Christian era. It is in the highest degree improbable that the Jews would allow a name consecrated through all the past "to the mountain of the Lord's house," to be capriciously transferred to another and a common part of the city. If Eusebius was guided by the language of the Psalms in his description, and by existing traditions, he must have employed the term in its usual sense, the Temple hill; or at any rate, before the idea of a change is admissible, we must have some proof when and wherefore that change took place.

[1] *Museum of Classical Antiquities*, vol. ii. p. 381. In Vol. ii. Part iv. there is an elaborate review and examination of the various Topographical Theories on Jerusalem, which I did not see till recently, but was pleased to find that the author " is inclined to believe that a trench ran across the parallelogram of the Haram."—Vol. ii. Supplement, p. 446.

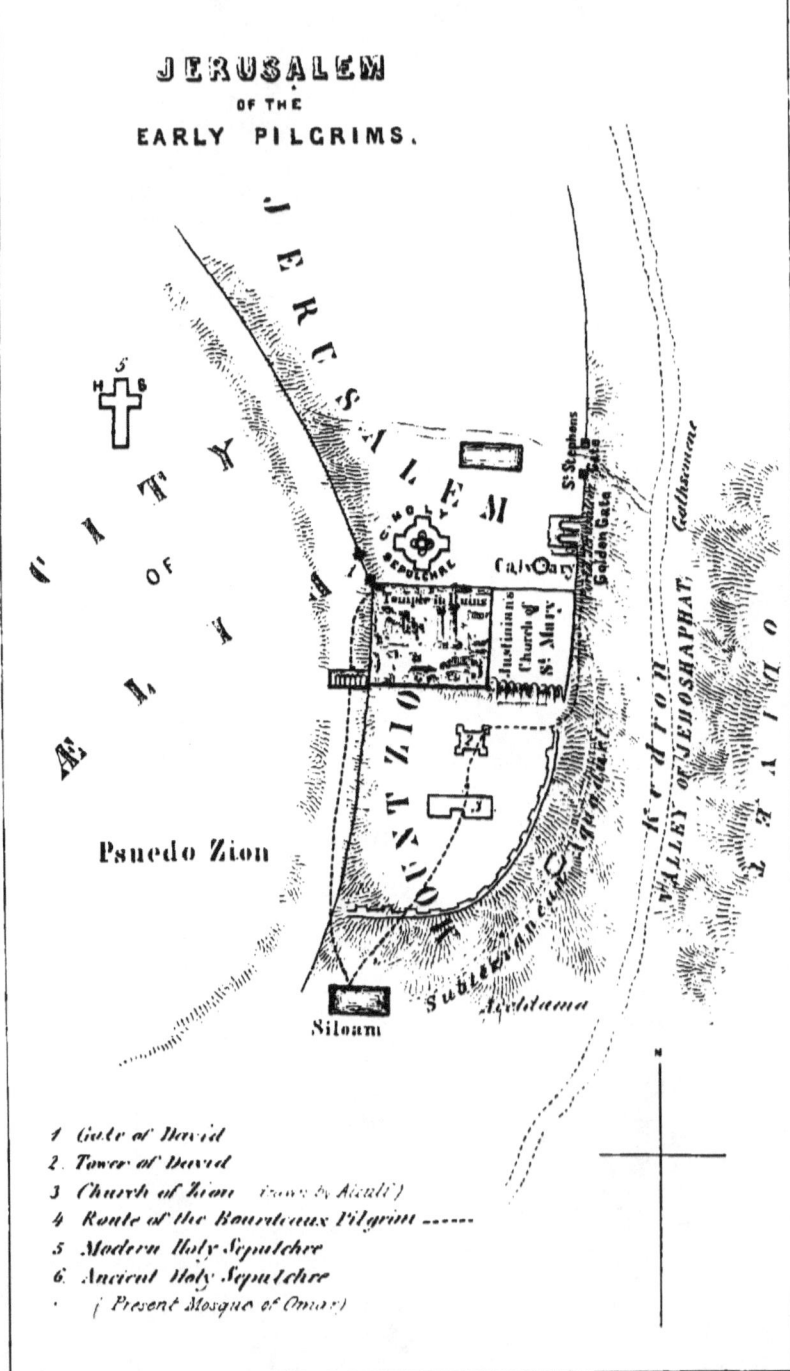

2. The pilgrim Arculf twice affirms that the Valley of Jehoshaphat was between Mount Zion and Mount Olivet. "Between these two mountains," he says, "lies the Valley of Jehoshaphat."[1] Again, he speaks "of Mount Zion and Mount Olivet and the intermediate Valley of Jehoshaphat."[2] This is intelligible if Mount Zion be the eastern hill, but the description is absurd if it was the western one, for that is distant from Olivet and the Valley of Jehoshaphat by the breadth of the Temple hill and the central valley of the city.

There is another pilgrim, Saewulf, in the twelfth century, who speaks of "the brook Kedron (Valley of Jehoshaphat) between Mount Zion and Mount Olivet." The locality even at that late time was unchanged, but by and by had to follow the Sepulchre to the western hill, in order to make the relative position of the places accord with the language of Eusebius.

3. Arculf represents Mount Zion as *without* the walls, for he says "that the city (*Hierosolymitana situs*) began from the northern brow of the Mount Zion."

It is, I affirm, until some proof be offered, utterly incredible that the present large portion of the city on the western hill, known as the modern Mount Zion, should at any time have been without the walls. The language is explained at once by a reference to the eastern hill. The temple site was held to be accursed by the Christians, and so it was left outside. The southern wall of "the Jerusalem community," as Arculf often calls it, enclosed the Holy Places, separating them from the

---

[1] Inter hos duos montes vallis Jehoshaphat media interjacet.—*De Loc. Sanct.* lib. i. cap 16.

[2] Montis Sion, montisque Oliveti et vallis Jehoshaphat interjacentis.—*Ibid.* lib. i. cap. 19.

Temple, and it seems likely that the traces of its presence can be detected across the breadth of the Haram es Sheriff at the present day.

Again, Arculf speaks of passing through the gate of David, and coming to a stone bridge raised on arches, *pointing straight across the valley* to the south. This gate is "on the west of Mount Zion;" "Mount Zion is on the left hand"[1] in passing through it. Now, he cannot here mean the present gate of David on the western hill, for it is on the crown of the ridge to the south. Nor can he refer to the Jaffa gate (as Dr. Robinson supposes), for no one can assert that the bridge he means was in the Valley of Hinnom. But there was anciently such a bridge in the central valley, and a portion of an arch is still seen springing from the Temple wall. The Gate of David then, I believe, was in that central valley; and if so, then Mount Zion, "on his left hand" as he passes out, was the Temple hill.

4. The Church of Zion. Arculf drew a plan of the church on Zion which included several sacred localities. It was the church where the last supper was held, where our Lord washed the disciples' feet; the church where the Holy Ghost descended on Pentecost; the church where Mary died, Church of St. Simeon, etc. Within its walls were a number of consecrated relics, the column where Christ was scourged, the stone of Stephen's martyrdom, the spear that pierced Christ, the cup with which the Apostles celebrated mass after the resurrection of Christ, etc. etc. Such was the Church of Zion, and

---

[1] Per eandem de civitate egredientibus portam, et Montem Sion proximum ad sinistram habentibus, pons lapideus occurrit, eminus per vallem in austrum recto tramite directis arcubus sulfultus.—*De Loc. Sanct.* cap. xii. Porta David ad occidentalem partem Montis Zion.—Cap. i.

I ask the reader to note its situation, which is well defined. "To the *south* of it," says Arculf, "was Aceldama," which is declared by Saewulf (A.D. 1106), to be at "*the foot of Olivet*,"[1] and on the way from Olivet to Siloam; and "to the *north* of it was the *Temple of Solomon*, having a synagogue of the Saracens" (Bernard).[2] I am unable to see how it is possible, without a most suspicious amount of quibbling with language, to maintain that a church *thus* defined can be anywhere except on the slope of the Temple hill, as our sketch represents.

As further corroborative of this, Antoninus, on his way from Golgotha to this church, visits the tower of David, where he says "Christians ascend for pious meditation, and hear about midnight murmuring voices rising from the Valley of Jehoshaphat." Here he is clearly on the Temple hill. But how came he there, if he is passing from the present Golgotha to the present Zion with its *Cœnaculum*, both on the western hill? His whole route from the Holy Sepulchre to Golgotha,[3] then to the place where the cross was found,[4] then to the tower of David,[5] and then to the Basilica of Zion, seems incompatible with the present traditions.

5. The same pilgrim speaks of the Church of St. Mary (built by Justinian) as on *Mount Zion*. This Church was, as all admit, built on the Temple hill, and in con-

---

[1] *Early Travels in Palestine* (Bohn), p. 42.   [2] *Ibid.* p. 28.
[3] A monumento usque Golgotha sunt gressus octaginta.
[4] De Golgotha usque ubi inventa est crux sunt gressus 50.
[5] *Inde* ascendimus turrim David, in quâ Christiani pro devotione ascendunt ad mansionem et circa medium noctis, spatium surgentes, audiunt voces murmurantium in Valle Jehoshaphat ad loca quæ respiciunt contra Sodoma et Gomorrha. Deinde venimus in basilicam Sion, etc.—*Itiner. Anton. Martyr. Acta Sanctorum, Ugolini Thesaurus*, p. 1208.

nexion with it he makes mention of "the ruins of the Temple of Solomon, where water comes down to Siloam."

These are the proofs that lead to the conclusion that Zion was in the early Christian centuries, as in the ancient time, the Temple hill. Let the reader mark the bearing of this on the main question before us. "Golgotha," says Eusebius, "was on the *north* of Zion."[1] The description answers exactly to its position as marked by Mr. Fergusson.

6. Before passing from this subject, I will venture to affirm, that this location of the Church of the Supper on the eastern hill, by the early traditions of the Christian Church, is the only one sanctioned by the incidents of the Gospel narrative. The Saviour with his disciples was coming from Bethany to Jerusalem : "And he sent Peter and John, saying, Go and prepare us the Passover, that we may eat. And they said unto him, Where wilt thou that we prepare? And he said unto them, Behold, when ye *are entered* into the city, there shall a man meet you, bearing a pitcher of water; follow him into the house where he entereth in" (Luke xxii. 8-10). "And his disciples went forth, and came into the city, and found as he had said unto them: and they made ready the Passover" (Mark xiv. 16). Now, if the *Cœnaculum* had been on the western hill, where modern tradition places it, it is impossible to understand how the disciples could have met such a man until they had traversed nearly the whole city, instead of when they *entered* it. On the eastern hill it can be well understood. After descending the slope of Olivet, they, on entering the city,

[1] Eusebius, *Onomasticon*, *voce* Golgotha.

might meet the individual referred to bearing the pitcher of water from the fountain of the Virgin or the pool of Siloam.

VII. I now call attention to a distinction made, I believe, by the early pilgrims between "Jerusalem,"—a name revived by the Christians and given to the district consecrated by the site of the Holy Sepulchre,—and Ælia, the name given to the old city by the Roman Emperor Hadrian. In his reign the Jews throughout Palestine once more made the attempt to throw off the Roman yoke. The revolt was put down after a terrible struggle, and the Emperor having rebuilt the city, planted there a Roman colony, and changed its name to Ælia. So completely did the old name of "Jerusalem" go out of use, that according to Eusebius, when a martyr at Cæsarea mentioned Jerusalem as his birthplace, meaning the heavenly city, the Roman governor Formilianus inquired what city that was, and where it lay?[1] It will be said that the name Jerusalem being soon afterwards restored, was used indifferently with Ælia to denote the entire city. This is a mistake, the rectification of which will greatly help our inquiry. Eusebius expressly says that the district so named, instead of embracing the old city, "*was opposite to it.*" The name had been restored when he wrote his *Onomasticon* (for he defines the position of Calvary, the recognition of which, with that of the site of the Sepulchre, was the cause of its restoration), but we shall find that it was never applied by him to the then existing city. He describes Jerusalem, indeed, with its suburbs, but he means the *old* city, " which once," he

[1] Euseb. *De Martyr Palest.* c. 11.

says, "belonged to the tribe of Benjamin," the city therefore that existed before the destruction by Titus. The *city of Hadrian*, if I mistake not, he never so names, nor does he use the word in speaking of the position of the towns and villages of Judah relative to their metropolis.

Ælia is the one term used, and Bethel, Bethlehem, Bethany, Bethhoron, Bethzur, Gadara, Remma, etc., are described by their distance and direction from *Ælia*, a fact not easily accounted for, if he could have used the restored name with equal propriety.

"Jerusalem" was restricted, as has been said, to that district of the city of Ælia dear to the Christians from its connexion with the passion and resurrection of Christ. St. John in the Revelation had spoken of the descent of the New Jerusalem from heaven, and Eusebius saw the prophecy verified in the churches of Constantine over these sacred localities. Hence his language, speaking of the directions of the Emperor to build a church: "On the *very spot* which witnessed the Saviour's sufferings, a *New Jerusalem* was constructed over against the one celebrated of old,"—"opposite to the city, the Emperor began to rear a monument to the Saviour's victory over death, with rich and lavish magnificence; and it may be that this was that second and *New Jerusalem* spoken of in the predictions of the Prophets, concerning which such abundant testimony is given in the inspired words."[1] The testimony of Socrates is to the same effect. To the early Christian pilgrims Jerusalem was a *holy name*, because thus appropriated, and they applied the heathen one, Ælia, to the ancient city, accursed of God, as they esteemed it, and

[1] Eusebius, *Vita Constantini*, cap. xxxiii.

"which" (to use the language of Eusebius), "since the foul stain of guilt brought on it by the murder of the Lord, had experienced the last extremity of desolation, the effect of Divine judgment on its impious people." Hence also the Temple site, as accursed, did not belong to their "Jerusalem;" and the early Bordeaux pilgrim speaks of going out *from it into Jerusalem*, that he might ascend Zion.

As the name exclusively of the Christian district, we can understand the constant use of the phrase of Arculf, *Hierosolymitana civitas*, and as descriptive of its situation, *Hierosolymitanus situs*. Let us bear in mind, that Jerusalem had before his time become a place of pilgrimage to the Mohammedans, in consequence of the sanctity attached to its Sakrah by Mohammed, many of their writers contending that he regarded it with a deeper veneration than even the Kaaba in Mecca.[1] Fifty years had elapsed since Omar had taken possession of the city, and his proclamation on that occasion refers to the *Jews* of Ælia, as well as the Christians. If, in addition to this, we reflect on the numbers of Mohammedans that then began to settle in the city, and to worship in the newly built Mosque of the Sakrah, as the historian affirms,[2] and whom the Christians pledged themselves not to insult, we must conceive of the city as containing a motley population of various races and religions, which forces us to recognise the distinctive use of Arculf's phraseology in such instances as the following:—

He narrates a strange story about the miraculous preservation of the napkin, "*Sacrosanctum Domini sudarium*," that was about the head of Christ in the sepulchre.

[1] Jelleladin, *History of Temple*, chap. vi.   [2] *Ibid.* chap. ix.

Strange though the story is, "all the Jerusalem people," he says, "affirm it to be true," *Totus Hierosolymitanus populus veram esse protestatur.* Speaking of a sacred relic, a coat woven by the hands of the Virgin, and which he saw in the same Jerusalem community (*in eâdem Hierosolymitana civitate*), he says all the people (*totus populus*) regard it with deep reverence. Referring to the spear that pierced the side of our Lord, he says, the Jerusalem community reverently kiss it (*Quam Hierosolymitana civitas osculatur et veneratur*). Nothing of all this could be said of the Mohammedan or Jewish population in the city; and this emphatic repetition of the epithet *Hierosolymitana*, confirms the idea that the pilgrims, so long as the other name *Ælia* existed, used the word Jerusalem in the sacred meaning, as defined by Eusebius. The truth seems to be, that then, as now, the different religionists inhabited different districts; the Jerusalem people were the Christians, the Jerusalem city was the Christian district, where the Churches of Calvary and the Resurrection were situated. This being kept in mind, the following evidence tends to show that "Jerusalem" was on the *eastern* side of the central valley, the next point to be established.

1. Eusebius, in the language quoted, affirms that the new Jerusalem was *opposite* the old one (now called Ælia). To explain his language more precisely, it will be necessary to notice to what extent the city was rebuilt by Hadrian, A.D. 135. It has been assumed on all sides, that the course of the walls of Hadrian was nearly identical with those existing now. This seems altogether a mistake, if for no other reason than the language of Eusebius, which represents the site of the

Sepulchre (wherever it was) "as *opposite* the city,"—an expression pointing to a locality *not enclosed* in the then inhabited city, however the traces of Agrippa's wall might be still discoverable beyond it.

The above assumption is most improbable in itself, for it was far from the object of the Emperor to recall the former grandeur of Jerusalem. His great policy was, to destroy its former prestige, to impress upon the Jews that its restoration was hopeless, and so crush the spirit of revolt. He changed the name, and stationed there a Roman colony, purely for military purposes, his one great object being to prevent the Jews approaching the city. If all this be so, the proper inference surely is, that he was content with the rebuilding the city on a scale by no means so extensive as the present area. And with this supposition we can better understand how the old name went so entirely out of use. Moreover, the usual theory implies that Hadrian enclosed the Temple area, whereas, by the statement of the Jewish writers and also of Jerome, the plough was driven over its site, as a symbol of perpetual doom, and a heathen temple erected there. Dr. Robinson, indeed, discredits the fact, though thus strongly alleged, on the ground that the Romans never so condemned the site of single edifices.[1] But it is obvious that this objection ignores the special emergency of the case, and the declared policy of the Emperor. His great object was to destroy the spirit of revolt among the Jews, the mainspring of which was their desire for the restoration of their Temple worship. He could have adopted no means for this purpose better than those of the doom and desecration which, without

---

[1] *Biblical Researches*, i. 370.

one dissentient testimony, he is alleged to have employed on the Temple site. Moreover, Eusebius, by his language formerly quoted, implies that the existing city in his time was impoverished and limited, and Socrates speaks of "what was once Jerusalem as then a lodge in a garden of cucumbers, according to the prophecy," and as "the old and *deserted* city."[1]

Regarding then the restoration of the city by Hadrian as limited, and moreover, merely with the design of a military occupation, we are led to the conclusion that the colony of Ælia was established on the western hill. From its natural position, it was the fittest for the declared purpose ; on that hill, moreover, Titus had left three great towers, expressly to render any military occupation effective, one of which remains to this day. I have only to add that this was emphatically the part of the ancient city named as Jerusalem, Josephus affirming the Temple to be over against the city. Thus the language of Eusebius, affirming the Sepulchre to be "opposite the city," directs our attention to its site on the eastern hill. Along with the adjacent Temple, and, like it, branded by the presence of a heathen temple, it lay unenclosed until Constantine built his church, the principal entrance to which was the Golden gateway in the line of the former wall of Agrippa.

2. Let us now notice how the situation of Jerusalem (*Hierosolymitanus situs*, as he calls it) is defined by Arculf. At the time of his pilgrimage, as already remarked, the Jerusalem community had become very large. After the Church of Constantine was erected, many pilgrims flocked to Jerusalem, and many fixed on it as their resi-

[1] *Historia Ecclesiastica*, B. i. 17.

dence. This increase to the Christian population explains how the bishops of the poor, persecuted church of Ælia, who had been hitherto subject to the metropolitan see of Cæsarea, soon afterwards attained the dignity of an independent patriarchate. Arculf declares that in his time Jerusalem had eighty-four towers and many large buildings. If, as has been shown, he uses the word as distinguished from Ælia (a name which he also quotes), then we must conceive of the city as stretching up the eastern ridge, far beyond the present wall, and on to the northern district of Bezetha. And this fact seems confirmed by the ruins of buildings and churches still found there. The whole appearance of the ground indicates that it had inhabitants subsequent to the siege of Titus, otherwise, indeed, it would by this time have completely assumed, as other portions about the city, the aspect of cultivated fields. The supposition that Jerusalem stretched up in this direction during the occupation of the Christians, may thus account for the ruins on the ridge, and the language of Arculf about its size and the number of its towers. At all events, his language points to the situation of Jerusalem as on that *eastern* hill, which is the great fact to be noticed.

This pilgrim affirms that a fair was annually held in Jerusalem, attended by an immense concourse (*innumera multitudo*) of different nations, and of course the crowds had to be accommodated for some days in this same hospitable city (*in eadem hospitâ civitate*). Its clean streets (*politanas platœas*) were covered with the pestilential refuse of the numerous camels, besides horses, asses, and various beasts of burden; but wonderful to state, on the night that followed the day of their departure, a copious shower descended upon "the same city," which thoroughly cleansed it. "For the situation of Jerusalem (*Hierosolymitanus situs*) is placed by God the founder" that the waters of the descending rain do not stagnate, but "flow through the *eastern* gates, carrying all the filth into the valley of Jehoshaphat, increasing the torrent Kedron."[1] After this cleansing of Jerusalem (*post talem Hierosolymitanam baptizationem*) the deluge ceases. He then affirms that the fact of this pollution being so speedily got rid of, indicates the high honour put upon this chosen and distinguished city (*hæc electa et predicabilis civitas*) because it encloses "within its walls the venerated sites of the Cross and the Resurrection."

Here again, the reader will observe we have the same emphatic repetitions of "the same city," "the Jerusalem situation," "the Jerusalem baptism," etc., which mark out a special district of Ælia as the object of his reference. For how can we explain them as so often recurring if he speaks of the entire city, and cannot possibly be referring to anything special about it? And what he here says about the flow of the water through the streets into the Kedron, proves that he cannot be speaking either of the whole city or the western hill, where the present church of the Sepulchre stands. For by no possibility could the waters from *its* streets have reached the Kedron. These must, as every one knows, have fallen into the central valley of the city, and thus have found their way to the valley of Hinnom. Only of the eastern hill can the pilgrim be said to speak, and there accord-

---

[1] Quæ scilicet cœlestium aquarum inundatio per Orientales interfluens portas, et omnia secum stercoraria auferens abominamenta, vallem Josaphat intrans, torrentem Cedron auget.—*De Loc. Sanct.*, cap. i.

ingly we are warranted to conclude stood the "honoured sites of the Cross and the Resurrection."

3. Let us now look at the statement of Antoninus. Journeying from Jericho, he descends by Olivet to Gethsemane. Coming up from the valley he speaks of himself as immediately entering by the gate Jerusalem (*porta Jerusalem*) into the holy community (*Sancta civitas*). On entering the gate[1] he prostrated himself reverently, and visited the Church of the Holy Sepulchre. Again, I affirm, we must understand it to be on the eastern hill, for the western site is half-a-mile away, and the intermediate ground must have been, in the view of the pilgrim, the reverse of consecrated, and not at all such as to induce this reverence and adoration. He speaks moreover of a fig-tree in the Valley of Jehoshaphat, where Judas hanged himself, and which was near "the gate of Jerusalem," and adds: "This gate adjoins the splendid gate of the ancient Temple,"—a statement which, place that gate where we may, implies the Jerusalem district in the eastern hill. The pilgrim refers, as I understand, to the present so-called Golden gate, built (as shown by Mr. Fergusson) by Constantine, and leading to the holy places of Golgotha and the Sepulchre, which buildings were the foundations of "the New Jerusalem."

VIII. *Connexion of the rock of Golgotha with Siloam.*—Antoninus, speaking of Golgotha, says: "Near its altar (*juxta ipsum altare*) is a crypt, where if you place your ear you hear the flowing of water, and if you throw in an apple, or anything that will swim, and go to

---

[1] Portam civitatis quæ cohæret portæ speciosæ quæ fuit Templi cujus leminare et tabulatio stat. Inclinanter proni in terram ingressi sumus in sanctam civitatem, in quâ adoravimus Domini monumentum.—Anton. *ut sup.* p. 1213.

the fountain Siloam, you will find it there." When in Jerusalem I had a conversation with Mr. Pierrotti, the architect of the Pasha, on his explorations in the Temple hill. Though opposing Mr. Fergusson's theory (on what grounds it remains to be seen), he yet contributes a fact which as much as anything else tends to confirm it. He informed me that his Arabs travelled by a subterranean passage (see Sketch) from Siloam (or the Pool of the Virgin[1]) up to the very spot fixed on by that writer as the rock of Golgotha. This, I submit, is very conclusive. None have ever pretended that there is any connexion whatever between the Calvary of the present church on the western hill and the fountain of Siloam.

IX. I have reserved the consideration of the statements of the Bordeaux pilgrim (A.D. 330) to the last, both because of the controversy connected with them, and because I believe they can be judged of more satisfactorily in the light of the conclusions to which we have come. Let us in candour endeavour to decide the question, whether he understood Zion to be the western hill, and the holy places to be where modern tradition has placed them? The affirmative has been most dogmatically asserted, nay, a single sentence from this Bordeaux pilgrim has been thought enough to dispose of the whole architectural theory of Mr. Fergusson! I daresay it might, were we to be content with mere assumptions and detached expressions of his record; but our conclusion will be very different, if we examine for a little the details of his route.

---

[1] Whichever of the two, matters little to the argument, for the Pool of the Virgin is connected with that of Siloam by a subterranean channel.

The following objections quite forbid the idea of this route being on the western hill, or the Holy Sepulchre as anywhere in the vicinity of the present church :—

1. After inspecting (as all admit) the ruins of the Temple, "he goes into Jerusalem to ascend Zion." One would fancy, on the ordinary theory, that he would simply cross the valley to the western hill; but instead of this, he goes down to the pool of Siloam! This is surely an extraordinary detour (be it remarked he expressly says, "that you may ascend Zion"), if the modern Zion be his aim.[1] After describing the pool of Siloam, he adds : " In the same part Zion is ascended." What, I ask, are we to make of this statement, as Siloam is not on the western hill at all ?

2. He sees on Zion the house of Caiaphas without the walls, and the palace of David within the walls. By " the palace of David," say some, " he means the present so-called Tomb of David." This is a strange mistake, to say the least of it. But admitting that such is the reference, how could he describe this site as within the walls, when it is farther *without* them than even the house of Caiaphas ? The present traditions therefore reverse the localities of the Pilgrim. But by the palace of David, say others, he means the tower at the Jaffa Gate, the present so-called Castle of David. Be it so ; let us go on with the further examination of his route.

3. He goes from this site to the Neapolitan Gate, which is affirmed to be the present Damascus Gate, and finds on his way thither Golgotha on his left.[2] I appeal

[1] Item exeunti in Hierusalem ut ascendas Sion in parte sinistrâ et deorsum in valle juxta murum est piscina quæ dicitur Siloa. Habet quadriporticum, et alia piscina grandis foras.—*In eadem* ascenditur Sion, etc.

[2] Inde ut eas foris murum de Sione, euntibus ad Portam Neapolitanam, ad

to a candid inspection of any map for an explanation how this could be, and whether he would not rather have found it on his *right*. Only by dexterous manipulation of his movements, and making him turn this corner and that, could he come into such a relative position to this locality as answers his description. A sketch of such a route to this Damascus Gate would, I believe, be sufficient to condemn it. Besides, where was the *wall* of Zion here, outside of which he passes?

4. He says that the crypt of the Sepulchre is distant from Golgotha "a stone's-throw." In the present church it is only about one hundred feet! Besides, he must have passed as near the one place as the other.

5. He sees on his right hand the house of Pilate in a valley. This is said to be the present so-called house of Pilate, part of the old castle of Antonia. Now this is *not* in a valley, but on a *height*.

6. When at the Damascus Gate he must have been outside the city. But the context shows that he went through the Porta Neapolitana *into* the city, for he next speaks of going out of Jerusalem into the Valley of Jehoshaphat.

7. That the Damascus Gate was the Porta Neapolitana, and so named from the city of Nablous (Neapolis), is an inadmissible assumption. The name in that case would, it is probable, have been a fixed one, and yet by no other pilgrim is it mentioned.

Such then are the great (and as I believe insuperable)

partem dextram deorsum in valle sunt parietes ubi domus fuit sive Pretorium Pontii Pilati. Ibi Dominus auditus est antequam pateretur. A sinistra autem parte est monticulus Golgotha, ubi Dominus crucifixus est. Inde quasi ad lapidem missum est cripta ubi corpus ejus positum fuit et tertia die resurrexit. Ibidem modo jussu Constantini Imperatoris Basilica facta est, id est Dominicum miræ pulchritudinis, etc.

difficulties which preclude the idea of this pilgrim taking the route by the western hill, as has been so confidently asserted.

It will be found that his route can be best understood by identifying the eastern hill as Zion, especially when we compare his statements with those of his successor, Antoninus, A.D. 600.

1. The Temple which he first visits is full of ruins, and so he requires "to go into Jerusalem" that he might ascend Zion. As Antoninus goes down from the Church of Zion to Siloam, so this pilgrim goes up from Siloam to Zion. He has passed down the central valley to that fountain, where, to use his own words, "Zion is ascended." He speaks of the house of Caiaphas, and the column where Christ was scourged, as near Siloam, but "without the walls."

2. "Within the walls" of Zion, which he has commenced to ascend, he sees the palace of David. This, I take it, is identical with "the tower of David" mentioned by Antoninus, where pilgrims were wont to repair for devotion, and "at midnight heard murmuring voices from the Valley of Jehoshaphat." We may understand how this earlier pilgrim should speak of it as *within the walls*, for the old wall swept up from Siloam, enclosing this district, and, passing on, joined the eastern wall of the Temple at "the Kedron ravine."

3. The pilgrim then "goes outside this wall (*de Sione foris murum*) to the New City gate."[1] Constantine had lately built the church of the "New City," and it is towards the splendid gate leading to it that the language points, in other words, "the Golden Gate." Another

[1] Porta Neapolitana.

name for that new city was the "New Jerusalem," and hence Antoninus calls the same gate "the Jerusalem Gate," which he asserts to be "near the gate of the Temple." The Bordeaux pilgrim, passing round the eastern corner of the present Haram, would go "*without the wall*" of Zion.

4. On his way he sees the prætorium or house of Pilate in the *valley* on the right hand. It may be said, "This is impossible, the house of Pilate was never here!" Even supposing this objection could not be got over, the difficulty would be equally insuperable on the other route, inasmuch as the house of Pilate there is on a *height*. But let us remember that we have to do merely with the traditions of the time, well or ill founded, and that in such sites as Pilate's house, this pilgrim might not care to be scripturally correct. Thus a little hill, a short way from Olivet, is termed by him the Mount of the Transfiguration! It can hardly be supposed, indeed, that the minor sites of Scripture localities could be accurately fixed at the time of the pilgrim's visit, as Constantine had but lately erected the Church of the Sepulchre, the centre of all. The question is, where was the traditional site of Pilate's house in this early time? and the answer, I contend, must be, Somewhere on this eastern hill. I appeal for proof to the statement of Antoninus. He tells us that he worshipped in the church *where our Lord was tried*, and in which was "the seat where Pilate sat," and this same church was "*before the ruins of the Temple of Solomon*, where water ran down to Siloam." In this neighbourhood, therefore, the earliest traditions located the prætorium of Pilate,—a fact in harmony with our pilgrim's route.

5. Passing on he sees the "*hill* Golgotha" on the left. It is remarkable that the expression, "the hill Calvary," has clung to the literature of the Christian Church ever since it was used by this pilgrim. The place would present, I believe, such an aspect to him on his route. Originally, on the spur of the hill overlooking "the Kedron ravine," into which the ruins of the Temple were tumbled, we can imagine that the depth (which was "frightful," according to Josephus) was not yet filled up to the level, leaving therefore the appearance of a knoll or mound—not artificial in this case, as that of the church on the western hill, but such as would be described by the phrase, the "Monticulus Golgotha."

6. From Golgotha to the crypt of the Sepulchre was a stone's-throw,—an expression suiting the distance from this spot to the Sakrah, or 150 yards.

7. Entering in by the Golden Gate, he *inspects* the Church of the Sepulchre, which he affirms to be "of wondrous beauty."

8. At all events, he *enters* the city by that gate, for he immediately speaks of going out from Jerusalem to Mount Olivet.

In this case then, as in others, where we candidly examine the *details* of the route, it will be found that Zion was the eastern hill, and our conclusion is that the statements of all the pilgrims, up to the eleventh century, do coincide with and confirm the location of the Holy Sepulchre as first fixed by the architectural argument of Mr. Fergusson.

X. The present Church of the Holy Sepulchre, then, is the result of a *transference*. For a fuller discussion of this subject, I must refer to the pages of Mr. Fergusson. The very idea has excited in some an uncalled-for amazement and horror, but most of my readers will be ready to believe that the priests of the middle ages would not scruple much at anything of this sort, if necessity required it, and if the interests of the church could be thereby defended or advanced.

In Jerusalem especially, the priesthood have ventured on strange expedients, presuming on the credulity of the devotees. Witness, for example, the scandalous miracle of the holy fire of the present day! Nothing has been left untried that tends to replenish the coffers of the church, and the wealth of individual priests; and the spirit of avarice was intensely active at the period when the transference took place. Bishoprics were openly disposed of for sale, bits of the sacred cross, of the holy coat, bones and relics of martyrs were multiplied to any extent, and sold through the length and breadth of Christendom. Pilgrimages were a great source of revenue, and must on no account be discouraged. Pilgrims, who visited Jerusalem after the Dome of the Rock had passed out of Christian hands, are not to be told that the new Church was not the real sepulchre, but an imitation raised on an opposite hill.

About the commencement of the eleventh century, a fierce persecution broke forth against the Christians in Jerusalem. When first taken possession of by Omar (A.D. 640), he pledged himself "that the people of Ælia should have security for their lives, their churches, their crosses, their lands, and all that appertains to their religion, that none should be exposed to violence for following their religion." For a long time this pledge was faithfully kept. But at last the storm of persecution raged under the Egyptian khalif El Hakim. This rapacious oppressor is said to have adorned his palace with the gold and silver treasures of 30,000 churches, to have destroyed and laid waste the Church of Golgotha, and stripped of its great wealth the Church of the Resurrection. It has been alleged that he utterly razed to the ground this church also; a fact earnestly brought forward by the advocates of the present Church to account for the absence of ancient architecture. But as has been said, surely some fragment of pillar or shaft would have remained as witness of the past. But there is none. Moreover, to destroy the tomb of Christ is the last thing that any Mohammedan ruler would do. Have they destroyed the tomb of David; the tomb of Abraham? On the contrary, they guard these with religious veneration, and much more would they be disposed to protect the tomb of Christ, whom they reckon a prophet next to Mohammed himself. But the principal answer to the idea of its destruction, is in the architectural proof that the building is still unchanged in its essential features since the days of Constantine. The Mohammedans destroyed the adjoining Church of Calvary (horrible to them as the spot where the Christians said that God was crucified), despoiled that of the Sepulchre of its treasures, destroyed its images—idols they regard them —and expelling the Christians from its precincts, appropriated the sanctuary for their own worship.

Driven from their sepulchre, the Christians had no resource but to erect another building in the north-west part of Jerusalem, where they were still allowed to dwell. The building, representative only at first, would soon be confounded with the original by the devout pilgrims who came to Jerusalem.¹ The priests certainly were the last that would let them into the secret. They succeeded then as now, in persuading the devotees to believe that this elevation of artificial blocks was the hill Calvary, and the cave of marble slabs was the sepulchre of Christ. In that dark time what could the pilgrims do but take on trust everything said to them? And they were in Jerusalem!

There are one or two incidental circumstances which can only be accounted for on the theory of a transference. One is, that when the Crusaders came, they found, besides the Church of the Holy Sepulchre, another building never heard of before, "*Templum Domini*," the Temple of our Lord. It was none other than the "Dome of the Rock," and the fact that they gave it this name and worshipped in it most reverently, while they used for their dwelling the adjacent Mohammedan mosque (built on the site of the Temple), indicated the Christian traditions that clung to the building. Bernard declares that one among the various opinions in his day affirms, that the Templum Domini had been built by Helena under the Emperor Constantine.² Again, in the time of Saewulf (A.D. 1106), while the Church of the Sepulchre had been erected on its present site, there was a report that Justinian built it.³ In his time Zion was still the

---

¹ It was common to construct churches in Spain, Italy, and France in imitation of the holy places at Jerusalem, and in some cases the votaries even there believed in the representation as the reality. How much more easily would this be the case in Jerusalem!

² De hujus templi restauratione, ut nunc est variæ sunt opiniones. Quidam enim sub Constantino imperatore, ab Helena matre sua reædificatum fuisse perhibent pro venerentia Sanctæ Crucis ab ea repertæ.—Quoted in *Museum of Classical Antiquities*, vol. ii. p. 386.

³ *Early Travels*, p. 37.

eastern hill, for it is "separated from Olivet by *the Valley of Jehoshaphat*. Aceldama also was yet at "*the foot of Olivet*," and visited on his way to Siloam. Even in Maundrell's time (A.D. 1697) there were two Aceldamas, this ancient one, and the present one in the Valley of Hinnom. Both Zion and Aceldama had to follow in due time in the wake of the Church of the Sepulchre, to the western hill, where they are now visited.

Before passing from this point, it is worthy of notice that several *Mohammedan* traditions also distinctly indicate that "the Dome of the Rock" was originally a Christian building. Jelal Addin, in his *History of the Temple of Jerusalem*, gives the discourse delivered here before the soldiers of the Sultan on their driving out the Crusader, and regaining possession of the city. The preacher, referring to the first Mohammedan occupation (A.D. 640), speaks of "Omar, the commander of the Faithful, as the first who removed from this consecrated house *the representations of the cross*" (p. 234). The writer also quotes from Omar, who says, that the *Franks* built a church on the *Sakrah* and erected just by the place of Mohammed's foot (the impress of which it bears), a little chapel, and said, "This is the place where Christ set his foot" (p. 246). It is also worthy of our attention, that with this locality the Mohammedans still associate the idea of the *Resurrection* —a tradition that can well be explained if the Church of the Resurrection was originally here.

From the evidence now adduced, I believe that the advocates of the present Church, while confidently appealing to tradition, are really untrue to it, and moreover, make Constantine responsible for a blunder in the choice of a site which a far inferior mind could hardly have fallen into, and one assuredly of which the great Emperor was altogether free.

Before passing from the consideration of the early tradition of sacred localities, it will be well for the reader to mark what the Bordeaux pilgrim says about the site of the house of Caiaphas. He sees it as he goes up from Siloam to Zion, *i.e.*, up the eastern hill. In harmony with this, another pilgrim (Bernard), speaking of the place where Peter denied our Lord, *i.e.*, the house of the high priest, says, "to the *north* was the Temple of Solomon." It is probable that the house of Annas, his father-in-law, was hereabouts also, as his tomb, referred to by Josephus, is identified near at hand in the modern Aceldama. While the traditional house of the high priests was *outside* the city in the time of the Bordeaux pilgrim, we are not to conclude it was so at the time of the Gospel history, as it is not easy to see in that case how they could have kept the Passover with the strictness which they so greatly affected. It is far more probable that this dwelling was within the city, near to the princely gardens of Siloam, usually the property of the high dignitaries of Jerusalem. At all events, it was near Siloam where Caiaphas and his father-in-law dwelt, and the recollection of this fact will aid us in the interpretation of the Scripture incidents relating to the scenes of the Passion and the Resurrection.

CHAPTER XIV.

THE HOLY SEPULCHRE—SCRIPTURE ARGUMENT.

The question remains, Admitting that Constantine *did* build the Dome of the Rock as the Church of the Sepulchre, was not this a greater blunder than if he had chosen the western hill ? Had the locality contended for been far from the Temple, and outside the present walls, it might have perhaps received more consideration than has yet been allowed to it. But the hypothesis here maintained is by many condemned as soon as propounded. "Absurd!" say they at once. "This is the Mosque of Omar, and built on the site of the old Temple!" and so it was, if we are to believe the fancies of modern authors, and cast the statements of Josephus to the winds. A candid consideration of his description (as has been shown by Fergusson, Thrupp, and Lewin, the two last earnest advocates for the present Holy Sepulchre) has clearly proved that this locality must have been outside the Temple ; and I have called attention to the ravine that, as I believe, divided them. Now, to the question whether Constantine was right in fixing on this precise spot, I believe the following evidence warrants us to return an emphatic affirmative :—

I. Let us look, first of all, at the presumptive evidence furnished by a consideration of the circumstances of the

Roman occupation of Jerusalem. Crucifixion, it is well known, was the doom of rebels and traitors; and judging *à priori* from the critical circumstances of the times, I believe this was the most likely place of all where that doom would be inflicted. As the reader knows, the Jewish people never submitted in quietness to their government, but again and again during its continuance rose in fierce and sanguinary revolt. In the time of our Lord, as the hints of Scripture indicate, the spirit of insurrection was still intensely cherished, awakening the keen vigilance and energetic arm of the conqueror. Many were then cast into prison for sedition; Pilate, to be revenged on their turbulence, had mingled the blood of the Galileans with their sacrifices; a word or sign against Cæsar was eagerly laid hold of; and the address of Caiaphas clearly indicates that any remaining fragment of independence hung by a precarious tenure, so that a very slight pretext would suffice to make the Romans "take away their place and nation."

We may then fairly ask, as bearing on the point before us, *Where* in such an unquiet period would the public place of execution naturally be? I reply, we might expect it, for one thing, to be near Antonia, the barracks of the garrison.

It had been strange, indeed, if in these critical times the Roman Executive had sent the criminal away to be crucified on the western hill. In that case he was led to a distance from the Castle of Antonia, attended by a guard of four soldiers,[1] and passes through the heart of the city, at the obvious risk of exciting sympathy and

[1] There were four soldiers around the cross of Christ, as appears from the proposed division of the garments into four parts, "to every soldier a part."

an attempt at rescue. It is much more probable, surely, that Golgotha lay under the shadow of Antonia, so to speak, just as Constantine seems to have supposed. With such a proximity, an attempt at rescue in any case was impossible; the sympathy of the excited populace would be kept in check, and the whole Roman legion would be at hand to enforce, if necessary, the execution of the law.

Again, it is a fair presumption that the place was near the Temple. "But it is *too* near," says the reader; "this seems the grand objection." I have to remind him, however, of the deep and marked valley which separated the two at this time. However filled up at the west end, it was very deep where it entered the Kedron. Here the northern colonnade met the eastern one of the Temple, and the depth was great, according to Josephus, even as far on as the time of the destruction by Titus; that is, fifty years after the crucifixion of Christ. Golgotha, then, was separated in the most marked way from the Temple; and this being kept in view, its proximity is an argument *in its favour*. For it was *in* the Temple that the spirit of revolt was most deeply felt, and there the appeals to insurrection were proclaimed, in the name of religion and law. The assembly of the people here caused special uneasiness to Herod, who provided against the danger, first, by building the connecting colonnades of Antonia; and, secondly, by forming an "underground passage to the eastern gate of the inner Temple."[1] The times of the festival were seasons of his special vigilance and activity, both because of the crowds and the excitement of religious feeling. We should therefore, I

[1] Josephus, *Antiquities*, xv. 11. 7.

repeat, expect the place of crucifixion to be near the Temple, so that those disposed to sedition should have clearly before them the consequences of provoking the vengeance of the Roman power.

So much then for the presumptive evidence in favour of this locality, when the character and circumstances of the age are duly considered.

II. I proceed to show that Constantine was guided to the spot by the strong and unquestioned tradition of his time.

Some of my readers are aware that Dr. Robinson disputes this opinion. Never doubting but that Constantine built on the site of the *western* hill, and finding this to be quite at variance with the tests mentioned in Scripture, he concludes that there was no established tradition in that age; that the Emperor undertook the discovery of the spot, animated by a pious but ignorant zeal; mistaking this for a supernatural intimation, on which, of course, we can place no dependence. In short, he "invented" a locality.

The following remarks are intended to show that Dr. Robinson and others after him have done injustice to the memory of the Christian Emperor, and have imposed an unwarrantable construction on the language of Eusebius, the contemporary historian of the whole transaction.

1. It appears, then, that on the rock of the Sepulchre a heathen temple had been erected, enshrining a statue of Venus, the worst idol of the Pantheon in the view o the Christians. This temple with its idol, Constantine destroyed, removing to a great distance the vast accu-

mulations of earth on which it had been reared. For the heathen "had brought a quantity of earth with much labour from a distance, and covered the entire spot; then having raised this to a moderate height, they paved it with stone, concealing the Holy Cave beneath this massive mound."[1] When this was cleared away, the rock appeared, showing, to the surprise of all, its cavern uninjured.

Now, in reference to this heathen temple Eusebius says, "It had been the attempt of impious men, or rather, let me say, of the whole race of demons, to consign to the darkness of oblivion that monument of immortality." In making this quotation Dr. Robinson remarks, "Such language would hardly be appropriate in speaking of a spot definitely known and marked by long tradition." In that case, one knows not what to make of it. It is precisely *such* language, repeated throughout the historian's statement, which establishes a tradition that clung to the spot despite of all attempts to destroy it.

The Doctor, indeed, understands Eusebius to say, that "the spot was consigned to utter oblivion,"[2] which, let the reader observe, he is very far from saying. All that he affirms is, "that the heathen *attempted* to consign that monument of immortality to the darkness of oblivion." The whole tenor of his account is to the effect that the attempt was utterly baffled. It is obvious enough, that if the Christians had allowed the spot to become unknown and uncared-for, then this "attempt" of the heathen was unnecessary, and the language of the historian is absurd. He goes on to characterize it "as the object of godless and impious persons to remove the

[1] *Vita Constantini*, chap. xxvi.   [2] Vol. iii. p. 258.

cave from the eyes of men." Here is an absurd statement also, if men never cared to see that cave, or to remember it was there! He affirms that this act of "burying the sacred cave beneath these foul pollutions, and preparing on the foundation a dreadful sepulchre of souls, by the erection of a shrine to the impure spirit, was a device of impious and wicked men against the truth. Unhappy men! they were unable to comprehend how impossible that their attempt should remain unknown to Him who had been crowned with victory over death," etc. It may be confidently asserted, that if there was no tradition consecrating the spot in the view of the Christians; if the heathen temple was erected here by mere chance, and no more slandered the locality and truth of the resurrection of Christ, than any temple in Athens or Rome,—the accusation of Eusebius is about as bigoted and false as can well be conceived. Throughout, he speaks of the doings of the heathen in connexion with the spot, as a deliberate and audacious insult to the cardinal truth of Christianity—the resurrection of Christ! If there is any truth in his charge, the conclusion is certain that "the spot *was* definitely known and marked by long tradition."

2. It has been alleged that Constantine felt himself moved to discover the locality by "a Divine impulse." This is a mistake. Eusebius affirms that he was animated by a Divine impulse to *erect a church* on the consecrated spot, which is quite a different thing. His language is as follows: "He judged it incumbent on him to render the blessed locality of our Saviour's resurrection an object of attention and veneration to all." The Christians necessarily kept aloof from it so long as the idol was

standing. "He issued immediate orders, therefore, for the erection in that spot of a house of prayer, and this he did, not on the mere natural impulse of his own mind, but feeling his spirit thereto directed by the Saviour himself."[1]

3. Again, it is said that the discovery of the locality is represented as "a miracle." I reply, that here also Eusebius is misunderstood. He tells us that "the devices of impious men prevailed against the truth till the days of Constantine." But what was the reason of this? Not certainly that Constantine was the first to gain a knowledge of the spot, but that up to that time "the governors had no ability to abolish the temple,"[2] owing, of course, to the heathen policy of the State. Constantine, he goes on to say, "acting under the guidance of the Spirit, could not *endure to see* the sacred spot buried by the devices of the adversaries under every kind of impurity, and gave orders that the place should be thoroughly purified." He is not then said to have received any fresh knowledge of the locality "by miracle and diligent inquiry," or in any other way, but to have possessed "the ability" of "overthrowing the dwelling-places of error, with the statues and evil spirits which they represented."

But, let the reader observe, while the locality was known well enough, the unharmed condition of the Sepulchre when laid open to the light of day, excited the idea of a Divine preservation. Here was "the miracle" of Eusebius. "As soon," he says, "as the original surface of the ground appeared (after clearing away the rubbish), then immediately, contrary to the expectation of all, the

[1] *Vita Constantini*, chap. xxv.   [2] *Ibid.* xxvi.

venerable and hallowed monument of our Saviour's resurrection was revealed." It was "this monument of the Saviour's passion, so long buried under ground, and unseen for a long series of years, now reappearing to his servants," which Constantine also has described as "a miracle that transcends the capacity of man sufficiently to celebrate or comprehend."

It was also deemed a miraculous interposition of Providence that the rock showed only one sepulchral chamber within it. They were not perplexed with any difficulty in fixing on the tomb of the Redeemer, inasmuch as there was but one *loculus*. "For it is wonderful," says Eusebius, "to see this rock standing out erect and alone on level ground, and having only one cavern within it, lest, had there been many, the miracle of Him who overcame death would have been obscured."[1]

No one will wonder that this preservation of the cave should in that age especially be spoken of as "a miracle," if he reflects on the fierce persecutions that had marked the previous history of Christianity, persecutions which were especially violent during what was called "the festival of the passion."

Remembering the past, the Emperor and his historian might naturally dread that the heathens would have mutilated or entirely destroyed the rock, and that the removal of the temple and the rubbish would reveal but faint and fragmentary traces of the Holy Sepulchre. Instead of which it rises to view entire and uninjured; hence, in the pious enthusiasm of the time, they exclaim —A miracle!

But this should not have led to the inference that the

[1] *Theophania*, translated by Dr. Lee, p. 199.

discovery of the locality was miraculous, which neither Eusebius nor his patron at any time pretend.

4. Still further, it has been attempted to cast discredit on the spot selected, by representing it as the choice of Helena the mother of Constantine. She was about eighty years of age when she visited Jerusalem; she found in the sepulchre, it is alleged, three crosses; and one of these, by its miraculous power of healing, was ascertained to be the cross of Christ. If the "*Invention* of the cross," as it is well called, settled the question of the Holy Sepulchre, then, indeed, a pious fraud was palmed off upon the aged pilgrim, and was at the bottom of the fancied discovery.

But once more, not a word of all this is to be found in Eusebius or any contemporary historian. He does mention, indeed, the visit of Helena, and ascribes to her the erection of two splendid churches, one at Bethlehem, the other on the Mount of Ascension. But never in any way does he connect her name with the Church of the Holy Sepulchre. It is Constantine that gives the orders to demolish the heathen temple; Constantine that writes to the Bishop of Jerusalem regarding the erection of a church, in a letter which says: "I have no greater care than how I may best adorn with a splendid structure that sacred spot, which, under Divine direction, I have disencumbered, as it were, of the heavy weight of foul idol-worship." It is Constantine who summons the bishops of the Christian world to the consecration of this one Church alone.

The assumption that Eusebius did not mention the name of Helena, whom Dr. Robinson suspects to have been "the prime mover" in the matter, because he wished to flatter his patron, is clearly refuted by these facts (especially the language of the letter), and by the whole strain of the historian's statements. He speaks as if the Emperor gloried rather in any praise bestowed on his mother, "whose memory he wished to eternize." "He honoured her so fully with imperial dignities, that in every province, and in the very ranks of the soldiery, she was spoken of under the title of Augusta and Empress, and her likeness was impressed on golden coins," etc.[1] To her is attributed all the merit of building the church at Bethlehem and that on Olivet; therefore it must be affirmed that if she had had any share whatever in the erection of that over the Holy Sepulchre, much more if she had been "the prime mover in the matter," her name would not have been so utterly passed by.

Dr. Robinson, admitting the silence of Eusebius as to any share of the Empress in the matter, goes on to affirm "that all the writers of the following century relate, as with one voice, that she was from the first instigated to discover the Holy Sepulchre and the sacred cross," "that a divine intimation pointed out to her the spot;" that on her arrival at Jerusalem she inquired of the inhabitants; and "that in consequence of the discovery of the crosses she caused a splendid church to be erected."[2] Now, passing over the fact that the writers he refers to write a hundred years after the event, whereas Eusebius was a contemporary, I submit that even their language does not bear out the inferences here alleged. Sozomen (A.D. 450) affirms that "Constantine had resolved to erect a church near the place called Calvary. At the same time his mother repaired to the

[1] *Vita Constantini*, cap. 41, 47. [2] *Biblical Researches*, i. 374.

city for the purpose of offering up prayers and visiting the holy places."¹ This exactly accords with the language of Eusebius, and there is no reference here to any search or discovery. Theodoret (A.D. 440) asserts that the heathen temple was still standing at the time of her visit, but his language distinctly implies the most complete assurance of the pilgrim that beneath that temple was the Holy Sepulchre. "When she arrived at the place where the Saviour suffered, she immediately ordered the temple to be removed."² Socrates (A D. 450) indeed speaks of the Empress making "careful inquiry," and the fact that a heathen temple stood on the spot having become known to her, she caused it to be thrown down. But does not this language also imply the existence of a tradition, otherwise wherefore any inquiry at all? Why, moreover, was such immense labour undertaken unless the tradition was strong and unanimous? In the sepulchre three crosses were found (the fraud likely of some cunning monk), one of which, "a miracle" revealed to be the cross of Christ. But it is not alleged that the discovery of these fixed the site of the locality. The language of Sozomen affirms, that with Constantine originated the resolution to destroy the heathen temple; and Theodoret, though he speaks of Helena ordering its destruction, represents her as carrying letters from the Emperor to that effect. Eusebius, the contemporary historian, emphatically ascribes to him the superintendence of the whole business. And there is no difficulty, or obscurity, or miracle at all as to the site. He has no dream, sees no sign, hears no revela ion, makes no inquiry, resorts to no pious fraud, but simply commands

---

[1] *Historia Ecclesiastica*, ii. 1.   [2] *Ibid.* i. 18.

the demolition of the heathen temple, whereupon the sacred cave comes to light uninjured and alone.

The Romans were not in the habit of insulting the religions of the countries they conquered, but in Jerusalem, they, in the most marked manner, vented their scorn both on Judaism and Christianity. For the Jew and the Christian alike denounced all idols, and refused to worship the statue of the Emperor. Hence their religion was looked on as a political offence, as treason to the State, and the perpetual source of irritation and revolt. It was therefore their policy to insult and trample it down. With this view, they placed the statue of Venus on the site of the sepulchre, and two statues of Hadrian (existing in the days of Jerome) on the site of the Temple. The fact settles the question of traditional reverence for both localities, and furnishes an argument for the genuineness of the site of the Holy Sepulchre which can be adduced in favour of none of the other holy places whatever.

I will only add, that those who deny the existence of tradition will find it somewhat difficult to explain how Constantine, without that sanction, dared to proclaim as "the most holy and blessed monument of the passion and resurrection," a spot defiled by the presence of an idol. It is the last thing he might be expected to do. If he wished "to invent" a place, surely many could have been found about Jerusalem free from the unholy contamination. In an age when the great duty of a Christian was to protest against and keep aloof from idolatry and all its pollutions, it seems the most incredible of all things that a man of his known temperament and character should have pitched upon such a spot. The attempt would have awakened the horror of Christendom, and few pilgrims would have come to worship. But how stands the fact? The proposal to build a church even here was, despite of the past defilement, hailed with universal joy; and from far and near the bishops hastened to its splendid consecration. In any view of the matter, then, we are led to infer that there was a clear and unquestioned tradition pointing to this locality, which no heathen devices had been able to efface.

III. I may remark further, that Constantine may have had another means of ascertaining the true locality in the abundant access which he possessed to the archives of the Roman government. Mr. Finlay, author of *Greece under the Romans*, contends, in his pamphlet on the Holy Sepulchre, "that in no department of the civil administration was the superiority of the Roman system of government over that of modern states more conspicuous than in the mass of statistical information in the possession of the executive power; that every private estate was surveyed, that maps were constructed indicating any locality possessing a name, and so detailed that every field was marked." He refers to St. Luke and Ulpian to show that Palestine was thus surveyed. Now, while we may not be prepared without further evidence to believe that the colony of Palestine was thus minutely surveyed, it can hardly be doubted that "the place called Calvary" would be marked in any map that may have been constructed, however vague and incomplete. For it was "near the city," the place of execution for great crimes, the well-known place of doom for rebels against the

Roman power. If Constantine, then, did need to make inquiry (which the previous evidence, I believe, shows was quite unnecessary), and so guard against mistake, he might gain information from the records and surveys transmitted from Palestine to the government at Rome.

IV. We now come to the evidences from Scripture, the most conclusive of all. There is some light thrown on the inquiry by incidents recorded in the *Old Testament*, which is not to be disregarded. Jerusalem, as other cities, had its own fixed place where criminals underwent the extreme penalty of law, and where the crime of idolatry was publicly branded and punished. This place, beyond all doubt, was in the vicinity of the Kedron, where we allege Golgotha to have been.

Thus we read, that Asa " removed his mother Maachah from being queen, because she had made an idol in a grove, and Asa destroyed her idol, and burnt it by the *brook Kedron*" (1 Kings xv. 13). Joash " brought out the grove from the house of the Lord, without Jerusalem unto the brook Kedron, and burnt it at the brook Kedron, and stamped it small to powder, and cast the powder thereof upon the graves of the children of the people."

Here also was slain the traitor-queen, Athaliah. "Jehoiada the priest brought out the captains of the hundreds that were over the host, and said unto them, Have her forth of the ranges, and him that followeth her, let him be slain with the sword; for the priest said, Let her not be slain in the house of the Lord. And they laid hands on her, and when she was come to the entering of the horse-gate by the king's house, they slew her there"

(2 Chron. xxiii. 14, 15). Turning to Josephus, we find this locality to have been at "*the ravine of the Kedron.*"

There is a remarkable passage in Jeremiah bearing on the point under consideration, where the name Golgotha has been identified with Goath. Jerusalem has been destroyed, and its inhabitants carried away captive, but the prophet foretells its returning prosperity: "Behold, the days come, saith the Lord, that the city shall be built to the Lord from the tower of Hananeel to the gate of the corner" (Jer. xxxi. 38). Here there is affirmed the restoration of the ancient walls. The next verse speaks of a vast increase to its extent, as marking the era of its coming glory: "And the measuring-line shall yet go forth over-against it upon the hill Gareb, and shall compass about to *Goath,* and the whole valley of the dead bodies, and of the ashes, and all the fields unto the brook Kedron, unto the corner of the horse-gate toward the east, shall be holy unto the Lord" (ver. 39, 40).

Goath, be it observed, must be in the vicinity "of the brook Kedron, and of the horse-gate toward the east," for all these mark the *termination* of the wall after its sweep over the hill Gareb.

Now here is situated the Golgotha for which we are contending. The prophet seems to refer to the large increase of the city that marked its later history, and which caused Agrippa to run a wall northwards over Bezetha, fetching it round afterwards till it terminated, as Josephus describes, "at the Kedron ravine." It thus corresponded in its sweep and termination with "the measuring-line" of the prophet.

I may add, that the Syriac version translates Goath

as "the eminence;"[1] such was its appearance, inasmuch as it overhung the steeps of "the Kedron ravine."

Here then in the time of the kings, near the fields of the Kedron, was their Goath or Golgotha, the place of punishment for daring crimes against religion and law. Thus the incidents of the Old Testament tend to support the Calvary in the eastern hill, as fixed on by Constantine.

We have now to examine the hints and incidents of the *New Testament narrative* in its representation of the scene of the crucifixion. These, I believe, accord completely with this locality, and gain immeasurably in their impressions and life-like interest. Let us especially note what is said on four points: 1. The way to the cross; 2. The name of the place of crucifixion, Calvary, and its position relative to the city; 3. The position and doings of the various groups of spectators, soldiers, people, and priests; 4. The garden of Joseph enclosing the sepulchre. In view of the features of this eastern hill, the slight hints of the record expand into high significance, and sketch for us a picture of graphic force.

I. *The way to the Cross, the Via Dolorosa.*—1. The language of the narrative intimates, as I understand it, that our Lord was led outside the city *as soon as* he left the Governor's house. That is to say, that the *Via Dolorosa* was outside the gate as well as Calvary. Every one knows that the present so-called *Via Dolorosa*, leading to the present so-called Calvary on the *western* hill, must have conducted from the judgment-seat of Pilate right into the city, our Lord passing through

[1] See Smith's *Dictionary of the Bible:* Art. "Goath."

the very heart of Jerusalem nearly all the way. Now, even admitting (a far-fetched supposition) that this site was *beyond* the walls, the language of the evangelist, I submit, will not allow of such a route to it. It leads us to conclude, that long before arriving at Calvary, and before Simon the Cyrenian is met " coming out of the country," the procession was outside the city. According to the testimony of St. Mark, " when they had mocked him, they took off the purple from him, and put his own clothes on him, and *led him out* (ἐξάγουσιν αὐτὸν) to crucify him." He then adds, that " they compelled Simon a Cyrenian, who passed by, coming out of the country, the father of Alexander and Rufus, to bear his cross." The procession, be it observed, had reached a road leading to the country, and must have been therefore considerably on its way, and yet it is implied that even before this it was without the city. The language of St. John confirms this conclusion, for he says, "Jesus, *bearing his cross*, went forth (ἐξῆλθεν) into a place called the place of a skull." Such expressions indicate that the procession was, from the starting-place, outside the city gate, Jesus bearing so far his own cross.

Now all this would happen in the route to the Calvary on this eastern hill. If any reader should object that he passes between houses even in this direction, I remind him that they are those of the suburb Bezetha, which were not enclosed by the wall of Agrippa till some years afterwards. At the Castle of Antonia, the judgment-seat of Pilate, the wall then existing terminated ; and in this wall doubtless was the gate of the city, through which our Lord passed at once, on the order of Pilate for his crucifixion. Thus the *Via Dolorosa* was nearly all along outside the city, and the language of Scripture is verified and explained.

2. It passed a road "coming out of the country." Such would happen on the route in question, for it would require to go eastwards to the point marked by St. Stephen's Gate, where such a road exists at the present day. Thence it turned down along the brow of the Kedron to Calvary. The reader asks, Why this detour? Why not go right across the plateau from the Castle of Antonia? I have to remind him of the nature of the ground. The procession, on emerging from the city gate, required to go eastwards along nearly the whole breadth of the castle, which stretched to the suburb Bezetha. There the larger pool of Bethesda adjoined, so that the course was still eastwards even to St. Stephen's Gate, as at the present day. There a road comes in from the country, and a glance at the rocky ground is sufficient to convince us that the present road was the same in the distant past. To this point, then, Christ had gone forth, bearing his own cross. It is distant from the present traditional Pilate's house (which there is no reason to doubt is correct) about 350 yards; in other words, it is along the present breadth of the northern side of the Haram es Sheriff. Over the remaining distance to Calvary, or that from the present St. Stephen's Gate to somewhere below the Golden Gate (about 150 yards), the cross is carried by Simon the Cyrenian. The entire distance was about 500 yards, or a quarter of a mile. Such I believe to have been the true *Via Dolorosa*, answering in these two points to the Scripture narrative. Its name too, as "the way of sorrow," will become more impressive to us, if we reflect that it led to Calvary along the brow of the Kedron, in

which valley was the Garden of the agony, and the tombs of the murdered prophets. The Saviour had all these scenes in the foreground of his view when from Olivet "he beheld the city, and wept over it :" "O Jerusalem, Jerusalem, thou that killest the prophets!"

II. *The name Calvary, and its position relative to the city.*—Here three things are to be remarked :—

1. It *was outside the gate.* One of the strongest objections to the site in the western hill is, that it must have been within the wall. To this eastern site the objection cannot apply. If Calvary be here, then Jesus "suffered without the gate." The enclosing wall of Agrippa, I repeat, was not yet built. The locality was open, as the sketch represents, and might still be described in the language of the Old Testament, "the fields of Kedron, without Jerusalem."

2. It was near the city. "The place where he was crucified was near the city" (John xix. 20).

3. It was the place called Golgotha, Calvary, *i. e.*, a skull. What are we to understand by this? The usual idea is, that the place was so named because it was the spot of public execution, of violent death. This idea, however, the best scholars are now giving up. In reference to it an able writer remarks : "According to Jewish law the skulls must have been buried, and therefore were no more likely to confer a name on the spot than any other part of the skeleton. In this case, too, the Greek should be κρανίων, 'of skulls,' instead of κρανίου, 'of a skull;' still less a skull, as in the Hebrew, and in the Greek of St. Luke." There is another explanation of the word. "It may come," says the same writer, "from the look or form of the

spot itself, bald, round, skull-like, and therefore a mound or hillock, in accordance with the common phrase—for which there is no direct authority—Mount Calvary."[1]

It can hardly be questioned that this latter explanation is the true one. In all languages, it would appear, a projecting hill or promontory is named by such a figure: thus "Cape" (*caput*), "headland," and in Arabic *Ras* (*head*), as Ras Attakah, the promontory of Attakah. Thus to apply the Hebrew term Golgotha in the way indicated, is sanctioned by the general usage of language. And we are shut up to such an interpretation all the more from the expression of the Evangelists, when strictly translated. In Matthew, it is "a place called Golgotha, that is to say, a place of a skull;" in Mark, "the place Golgotha, which is, being interpreted, the place of a skull;" in Luke, "the place that *is called a skull*;" in John, "the place of a skull, which is called in the Hebrew, Golgotha." This would be a strange way, assuredly, of expressing the circumstance, that it was a place of public execution; but it is natural, and in harmony with the analogy of language, if employed to describe a bare projecting spur or promontory.

Again, we have seen that Goath or Golgotha is expressed by the Syriac *Ieromto*, " an eminence;" and yet further, as early as the fourth century, the place was called "the hill Calvary" by the Bordeaux pilgrim, who visited the spot when Constantine was building the adjacent Church on the rock of the Sepulchre. Ever since, the phrase has been adopted in all Christian literature, a fact for which we can account only by adopting the above explanation of the word.

[1] Smith's *Dictionary of the Bible*: Art. "Golgotha."

Let the reader then remark that there was precisely such a projecting ridge or "cape" at this place on the eastern hill. "The Kedron ravine" here entered "the Kedron" or Valley of Jehoshaphat, and thence there resulted a prominent ridge, the bare rocky summit of which was Golgotha, "the skull-shaped hill."

III. Let us now see how this locality accords with what is said of the various groups at the crucifixion—*Soldiers, People,* and *Priests.*

1. *Soldiers.*—It has been already shown from a consideration of the revolutionary spirit of the time, that it is highly probable that the place of crucifixion was near Antonia, the barrack of the garrison. There are two incidents mentioned in connexion with the doings of the soldiers at the crucifixion, which have a natural explanation on such a supposition, but which cannot be well understood if there was any great distance between the localities.

We are told that "the soldiers also mocked him, coming to him and offering him vinegar (προσερχόμενοι καὶ ὄξος προσφέροντες αὐτῷ), and saying, If thou be the King of the Jews, save thyself" (Luke xxiii. 36). This vinegar, as is well known, was the *posca* or cheap acid wine mixed with water, which was the common drink of the Roman soldiers. What soldiers then were these who thus brought the vinegar to Christ in mockery? "The soldiers that crucified him," is the usual understanding. This I am persuaded was not the case. The party in charge of the crucifixion had other work appointed them, which the Evangelists record. They offer the victim the medicated cup to deaden the suffering (which Christ refused), and nail him to his cross. They are but four in number, but instead of dividing "the garment into four parts, to every soldier a part," they cast lots for it. And then it is said, "Sitting down they watched him there" (Matt. xxvii. 36) while "the centurion (their commander) stood over against him" (Mark xv. 39). It was theirs not to insult or aggravate the agony of the victim (however others might do this), but to see that the sentence was completely carried out, and the body not taken away, and the expressions above quoted show that they were faithful to their trust. Besides, they were already *at* the cross, whereas the soldiers that mocked Christ are said to have come to him (προσερχόμενοι), and to have carried to him (προσφέροντες αὐτῷ) the vinegar. These were therefore the other soldiers of the garrison, part of the "whole band" who insulted him on the judgment-seat of Pilate, and now they come out with the crowd to mock at his agony and shame. And the fact that they thus carried to him the vinegar, or posca, implies that the garrison was near the scene of his suffering.

Again, after the cry, "Eli, Eli, lama sabachthani : My God, my God, why hast thou forsaken me?" the sufferer, experiencing one of the most intolerable agonies of this mode of punishment, and "knowing that all things were now accomplished, that the Scriptures might be fulfilled, saith, I thirst" (John xix. 28). This Evangelist adds,—Σκεῦος οὖν ἔκειτο ὄξους μεστόν : "Then was set a vessel full of vinegar" (John xix. 29). From the other Evangelists we learn that one ran to fetch it : "Straightway one of them ran and filled a sponge full of vinegar" (Matt. xxvii. 48 ; Mark xv. 36). This also was the posca ; and consequently the runner was a soldier, one probably who, like the centurion, regarded the sufferer with compassion: "When Jesus therefore had received the vinegar, he said, It is finished, and he bowed his head, and gave up the ghost." Again, the narrative is natural and intelligible on the idea that Antonia was near. The messenger had but to cross the plateau to secure a fresh supply of the posca.

2. *The People.*—On the way to the cross there followed Jesus a great company (πολὺ πλῆθος) of the people (Luke xxiii. 27). Foes were among the crowd—Scribes, Pharisees, Sadducees—hypocrites no longer in this respect; but also friends, whose hearts protested against the injustice of his doom, and who "smote their breasts" in grief at the spectacle. Gathered as they were from different parts of Palestine to the festival, they were numerous. "All the people," or rather all the crowds (πάντες οἱ ὄχλοι) "that came together to that sight, beholding the things that were done, smote their breasts, and returned. And all his acquaintance, and the women that followed him from Galilee, stood afar off, beholding these things" (Luke xxiii. 48, 49). Now on the opposite side of the Kedron rose the slopes of Olivet, where *thousands* could have witnessed the spectacle.

While his friends and sympathizers thus viewed the tragedy from a distance, his foes press near to mock around the cross. It is said "the people (ὁ λαὸς, that had clamoured for his death) stood beholding; and the rulers also with them derided him, saying, He saved others; let him save himself, if he be Christ, the chosen of God" (Luke xxiii. 35). These would cover the plateau and slopes of the Kedron. Of another party of mockers belonging to the people, it is said: "They that passed by railed on him, wagging their heads, and saying, Ah! thou that destroyest the temple, and buildest it in three days, save thyself, and come down from the cross" (Mark xv. 29). This incident also finds a natural place in such a locality. It was the 15th day of Nisan, the first day of the festival of the Passover (it lasted for seven days), on which many additional sacrifices were offered. "Many voluntary sacrifices and freewill offerings were made by private individuals and families."[1] Now the party in question, we may believe, had been on such an errand, and were carrying, as was the custom, some portion of their sacrifices to be shared with their friends and families on the festive occasion. They had issued from the northern gate of the Temple,[2] and were making for the suburb Bezetha, necessarily "passing by" the cross. The Temple they have left is in all its glory, showing no trace of decay; and here, close to it, is Jesus of Nazareth dying in disgrace and agony. Perverting his language they naturally draw the contrast as they pass, and hurl it at him as the bitterest of sarcasms.

3. *The Priests.*—The question here is, Whither did these dignitaries resort that they might witness the scene? The only answer, I believe, is, To the Temple itself; and if this can be made out, then Calvary must have been near at hand, as is all along contended for. We have already looked at the presumptive evidence for this proximity, on the ground that the Temple was the scene where revolt was most apt to break forth,—that rebellious spirit which the punishment of crucifixion was intended to keep in check. From the northern wall of

[1] See Robinson's *Harmony*.   [2] Josephus, *Bell. Jud.* ii. 19. 5.

the Temple, I believe, the priests looked across at this deed of savage Jewish spite, and of barbarous Roman arrogance, while they launched their sneers at the victim before them. It is usual to suppose that the priests followed with the crowd to Calvary; but the narrative indicates the contrary. In the previous scenes "the priests" and "the people" are mentioned as mingling with each other and acting together. Thus "Pilate said to the *priests* and *people*, I find no fault in the man." At the bar of Herod, "the priests and scribes stood and vehemently accused him." On his return to Pilate, the Roman governor called together the *chief priests* and *the rulers* and *the people*, and said unto them, "I find no fault in this man, touching those things of which ye accuse him: no, nor yet Herod. I will therefore chastise him and let him go." "They (the people) were instant with loud voices, requiring that he should be crucified, and the voices of *them* and the *chief priests* prevailed," etc. In view of these passages, I submit that if "the priests" *had* joined in the procession to the cross, it would have been expressly mentioned. But it is said simply, "There followed him a great company of people" ($\pi o \lambda \grave{v}$ $\pi \lambda \hat{\eta} \theta o s$ $\tau o \hat{v}$ $\lambda a o \hat{v}$), no mention being made of the priests,—an omission which proves that they had gone elsewhere. The language of St. Matthew indicates that the members of the Sanhedrim, the chief priests, the scribes, and elders, were together as they mocked; and that of St. Mark indicates that they *were apart from the crowd.* "Likewise also the chief priests, mocking, said *among themselves* ($\pi \rho \grave{o} s$ $\dot{a} \lambda \lambda \acute{\eta} \lambda o v s$), with the scribes, He saved others; himself he cannot save." That they should keep apart, may be also inferred from their fear of defilement during the period of the Passover festival.

They were in the Temple. Not to dwell on the fact that a number of sacrifices were being offered, requiring the presence of many of them there, I direct the attention of the reader to what is said about the conduct of Judas in the repayment of the thirty pieces of silver. The sentence had been passed on the Saviour, and all parties had betaken themselves to their respective positions to gaze on the scene. "Judas," it is said, "who had betrayed him, when he *saw that he was condemned*, repented himself, and brought again the thirty pieces of silver to the chief priests and elders, saying, I have sinned, in that I have betrayed innocent blood. And they said, What is that to us? see thou to that. And he cast down the *pieces of silver in the Temple*, and departed, and went and hanged himself. And the *chief priests* took *the silver pieces*," etc. (Matt. xxvii. 3-7.)

Thus then the *chief priests were* in the Temple, and thence shout their derision at the crucified. But if so, it must have been near Calvary, as the sketch represents.

Hence this locality agrees perfectly with the slight references of the narrative, respecting the position of the various groups at the crucifixion, and the feeling and conduct which they displayed. If any other site can be pointed out, as equally verifying and illustrating the language, then by all means let it be tried; for my part, I know not where it is to be found.

IV. *The Sepulchre.*— 1. It must have been *large*. The women enter into it, and "see a young man sitting on the right side, clothed in a long white garment" (Mark xvi. 2). Mary Magdalene, stooping down, sees "*two* angels in white, sitting the one at the head, the other at the feet, where the body of Jesus had lain" (John xx. 11). "Simon Peter went into the Sepulchre" (John xx. 6). We must therefore conceive it to have been a *cavern* of some considerable dimensions,—a condition perfectly met by the appearance of the cave under the Dome of the Rock.

2. They "*stooped down*" to look into and enter the Sepulchre (John xx. 5, 11). This cave is several feet below the surface of the ground.

3. "It was *a new* tomb, hewn out of the rock, wherein man was never before laid." This circumstance is fatal to the supposition that it was somewhere in the Valley of the Kedron, as has of late been supposed by some, full as that was of the "graves of the children of the people." Besides, it was in a garden. If we remember that the rock overlooked the ravine anciently consecrated as the Sepulchre of the Kings, and thereafter, when the ravine was so far filled up, lay between Antonia and the Temple, and so belonged to ground jealously watched by Jews and Romans, we may understand how it was so long unused for burial, and fell to be purchased by Joseph, "a rich man of Arimathea," "a councillor," and apparently a friend of Pilate as well as of the Jews.

4. Around the Sepulchre *was a garden*. That the plateau here was of considerable extent, and moreover was vacant ground (so far as regards the building of houses), is evident from the fact, that Titus and a portion of his army came up here, and were assailed by the Jews "both from the north wall of the Temple and the castle

of Antonia." The garden of Joseph may have been bounded by the side of Antonia on the north, and its connecting colounades on the west, and so covered a considerable part of the present platform of the Dome of the Rock, which is (to give it roughly) a square of 500 feet. The garden was enclosed as being of some extent (it had a gardener, John xx. 15), and moreover as being near, or rather at, the place of crucifixion. "In the place where he was crucified, there was a garden, and in the garden a new sepulchre, wherein was never man yet laid. There laid they Jesus, therefore, because of the Jews' preparation-day, for the sepulchre was nigh at hand."

V. We may further glance at two incidents that occurred on the morning of the resurrection, which have a natural and unforced explanation in connexion with this locality.

1. The angels, who appear to the women at the Sepulchre, bid them go quickly and tell the disciples that their Master had risen from the dead. "They did run," it is said, "to bring his disciples word; and as they went to tell his disciples, behold, Jesus met them, saying, All hail. And they came and held him by the feet, and worshipped him" (Matt. xxviii. 9, 10). It is fitting surely that we image to ourselves this scene of worship as taking place in some *secluded solitude* outside the city, instead of in the heart of it, as seems inevitable if they had been at the locality marked by the present church. It has been shown that the more ancient tradition fixed the *Cœnaculum* on the slope of the Temple hill. It was probably not far from Siloam where the

disciples entered the city, and found a man carrying the pitcher of water, as their Master had predicted. The early tradition indicates that this was also the place where the disciples received the Holy Ghost, which seems to agree with the hints of Scripture on Christ's reappearance to them as they sat at meat. The upper room was probably hired for the eight days of the Paschal festival. In this quarter then the disciples were dwelling, and the *Latibulum Apostolorum*, "the retreat of the apostles," is shown near Siloam at this day. To *this part* of the city then the women are hurrying with the tidings, and on leaving the Sepulchre, their route would be down the Valley of the Kedron. Accordingly, in some part of that valley, all silent and secluded, in the early morning, they meet and worship their Lord.

2. "Now, when they were going, behold, some of the watch came into the city, and showed unto the chief priests all the things that were done" (Matt. xxviii. 11). As "the watch" were not at the Sepulchre when the women arrived, they must have been in the city before them, and the true inference from the statement seems to be, that the women met them in the *same part* of the city whither they were bound. Before showing how that could be, I must remark, that the usual idea of this watch being composed of Roman soldiers, seems an assumption altogether untenable. Considering the jealousy and hatred between the Jews and Romans, it seems unaccountable that Roman soldiers should go with the tale to the chief priests instead of their own commander. And still more unaccountable is their consenting to propagate such a falsehood as they were bribed to tell. It was the proclamation of their deepest disgrace, and the decree against

it was death. Even in ordinary circumstances this stern sentence was executed, but much more would it be carried out when Pilate had to deal with such a turbulent people, and his only hope lay in maintaining the strictest discipline among his troops. The priests indeed assured " the watch" against any evil consequences from the wrath of the Governor ; but Roman soldiers would not have been duped by such a promise, well aware of the heinousness of the fault on their own part. They were bribed too, not to keep silence, but actually to propagate the story ! Still further, the priests conjecture that after all Pilate may never hear of it ; as possibly he never did. Yet how could he fail to know, if the guard consisted of his own troops, to be relieved only under the orders of their superior ? "The watch" at Christ's tomb seems to have been part of the Jewish guard of the Temple. The Pharisees presented a request to Pilate for a Roman guard ; he dismisses them with a refusal. "Ye *have* a watch," he says (your own watch took him captive and brought him to me) ; "go your way, and make it as sure as you can." He is in truth ashamed of the part he had already taken, has refused their request to alter the inscription on the cross, and will refuse this other also. As he had given the body of Christ to Joseph to be buried in his own tomb, he might be displeased to hear that it had been allowed to be stolen away. Still, considering that it was an affair of the Jews, and had happened under their own watch, it is not likely that he would be inclined to take severe measures. It is easy then to conceive how the priests might persuade this guard from the Temple to propagate their version of the story.

Let us now see how the meeting of the women with the watch can be explained. At the appearance of the angel "the keepers became as dead men." They had fled in terror from the scene before the women reach the Sepulchre. They take immediate refuge, it is likely, among the guard of the adjacent Temple. After a space they recover from their terror, and hasten with their tale to the residences of the priests, Annas and Caiaphas. Now these were, as tradition indicates, in that district of the city to which the women are bound, and accordingly soon after entering at the gate near Siloam, they might meet the watch as the narrative describes.

I have thus endeavoured to show that the site of the Sepulchre beneath the Dome of the Rock agrees with and throws light upon the incidents of the inspired narrative. If these can be held to agree with any other spot, it certainly behoves those who advocate it to exhibit this correspondence. For its capability of accommodation *to details* must ever be the grand test of any theory that may be hazarded; and if this be shrunk from, no asseverations, however dogmatic and abundant, will be able or can be expected to command belief.

CHAPTER XV.

CLOSING SCENES OF THE GOSPEL NARRATIVE.

I SHALL now endeavour, following the *order of the narrative*, to present the eventful scenes of the last day of our Lord's passion, from the supper in the upper chamber on to the events of the resurrection, with the illustration and commentary which their localities supply. On these events the Evangelists have dwelt with special minuteness, and they are those surely which the Christian reader wishes to realize as vividly as possible. It is not easy to do this when the localities are uncertain and disregarded; the sketches of the painter, however successful in catching the expression and spirit of the actors, are felt to want an appropriate background. By the union of the two, on the other hand, a living picture rises on the view, and hints and phrases of the writer, apt otherwise to be overlooked, receive often striking illustration and enforcement. Moreover, this treatment of Gospel history is one of the best antidotes to the spirit of modern criticism, calling itself *eclectic*, and which would eliminate so many of its incidents on what to many a reader seem the most capricious pretexts. Regarding the time and place of their occurrence, the scenes of the passion, as depicted by the Evangelists, rise before us with a vividness and power which the most fanciful sketch but feebly imitates. It is to these scenes that the doctrines and symbols of the Christian faith impressively summon our thoughts, and the view of them, in connexion with their localities, will fitly close this portion of the book which has aimed to develop the topography of ancient Jerusalem.

After partaking of the broken bread and the poured out wine, our Lord seeks to console and instruct the perplexed disciples by the wonderful exhortation recorded in the fourteenth chapter of St. John. At its close he says, "Arise, let us go hence;" and then, along with his disciples, moves out towards Olivet. They pass out of the city (as they had entered it from Bethany during the day) by the gate near Siloam, and issue into the quiet Valley of the Kedron. Gethsemane is distant about three-quarters of a mile. In the way, our Lord delivers the injunctions in the fifteenth and sixteenth chapters of St. John's Gospel.[1]

These words of counsel to the disciples closed with the prediction, that they would all forsake him in the dark hour that was now impending. Turning to the state-

[1] Some maintain that these discourses and the prayer that followed were really delivered in the upper room, because this Evangelist uses the expression, "Jesus went out" ('Ιησοῦς ἐξῆλθε) in chap. xviii. 1. I have inclined to the view adopted above: (1.) because of the emphatic statement at the close of the 14th chapter, "Arise, let us go hence," which indicates that they at that time left the upper chamber. (2.) In chap. xvi. 32, our Lord tells his disciples, that in that hour they should be scattered and leave him alone. Two Evangelists record this statement as made to them *after* they had left the chamber for the Mount of Olives; Matt. xxvi. 31; Mark xiv. 27. (3.) The phrase, "lifted up his eyes to heaven" (chap. xvii. 1) favours the idea that the prayer was uttered beneath the open sky, and not in the upper room. (4.) We can explain the expression in question (ἐξῆλθε) by the fact that the Evangelist specifies the distance to which they had by that time proceeded from the city, "over the brook Kedron." No fitter scene can be imagined for the utterance of these discourses and of that prayer than the quiet Valley of Kedron on that eventful night.

ments of the other Evangelists, we find that all of them protested against the idea with a self-confidence which proved how little they knew their own strength and their need of that Divine protection and help which formed the burden of the prayer that followed. With characteristic vehemence Peter protests that however the others might act, he would stand faithful to the last. He received for answer the warning addressed to him in the upper room: "Verily I say to thee, Before the cock crow twice thou shalt deny me thrice. But he spake the more vehemently: If I should die with thee, I will not deny thee in anywise. Likewise also said they all."[1] Our Lord now offered the prayer (John xvii.), asking the protection and guidance of the Father for the disciples he was leaving, and arriving at the Garden, urged them to supplicate heavenly aid for themselves: "When he was at the place, he said unto them, Pray that ye enter not into temptation!" (Luke xxii. 40.) He goes into the depth of the Garden with Peter and the two sons of Zebedee, James and John, and "began to be sorrowful and very heavy. Then saith he to them, My soul is exceeding sorrowful, even unto death: tarry ye here, and watch with me." Again during the agony he rebukes their slumber, and urges to imitation of his example: "Why sleep ye, rise and pray, lest ye enter into temptation!"

Meanwhile the traitor with the Temple guard—"the band received from the chief priests and officers of the Temple"—have assembled, probably at the high priest's

---

[1] Matthew and Mark distinctly affirm this scene to have taken place after the company had left the upper room and gone out to Olivet. It should not therefore be confounded with what had occurred at the table, when Peter alone was addressed.

house. They also steal out of the gate near Siloam and pass up the Kedron to Gethsemane, "for Judas knew the place." They form a numerous group, and are armed with swords and staves; for they have a strange undefined dread of Him they are going to seize. They have torches and lanterns with which to explore the caverns on the sides of Olivet, should he be tempted to hide himself. Arriving at the Garden, they see the forms of the disciples in the moonlight, thus ascertaining that the object of their search is indeed here. "Judas went before them, and drew near to Jesus to kiss him,"—the preconcerted sign. Jesus advances towards his enemies with the question, "Whom seek ye? They answer him, Jesus of Nazareth. Jesus saith unto them, I am he. As soon as he had said unto them, I am he, they went back and fell to the ground." What was it that produced such a shock? Was it the altered aspect of his countenance, so deeply imprinted with the traces of the agony, serenely sad, and revealing "the divine depths of sorrow"? or did they dread some self-defensive if not vindicatory manifestation of that power, which they could not deny him to possess, however they might account for it? But he stands before them meek and forbearing, and, as they rise to their feet, simply asks that his disciples be allowed to depart unharmed. The latter, animated to courage by the spectacle of the prostrate throng, had begun to strike with the sword at their renewed movements. But the Master forbade such an attack, healed the wound inflicted, and surrendered himself, the band closing around him with their swords and staves. They passed down the Valley of the Kedron, and entering the city again by the gate at Siloam, led the prisoner first to the house of Annas, in the immediate vicinity. Annas ordered fetters, and "sent him bound unto Caiaphas the high priest." The house of Caiaphas was adjacent, where, passing through its outer court, he was led into one of the inner apartments for examination. When the high priest "asked Jesus of his disciples and of his doctrine," He answered that all his teaching had been open and public, and that he had no plan or purpose different from that which had been openly avowed. He referred Caiaphas, therefore, to those who had heard his teaching for the information he desired. His reply was considered insulting, and one of the officers present struck him, although bound, with the palm of his hand.

While His examination was proceeding within, the outer court or quadrangle was open to the sky, and there a fire had been kindled "because of the cold." By the influence of John, who knew the high priest, Peter had got access to the palace. He was not now with his Master, but as the Evangelist says, "sat *without* in the palace," and warmed himself at the fire with the officers and servants. Then occurred one of the most touching incidents of the eventful night—Peter's denial and repentance. A certain damsel (who had probably got the information from her fellow-servant that kept the door) "came unto him, saying, Thou also wast with Jesus of Galilee; but he denied before them all, saying, I know not what thou sayest." After this he skulks from the light of that fire, with the dark inquisitive eyes of the group around it, and seeks the obscurity of the porch. "And he went out into the porch, and the cock crew." Here another maid saw him, being none other indeed than "the damsel that kept the door," and who recognised him as the friend she had let in at the request of John. She said to them that stood by, "This is one of them." Peter, in answer to one of the group who was enforcing the accusation, saith, "Man, I am not."[1] His Master is meanwhile within, and hence no warning issues from his look to check or remonstrate with the cowardly and lying disciple. But it was different at the *third* denial. Annoyed even in the dark porch by the second challenge, he returns to the fire of the quadrangle, and here, "as he stood and warmed himself," he is subjected afresh to the questionings of the bystanders. Evidence is now produced. "He is a Galilean;" "his speech betrayed" him. The kinsman of him whose ear Peter had cut off, asks, "Did I not see thee in the garden with him?" "Then began he to curse and to swear, saying, I know not the man." This took place about an hour after the previous denial. By this time it is the dawning, and his Master is conducted into the

---

[1] There are various ways of seeking to harmonize the statements of the Evangelists in reference to the account of Peter's denial. It appears to me that this is satisfactorily reached by viewing the account in John as the record of *two* denials only. Mark and Luke distinctly affirm that the first denial was at the fire "in the midst of the hall." Matthew also implies this, for he speaks of the second denial as made after Peter had gone out into the *porch*. The second denial was therefore in the porch, as Matthew and Mark testify. The challenge in this case was made by a maid, and the answer recorded by Luke, "*Man*, I am not," is explained by the fact that she "spake to them that stood by," who endorsed it, and to whom therefore the answer was returned. It is of this *second* challenge that John first speaks (xviii. 16-18), affirming it to be given by "the damsel that kept the door." His further account (ver. 25-28) seems to refer to the third and last denial alone. True, he instances there Peter's denial as given *twice over*. But the repetition was owing to the fresh evidence of the kinswoman of the High Priest's servant. That it was given on the same occasion is sanctioned by the present tense (λέγει) being employed. John does not indicate an interval here, such as is indicated in the three distinct denials of the other accounts.

quadrangle, ready to be led away to the Sanhedrim for formal trial. Accordingly he witnesses this *last* and worst exhibition of his disciple's cowardice and falsehood. All is as he predicted. "Immediately while he yet spake the cock crew. And the Lord turned and looked upon Peter; and Peter remembered the word of the Lord, how he had said unto him, Before the cock crow thou shalt deny me thrice. And Peter went out, and wept bitterly."

"As soon as it was day, the elders of the people and the chief priests and the Scribes came together, and led him into their council." Jesus was led up the hill, passing, it is likely, through the courts of the Temple; and thereafter, by one of its western gates, was conducted to the council-chamber of the Sanhedrim. At that hour, in the Temple courts, the lamb for the morning sacrifice would be offered. Bringing him into the council-chamber, they proceeded to search for the witnesses, for they were careful to observe the *forms* of the law. Many came, but their witness proved false. It could not stand cross-examination. "Their witness," says Mark, "did not agree together." It is likely Nicodemus was there, and also Joseph of Arimathea, who was a "good man and a just, and had not consented to the counsel and deed of them." These members may have suggested and enforced the questions which falsified the testimony, and exposed its contradictions. But time pressed. It would soon be clear day, when a holiday crowd would be astir. And as many of these were friends of Jesus of Nazareth, they might create a troublesome uproar because of his capture, stealthy and treacherous as it seemed. If the priests could but get the victim condemned in some formal way, and delivered to the custody of Pilate, then all were well. The high priest devises a plan which brings matters to a point. He makes a solemn appeal to the prisoner : " I adjure thee by the living God, that thou tell us whether thou be the Christ, the Son of God." On which, with calm dignity, Jesus of Nazareth assents to the demand, and unequivocally claims the title of Messiah as his own. " Then the high priest rent his clothes, saying, He hath spoken blasphemy; what further need have we of witnesses ? behold, now ye have heard his blasphemy; what think ye ? They answered and said, He is guilty of death ; and some began to spit on him and to cover his face, and others smote him with the palms of their hands, saying, Prophesy unto us, thou Christ (self-constituted *Messiah*), who it is that smote thee ; and many other things blasphemously spake they against him." They now passed up the central valley of the city, the Tyropœon, to the Castle of Antonia, the residence of Pilate. Arriving at the gate, they delivered their prisoner to the soldiers as a malefactor, and demanded an immediate sentence on his case. They did not themselves enter the precincts of the Castle, either now or at any other time, " lest they should be defiled," and so made unfit for duly celebrating their paschal festival. " Pilate then went out to them, and said, What accusation bring ye against this man ? They answered and said, If he were not a malefactor, we would not have delivered him unto thee." A charge more specific must be made if Pilate is to take action. " And they began to accuse him, saying, We found this fellow perverting the nation, and forbidding to give tribute to Cæsar, saying that he himself is Christ, a king." The prisoner had remained in custody within.

"Then Pilate entered into the judgment-hall (the Prætorium) and called Jesus, and said unto him, Art thou the King of the Jews? Jesus answered, Sayest thou this thing of thyself, or did others tell it thee of me?" He affirms that he is a king, but that his kingdom is not of this world. He is the King of truth and King of all who love truth. "Every one that is of the truth heareth my voice." "Pilate saith unto him, What is truth?" It was clear to him, in any case, that here was no rival to Cæsar, but an enthusiast only, claiming some abstract, impalpable, uncertain, unintelligible empire, which he calls "Truth." A ridiculous, harmless delusion! Then Pilate "went out again to the Jews, and saith unto them, I find in him no fault at all." He took the prisoner along with him as he announced the decision. "And when he was accused of the chief priests and elders, he answered nothing. Then said Pilate unto him, Hearest thou not how many things they witness against thee? and he answered him to never a word, insomuch that the Governor marvelled greatly." One of the accusations against him was so expressed as to induce Pilate to send him to Herod for examination. "He stirreth up the people, teaching throughout all Jewry, beginning from Galilee to this place. When Pilate heard of Galilee, he asked whether the man were a Galilean; and as soon as he knew that he belonged to Herod's jurisdiction, he sent him to Herod, who himself also was at Jerusalem at that time."

Our Lord now passed up to the Palace of Herod, on the north-west of the city, and so the present Via Dolorosa might be applied, in respect of *that* journey. "Herod questioned him in many words, but he answered him nothing." The chief priests and scribes "vehemently accused him, and Herod with his men of war set him at nought, and mocked him, and arrayed him in a gorgeous robe, and sent him again to Pilate." The robe was of white, the lampra, the royal colour of the Hebrews, here designed to throw ridicule upon his pretensions as a King.

On his being brought back to the Castle of Antonia, Pilate sees that Herod regarded the prisoner as a fit object of mockery, and therefore it was all the more preposterous to entertain the idea of any capital charge. This being in accordance with his previous convictions, he again announced to the chief priests and the rulers and the people, that he "found no fault in the Man touching the things whereof they accuse him." He adds, however, "I will chastise him, and let him go." A strange decision if the prisoner be innocent, as he so often alleges! But just here the dastardly Governor exhibits that fatal tendency which was *his* crime in the great tragedy. He wants courage in his high place to maintain law, to act according to his own convictions, and inclines to give way before the popular clamour. He yields but little at first, he will soon yield all. His judgment-seat, sometimes moveable (*sella curulis*), sometimes a fixed platform, is outside the castle on a level esplanade, in a place called the Pavement, but in the Hebrew, Gabbatha.[1] Pilate takes his place in it, inasmuch as matters are so far ripe for a judicial decision. But the people and priests will not have what he pro-

---

[1] This cannot be (as Dr. Robinson suggests in his *Harmony*) the Pavement which Josephus refers to, for that was the lining of the steep rock on which the Castle of Antonia was built, so as that none might clamber up.—Josephus, *Bell. Jud.* v. 5. 8.

poses, that their victim be released after the scourging. Pilate then reminds them that at such a feast, a prisoner, even though convicted of a capital crime, could be set free. He proposes to release Jesus of Nazareth, and is all the more urged to it by a message that arrives from his wife: "Have thou nothing to do with that just man, for I have suffered many things this day in a dream because of him." Also he "knew that for envy they had delivered him." "Will ye, then," he asks, "that I release to you the King of the Jews?" "But the chief priests moved the people that he should rather release Barabbas unto them. Then cried they all again, Not this man, but Barabbas; now Barabbas was a robber," and "for sedition and murder was cast into prison." "Pilate therefore, willing to release Jesus, spake again to them," and still they cry, "Barabbas, Barabbas." "What then," asks the bewildered governor, "shall I do with him that is called Christ?" All say unto him, "Let him be crucified! Crucify him! Crucify him!" "Why, what evil hath he done? They cried out the more exceedingly, Crucify him." Appalling spectacle! These are not heathens and savages that so clamour! They have for ages possessed psalmists, prophets, and the Temple; they reckon themselves the children of Abraham, the children of God! Well might their own prophet, seeing the scene through the vista of time, exclaim, "Who shall declare his generation, for *he* was cut off from the land of the living." And yet it is in keeping with their antecedents of old: "O Jerusalem, Jerusalem, that killest the prophets! It cannot be that a prophet perish out of Jerusalem."

"When Pilate saw that he could prevail nothing, but

that rather a tumult was made, he took water and washed his hands before the multitude, saying, I am innocent of the blood of this just person!" Yet another effort however will he make to rescue Jesus of Nazareth. He delivers Jesus to be scourged; the soldiers lead him into the Prætorium, and calling together the whole band, heap upon him every mockery that occurs to them. "They clothed him with purple, and platted a crown of thorns and put it about his head, and put a reed in his right hand, and they bowed the knee before him, and mocked him, saying, Hail, King of the Jews! and they spat upon him, and took the reed and smote him on the head." This over, Pilate went forth again to the esplanade where the crowd awaited the result. Once more he affirms, "Behold, I bring him forth to you, that ye may know that I find no fault in him. Then came Jesus forth wearing the crown of thorns and the purple robe, and Pilate saith unto them, Behold the man!" Have pity, O ye priests and people, urge not the sentence of crucifixion; let this ignominy and scourging suffice. "When the chief priests and officers saw him, they cried out, saying, Crucify him! Crucify him!" Serpents, generation of vipers! Pilate, angry at the increasing cry, exclaims, "Take ye him and crucify him, for I find no fault in him!" But they throw back an accusation, which in his then mood greatly influenced him. The Jews answered him, "We have a law, and by our law he ought to die, because he made himself the Son of God." Pilate, familiar with the heathen mythology, which is throughout pervaded by the idea of gods and demigods moving on earth, is tempted to think that his prisoner may be one of the gods in the likeness of men. We read, that "when he heard that saying, he was the *more afraid*, and went again with his prisoner into the judgment-hall, and saith unto Jesus, Whence art thou?" But Jesus again gave him no answer. "Then Pilate saith unto him, Speakest thou not unto me? knowest thou not that I have power to crucify thee, and have power to release thee?" Our Lord gave an answer which did imply the superhuman dignity, about which Pilate was so anxious; which moreover asserted his freedom from all crime that could fitly bring him within his jurisdiction: "*Thou* couldest have no power at all against me, except it were given thee from above; therefore he that delivered me unto thee hath the greater sin." The language deepened Pilate's conviction of his innocence. From thenceforth he "sought to release him; but the Jews cried out, If thou let this man go, thou art not Cæsar's friend; whosoever maketh himself a king speaketh against Cesar." Here is a cry that stings Pilate to the quick. Already under suspicion of the imperial government, he dreads a fresh accusation of disloyalty on any pretext. So once more he takes his place on the "judgment-seat," and decides to give sentence in such wise as will tend to restore him to the favour of Cæsar, and secure his continuance in office. "When Pilate therefore heard *that* saying, he brought Jesus forth, and sat down on the judgment-seat, in a place that is called the Pavement, but in the Hebrew, Gabbatha. And he saith unto the Jews, Behold your King! but they cried out, Away with him, Crucify him! Pilate saith unto them, Shall I crucify your King? The chief priests answered, We have no king but Cæsar. Then delivered he him therefore unto them to be crucified."

So "the Holy One of God" was doomed to the cross. The world perpetrated its greatest crime in the name of religion and law. The martyr was not a mere victim to the passions of a lawless mob. The high priest delivered sentence against him in the assembled council —the Roman governor from his high judgment-seat. It was judicial murder; and on the pretext of order, justice, and religion, the Just One was with wicked hands crucified and slain. But he was so to submit and suffer, as to accomplish by his death the world's redemption, the great end of his mission; to transform the ignominy of the cross into the symbol of all that is holiest and most Divine, rendering it "the power of God unto salvation to every one that believeth."

We are informed by one Evangelist, that when Pilate sat down on the judgment-seat, it was about the sixth hour. This computation, as has been well suggested,[1] is according to the hours of the Roman civil day, which reached from midnight to midnight, and consisted of sixteen parts.[2] One hour, therefore, equalled an hour and a half of our time; accordingly, reckoning from midnight, the sixth hour indicated nine o'clock (*mane*) in the morning. The statement thus exactly agrees with the time of another Evangelist, Mark, who, speaking by the Jewish time, says, "It was the third hour, and they crucified him," so that the sentence was pronounced, we may conjecture, from the judgment-seat of Antonia about half-past eight o'clock; and the procession arrived at the place of crucifixion at the third hour, *i.e.*, nine o'clock— the entire distance being about a quarter of a mile.

---

[1] Dr. Davidson, *Opinions concerning Jesus Christ*.
[2] Adam's *Roman Antiquities*, p. 269.

The priests having accomplished their object, retire to the Temple, whither, on that day, many come with sacrifices to them, a source of gain. No prophet is there to thunder in their ears this day, "Your new moons and appointed feasts my soul hateth: they are a trouble unto me; I am weary to bear them. And when ye spread forth your hands, I will hide mine eyes from you; yea, when ye make many prayers, I will not hear; *your hands are full of blood.*" They resort to the Temple the more eagerly, because from its northern wall they can look on and enjoy the agony and death of their victim.

But the procession passes out of the gate of the city. It is a holiday, and the crowds are large. Some are friendly, others hostile. Eastwards along the breadth of the castle, along by the Pool of Bethesda, to the brink of the Kedron, does Jesus bear his cross. But here he faints; exhausted with the scourging, the reproach, the agony. At this point is a road coming in from the country. It is the road that he had walked, how often, to the peaceful home of Bethany! He sees, immediately beneath, the garden of the agony. Simon the Cyrenian, on coming up the hill, is pressed into the service to bear his cross the rest of the way along the ridge. The sufferer, relieved from the burden, has a word of pity for " the women that bewailed and lamented him;" who remember his pity, his gentleness, his blessing their little ones, his miracles of healing to those they most dearly loved. He foretells the terrible siege of their city, and the destruction of its people. He foretells that the Roman power, that has condemned him though confessedly innocent, will wreak terrible vengeance, when its fury is raised by the pretext of a guilty revolt. "Daughters of Jerusalem, weep not for me, but for yourselves. For, behold, the days are coming, in the which they shall say, Blessed are the barren, and the wombs that never bare, and the paps which never gave suck. For if they do these things in a green tree (the innocent), what shall be done in the dry (the guilty)?" They come at last to "the place that is called Calvary," a rocky eminence overhanging the Kedron ravine.

The slopes of Olivet are dark with the crowds, beholding him "afar off." Around his cross are "the rulers and the people." The priests are in their Temple, where, after dismissing the traitor Judas to his doom, with the cold, heartless query, "What is that to us? see thou to that," they pass out to the colonnades for a view of the scene. The soldiers of the Castle move about on the plateau. The party in charge of the execution nail him to his cross, putting up the inscription, "This is Jesus of Nazareth, the King of the Jews," which Pilate will not alter. They offer him the cup of myrrh to deaden his sufferings. This he refuses. And with him they crucify two thieves, the one on his right hand, the other on his left. While the soldiers that crucify him "sit down to watch him there," and the centurion in command "stood over-against him," the other spectators—soldiers, people, and priests—join in mockery and insult. Likewise those that "passed by" railed, reminding him of his words about the Temple, from which they had just come, and which they probably have heard reiterated by the priest that offered their sacrifices. As regards the great Sufferer himself, we have the inspired language of the Psalms as our only fit expression of his mental anguish, so far as human imagination is allowed to conceive of it. "Many bulls have compassed me, strong bulls of Bashan have beset me round. They gaped on me with their mouths, as a ravening and roaring lion. I am poured out like water, all my bones are out of joint, my heart is like wax; it is melted in the midst of my bowels. My strength is dried up like a potsherd; and my tongue cleaveth to my jaws; and thou hast brought me into the dust of death. For dogs have compassed me; the assembly of the wicked have enclosed me: they pierced my hands and my feet. I may tell all my bones: they look and stare upon me. They part my garments among them, and cast lots upon my vesture." Is there then no kindly human look near?

On one unutterably affecting interchange of looks, we are permitted to dwell in thought, between the cross and her who stood near it,—as says the devout hymn of the mediæval church,—

> "Stabat Mater dolorosa
> Juxta crucem lachrymosa
> Dum pendebat filius."

"When Jesus therefore saw his mother and the disciple standing by whom he loved, he saith unto his mother, Woman, behold thy son! Then said he to the disciple, Behold thy mother! and from that hour, that disciple took her unto his own home." It is now mid-day, and a preternatural darkness covers the scene. It lasted for three hours, and seems to have quelled the mockery. We read of no ridicule after this. About its close, a cry arises from the sufferer, which the Jews, if still present, would have understood as only a fresh blasphemy, but which the soldiers around him could not well interpret, as it was expressed in the Hebrew tongue,

—" Eli ! Eli ! lama sabachthani !" It seems to some a cry for Elias, the name of the deliverer whom the Jews were expecting. One other exclamation is heard, and is intelligible, " I thirst !" and a soldier runs across to the Castle for a vessel of the posca, and dipping in the sponge, presents it to the sufferer's lips. " When Jesus therefore had received the vinegar, he said, It is finished ! and he bowed his head, and gave up the ghost." It is by this time the ninth hour, when the priests in the Temple are offering the evening sacrifice. The cross stood fronting the Holy of holies, screened from view by the great veil, which, according to Josephus, was generally " embroidered with blue, and fine linen, and with scarlet and purple cord, of a contexture that was truly wonderful." At that cry of death, " behold, the veil of the Temple was rent from the top to the bottom!" The mind welcomes the reflection that the last exclamation heard on the occasion, at that cross where so much ridicule had been uttered, is one of homage to the preternatural occurrences, and likewise to the superhuman dignity of the Sufferer : " Truly this was the son of God !"

It is but three hours to the Sabbath, and now, with a view to assure themselves of the real death of the chief sufferer (whom they would dread all the more because of the circumstances attending his death), the Pharisees besought Pilate that the legs of the victims " might be broken, and that they might be taken away." But Jesus of Nazareth is dead, and the care of Omnipotence withholds their hands, though they were unaware of it, from the injury they designed against him. " It was written, A bone of him shall not be broken. But a soldier pierced his side with a spear (to prove the fact in question), and forthwith came there out blood and water."

"The Sabbath drew on." "Joseph of Arimathea went to Pilate and begged the body of Jesus." Pilate, willing to do anything that might blunt the stings of an accusing conscience, consented, and "he took down the body." "And there came also Nicodemus, who at the first came to Jesus by night, and brought a mixture of myrrh and aloes, about an hundred pound weight. Then took they the body of Jesus, and wound it in linen clothes with the spices, as the manner of the Jews is to bury." Joseph's own garden, with "a new tomb wherein never was man laid," is "nigh at hand," or rather at the place itself. They reverently and lovingly bear the body across to this spot, and there, amid the deepening shadows of the citadel and the Temple, and while the rays of the sunset are still lingering on the top of Olivet, they complete that strange burial,— the burial of the promised Hope of Israel, extinguished thus before it seemed to reach its prime.

While Mary his mother, after the words uttered by the expiring Saviour, had been led home by John, "Mary Magdalene and the other Mary," who had stood with her by the cross, remained "sitting over-against the sepulchre." "And the women also who came with him from Galilee, followed after, and beheld the sepulchre, and how his body was laid; and they return and prepared spices and ointments, and rested the sabbath-day, according to the commandment." But the chief priests and Pharisees did not rest. Haunted by a dread of Him whom they had crucified, they went to Pilate with a request for a guard of Roman troops to watch the tomb. It now appeared that they could correctly enough interpret the drift of his language : " Destroy this temple, and in three days I will raise it up." It had suited their purpose to misrepresent the words in their council, but now they indicate the real meaning to Pilate : " Sir, we remember that that deceiver said, while he was yet alive, After three days I will rise again. Command therefore that the sepulchre be made sure until the third day." Pilate refuses the request. He will have no more to do with the transaction ; if they wanted to guard the tomb, they might do as they thought best with their Temple-guard, who had already been so prompt to capture and imprison him. " Ye have a watch, go your way, make it as sure, as ye know how."[1] " So they went and made the sepulchre sure, sealing the stone, and setting a watch." It could be easily relieved, as the Temple was adjacent. The unusual precaution would serve to attract the attention of the multitudes that thronged the courts on the Sabbath, and thus give energy to the feelings of the audience on the day of Pentecost, when the fact of the resurrection was demonstrated with an emphasis which they could not resist.

"When the Sabbath was past, the Angel of the Lord descended from heaven, and came and rolled back the stone from the door, and sat upon it. His countenance was like lightning, and his raiment white as snow ; and for fear of him the keepers did shake, and became as dead men." They flee in terror to their comrades in the Temple. The women come to the Sepulchre, bringing the spices they had prepared, and find the stone rolled away. " And they entered in, and found not the

---

[1] ὡς οἴδατε, Matt. xxvii. 65.

body of the Lord Jesus." Mary Magdalene instantly hastened away to have the counsel and help of Peter and John at this unexpected calamity. The other women linger, examining the garden and adjacent ground, but can discover no trace of the body. "And it came to pass, as they were much perplexed thereabout, behold, two men stood by them in shining garments, and, as they were afraid, and bowed down their faces to the earth, they said unto them, Why seek ye the living among the dead? He is not here; he is risen. Remember how he spake to you, when he was yet in Galilee, saying, The Son of man must be delivered into the hands of sinful men, and be crucified, and the third day rise again. And they remembered his words." They now with joy re-entered the empty tomb. But on this *second* visit "they saw a young man sitting on the right side, clothed in a long white garment, and they were affrighted." This angel likewise affirmed that Jesus of Nazareth had risen, and bade them "see the place where the Lord lay, and go quickly and tell his disciples that he is risen from the dead." Thus doubly assured of the blessed fact, "they departed quickly from the sepulchre, with fear and great joy, and did run to bring the disciples word." They descend the slope to the Valley of Kedron, and are hasting down to the gate of Siloam, near which the disciples lodged. "And as they went, behold, Jesus met them, saying, All hail!" Has he come back from among the mysteries of another world, from the "state of separate souls" in that *Hades* where the dying thief had "been with him" in the interval —now in the early dawn of the great Resurrection Day, tranquilly to revisit the scene of suffering, the very garden of agony? His language is that of congratulation and of victory. "And they came, and held him by the feet, and worshipped him." He does not now reject this mode of their instinctive salutation, but at the same time also bids them haste to tell the disciples. They pass down the valley, enter the city, and there meet some of the watch, who have descended from the Temple with the startling intelligence to Caiaphas. Meanwhile, in receiving the prior intelligence from Mary Magdalene that the body was taken away, "Peter went out (of the city), and that other disciple (John), and came to the sepulchre. They ran both together (up the valley), and the other disciple did outrun Peter and came first to the sepulchre." When they entered the body is not to be seen; and so "they believed the report" of Mary Magdalene, "for as yet they knew not the Scriptures, that he must rise from the dead." "Then the disciples went away again to their own home." "But Mary Magdalene stood without at the sepulchre, weeping; and as she wept, she stooped down into the sepulchre, and seeth the two angels in white, sitting, the one at the head, the other at the feet, where the body of Jesus had lain. And they say unto her, Woman, Why weepest thou? She saith unto them, Because they have taken away my Lord, and I know not where they have laid him." She hears a footstep behind her of one who had entered the garden. "She turned herself back, and saw Jesus standing, and knew not that it was Jesus. She, supposing him to be the gardener, saith unto him, Sir, if thou have borne him hence, tell me where thou hast laid him, and I will take him away. Jesus saith to her, Mary!" Who can express the Divine fulness of this simple word, or depict the look of rapture that beamed from that tearful face, as, turning to the speaker, Mary recognised her risen Lord!

But the sun is now rising, and multitudes will gather when the news is spread. The Saviour intimates to her that not now was the time for a prolonged interview; he dismisses her to the disciples with a message, assuring them of his abiding union to them in his new resurrection-life. "Jesus saith to her, Touch me not" (detain me not now), "but go to my brethren, and say unto them, I ascend to my Father, and your Father, and to my God, and your God." So the scene of angels passes away; the Lord of angels and of men, though still on earth, reserves himself from all unnecessary view; secluded valley and populous city are now alike to the new conditions of his glorified presence. Mary pursues her way down the Kedron to the city, "to tell the disciples that she had seen the Lord, and that he had spoken these things unto her." They are not convinced, however, until he appears to them in the evening, as they sit at meat in the upper room, which they had hired for the days of the festival. During the day, the spot itself was doubtless visited by crowds, impelled thither by the story of the watch, which they tell as bribed by the chief priests,—a lie, however, which many would cease to believe after the sermon by Peter on the day of Pentecost.

I have thus endeavoured to show that the Scripture narrative relating to the incidents of the Passion and Resurrection can be read in harmony with, and receive additional illustration from, the localities here contended for. If the theory here advocated should gain ground, then the present enclosure of Haram es Sheriff will come to be regarded as by far the most interesting spot on earth; and the Mohammedan fanaticism that now guards it must soon give way to the eager desire for its more thorough examination on the part of the Christian world. Rich discoveries await the excavations to be made there, precious relics of the ancient Temple, the rock-chambers of the sepulchres of the kings. On its eastern side overlooking Gethsemane and the slopes of Olivet, the Christian pilgrim will visit "the place called Calvary," and ascending the central platform, he will enter the true "Church of the Holy Sepulchre," and see in very deed "the place where the Lord lay."

FINIS.